SAMUEL KINSER is an associate professor of history at Northern Illinois University. He received his B.A. degree from Carleton College, in Northfield, Minnesota, in 1953 and his Ph.D. degree from Cornell University in 1960. From 1960 through 1965 he was an assistant professor of history at Washington State University. He studied at the University of Bonn, in Germany, on a Rotary Foundation Fellowship (1953–54), and in Paris on a Fulbright Fellowship (1958–59); he is currently on leave from Northern Illinois University as a Fellow at the Institute for Research in the Humanities at the University of Wisconsin (1968–69). Mr. Kinser has also published *The Works of Jacques Auguste de Thou.*

ISABELLE CAZEAUX is assistant professor of music at Bryn Mawr College. She received an M.A. in music from Smith College in 1946 and a Ph.D. in musicology from Columbia University in 1961. Her graduate and postgraduate work have included the completion of separate music programs at the Ecole normale de musique and the Conservatoire national supérieur de musique in Paris, as well as other advanced studies. Miss Cazeaux's professional activities have ranged from teaching private lessons to giving violin recitals, and from cataloguing music (she holds an M.S. in Library Science) to translating and writing. She has published numerous articles in both French and English.

VOLUME ONE

THE MEMOIRS OF PHILIPPE DE COMMYNES

Book One: The War for the Public Good, 1465 / Book Two: The Wars against Liège and the interview at Péronne, 1466– 1468 / Book Three: The War over the Somme River Towns, 1470–1472 / Book Four: The Franco-English War of 1475 and the betrayal of the Count of Saint-Pol / Book Five: The fall of Burgundy, 1476–1477

EDITED BY SAMUEL KINSER

TRANSLATED BY ISABELLE CAZEAUX

University of South Carolina Press / Columbia, South Carolina

In this book, designed by Damienne Grant, the typeface used for both text and display is Janson, a typeface noted for its well-matched roman and italic. The initial letter on the title page and the ornament used throughout the book were selected from the early typographic decorations of Erhard Ratdolt (1442–1528), German printer and type cutter, which were used widely in Commynes' day.

FIRST EDITION

Copyright © 1969 by Samuel Kinser. Published in Columbia, S.C., by the University of South Carolina Press, 1969. This edition is published under an arrangement with Harper Torchbooks, Harper & Row, Publishers, Inc.
Library of Congress Catalog Card Number: 68–9363
Standard Book Number: 87249–130–7
Manufactured in the United States of America
Composition by Heritage Printers, Inc., Charlotte, North Carolina
Offset lithography by Universal Lithographers, Inc.,
Lutherville-Timonium, Maryland
Bound by L. H. Jenkins, Inc., Richmond, Virginia

Acknowledgments

The contributions of Isabelle Cazeaux of Bryn Mawr College, translator of this edition of the *Memoirs*, to the preparation of the manuscript go far beyond the transcription of Commynes' words. Her gentle good humor and unfailing energy in solving the word-puzzles presented by a five-hundred-year-old text have made our collaboration warm and easy. I should also like to thank Hugh Van Dusen of Harper and Row, Publishers, whose enthusiasm for his work is as catching as a cold, and whose sympathy with overscrupulous scholars must be kept a secret from all others in our tribe for fear that they will usurp his services. As for the kicks and blows of all sorts which Sandra Kinser and Hyman Drell bestowed upon this manuscript and its author, I can only say that I warned them when they first came around that an antiquary absorbed in his work is, like Calvin's church, *une enclume qui use beaucoup de marteaux.*

Contents

Illustrations

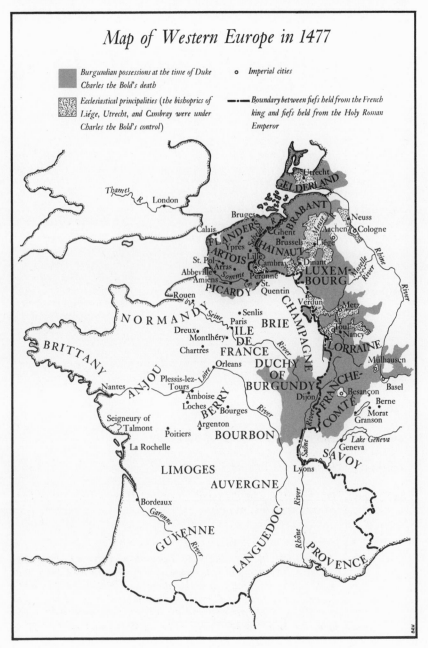

Map of Western Europe in 1477

▨ Burgundian possessions at the time of Duke Charles the Bold's death

▨ Ecclesiastical principalities (the bishoprics of Liége, Utrecht, and Cambray were under Charles the Bold's control)

○ Imperial cities

▬ ▬ Boundary between fiefs held from the French king and fiefs held from the Holy Roman Emperor

Thames R.
London
Utrecht
GELDERLAND
Bruges
Calais
Neuss
Cologne
FLANDERS
Ghent
Brussels
Aachen
Liège
Ypres
HAINAUT
St. Pol
Lille
Cambray
Dinant
LUXEM-
Arras
Somme
Péronne
BOURG
Abbeville
St.
Amiens
Quentin
Verdun
Metz
PICARDY
Rouen
Toul
Nancy
Senlis
Paris
BRIE
NORMANDY
Seine
Dreux
ÎLE
Montlhéry
DE
CHAMPAGNE
LORRAINE
Chartres
FRANCE
Mulhausen
Orleans
DUCHY
BRITTANY
OF
ANJOU
Loire
BURGUNDY
Besançon
Basel
Nantes
Plessis-lez-
Tours
Dijon
FRANCHE-
Amboise
Berne
Loches
BERRY
Morat
Bourges
River
COMTÉ
Granson
Seigneury of
Argenton
Talmont
Poitiers
BOURBON
Lake Geneva
La Rochelle
Geneva
Saône
SAVOY
LIMOGES
Lyons
AUVERGNE
Bordeaux
Garonne
River
GUYENNE
Rhône
River
LANGUEDOC
PROVENCE
Meuse
Scheldt
Moselle River
Rhine River
Rhine
River

Chronological Table

for Volume One

	tion between the dukes continues in desultory fashion until the death of the king's brother and the peace which Louis made separately with the duke of Brittany in 1472. (See Books 1 and 3)
1465–1468	*The prince-bishopric of Liége resists Charles the Bold's aggression. Louis XI aids Liége and threatens Charles's possession of the towns along the Somme River. Peace is made between Louis and Charles at Péronne (October, 1468) and Liége is razed by the Burgundian army with both Charles and Louis present. (See Book 2)*
1475	*The Burgundian siege of Neuss, Germany, and the intended joint Burgundian-English invasion of France fail because Charles the Bold, England's ally, is torn between ambition to expand in Germany and desire to free himself from Louis XI's intrigues against him. The constable of France, Saint-Pol, is executed by Louis XI in Paris with the cooperation of Charles the Bold. (See Book 4)*
1475–1477	*Charles the Bold conquers Lorraine, and then moves against the Swiss who had sent some troops against him. He is defeated, chiefly by the Swiss, at Granson and Morat, and falls in battle at Nancy. His death provokes a three-way struggle for control of his territories between Louis XI, Mary of Burgundy, and local lords and towns, such as the lord of Cordes and the city of Ghent. (See Book 5)*

Principal Events

of Commynes' Life

1486 | Condemned by the Parlement of Paris to give up his property of Talmont.

1487 | Arrested as conspirator against the regent Anne de Beaujeu. Imprisoned for some months in an iron cage in Loches castle. Transferred to Paris, where he is imprisoned twenty months in the high chamber of the tower of the Conciergerie overlooking the Seine.

1489 | Pleads his own case before the Parlement of Paris. Sentenced to ten years' exile at Dreux, one of his castles, to confiscation of one-fourth of his property, and to a bail of ten thousand gold écus.

1490 | Receives right of freedom of movement outside Dreux.

1491 | Returns to court, where his pension is renewed. Makes final settlement with La Trémoïlle over possession of Talmont in July.

1493 | Negotiates the Treaty of Senlis between Charles VIII and Maximilian of Austria, regulating affairs concerning Charles the Bold's heirs. Involved in receiving Italian ambassadors, and in counseling the king on the coming Italian campaign.

1494 | Accompanies French army to Italy, and is then sent to Venice as ambassador.

1495 | Recalled from Venice after failing to prevent the formation of an anti-French alliance between Venice, Milan, and other Italian powers.

1498 | When Louis XII becomes king, Commynes suffers eclipse at court.

1505 | Through Queen Anne's favor, appointed chamberlain at court and pension of three thousand livres is restored.

1507 | Accompanies Louis XII's expedition against Genoa.

1508 | Argenton, Commynes' residence, placed in sequestration. Commynes' family allowed to live there as renters until 1515.

1511 | Dies at Argenton.

xv

Introduction

France in the fifteenth century showed the signs of a society in crisis. Her kings were beset by coalitions of disloyal vassals. Her peasants were plundered by tax collectors and mercenary soldiers. During the Hundred Years' War (1340–1453) all sense of unity, administrative or patriotic, was lost and the country was carved into pieces by factious nobles allied with France's powerful neighbors, England and Burgundy.

The plight of fifteenth-century France defined—indeed, made possible—the meteoric careers of two of her most famous countrymen: Jacques Coeur and Joan of Arc. Both were humbly born, both saved France from ruin at a critical moment in the Hundred Years' War—the one financially, the other militarily—and both were abandoned by the monarch they rescued shortly after their most spectacular services had been performed.

Social mobility of the sort first exploited and later suffered by the peasant's daughter who commanded an army and the artisan's son who commanded the royal mint reflects institutions either in extreme decay or in early formation. Or perhaps decay of the old and formation of the new are synonymous terms. At any rate, less than a century after the death of Joan of Arc and Jacques Coeur, France was one of the most unified, powerful states in Europe, and her leading men came once more from traditional elites. Many of the steps by which France regained unity, some of the early attempts to reknit the social fabric from the tattered remnants bequeathed by King Charles to his son in 1461, are recorded in Philippe de Commynes' *Memoirs*.

Commynes was a minor Burgundian nobleman who deserted the duke of Burgundy to enter the service of King Louis XI of France in 1472. He became very close to the king—in fact, when Louis suffered apoplectic attacks which deprived him of speech in his last years, he kept Commynes by his side day and night as the one who could best interpret the feeble signs by which he expressed his desires.[1] Commynes was rewarded

1. See Joseph Calmette's edition of the *Memoirs* (Paris, 1924–1925), II, 281. In Volume One of the present translation, page references to Books 6, 7, and 8, which

3

lavishly with lands and money for his services, and as might be expected, therefore, his interpretation of how Louis succeeded in defeating his adversaries and in refounding French unity is not an impartial account. But it is not consciously biased, either. Commynes says in his Prologue that he does "not wish to lie," and that he has reported unfavorable as well as favorable facts about Louis XI.[2] Although some authors have interpreted these words as an attempt to disguise what they see as an apology for Louis XI's reign, there is considerable evidence to indicate that Commynes' words are sincere, as I shall try to show in the course of this Introduction.

More important than Commynes' conscious attempts to control his partiality were his unconscious loyalties. These loyalties were aristocratic and Christian as well as French. Attitudes which in later centuries were to characterize the bureaucrat and bourgeois also influenced his writings. The codes of behavior demanded by these allegiances and proclivities conflicted in many respects, and one of the strangest aspects of the *Memoirs* is Commynes' apparent unawareness of these conflicts.

The reason for Commynes' unawareness was, in large part, cultural. Culture, like politics, was in crisis in the fifteenth century, a crisis which several generations of students have interpreted through the medium of Johan Huizinga's book *The Waning of the Middle Ages*. When we speak of the "late" Middle Ages, or its "waning," however, we are talking about the crisis of a class, not the end of a society or civilization. That class was the feudal elite which still retained in the fifteenth century an almost total monopoly of social privilege and artistic patronage, even though patterns of economic productivity, social dependence, and artistic creativity had changed radically. From this cleavage between privilege and productivity, a fragmentation of institutions and ideologies resulted; what men did, more often than not, was different from what they said, and what they said was usually not what they believed. The *Memoirs*, with their medley of uncoordinated and conflicting ideas, reflect these gaps between belief, word, and deed. If Commynes is unaware of the contradictions among the values he cherishes, he shares this quality with most men of his time. Medieval atavisms and precocious modernity flourish side by side in his work,

---

will be included in Volume Two, will be to Calmette's edition, cited henceforth thus: Calmette, II, 281. Corresponding page numbers in this translation will be given in an Appendix to Volume Two.

2. See p. 91 of this translation of the *Memoirs*. References to this translation will henceforth be given as follows: M, p. 91.

and his writing offers in this sense a concentrated reflection of the epoch through which he lived.

A fresh look at the *Memoirs* may lead us to modify Huizinga's rather static picture of a world of decay. As old forms of life withered, new ones acquired room to grow; such was the case in France, at the court of the king, where Commynes, fascinated by the turbulent course of political life around him, observed and recorded many of the early signs of that transition from institutional debility to national greatness which began in his time.

1/BIOGRAPHY

Family background, personal opportunities, and a cool intelligence combined in Commynes' life to create a brilliant if checkered career. Two dates stand out as turning points: August, 1472, when Commynes deserted the service of his native lord, Charles the Bold of Burgundy, to enter the pay of Charles's arch-rival, King Louis XI of France, and January, 1487, when Commynes was arrested and imprisoned for plotting against King Charles VIII, Louis' son.

Philippe de Commynes was born about 1447,[3] the son of Colard van den Clyte and Marguerite d'Armuyden. We know little about Commynes' mother beyond the fact that she died within a year or so of Commynes' birth. The van den Clytes (the name probably comes from the hamlet Clyte near Ypres, Belgium) are recorded as town officials in Ypres from the early fourteenth century. Jean van den Clyte, Philippe's great-grandfather, aided the count of Flanders to put down the revolt led by Nicholas Zannekin and supported by his own city of Ypres during 1326–1328. Colard, Philippe's grandfather, after obtaining the office of bailiff of Ghent and later of princely counselor under Count Louis de Male of Flanders, signed a charter in 1377 annulling the privileges of Ypres. These facts are recounted with some relish by Kervyn de Lettenhove, an important nineteenth-century Belgian historian, who could not forgive Commynes' desertion of his ancestral home in the duke of Burgundy's territories.[4] Kervyn seems to be saying that betrayal of the

---

3. Neither place nor date of Commynes' birth is certain. See Calmette, I, ii, for the controversy concerning the date of Commynes' birth.
4. Modern Belgium consists of the northern territories once held by the duke of Burgundy and has often been called a descendant of the medieval Burgundian state.

family origins was a habit with the van den Clytes ever since the beginning of their rise as the officers of princes.

The facts which Kervyn recounts about Philippe's father bear out his theme. As bailiff of Cassel, Colard increased the feudal dues owed to his employer, Duke Philip the Good of Burgundy, and thus to himself as the duke's administrator, by some 600 per cent. The inhabitants revolted, razing Colard's chief place of residence. With the aid of Duke Philip, Colard's castle, Renescure, was restored eventually, and the revolutionaries were forced to pay a double indemnity. Nevertheless, when Commynes' father died in 1453, the family was forced to sell Renescure in order to pay Colard's enormous debts (he seems to have bought land far beyond his capacity to pay for in full) and in order to straighten out the allegedly irregular accounts from Colard's officeholding under the duke. Upon his father's death, Commynes became the ward of his father's brother, and this, incidentally, is probably why he is known as Commynes, not van den Clyte.

Philippe de Commynes takes his surname from his grandmother Jeanne de Wazières, who married Commynes' grandfather about 1373 and brought the fief of Commynes into the family. Philippe, interestingly enough, never possessed the fief of Commynes, which passed to his grandfather's eldest son Jean, Philippe's uncle and guardian, and thence to Jean's children. The lordship of Commynes was famous and venerable, having belonged to a noble who took part in the first Crusade. Philippe's use of the name to sign his letters probably reflects his residence with his uncle between the ages of six and sixteen. It may also represent a pretension to respectable and well-attested nobility, natural enough in the orphaned, penurious son of the recently ennobled van den Clytes.[5]

We know nothing of Philippe's childhood. It cannot have been pleasant. He lost his mother as an infant; he shared his improvident and ambitious father's affections with a bastard brother and two illegitimate sisters until the age of six, and then went to live with his rich cousins.[6] If in later life he showed himself avid for money and unscrupulous in obtaining it, his early experiences and family background provide explanation enough.

Philippe de Commynes entered the service of Duke Philip's son,

5. Documentation of the material in the preceding paragraphs may be found in Kervyn de Lettenhove, *Lettres et négotiations de Philippe de Comines* [sic], I (Brussels, 1867), 40–47. "Comines" is a form of the memorialist's name frequently found in nineteenth-century publications.
6. *Ibid.*, p. 47.

Charles the Bold, in 1464. His rise in Charles's favor was rapid. He held the offices of counselor and chamberlain to Duke Charles from 1467, and by 1469 he had secured remission of the debts still owed by his father's estate to the ducal treasury. For the rest, his activities from 1464 to 1472 are recorded in the *Memoirs*—though they do not mention, characteristically enough, his selection by Duke Charles as one of the twenty-five Burgundian knights who jousted in honor of the duke's marriage to Margaret of York in July, 1468.[7] Commynes had no use for the decorative aspects of knighthood.

Charles rewarded his servant for diplomatic services: a contract with the city of Ghent in 1467, others with Courtrai and Ypres in 1468 and 1469, and negotiations with the English at Calais in 1470. The most important of Commynes' diplomatic services during this period took place in October, 1468, at Péronne, where Commynes acted informally but, according to himself, decisively, in the negotiations between Charles the Bold and Commynes' future employer, Louis XI. This was Louis' first acquaintance with Commynes, probably, and Commynes performed services for Louis on this occasion which led the king to tempt the diplomat to desert Charles a few years later.

Commynes' Desertion   In 1471 Commynes was sent by Charles to negotiate with Louis' enemy, the duke of Brittany, and perhaps also with the duke of Guyenne and the king of Castile, equally Louis' adversaries. Using the pretext of a pilgrimage to Santiago de Compostella, the ambassador went first to Brittany and then southward across France. En route he visited Louis XI at Tours, as Duke Charles intended him to do. But while at Tours he accepted from the king a pension of six thousand livres, which Charles certainly did not intend. This pension was the bait which Louis used to attract Commynes into his camp.[8]

7. See *ibid.*, pp. 49–66, for this and some few other facts about Commynes' life during these years not reported in the *Memoirs*.

8. The evidence for Commynes' acceptance of money from Charles the Bold's adversary in 1471 is indirect, but hard to explain in any other manner than as treachery. Dupont has printed an undated letter to Charles from Simon de Quingey, the duke's ambassador at Louis' court, which reports that Louis is irritated because he has learned that although Commynes is going to Santiago, he does not intend to visit the king. Charles the Bold has written in the margin of this letter, according to Dupont: "Commynes a esté rencontré à Orléans, dont ne peut faillir de passer par vous [i.e., at the king's court]." See Commynes, *Mémoires*, ed. Dupont, III (Paris, 1847), 6. As Karl Bittmann has recently shown, Charles was pursuing several diplomatic maneuvers at this time. On one hand, he tried to cement bonds between himself and the dukes of Brittany and Guyenne, his untrustworthy allies against Louis XI. On the other hand, he undertook secret negotiations with Louis himself in order

Introduction

Charles the Bold attacked the king in 1472, laying waste north France and massacring the inhabitants of Nesle with a cruelty which displeased Commynes greatly. The duke of Burgundy then laid siege to Dieppe in Normandy. While he was thus occupied, Commynes fled from the Burgundian camp to that of the king at Ponts-de-Cé during the night of August 7, 1472.

to end the war which he had begun in 1471. See Karl Bittmann, *Ludwig XI und Karl der Kühne*, I (Göttingen, 1964), 551–52. Commynes may have been sent to serve both these ends. At any rate, Charles's comment in the margin of Quingey's letter indicates that he expected Commynes to see Louis XI. Was Louis XI's irritation at the failure of Commynes to appear, therefore, a feint? Had Commynes seen Louis secretly, accepted a pension in anticipation of his later desertion, and asked Louis to act as if he had not appeared at court? If so, Charles can hardly have entrusted important negotiations with Louis to Commynes, or Commynes would not have dared to fail to appear openly at Tours.

We are certain of only one thing in regard to Commynes' pension of 1471: sometime before August 8, 1472, Louis issued an undated letter to one of his officers, which begins: ". . . Nous avons esté acertenez par aucuns de notre hostel que le Sr de Renescure, Bourguignon [i.e., Commynes], a en garde et deppost en notre ville de Tours la somme de six mil livres tournois; et pour ce que luy et autres Bourguingnons, comme noz rebelles et desobeissans subgetz, ont forfait envers Nous corps et biens, Nous avons aujourd'uy . . . commandé . . . pour contraindre Jehan de Beaune, marchant de Tours, que on dit qui a ladicte somme en garde et deppost . . . à bailler ladicte somme à ce porteur pour le nous apporter incontinent. . . ." (Dupont, *op. cit.*, III, 7–8.) Commynes' biographers have always assumed that Commynes received this money from Louis while on his "pilgrimage," and that Louis confiscated it sometime in 1472 in order to force Commynes to desert Charles's service for his own. In August, 1472, Commynes did desert and on October 28, 1472, Louis XI granted Commynes an annual pension of six thousand livres for the future (*ibid.*, pp. 20–24). It seems probable that this was a restoration, not the beginning, of Commynes' salary.

How could the enormous sum of six thousand livres have been deposited in Tours for Commynes without either Commynes or Louis putting it there? Where could Commynes, a penurious noble, have obtained such a sum except from Louis, Charles, or the duke of Brittany, the latter two of whom would hardly want such a sum left in Louis XI's territories by their secret agent? The mere fact that this amount, six thousand livres, remains the amount which Commynes received as an annual pension from Louis after 1472 indicates that Louis began paying Commynes not after his desertion, but one year before.

It is possible that Commynes was in secret contact with Louis from their meeting at Péronne onward. (See p. 30, n. 67, concerning money which he probably received at Péronne.) In that case, he may have initiated the request to go to Santiago himself as a pretext enabling him to meet Louis XI in secret. Charles may then have acquiesced on condition that Commynes carry messages to the duke of Brittany before starting southward to Spain. Note that in Louis' letter the ostensible cause of confiscating Commynes' money is Commynes' collusion with Louis' "enemies." In another part of the letter Louis states that by "enemies" he means the duke of Brittany. Commynes' announced intent, a pilgrimage, could hardly have been taken seriously by anyone, however. Charles the Bold and Louis were officially at war; for Louis to allow one of Charles's privy counselors to pass through his territories must have required some secret understanding—probably the negotiations mentioned at the beginning of this note.

Commynes' desertion has aroused impassioned denunciation from generations of Belgian historians. Yet the act seems quite simple. Commynes was poorly paid (he received eighteen sous per day).[9] His employer would not listen to him (Commynes distrusted war as a measure of policy and found the actions of the duke increasingly ill-chosen and uncontrolled). Other more prominent men than Commynes had already abandoned the duke (including Baldwin, one of Philip the Good's illegitimate sons and thus Charles's half-brother).[10] And in any case the king of France was in feudal law Commynes' ultimate suzerain, just as he was Charles the Bold's. The concept of nationality was of course extremely fluid in Commynes' time, and to charge Commynes with treason is an evident anachronism, for it presupposes that Burgundy was a nation and capable of being betrayed.[11] What Commynes did was to break his personal obligations to a dynasty which had furthered not only his own career but that of his father and his grandfather. His family had received property and offices in return for their loyalty. After his desertion Charles the Bold confiscated that property and struck the name of Commynes from the list of his officeholders. Both sides undoubtedly thought of the affair, insofar as it had a public side, in feudal terms, and with these confiscations both sides no doubt considered the matter juridically closed.

On the private side, however, Commynes may well have felt that he continued rather than broke with a family tradition. The van den Clytes had always shown that they could pick the winning side. Having abandoned Clyte for Ypres and Ypres for the Burgundian court, their contemporary representative now abandoned Burgundy for France. Sure enough, Burgundy, like Ypres, and like Clyte, shortly afterwards succumbed to the larger power.

Commynes' decision was certainly not sudden. During the preceding eight years he had experienced repeatedly and at close hand both the clumsiness of Charles in exploiting his material advantages and the craft of Louis XI in escaping from his enemies. The tense situation at Péronne, when Commynes acted to save King Louis from what was apparently a

9. Kervyn, *op. cit.*, I, 71.
10. See M, p. 202.
11. I base this point on the evidence supplied by Johan Huizinga in his series of three articles entitled "L'état bourguignon," *Moyen Age* (1930–1931). Jean Dufournet denies Huizinga's assertion that Burgundy never became a nation in his book *La destruction des mythes dans les Mémoires de Ph. de Commynes* (Geneva, 1966), p. 32. For Dufournet, whose seven-hundred-page book is the lengthiest study of the *Memoirs* ever written, Commynes did commit treason, therefore; this assertion provides the basis for most of his interpretations of Commynes' words and actions in the rest of his book.

threat of bodily injury, may illustrate how he was brought to observe the difference between the two princes. Commynes tells us how Charles, convinced that Louis had tried to trick him, was unable to sleep at night for anger, throwing himself on his bed and then arising and stalking about the chamber. Commynes himself was sleeping that evening, as he often did, in the same room with Charles, and he attempted to calm the duke by accompanying him on his prowls. But "the next morning he was angrier than ever, made all sorts of threats and was ready to put some great plan into execution."[12] Commynes thereupon spoke to Louis secretly, telling him what concessions would be necessary to calm the duke of Burgundy, and the king followed Commynes' advice. One almost perceives a secret current of sympathy flowing between the two men. Certainly Commynes' instincts were more akin to Louis' than to Charles's: he was conservative, opposed to violence, and inclined to view politics as a chess game, won by the coolest, most calculating player, rather than by the most aggressive.

Commynes' action at Péronne in favor of Louis was probably not only in expectation of gain but also in fulfillment of some vague belief in the greatness and sanctity of kings, a feeling buttressed by his religious principles, which were as divine-rightist as those of King James I of England. Once performed, Commynes' favor probably stimulated Louis XI's curiosity; the chronicler tells us how the king habitually sought to recruit the ablest of his adversaries' counselors,[13] so his eye would naturally have been attracted to Commynes. Correspondingly, the contrast between the king's character and that of his own master must have begun to work in Commynes' mind from the time of their interview at Péronne onward.[14]

Confidant of Louis XI   Louis was lavish in his gifts to the new counselor. In addition to an annual pension of six thousand livres, Commynes was given the principality of Talmont, a huge territory in the west of France with some seventeen hundred dependent fiefs. In January, 1473, Commynes' marriage to the rich heiress Hélène de Chambes was arranged; the prince of Talmont became in addition Lord Argenton, and this latter title is that by which Commynes was henceforth known in France. Other offices and titles followed, often in a rather unwhole-

12. M, p. 178.
13. M, p. 130.
14. See M, p. 184, where Commynes admiringly contrasts the promptness of mind of the king with the clumsiness of Charles the Bold in handling an emergency during their joint attack on Liége.

some manner.[15] Not only was Louis' right to dispose of Talmont disputed by the La Trémoïlle family, its former owner, but the new lands and pensions which Commynes accepted in September, 1477, were confiscated from the property of the duke of Nemours after a notorious trial in which the duke was executed for lese majesty. This was a charge of which nearly every great noble of France was guilty at one time or another during Louis' reign, of course, and therefore Louis' confiscations and those who benefited from them were hated by the rest of the nobility.

Commynes was avaricious. He felt little compunction about it. As he reports concerning one of the defeats of the duke of Burgundy in 1477:

Many people kept their ears open in order to be the first to hear the news and report it to the king [Louis XI], for he usually rewarded the first to bring him important news, without forgetting the messenger besides. And he liked to speak about prospective news before it arrived, and said: "I shall give so much to the first man who brings me news of this." My lord of Bouchage and I received the first message about the battle of Morat, and we went together to inform the king about it. He gave each one of us two hundred silver marks.[16]

Commynes received money from Lorenzo and Piero de' Medici, unofficial rulers of Florence, in return for information on court affairs in France, and he probably received gifts from the Milanese court as well. Commynes also claimed that he had money deposited with the Medici bank in Lyon which was collecting interest, and the tedious avidity of his letters to the Medici trying to collect these deposits with their interest makes as distressing reading as the record of his decades-long court fight with the La Trémoïlle family for possession of Talmont.[17]

The difficulty in the Talmont affair was Louis XI's poor grounds for confiscating the territory in 1470, before giving it to Commynes in 1472. As in the case of the duke of Nemours' lands, Commynes cannot be held responsible for the unjust manner in which the king acquired these territories. But Commynes never admitted that his pretentions were founded on poor claims of the king, and the unremitting legal chicanery to which he resorted in order to stave off repossession of Talmont by the heirs of the La Trémoïlle family—including outright lies in court

15. See Calmette, I, vii, n. 3, for a list of Commynes' most important possessions.
16. M, p. 327.
17. See L. Sozzi, "Lettere inedite de Filippo de Commynes a Francesco Gaddi," in *Studi in onore di Tammaro de Marinis*, IV (Verona, 1964), 227 ff., for a modern edition of the letters to the Medici and a convenient summary by Sozzi of the cases of Commynes' venality known at present.

and an attempt to burn incriminating documents—was petty and futile in addition to being dishonest.[18] The only mitigating factor in the story of Commynes' pursuit of riches is his use of the lands granted him. Besides draining the marshes around Olonne and aiding the efforts of the townsmen to develop Olonne as a port, Commynes spent some 200,000 livres on his lordship of Argenton, building mills, bridges, and stables, establishing fairs and markets, rebuilding castles, endowing churches and chapels, and aiding the peasants by distributing grain.[19]

Nineteenth-century commentators on Commynes misinterpreted his statements concerning the injustice of taxation without consent. Far from making Commynes a constitutionalist, concerned with limiting the power of the king by representative estates, these statements reflect his avarice or, more kindly, his sense of property. They do not indicate Commynes' disposition to identify his future with that of the feudal class, for all Commynes' work as royal counselor, all his praise of Louis XI's astuteness in putting down feudal revolt and centralizing and rationalizing the government of France, point in the opposite direction. Taxation is wrong in Commynes' eyes because it injures people's property, not because it concentrates too much power in the hands of the prince.[20] Declaring war, too, should be done only after securing one's subjects' consent, as is done in England, for war always costs money. These are the only differences between just kings and tyrants: for the rest, royal authority, in Commynes' opinion, should be unrestrained.[21]

The most precious of Louis XI's gifts to Philippe de Commynes was not, however, a piece of property. It was his confidence. Commynes' sympathy with Louis XI's political style, perhaps sensed by the monarch as early as 1468 at Péronne, rapidly allowed Commynes to become Louis XI's intimate. This kind of tie to the king was essential to a parvenu such

18. See Dupont, *op. cit.*, I (Paris, 1840), xl–xlii, lxiv–xc, for details of the court hearings over Talmont.

19. C. Hippeau has summarized the improvements which Commynes made, basing his work on the research of C. Fierville. See Hippeau, "Documents inédits sur Philippe de Comines," *Revue des sociétés savantes*, series 7, IV (1881), 134–37.

20. See W. Bouwsma, "The Politics of Commynes," *Journal of Modern History*, XXIII (1951), 320–22. Bouwsma's interpretation is confirmed by Commynes' comments on Mohammed II, conqueror of Constantinople: Mohammed is one of the three greatest kings that have reigned during the preceding one hundred years. His chief claim to merit, aside from his conquests—achieved through the use of "sense and cunning rather than valor and boldness," the same antithesis which Commynes uses to contrast Louis XI and Charles the Bold—was that on his deathbed he abolished a tax which he had recently imposed without the consent of his subjects. See Calmette, II, 337–40.

21. See M, p. 361, and Calmette, III, 17 and 18, for Commynes' identification of tyranny with unjust taxation.

as Commynes. Like his forefathers, he was a personal servant, made great because of the value of his intelligence and character, not because of his social position. Louis XI, for his part, seems to have been the sort of closed, suspicious person who could feel safe only with confidants, men bound to him by dangerous secrets and mutual cunning rather than by public ties and an official morality. Commynes was able to play that role without becoming proud or presumptive. His conventional piety, his passionless intelligence were made to observe and admire rather than to suggest new policies or to nourish private projects against the king.

Louis' successors, however, required prime ministers, not intimates. Of narrow talent themselves, they relied on project-makers for ideas, and were not devious or mentally complicated enough to need release in personal confidence. Thus, after eleven years of almost uninterrupted intimacy with the king, Commynes found himself threatened with a loss of his position when in August, 1483, Louis XI died.[22]

Fall from Power   Commynes' fall was not precipitate. During the first months of the regency of Louis XI's daughter, Anne de Beaujeu, for the eight-year-old King Charles VIII, Commynes continued to sit in the king's council. Soon, however, he joined the party of the duke of Orleans against the regent. Commynes' subsequent involvement in plots against Anne de Beaujeu's power over the king led to the second turning point in his career: his imprisonment. Commynes was removed by the regent from the military command he held, the captaincy of the castle of Poitiers, in September, 1485; in January, 1487, he was arrested for conspiring against the king. Although he was released and allowed to return to court by 1490, his place at the elbow of sovereigns was gone forever. His fortune, too, was greatly diminished by action of the courts during his imprisonment. Pensions, lands, and offices had been stripped from him, and he never regained much of what he lost.

The year 1472 had been a turning point in Commynes' life because it set the seal on a solitude which had pursued him from infancy. Left to

22. Commynes was not Louis XI's only, nor always his most important, favorite. Du Bouchage, Olivier le Dain, and many others were used or discarded by Louis XI because of their possession of the same talents as those ascribed to Commynes here. Commynes expresses his sense of rivalry with these men, and especially with the favorites of Charles VIII, again and again in the *Memoirs*. The most important negotiations conducted by Commynes for Louis XI are listed in the Principal Dates preceding this Introduction (See p. xiv). Not all his activities are listed, particularly for the period of his ascendancy under Louis XI, for Commynes himself is extremely closemouthed in indicating his responsibilities. He was certainly, however, one of Louis' principal advisers on Burgundian and later on north Italian affairs.

fend for himself by the loss of his mother, his father, and his patrimony, Commynes had risen in Charles the Bold's service by virtue of his talents more than his name. If he had remained in Charles's service, a modest but secure position among the upper class in Burgundian society would have been almost certain. The loneliness experienced as a child would have been overcome, and social factors such as class ties and family heritage would probably have engrossed more and more of his action and thought. Commynes' desertion made that sort of security impossible, lifting him beyond the reach of what slowly acquired ties of trust and mutual self-interest can do to give human existence solidity. After 1472 Commynes found himself isolated on the pinnacle of his instinctive sympathy with King Louis and his special knowledge of Louis' archenemy, Charles.

He sometimes felt that he was alone: "I would counsel a friend of mine, if I had one . . . ," he remarks in the course of recommending a certain policy in the *Memoirs*.[23] And he had perhaps learned something from loneliness: "I have seen few people in my life . . . who knew how to flee at the right time. . . ."[24] But he does not seem to have experienced the despair which sometimes follows loneliness until 1487: "Our only hope should rest in God. . . . But each of us realizes this late in life, after we have been in need of Him."[25]

According to Jean Liniger, these last words refer to Commynes' discovery of God in prison after he had lost all that had made his life rich up to then.[26] The fact that Commynes gave the chains which had held him in Loches dungeon to the monastery of Notre-Dame-La-Ronde near Dreux in thanksgiving after his release seems to strengthen this interpretation.[27] The judicial decree granting permission to Commynes to hear Mass regularly in his prison in Paris a little more than a month after his transfer there from Loches again argues for the hypothesis of a turn toward piety in a man who until then may have been accustomed to thank only his own talent and sharp sense of occasion for his spectacular career.[28]

23. M, p. 244. Of course, this is not to say that Commynes was without friends or incapable of friendship. See e.g., M, p. 313, where Commynes emphasizes the usefulness of friendship.

24. M, p. 285.

25. M, p. 145.

26. I am indebted to Jean Liniger, *Le monde et Dieu selon Philippe de Commynes* (Neuchâtel, 1943), for the references to the preceding three quotations, as well as for this last point. See especially p. 42 of his book.

27. See Gustave Charlier, *Commynes* (Brussels, 1945), p. 50. Charlier gives no source for this information, and I have been unable to trace it elsewhere. Possibly it is apocryphal.

28. This decree is reprinted in Dupont, *op. cit.*, III, 142–43.

Liniger's ingenious speculation, which I have adopted in emphasizing January, 1487, as a second turning point in Commynes' life, may perhaps never be confirmed. But if Liniger is wrong, why does Commynes insist that God is not only the ultimate cause and the ultimate judge of human events but also the ultimate refuge of erring, imperfect man? This assertion stands in such discontinuity with his didactic emphasis on the necessity for calculation and watchfulness in political life that it seems likely that a conversion, or at any rate a decisive deepening of religious experience, did take place in the lonely man which Commynes found he had made himself.

"One's first refuge is to return to God, and consider whether one has offended him in any way, to humble oneself before Him, and to acknowledge one's misdeeds; for He determines the course of such affairs and no one can say that he makes a single error."[29] Whether we interpret these words, occasioned by the actions of Charles the Bold, as reflecting Commynes' experiences in prison or not, they do express one of the key organizing principles of the *Memoirs*. Every major change in human affairs which he records—deaths, military victories, sudden success or failure—is seen as a result of God reaching into history to punish the wicked or, more rarely, to reward the good. Commynes uses history to moralize. Taken singly, his descriptions of the power of God behind or within the tight network of Franco-Burgundian and Franco-Italian power politics impress one as eruptions of medieval superstition in an otherwise commonsensical, slightly cynical mind. Taken together, however, they disclose a coherence almost as tight as that which Commynes portrays operating among the elements of politics. Such a systematizing of God's actions in history can only have been the result of profound meditation and conscious intent. Or, if the moralizing was not conscious when Commynes began writing his *Memoirs*, it shortly became so, as we shall see when we examine the motives he gives for his composition.

The two central events in Commynes' life were Janus-faced. His desertion isolated him from stable social ties and thus reinforced his tendency toward avid, calculating opportunism. But it thereby also

---

29. M, p. 313. Commynes is commenting upon Charles the Bold's depression after the battle of Granson. "Such," he says, "are the passions of those who have never experienced adversity and who do not know how to find a remedy for their misfortunes, especially proud princes." The sentence quoted in the text follows, and following this comes the material on friendship mentioned in note 23 above. The passage as a whole seems to me to show that Commynes is generalizing from personal experience, although he does so in his usual cool, impersonal manner. His imprisonment was certainly not his only misfortune in life, but it was probably the most signal misfortune and probably uppermost in his mind when he wrote this passage. This passage was probably written within two years of his release from prison and at most within four years.

sharpened his ability to observe others without the prejudices of vested interest. Commynes' coolness in describing deceptions and betrayals in his *Memoirs* is not the expression of an inhuman, amoral temperament, but that of a man looking on from the outside. Commynes is one of the most objective observers of his time because he had very little social or ideological stake in his reporting. Similarly, Commynes' imprisonment exposed the precariousness of his chosen isolation and removed him from influence upon royal counsels. But it also led to a deepening of his religious sense and to an enforced leisure during which he decided to commit his knowledge of politics to paper. Commynes' misfortune was posterity's gain. Between the spring of 1489 and the spring of 1491 he dictated the first six books of his *Memoirs*.[30]

Purpose of the Memoirs   In the dedicatory letter which prefaces the first book of the *Memoirs*, Commynes tells us why he is writing. Angelo Cato, Archbishop of Vienne and one of Louis XI's physicians, has asked him for materials about the life of Louis with a view to writing a history of Louis' times in Latin. Commynes has decided to set down his recollections in order to comply with Cato's request. But the memorialist does not content himself with this explanation. He explains why he is complying, and here both the influence of his imprisonment upon his decision to write and the extraordinary coolness with which he could speak of the most painful personal experience is expressed:

. . . Due to the obligation of honor and because of the great intimacies and kindnesses which were to be uninterrupted until the death of one or the other of us, no one should be in a position to remember him [Louis XI] better than I am. The losses and afflictions which have befallen me since his death also serve to remind me of the graces which I received from him. It is not unusual that after the decease of so great and powerful a prince great changes should take place. Some people lose from this, and others gain. For goods and honors are not divided up according to the desire of those who request them.[31]

30. See Calmette, I, xiii–xiv; some finishing touches to Book 6, at least, were added in 1493. The conversational style of the *Memoirs* indicates that Commynes dictated rather than wrote his work. A miniature which shows Commynes dictating his *Memoirs* confirms this impression, and Calmette has pointed to one error in the manuscripts of the *Memoirs* which could only have arisen through dictation (I, xviii, n. 3). Although some revision of the text was undertaken by Commynes (*ibid.*, xiii), the *Memoirs* retain the syntactical flavor of speech, and some of their repetitiousness and chronological imprecision comes from their quality as spoken rather than written work.

31. M, p. 92.

Commynes began the dictation of his *Memoirs* from a sense of duty and gratitude to his dead benefactor Louis. And by praising Louis, Commynes also praised himself. By demonstrating the success of Louis' policies, Commynes vindicated his own adherence to the king and the value of his past services to France. Vindication and self-praise were probably not consciously sought by Commynes in his *Memoirs*, but certainly the choice of his subject and the manner in which he explained events served these motives, conscious or not.

In terms of his stated purpose, Commynes began composition as Joinville had in writing the *Life of Saint Louis*: the *Memoirs* were simply to record memories of a prince to whom Commynes was personally bound.[32] Commynes' method of composition reflects the informality of this purpose. Avoiding digressions concerning his own actions and never searching out, so far as we can tell, what others might know of Louis, Commynes tells Cato only what he happens to remember. "I am merely sending you what I could readily call to mind, hoping that you are requesting this in order to make use of it in some writing which you intend to compose in Latin. . . ."[33]

The *Memoirs* begin as draft notes, primary source materials for Louis XI's biography. But within ten pages of the beginning of the narration, Commynes so far departs from this modest purpose as to offer a general interpretation of the fall of the duchy of Burgundy. The duke's territories before the fall, he says, "could be called promised lands." After describing the peace and prosperity reigning then, he concludes:

Today, however, I know of no other house so desolate and I suspect that the sins which its members committed during the time of its prosperity have contributed to their present adversity, especially since they did not realize that all these benefits were gifts of God, who distributes them according to His pleasure.[34]

Commynes cannot refrain from adding moral comments to his recollections. Thus it is not surprising that by the end of Book 3, a new purpose emerges alongside that of commemoration: the instruction of princes.

I do not mention these things [how a prince should treat ambassadors] to reflect on the person or persons I am speaking of, but only to describe the events as I saw them happen. Besides, I assume that stupid or simple people

---

32. Commynes calls his work "memoirs" several times (see, e.g., Calmette, II, 299), and suggests in one passage that commemoration is the chief value of all books (M, p. 170).

33. M, p. 92.   34. M, p. 100.

will not amuse themselves by reading these memoirs; but princes or courtiers will find some good advice in them, I think.[35]

The clearest statement of Commynes' didactic purpose occurs near the beginning of Book 6:

I say these things principally to show how the affairs of this world are managed, so that one may either aid oneself or protect oneself, for perhaps this may be of service to those who have great matters in hand and who may see these memoirs. For no matter how great their sense may be, a bit of advice is often useful.[36]

As the last sentence indicates, Commynes never thought of his work as an ordered treatment of politics or diplomacy. His didacticism was never systematized. But it became more and more explicit in his later books. As it did, Commynes' idea of noting down reminiscences to be elaborated with other materials into a Latin history by Angelo Cato was superseded. Cato died in early 1496, but Commynes continued working on the *Memoirs* until 1498. As Commynes' audience changed from a private friend to a political class, his book acquired a worth of its own.

The popularity of the *Memoirs* in the sixteenth and seventeenth centuries, the apocryphal tales of Charles V reading the book in his camp-bed, do not reflect an enthusiasm for the details of Louis XI's campaigns, but rather the idea that Commynes' words taught perennial political wisdom. The notion that history's prime value lies in its usefulness to politicians is of course still with us; it received particular credit during

35. M, p. 228. Commynes offers advice to princes before Book 3. Little lessons for diplomats and princely counselors appear alongside the admonitions to princes before the end of Book 1 (see e.g., M, pp. 129–30, where Commynes offers advice on the proper conduct of negotiations). In Book 2 he reprimands Charles the Bold and Louis XI for proceeding to meet each other without proper diplomatic preparation (M, p. 168); in Book 3 Commynes considers in detail the way for a prince to treat foreign embassies. His conclusion is significant, for it shows that he had not yet made these little didacticisms a conscious part of his purpose. Commynes excuses himself for digressing to offer advice and tries clumsily to show how his moralizing might be called an aspect of his memorializing: "I have been rather lengthy in speaking of these ambassadors and how one must keep an eye on them, but it was not without cause, for I have seen so many deceits and wicked acts carried on under the color of friendly embassies that I could not refrain from mentioning these things, nor treat the subject more shortly." (M, p. 228.) On the following page the quotation given in the text here occurs. Note that Commynes reiterates the intention which he expressed in his dedicatory letter, to narrate what he has known without judging the actions involved, while at the same time suggesting that politicians may improve their judgment of affairs by attending to his words.
36. Calmette, II, 247.

the Renaissance and was not foreign to medieval historiography. One reason why Commynes never went to great lengths to emphasize his intention to inculcate morality in general and instruction in politics and diplomacy in particular was that both he and his audience took that purpose for granted. As I shall try to show in the next section of this Introduction, this unspoken assumption has in the long run damaged Commynes' reputation. The aura of impartiality and profundity with which French writers in particular have surrounded the *Memoirs* has evaporated in the light of recent study.

Commynes regained prominence at court in 1491, and shortly became involved in the preparations for the French invasion of Italy which occurred in 1494. After acting as ambassador to Venice during the period of the invasion and negotiating the treaty of Vercelli which aided the French to return safely home in the face of a hostile coalition of Italian states, Commynes seems once more to have lost what little influence he had at court. He dictated most of Books 7 and 8 of the *Memoirs* in 1495–96, revising and completing them in 1497–98. His participation in public affairs was henceforth inconsequential, and he died quietly at home in Argenton on October 18, 1511.

2 / HISTORICAL METHOD

One of the most famous passages in Philippe de Commynes' *Memoirs* is the description of the interview of Louis XI and Charles the Bold at Péronne in October, 1468. Commynes uses this dramatic encounter to juxtapose the psychological peculiarities of the two arch-enemies and to indicate adroitly how Louis escaped from the overwhelmingly superior material force on Charles's side. The outcome of the Péronne interview has often been taken as a forecast of the outcome of the whole struggle between France and Burgundy in the later fifteenth century.

Karl Bittmann's multi-volume study of Commynes' trustworthiness as a historical source has shown, however, that Commynes' picture of the Péronne interview depends upon false facts and the omission of many true ones. In Bittmann's view Commynes' description of the Péronne interview is a subtle defense of Louis XI's actions. I would add that it is also a not-so-subtle demonstration of several of Commynes' favorite didacticisms.

Thanks to Bittmann's exhaustive study of the many accounts of the interview written at the time and since, Commynes' description of it offers us an excellent opportunity to examine how he engaged himself as an historian. I have chosen four of the many issues discussed by Bittmann to illustrate Commynes' methods as a historical writer: the so-called "revolt" of Liége, the surprise attack at Tongres, the occasions of Charles the Bold's anger at Péronne, and the peace following the Péronne interview.

After mentioning briefly the situation which prompted Louis XI suddenly to seek a peace conference with Charles the Bold at Péronne, Commynes interrupts his narration to comment on Louis' ardent desire for peace:

War between two great princes is easily started but difficult to stop because of various things which occur and their consequences; for many intrigues take place on both sides in order to harm the enemy, and they cannot suddenly be recalled.[37]

In the case of Péronne, the intrigue which Louis XI failed to call off—indeed "forgot"!—was a "revolt" against Charles the Bold at Liége. The result, described by Commynes some pages later, was that Charles, "surprised" by the revolt, flew into a rage at Louis' treachery and imprisoned him in Péronne castle, from which Louis narrowly escaped with his life. The way to prevent such dangerous consequences of a slip of the memory like Louis' at Péronne is, in Commynes' opinion, to avoid personal interviews between great princes, and to settle their differences "through the mediation of wise and worthy ministers."[38] This thesis is so important to Commynes that he interrupts his narration of the Péronne interview again at the point at which Charles grew angry at Louis, and inserts five pages describing other princely interviews which, according to Commynes, served no good purpose.[39] Toward the end of his account he pauses a third time: "Observe how a very great and powerful prince can suddenly fall into disadvantage through the action of very few enemies; that is why all undertakings should be well weighed and discussed before they are put into effect."[40]

The selection of events and their ordering in Commynes' *Memoirs* are determined by didactic and apologetic purposes at least as much as they are by motives of simple commemoration: Commynes wishes to emphasize the necessity of good counselors (such a man as himself, for example, currently unemployed) and of careful, conservative action

37. M, p. 168.
38. M, p. 173.

39. M, pp. 173–77.
40. M, p. 185.

(such as good counselors advise) which Commynes believes neither Charles nor Louis pursued at Péronne. To drive these lessons home Commynes asks his reader to accept a number of historical oversimplifications and omissions. For, as we now know, and as Commynes must then have known, the Péronne meeting was not decided upon on the spur of the moment, Louis did not "forget" the revolt being prepared at Liége at the same time as the interview, and Charles was not surprised when he heard of the revolt. In fact, the "revolt" of Liége was, juridically speaking, not a revolt against Burgundy at all, but a defense of her independence.

The "Revolt" of Liége   What actually had happened was, very briefly, as follows. Liége was an ecclesiastical principality, consisting of two large cities, Liége and Dinant, together with many smaller towns and a large rural area. Its ruler was a prince-bishop, who owed allegiance ultimately to the pope. Since Burgundian territories almost surrounded Liége, the dukes of Burgundy had from the beginning of the fifteenth century tried to incorporate the principality into their state. In 1456 Duke Philip the Good had his nephew, Louis de Bourbon, elected prince-bishop to further his aims. Louis, however, was not anxious to become the puppet of his uncle. He did not want to become the tool of the Liége bourgeoisie either, which had in the course of several hundred years acquired a large share in government through insurrections subsequently legalized by revisions in the town charters. Louis sought to escape the control of both the dukes and the bourgeoisie by using his ecclesiastical prerogatives. In October, 1461, he placed an interdict on Liége for rebelling against his rule, an interdict confirmed by the pope in 1462. The townsmen refused to give in, turning for protection to the king of France, and so the bishop in turn was forced to ask the duke of Burgundy for aid.

By mid-1465, therefore, the two traditional governmental powers in the state of Liége, the prince-bishop and the townsmen organized in guilds, had each acquired an external ally. For geo-political reasons this insertion of the constitutional struggles of the Liégeois into the larger framework of the duel between France and Burgundy was perhaps inevitable. But the important thing to note is that the interference of either France or Burgundy in Liége could take place legally only by means of a treaty with the composite government of Liége, the prince and the representatives of the towns, a treaty ultimately to be confirmed by the pope. Such a treaty was unobtainable, since the townspeople, in response to the papal interdict of 1462, had deposed the bishop and elected a German lay protector in his stead, thereby ending all hope of composite government. The bishop was potentially in the most legitimate position, for he could pose as the defender of the traditional constitution against the rebelling bourgeoisie. In fact, of course, he too sought more than a return to the situation before the rebellion; his aim was a lordship over the principality which would eliminate the share in government which the townsmen had gradually acquired.

None of the parties to the dispute, therefore, desired ends compatible with the aims of any other. The situation was representative of the institutional crisis which, as indicated at the beginning of this Introduction, beset many areas of Northern Europe in the fifteenth century. It was a situation in which the available institutions no longer functioned to channel strife into legal forms and yet also one in which the institutions, inadequate as they were, were well-organized and mature enough to prevent the outright success of simple military aggression. In this situation, time, circumstance, and diplomatic cunning played roles as determining as those of legal norms and power politics. Commynes, in his account of the so-called revolt of Liége, shows that he is sensitive to the interplay of time and circumstance with cunning and force—but only when it suits his purposes to be so. On the other hand, Commynes neglects entirely to place the working of these four factors in relation to the fifth—the larger juridical and institutional framework of fifteenth-century politics, decrepit and tottering though it may have been.

The memorialist's suppression of facts and also his insensitivity to institutional factors can be illustrated by reference to the first acts of war involving all four parties to the disputes over Liége—bishop, bourgeoisie, France, and Burgundy—which took place in the fall of 1465. Louis XI had signed a treaty in the spring of 1465, promising never to make peace with Charles the Bold, the prince-bishop's ally, without including Liége in the peace on favorable terms. Nevertheless, on October 5, 1465, Louis XI signed a peace at Conflans with Charles the Bold in which, abandoning Liége, he stated that he would not interfere with any action taken by Charles against the city. Two weeks after signing the treaty of Conflans Louis wrote to the Liégeois, not of course to inform them of his perfidy, but to pose as their ally and to encourage them to continue in their revolt, assuring them that they would be included and safeguarded in any treaty between Charles and himself![41] By this means, Louis hoped to hasten Charles's departure from France in order to put

41. See Henri Pirenne, *Histoire de Belgique*, II (Brussels, 1905), 279, for this point.

down the Liége revolt, leaving the king free to violate the terms of the peace just signed at Conflans. No word of this delicate interplay of time with diplomatic shrewdness on the part of his hero, Louis XI, is included by Commynes in the *Memoirs*, presumably because, as I shall show later, it was part of Commynes' strategy in explaining events at Péronne to minimize the king's involvement in the Liége dispute until the days immediately preceding the Péronne interview. As for the memorialist's neglect of the influence of legal norms on the development of the Liége dispute, it is amazing to note that although Commynes mentions the treaty of Saint-Trond of December, 1465, which followed Charles the Bold's invasion of Liége, he does not refer to its most important clause. This clause proclaimed the duke of Burgundy and his successors "guardians and advowed sovereigns" of the churches, cities, and countryside of Liége.[42] In effect, the treaty of Saint-Trond, if it had been confirmed by the pope, would have legalized a Burgundian over-lordship over Liége.

The pope did not confirm the treaty of Saint-Trond, but Charles the Bold used it nevertheless as the basis for further intervention in Liége. Fighting between the unreconciled parties broke out again in the summer of 1466, when Charles the Bold sacked Dinant,[43] and in the summer of 1467, when Charles and the bishop defeated the Liégeois at the battle of Brusthem.[44] Following this decisive victory, Charles destroyed the Liége fortresses threatening his frontiers, imposed new taxes to pay for the expenses of his campaigns, and eliminated the right of the rebellious craft guilds to representation in city government.[45]

While these measures were being taken, a papal legate arrived (April, 1468) and warned Charles through his local representative, the lord of Humbercourt, that any clauses in the peace treaty made at Brusthem which injured church rights and property were void. On July 14, 1468, Bishop Louis de Bourbon wrote to the legate, Onofrio da Santa Croce, pleading for help in the face of the duke's ruthless proceedings in Liége. The legate sought an interview with Charles, and a conference between bishop, legate and duke was arranged for August 10. It was a stormy meeting. Charles flew into a rage at Bishop Louis' suggestion that the peace of Brusthem needed revision in some respects, and accused the bishop of breaking his word, "as the king of France was accustomed to do." Finally, however, the duke agreed that the legate and bishop might

42. *Ibid.* See M, p. 142, for Commynes' only mention of the peace made at Saint-Trond.
43. See M, pp. 149 ff.
44. See M, pp. 153 ff.
45. See Bittmann, *op. cit.*, I, 217, and Pirenne, *op. cit.*, II, 284–85.

return to Liége to draw up a list of articles needing modification before making the Brusthem settlement final.[46]

In all this King Louis of France had taken little direct part, although he had posed as the ally of the bourgeoisie against the bishop and Burgundy in the campaigns of 1466 and 1467. Louis had been busy preparing a war himself against Charles the Bold, with a view to seizing the so-called "Somme towns," ceded by France to Burgundy in the treaty of Conflans of 1465.[47] Charles therefore left the conference with the bishop and legate to hasten southward to defend the Somme towns, in the vicinity of which Louis' troops hovered threateningly. With Charles out of the way, however, the legate was able to bring about an agreement between the bishop and the leaders of the Liége rebels. The bishop prepared to enter Liége and to order everything in accordance with the legate's mediation—without prejudice, however, to the interests of the duke of Burgundy, as the bishop said in a letter to Charles. The duke wrote back threateningly that he was happy to hear of the reconciliation between bishop and city, but that if this reconciliation impaired in any way the treaties of Saint-Trond and Brusthem, Charles would declare war.[48]

With this declaration the duke of Burgundy lost most of the basis for his presence in Liége. Until October 1, 1468, the date of his last letter to the bishop, Charles posed as the bishop's ally, an aid to traditional authority against the rebelling townsmen. Now that a settlement between bishop and townsmen had been achieved by the papal legate, the bishop no longer needed or wanted Charles's interference in Liége, as Charles clearly saw. The duke's only hope for continued control of Liége affairs lay in the ratification of the treaties of Saint-Trond and Brusthem, making him "guardian" of Liége. He therefore threatened to intervene militarily if these treaties were modified, as they certainly would be by the legate's settlement. Since these treaties were not yet law, not having been ratified by the pope, there was no reason why they could not be modified, and there was no legal way for Charles to intervene.

To Commynes, on the other hand, who had served in Charles the Bold's diplomatic service and had been privy to the duke's policy-making ever since the beginning of the wars over Liége in 1465, Burgundy's right to intervene seemed unquestionable. Commynes offers

46. Bittmann, *op. cit.*, I, 218–23. Charles's irate words are reported by the legate in his report, which Bittmann quotes on p. 222 in n. 21.

47. See M, p. 98, n. 6, for the importance of the Somme towns as a cause of war between France and Burgundy in this period.

48. Bittmann, *op. cit.*, I, 225–31.

only one overview of the Liége revolt: the Liégeois have always been rebellious; ever since the time of Duke John the Fearless (d. 1419) they have committed crimes against Burgundians and they have never kept the promises which they made to the dukes.

This [1468] was the fifth year that the duke had come in person and made peace, and invariably they broke it the following year. They had already been excommunicated for many years, owing to their cruel behavior toward their bishop, but they never respected or obeyed the commandments of the church in relation to this conflict.[49]

The year 1468 in fact was the third, not the fifth, during which the Liégeois fought Burgundy,[50] and the crimes they committed were simply attempts to retain independence from the Burgundian behemoth allied with their prince. Commynes, the parvenu noble whose fortunes depend on the power of the centralizing prince, cannot understand the Liégeois' defense of their municipal liberties, any more than his great-grandfather apparently understood the revolts of his hometown, Arras.

Liége was burned to the ground by the combined troops of Charles the Bold and Louis XI after the Péronne interview, some five thousand people were massacred, and Commynes clearly thinks this fate not undeserved because the Liégeois do not keep promises and do not respect their bishop and the church. We have just learned, however, that the bishop and townsmen came to terms in September, 1468, largely through their cooperation with the highest local representative of the church, the papal legate. Commynes, of course, includes no word in the *Memoirs* of any of the frantic exchanges and desperate negotiations between bishop, legate, city leaders, and Charles the Bold, which led to this last-minute reconciliation. The reconciliation, precarious as it was, was shortly disrupted—not because the Liégeois broke their promises but because Charles the Bold refused to accept it. The modern historian must conclude that it was the duke of Burgundy, not the Liégeois, who showed no respect for the church, utterly destroying one of its most flourishing principalities with acts of horrifying cruelty.[51]

In order to give some color to his view of the Liége revolt as an insurrection against Bishop Louis which Duke Charles obligingly put down,

49. M, p. 192.
50. Commynes seems to be speaking purely of the city, not the entire principality of Liége. The city took arms against Charles in 1465, but not in 1466. It fought again in 1467 and 1468. Even if Commynes is referring to the insurrection of Dinant in 1466 as well, it would make only four years.
51. The hypocrisy of Charles the Bold, and Commynes' own indifference to the fate of ecclesiastics who were not on his side politically, is illustrated by Commynes' account of the capture of the legate after the fall of Liége (M, pp. 180–81).

Commynes reduces the bishop to the status of one of Charles's officers, and represents the duke as a conciliating peacemaker: "In order to straighten matters out at Liége, the duke had the bishop of Liége retire, since the whole quarrel had taken place on his account; and with him retired the lord of Humbercourt, the duke's lieutenant in that country, and many others."[52] In point of fact, the duke was unable to persuade the bishop to "retire"; Louis de Bourbon remained in or near Tongres, a town ten miles north of Liége, from September 28 onward, torn between his desire to re-enter the capital of his principality in triumphant reunion with his subjects and his fear of the powerful displeasure of Charles the Bold.

As for Commynes' assertion that Humbercourt retired along with the bishop, this would seem to be a lie of which Commynes, serving at the time at Duke Charles's side, must have been perfectly conscious: from September 17 onward Humbercourt had been hastily gathering an army in order to proceed against Liége with force, as the duke had informed the bishop in a letter of that date. Advancing toward rather than retiring from Liége, Humbercourt arrived at the bishop's residence at Tongres with five thousand Burgundian troops on October 9.

Surprise Attack at Tongres   Humbercourt revealed to the bishop his orders: on the following morning, October 10, he would storm the city. While the bishop and the legate (also at Tongres from October 2 onwards) tried to convince Humbercourt that his orders would lead to disaster for everyone, a new dispatch from Charles arrived, commanding Humbercourt to undertake nothing without the bishop's consent. Perhaps this dispatch is what Commynes is thinking of when he states that the duke ordered the bishop and Humbercourt to retire. At any rate, it raised the hopes of the bishop and legate once more that a peaceful solution might be found. That very night, however, the Liége rebels, who had heard nothing of the actions of bishop and legate since October 2 and suspected them of forming plans with the Burgundian enemy, attacked Tongres by surprise.

The attack at Tongres was part of a war declared not by the Liégeois or their bishop but by Charles the Bold after the city took arms against the brutal Burgundian administration. The Liégeois seized the initiative at the last possible moment before the Burgundian army was to arrive at Liége, and with full success: Humbercourt and his army were taken captive and led back to the city on October 10. The bishop embraced

52. M, p. 167.

the rebel captains and sent a messenger posthaste to assure Charles the Bold that matters had turned out much better than many had hoped and that he and Charles's army were all safe. The legate accompanied the bishop, rebels, and Humbercourt's army back to the city.

Some few members of Humbercourt's army, however, managed to escape. Making their way to Charles the Bold's camp at Péronne, they reported, says Commynes in the *Memoirs*, that the bishop, Humbercourt, and many others had been murdered!

They affirmed that they had seen the king's ambassadors in this company and they named them. All this was reported to the duke, who immediately gave credit to it: he became very angry and said that the king had come to deceive him.[53]

Here, then, is the immediate occasion of that eruption of Charles the Bold's anger which so jeopardized Louis XI's safety at Péronne: Charles was so enraged, Commynes assures us, that it took all the persuasive arts of Commynes and two *valets de chambre* to persuade the duke not to imprison the king.[54] In contrast to these assertions of Commynes, however, four other sources on the interview at Péronne, each independent of the others, reveal the duke's anger exploding not once or twice but three times, all of them for reasons not mentioned by Commynes, none of them because of the surprise attack at Tongres. Furthermore, the surprise attack, like the whole of the Liége "revolt," cannot be construed as a stratagem of Louis XI to distract Charles the Bold's attention from events in France, for the king had done little more to further the Liégeois' cause in 1468 than he had done in 1465, 1466, or 1467. The two royal ambassadors seen by Humbercourt's fleeing soldiers at Tongres had been sent not to Liége but to the papal legate's camp, and not until September 30, that is, two weeks *after* Charles the Bold had mobilized against the revolt which Louis' ambassadors supposedly caused.[55]

The gripping scenes in the *Memoirs* in which Commynes depicts the rage of his lord and his own efforts to calm him are probably not fabricated. The memorialist has simply explained them in a manner which allowed him to emphasize the importance of good counselors and the dangerousness of personal negotiations between princes, rather than in

53. M, p. 172.   54. *Ibid.*
55. Cf. Bittmann, *op. cit.*, I, 232 and 242 with M, p. 171. No other royal ambassadors are mentioned in any source concerning the Liége revolt in the autumn of 1468. The two ambassadors mentioned by Commynes on M, p. 167, are the same as those mentioned on M, p. 171.

a way which connects the events at Péronne with Charles's political policies. In order to show how unfortunate hasty interviews between princes are, Commynes portrays Charles and Louis as victims of circumstance, unable to make any move without entangling themselves. In fact, however, it was the continuing aims and policies of the two princes, quite as much as events at Tongres and elsewhere, which determined the course of events at Péronne.

The cause of Charles the Bold's initial anger at Péronne was due to the conflict between long- and short-range goals. In the long run, Charles, like Louis, wanted peace with his chief adversary, in order to concentrate on less formidable enemies. This is why he agreed to meet Louis at Péronne. In the short run, Charles wanted to destroy Liége. This intention dates from the return of the Liége exiles to power at the beginning of September. From October 1 onward Burgundian cannons lumbered toward Liége.[56] Charles set October 8 as the date on which he would join the army to lead the final assault. This plan was changed at the last minute when negotiations to meet Louis XI at Péronne on October 9 proved successful; Charles now hoped to postpone the Liége affair until he had made peace with France. The attack on Tongres showed that this hope was vain. Not an unexpected attack by an enemy secretly egged on by Louis XI, but frustration at not being able to carry out the destruction of a well-known enemy first unleashed Charles the Bold's passionate temperament.

The second occasion of his fury can be ascertained by straightening out the time sequence at Péronne which Commynes compressed or expanded—here as elsewhere in the *Memoirs*[57]—in accordance with the lesson he wished to teach. "Three or four days" after the arrival of Louis XI at Péronne, says Commynes, news of the attack at Tongres arrived.[58] The memorialist tells us nothing of what went on during those days. Louis arrived in fact about noon on October 9 at Péronne.[59] News of the attack on Tongres arrived late October 11—that is, two or three days later, depending on whether one counts October 9 as one day.[60] Mean-

56. Bittmann, *op. cit.*, I, 258, n. 24.

57. See note 50 above, and Calmette, III, 299 and 309 for other examples of this tendency. The inconsistency between the economic sense of quantity which accounts for many of Commynes' insights in politics, as shown in section 3 of the Introduction, and Commynes' many chronological errors in the *Memoirs* is only apparent. Commynes' sense of quantity is related more to his need to rationalize reality than to a desire to historify it. That is, he gives us numbers, time, and place in order to show how events fit together to form schemes of order and moral balance more than to show exactly what happened when.

58. M, p. 171.

59. Bittmann, *op. cit.*, I, 246–47.   60. *Ibid.*, p. 252.

while, on October 10, 11, and 12, negotiations for a permanent peace were pursued, and Louis XI finally on October 12 declared himself ready to agree to anything—even the accompaniment of Charles the Bold on his expedition against Liége—if Charles would swear in return to forsake all his allies and ally himself solely with the king. Charles the Bold hesitated, and finally sent to the king the answer that he could not swear this oath.[61] On the morning of October 13, accordingly, Louis XI withdrew his promise to accompany Charles against Liége. Charles in response closed the castle gates and beset it with a guard at noon, virtually imprisoning the king.[62] The king's withdrawal of his promise, therefore, a withdrawal which suggested that Louis was merely trying to amuse him while the Liége rebellion went on, occasioned Charles's second burst of anger.

The third occasion was Louis' attempt to escape from the guarded castle of Péronne during the night of October 13, an attempt which failed.[63] Commynes says nothing of this attempted escape, committed as he is to emphasis upon only one cause for the eruptions of the duke's anger: the king's supposed instigation of the surprise attack at Tongres. We may grant that Commynes might have confused the real cause of the first two occasions for the duke's anger, due to faulty recollection of circumstances which took place twenty-two years before he dictated the *Memoirs*. But Commynes' complete omission of the third occasion, the king's attempted escape, cannot be explained as faulty memory, even when combined with didactic zeal. For Commynes himself tells us that the duke's anger subsided on October 13,[64] and yet erupted again with redoubled force the next morning.[65] The memorialist offers no explanation whatever for this new passion, which seemed so dangerous to Commynes that he went secretly to Louis XI and told him what he must promise to Duke Charles if he wished to avoid serious danger to his person.

It seems almost certain that Commynes' suppression of the cause of Charles's new anger and his secret aid to the king are tied together. The memorialist himself offers an oblique clue to his motives in his description of the king's actions on October 13. Louis, in semi-imprisonment

61. *Ibid.*, pp. 251 and 264.   62. *Ibid.*, pp. 266–68.
63. *Ibid.*, pp. 278–79.
64. M, p. 177: "On the first day there was great terror and murmuring in the town. But on the second day the duke calmed down somewhat." The first day must be October 12, the day following arrival of the news from Tongres during the evening of October 11. The second day therefore must be October 13.
65. The night of October 13—"the third" counting from October 11 when the news of Tongres arrived—the duke could not sleep, and Commynes tried to calm him. Nevertheless, "The next morning he was angrier than ever. . . ." M, p. 178.

due to his withdrawal of his promise to aid Charles, "had overtures made to all those whom he considered to be in a position to help him; and he did not fail to make generous promises. He gave orders to have fifteen thousand gold *écus* distributed among them; but the person who had been assigned to do this kept part of it for himself and acquitted himself most improperly of this task, as the king was to discover later."[66] As Joseph Calmette has suggested, Commynes seems to voice personal discontent here. He was almost certainly among those approached by the king's agents, given his intimacy with the duke. Commynes' avarice is one characteristic on which all students of the memorialist have agreed. It is very difficult, therefore, not to reconstruct affairs thus: Commynes accepted an offer of the king's gold, fulfilled his promises by reporting Charles the Bold's threats to Louis, became discontented when the king's agent did not pay him off in full for his information, and told the king about it after his desertion of Charles in 1472. Twenty years later, in dictating his *Memoirs*, Commynes still cannot forget his indignation at not having been properly rewarded for his betrayal of the duke's confidence.[67]

From Louis XI's point of view, of course, any news of his attempted escape would be almost an admission of his guilt in relation to the Liége revolt, and of his insincerity in seeking peace with Burgundy. Thus, Commynes suppressed the cause of Charles the Bold's anger with Louis on October 14 because it was too damaging to the reputation of his future employer.

The Peace of Péronne   According to Commynes, the king took the memorialist's advice, renewed his promise to accompany the duke against Liége, and swore an eternal peace with Burgundy upon Charlemagne's crucifix.[68] But Commynes fails to indicate a third promise which alone gave meaning to the other two: Louis XI promised to disband his army. As long as the French army hovered on Burgundy's southern frontier, ready to attack at the first sign of a break in the truce arranged between the two princes, Charles the Bold could not risk sending his

66. M, p. 177.
67. See Calmette, I, 142, nn. 1 and 2. Bittmann, who discusses the distribution of gold at Péronne at some length, showing that much larger sums of money were distributed than Commynes indicated, does not include Commynes' name among the receivers of gold. But the archival records which he used included the names of only the four chief recipients of money, and the absence of more names does not disprove the probability of there being more recipients.
68. M, p. 179.

own army in full strength against Liége. To risk it would have fairly invited Louis to occupy the southern part of Burgundian territory, including the Somme towns, while the duke besieged Liége. Only if the French army no longer threatened Charles's rear could the duke proceed against Liége. Accordingly, Louis wrote on October 14 to the commander of his forces to disband the army immediately. But this was not enough in Charles's eyes, for how could he be certain that the king would not send secret instructions to the contrary of his public ones? There was one way, and Charles took it. By forcing the king to accompany him in the assault on Liége, he could be certain that the French would not attack him from behind. Bittmann states it emphatically: forcing Louis to go to Liége was not an act of humiliation, an exposure of the Liégeois' erstwhile protector as powerless; it was an act of security without which Charles would scarcely have dared to proceed against Liége at all.[69]

The peace to which the two princes swore on the morning of October 14, just before riding off together to destroy Liége, was not dictated by Charles the Bold in Péronne castle. The king's unconditional surrender on all the points still at dispute between them was worked out in Brussels during the month of November by one of Louis' royal secretaries, equipped with the royal seal, and by Charles the Bold's counselors. The peace consisted of forty-two articles, each of them minutely worked out and all in favor of Burgundy. In return for these favors, Charles promised to swear fealty to the king of France for those territories held from the crown. Article 42 stipulated, however, that if the king violated any of the foregoing articles, then the duke would be henceforth not only free of his promise to swear fealty, but would never again be considered a vassal of the king, a subject of the realm of France, at all.[70] Such a clause betrays Charles the Bold's feeling that Louis could not be trusted to keep his promises, no matter how solemnly sworn. Just as he could find no way to protect himself from the king while proceeding against Liége except by making the king accompany him, so he could discover no method to guarantee a peace entirely in his favor except to threaten to liberate Burgundy completely from her feudal ties to France.

The duke was correct, of course, in supposing that the treaty would be broken. King Louis instructed his lawyers to draw up briefs proving the nullity of the peace of Péronne, in which he claimed that he had

69. Bittmann, *op. cit.*, I, 288. Commynes was aware of Charles's motive in forcing Louis to accompany him. He related this motive not to Charles's actions at Péronne, however, but to Louis' feelings at Liége two weeks later. See M, p. 187.

70. Bittmann, *op. cit.*, I, 293.

never accorded any of the articles nor ever seen them before, and that in any case he had been forced against his will into all the decisions at Péronne. Moreover, Louis sent secret instructions to France on October 14, the very day on which he swore peace, which, when successful, nullified one of the chief objects of the treaty. These instructions concerned the fiefs to be granted to Louis XI's brother, Charles of France, with whom the duke of Burgundy had been allied.[71] Commynes, as was necessary in view of these actions of his sovereign, says as little as possible about the peace of Péronne, but he does mention the clauses concerning Louis' brother, and he tries to explain why they were not carried out. After the destruction of Liége, when Louis XI took leave of Charles to return to France, "the king asked him: 'If by chance my brother, who is in Brittany, should not be content with the share I am giving him for your sake, what would you have me do?' The duke replied immediately, without realizing what he was saying: 'If he refuses this appanage but you see to it that he is satisfied, I shall leave it up to the two of you.' This question and answer were to have important consequences, as you shall hear shortly."[72] Several pages later, Commynes speaks of how the peace of Péronne was broken:

After the king had taken leave of the duke, he returned with great joy to his kingdom and did not stir against the duke on account of the way in which he had been treated at Péronne and Liége. . . . But the duke of Burgundy, by the advice of his officers, wanted to extend his boundaries; and certain shrewd moves were made to re-establish discord, as I shall explain when it is time. My lord Charles of France, the king's only brother, and formerly duke of Normandy, who was informed of the treaty of Péronne and of the share that was allotted to him, sent a request to the king, begging him to agree to carry out the terms of the treaty and to give him the lands which he had promised. . . . Messengers were sent back and forth on the question of the distribution of the land, for the king had no intention of giving up the territory which he had promised. He did not want his brother and the duke of Burgundy to be such close neighbors; and so he negotiated with his brother to try to make him accept Guyenne and La Rochelle. . . .[73]

In the end Louis succeeded in making his brother exchange the lands near Burgundy for the distant duchy of Guyenne, which was of no strategic importance to Charles the Bold. While Commynes asks us to believe that the duke himself allowed this turn of events with his casual remark to the king on November 3, the secret instructions which Louis

71. *Ibid.*, pp. 297–99. It should be noted that Bittmann offers no certain proof that these instructions are about Charles of France. The circumstantial evidence seems convincing, however.

72. M, p. 191.   73. M, pp. 193–94.

XI sent on October 14 prove that the king never intended to keep his promise about his brother's appanage. While Commynes places the guilt for breaking the peace of Péronne on Charles the Bold's head, with a vague reference to the duke's aggressive designs, the fact is that thirty-six of the forty-two articles of that peace—all declared void by Louis' lawyers, as we have noted—were agreed to by representatives of the two princes at a conference at Ham before the Péronne conference began,[74] and re-read and agreed to anew by the king, according to Commynes himself, just before Louis returned to France on November 3, 1468, after the destruction of Liége.[75] Commynes' description of the breaking of the peace, like his description of the events before and during the Péronne interview, carefully conceals Louis XI's perfidy.

Commynes has few criticisms of Louis XI's actions anywhere in the *Memoirs*, but the very manner in which he analyzed the Péronne affair obliged him to blame the king in one respect. In the description of Louis' character which he inserts near the beginning of the *Memoirs*, Commynes states that Louis' overriding fault was his impetuosity in prosperity.[76] Having succeeded in splitting the alliance between the dukes of Brittany, Normandy, and Burgundy, Louis rushed to conclude a peace with Charles the Bold. His desire for peace is offered by Commynes as sufficient cause for the Péronne conference, and thus when difficulties arose there, Louis had no one but himself to blame if he did not prepare the conference carefully and rely on his counselors to carry matters through.[77]

The *leitmotiv* of Commynes' thinking about politics is this: the coolest customer wins the game. I use the argot of business intentionally, for Commynes does too: to negotiate is to "haggle" (*marchander*), the "smartest" (*le plus saige*) negotiator wins,[78] and the one who "collects

74. Bittmann, *op. cit.*, I, 293.   75. M, p. 191.
76. M, p. 131.
77. Note that Commynes' attempt to establish this didactic point is also based on a falsehood. Louis did not rush to conclude peace; he had been negotiating with Charles at Ham for many weeks before the Péronne interview occurred, and many articles had already been agreed upon at Ham. As Bittmann has shown, *op. cit.*, I, 306 ff., Louis made efforts to meet with Charles to make peace from as early as February, 1468.
78. *Saige* or *sage* means literally "wise," and cannot be considered slang. But Commynes' use of it is such that "wise" is scarcely ever a correct translation: it nearly always means "shrewd" or "skillful"—a practical rather than speculative virtue. It seems to me that the closest translation of the word as Commynes uses it would be the colloquial "smart," as it is used by middle-class Americans today. P. Archambault argues in "Commynes' *Saigesse* and the Renaissance Idea of Wisdom," *Bibliothèque d'humanisme et Renaissance*, XXIX (1967), 613–32, that most of Commynes' uses of *saige* have moral and conceptual overtones, a position with which I cannot agree. See also n. 107 on p. 46 below.

the profit" from a political encounter will also collect the honor, no matter how devious his methods.[79] In the long run Louis XI, the smartest negotiator among the princes of his time,[80] won the battle against Charles the Bold, who was anything but a cool player in politics. At Péronne, however, Louis did not play coolly, and so, says Commynes, he was in personal danger for a time. As a special pleader for wise counselors, Commynes was bound to make Louis XI responsible for the fiasco of his attempt to make peace at Péronne. But as Louis' admirer, Commynes wished to preserve the picture of the king's shrewdness in politics. So he credited the king with engineering a revolt at Liége to forestall Charles's armies from marching on France, and then blamed the king for forgetting this stratagem and overestimating his personal powers of diplomacy when he went to meet Charles to make peace. Reduced to these terms, Louis' reputation is scarcely impaired, but then not many of the historical facts about Péronne are included or explained by such a schema, either.

Commynes' explanation is so patently oversimplified, in fact, that one wonders how he managed to think it up and to satisfy himself with it. Perhaps, as Karl Bittmann has suggested in reference to another episode in the *Memoirs*, Commynes didn't think it up. Perhaps instead he heard his "master," Louis XI, reminisce about it in this manner years later, after the two had become intimate and the particular events, aside from those involving the two confidants directly, had begun to fade from memory. If this is so, it would explain why Commynes' narration conceals Louis' perfidies so completely, for even if Commynes had had no compunction about praising such dealings, Louis would not have wished such things known. It would also explain why a few dramatic encounters between Charles and Louis or Charles and Commynes are reported with sharp detail, and yet are embedded in a morass of chronological inconsistencies and omissions. Above all, it would explain why the Péronne interview is seen in the *Memoirs* so exclusively from the perspective of the duel between Louis and Charles, rather than from the perspective of the duel between Charles and Liége. If Commynes had connected the surprise attack at Tongres with the battle of Brusthem and the sack of Dinant rather than with events in France and the controversy over the Somme towns, his explanation of the Péronne interview would necessarily have been different, though no less biased.

The Memorialist's Perspective   While special pleading is a major reason for the shape of the *Memoirs*, it is not the sole cause of Commynes' deficiencies as an historical writer. For however Commynes chose the perspective from which he regarded events, it always led him into bias and oversimplification. The reason for this is that his perspectives, or methods of describing historical process, are always taken from inside the circle of action described, rather than from both outside and inside that circle. That is, one method of avoiding bias in one's narration is to try to understand how each of the participants in a historical action felt and acted from their individual points of view, and then to step outside these individual perspectives and observe how they interweave with each other to form a continuous pattern of feelings, intentions, and gestures which touch upon and modify each other in a multiplicity of ways. Such a narration of events attempts to account both for the perspectives of the individual participants—modified and influenced as they are, each by the others—and for the shape and outcome of the action as a whole, a shape which in turn effects the next set of events in time's unbroken web. Commynes, in contrast, is only occasionally aware that more than one perspective on a set of events is even possible. This is because he was often physically involved in the events which he later decided to narrate. As a participant in the events, even if only as an observer, Commynes inevitably took a point of view which not only conditioned his perception of what the other persons present were doing, but also influenced the subsequent behavior of those other persons.

It is clear, for example, that Charles the Bold expressed his anger differently in the presence of two *valets de chambre* and Commynes, who must have often cautioned the prince to act with moderation, than he would have done in the presence of his general, Humbercourt, or than he actually did when he confronted Louis XI. Similarly, Commynes could not help but tend to side with one or the other of the two princes confronting each other in wrath and suspicion at Péronne, especially since one of those princes had probably bribed him. But since Commynes was not ostensibly the actor in these events or in most of the others which he reports in the *Memoirs*, he perhaps tended to assume that his view came from outside the circle of action and was therefore objective, requiring no amplification by other points of view.

When he set down what he knew of the events at Péronne twenty-odd years later, he did not exchange the point of view which he had had as participant for that of a historian seeking to avoid the biases of personal involvement. He reports his perceptions of the actions going on, and then he reports his interpretations of the plans and thoughts and feelings of the actors which led apparently to those actions. He never steps out of himself to judge Louis and Charles from the point of view of other participants at Péronne, nor does he ever consider how he himself appeared to Charles and Louis. The relation between psychology and circumstances is one-directional and discontinuous for Commynes, and so his narrative tends to fall into little descriptive bundles of feelings or intentions connected with actions. These bundles of feelings and actions stand side by side with little connection between them syntactically or conceptually.[81]

If Commynes had been more of a maker of politics, he would probably have discovered through unhappy miscalculations that his interpretations of the actions of others were distorted by his involvement in the situation. But Commynes was rarely a decision-maker. He was, moreover, solitary and retiring; in his unobtrusive ability to observe others consisted much of his value to his princely employers. The discontinuity between observation and action, between perception and participation, which Commynes found profitable in life was reproduced in his work; for this reason, as much as for his special biases, he is a poor guide through the maze of events in which he was involved.

The *Memoirs* of Philippe de Commynes, however, are more than an attempt to recapture a past in which the author played a part. For beyond this effort of memory—and it is a dazzling display of recall, whatever the biases—Commynes added a new element to his original thoughts and actions. From all that he had felt and thought as an observant bystander, he distilled the moral and political lessons which dot his manuscript. These lessons are not inserted in any planned manner. We have noted how Commynes only gradually became aware that he wished to instruct his reader as well as to inform him. Like a confidence made to a friend during the course of conversation, the generalizations which Commynes derived from his experience emerge without warning in the midst of his narration of events. As in conversation, too, these suddenly announced generalizations very frequently lead on to a series of reflections in which Commynes' interest gradually shifts from the situation at hand to the demonstration of his thought. After some pages of this, the memorialist mentally shakes himself, saying, "To return to the af-

---

81. A limited exception to this occurs in M, pp. 233–35, where Commynes does attempt to see a situation from two sides. After writing this explanation of Commynes' biases, F. Ernst's brilliant article "Zeitgeschehen und Geschichtsschreibung," *Archiv für Kulturgeschichte*, XVII (1957), 139–189, came to my attention. Ernst applies to all "contemporary historiographers" and "historians of the last generation" what I have asserted about the memorialist's perspective. Commynes' mode of historical perception, insofar as it arises from his temporal relationship to his subject matter, is the predominant mode occurring in European historical writing, according to Ernst.

fairs I was narrating," or "I felt I had to include this for the profit of my readers."

These reflective passages have a coherence among themselves; they express the view of life and of history which gives the *Memoirs* their distinctive flavor. Their force is that of personal avowal; each reflection throws light on the next in the same way that fervently held truths cohere in the personality without being logically connected. The attempts of scholars to schematize Commynes' theories about God, man, or government are therefore misguided. Commynes' reflections have no systematic character; they are not thought out, but instead develop in reciprocal relation with his recall of the past. Each reflection is discontinuous with the next, just as each cause-effect bundle is discontinuous with the next set of feelings and events in Commynes' narration. Just as each of Commynes' reflections throws light on the next, enlarging each time our sense of the whole of Commynes' personality, so each narrative series, discontinuous as it is with the next set of events, enlarges our sense of the historical situation as a whole. Commynes' *Memoirs* present, strangely enough, a distorted image of individual events, and yet a true mirror of the times. In the same way, Commynes' *Memoirs* include almost no elements of autobiography, while the character of their author is still extremely vivid to the reader.

The word "discontinuous" describes Commynes' historical method in two respects. On the one hand it makes clear the difference between Commynes' notion of the causality or interconnection of events and that of the historian who seeks multiple perspectives. On the other hand, it describes the relation between each of Commynes' reflections and the next, and, in so doing, distinguishes the repetitious, rambling, and yet cohesive structure of the *Memoirs* from the logical, systematic organization of political theories or philosophies of history.

Commynes' amalgam of recollection and reflection constitutes both the strength and weakness of his book. We can see now that the distortions of the Péronne interview analyzed here were absolutely necessary to Commynes, not simply to prove this or that about his hero, Louis XI, but in order to defend his own personality. Distortion is, in fact, too harsh a word. Commynes did not willfully glorify Louis, villify the Liége rebels, or expose Charles as acting with ineffectual rage. His judgments were the expression of convictions rooted in his personality, which his historical method helped him to preserve rather than transcend. The discontinuous character of his thought, constantly lifting him out and apart from events rather than propelling him forward, into, and around the circle of cause and effect, made it only too easy for him to recall the past in such a way that it would evoke the lessons on which he had based his own career. The didacticism which condemned Louis XI for his foolhardy venture into the enemy's arms at Péronne was rooted in Commynes' sense of caution in running his own life, while at the same time this sense required Commynes to arrange events at Péronne so that they too harmonized with the lesson of caution: Louis' shrewdness in politics *had* to win out against Charles's boldness.

Commynes has no intention of organizing his recollections either chronologically or thematically to show the evolution of events.[82] His purpose was rather to extract from the flux of time the lessons which would endure. Commynes wished to relive his experience in the light of eternity. This goal led him to justify himself first of all, and then the actions of all those he served—Charles the Bold, Louis XI, Charles VIII: how could he condemn these men, not just for this or that, but for the very essence of their lives, without condemning his own life, and no less important, his ambitions?

Out of this purpose, only half-conscious, arise the lacunae in exposition, the repetitions of style—Commynes was interested in clarity, not beauty or precision—the chronological errors, the partialities and prejudices of all sorts noted in our analysis of the Péronne interview. Commynes relied on his memory, and his memory selected events or suppressed them, arranged them or provoked didactic interruptions, in accordance with the needs and biases, equally only half-conscious, of his personality.

It is Commynes' very indifference to the traditions of historical writing which has made his *Memoirs* immortal. Commynes' recollections of events are told with a freshness which his contemporaries and superiors in historical technique, such as Georges Chastellain, or Thomas Basin, never achieved. The very naïveté of Commynes' moralisms lend them an expressiveness and relevance which more learned or more pious men seldom matched. This is the meaning of the paradox that all Commynes' commonplace judgments yet lead him on to illuminate a historical situation in a far from commonplace way. This is why Commynes' *Memoirs* founded a new genre of historical—or perhaps "parahistorical" —writing in France: memoirs are something between the private diary and the town or dynastic chronicle, a hybrid born of matching extraordinary political experience with conceptual and methodological artlessness. Commynes is the father of a glorious, and almost exclusively

82. M, p. 210: "I am not observing the order of writing used in histories, and I am not mentioning the years or the exact times during which these events took place...."

French, family of writers; Blaise de Montluc, Cardinal de Retz, the duke of Saint-Simon, and Charles de Gaulle are among his descendants.[83]

3 / POLITICS AND RELIGION

Feudal institutions still prevailed in northern Europe in Commynes' time. But urbanization, commercial intercourse, and technology had advanced so far that the feudal system was beginning to constrict social life rather than to facilitate it. In a few especially developed areas these new economic and social forces had already brought about the demise of feudal-manorial institutions. Among these limited areas were most of Flanders and Brabant, possessions of the duke of Burgundy, and Liége, which succumbed to the duke in 1468, as we have seen. Here the effect of the new urban-centered economy had spread even into the country-side: subsistence farming was often replaced by cash-crop agriculture, and manorial lords by capitalist investors. Here the woolen industry, supported by a vast system of well-situated waterways, had facilitated the growth of the largest trading and manufacturing centers in Northern Europe. These centers nourished and were controlled by a wealthy bourgeoisie. Bureaucrats, representing at first the local authorities, then the county or duchy, and finally the Burgundian dukes, gradually built up a sense of regional interdependence which overcame the intense local patriotisms of the High Middle Ages. Regional loyalties emerged, which were first used by the dukes of Burgundy and which finally found expression in the monarchies of Belgium and the Netherlands.[84]

83. Joinville, as I have intimated on p. 17 above, might be called the "grand-father" of this kind of writing. Eduard Fueter, in his *Geschichte der neueren Historiographie* (Berlin, 1911), emphasizes Commynes' shaping of memoir-writing into a form which became an important genre of modern historiography. But my definition of memoirs here is somewhat different from his. See also F. Ernst's excellent comments on the peculiarity of Commynes' type of memoir-writing in the Introduction (pp. xxiii ff., and especially p. xxxiv) to the German translation of the *Memoirs* cited on p. 82.

84. The duke of Burgundy possessed power in the various parts of his realm only by virtue of being confirmed as count or duke or lord by local authorities. The duke originally acquired his possessions through marriage or conquest. In the case of Flanders, Duke Philip the Bold married the only child of the count of Flanders and was confirmed in his possession of the county after the death of his wife's father in 1384 (See Chronological Table, p. xii). This confirmation took the form of an "entry" into the important cities of Flanders, at which time the duke confirmed or modified the privileges accorded to these cities by his predecessor. Whether and how he confirmed them depended on the power which he could muster at the time against the city; such a process is described by Commynes with reference to Ghent

Introduction

Only in Italy had the breakdown of feudal institutions gone further, integrating much of the peninsula into a group of regional states which were usually urban and commercial in character and sometimes influenced by classical republican ideas of polity. The term "public good," or *res publica*, used by the barons of France in Commynes' time to designate the interests of those who profited from maintaining the traditional feudal hierarchy,[85] often meant in Italy a corporate good, involving a calculation by city government or despot of the varied interests and powers of relatively unordered and mobile classses within state frontiers.

Even in Italy, of course, this sort of thinking was still mixed with and influenced by the older concept of government as the private property of feudal lords. Compared with Italy, almost all governmental authority within Burgundian frontiers was unrepublican; most of the territories of the duke were still feudal in structure and rural in economy. Compared with Italy and Burgundy, the rest of the continent showed little influence of the new economic and social movements on the structure of politics. Thus, even though most princely administrators in fifteenth-century Europe were trained in the centralizing prerogatives of Roman law and regularly overrode the prescriptions of feudal custom, even though the military power of monarchs consisted mainly of mercenary infantry rather than of a feudal array of armored knights, even though kings could count on the returns from a steadily increasing number of direct and indirect taxes to finance public affairs, the day-to-day making of politics remained enmeshed in feudal forms almost everywhere. There were two main reasons for this.

In the first place, urbanization and growing commercial and political intercourse was founded, even in Flanders, Brabant, and Liége, on a precarious base—a narrow agricultural surplus which famine, plague, and war could wipe out in a single season, causing such constriction that patterns of local subsistence tended to re-emerge. Famine: the price of rye,

---

in M, pp. 163 ff. It was therefore only as count of Flanders, not as duke of Burgundy, that Charles the Bold was recognized in Flanders as their sovereign. There was no juridical name for all the duke's possessions as a unit; because the duchy of Burgundy was the oldest and largest of these units, all his possessions were conventionally called Burgundy.

85. *Res publica* refers literally to the good of the community as a whole and was a familiar political concept both north and south of the Alps from the twelfth century onward. But the concept masked increasingly divergent social realities in these two areas of Europe. Commynes was well aware of this masking effect, as indicated by his comment on the War of the Public Good in 1465 (M, p. 136): At the conference concluding the war, he says, the public good was converted into the good of certain great princes.

basic food for the mass of town and country folk, rose 90 per cent or more during the course of the years 1460, 1478, 1490, 1493, 1497, 1501, 1513, 1517, 1521, and 1524—the era during which Commynes lived —on the grain market at Brussels.[86] Plague: Bruges lost 20 per cent of its population by plague in 1438, Pavia 42 per cent in 1485. London experienced twenty epidemics in the fifteenth century, Frankfurt eighteen, Hamburg ten.[87] War: military operations in the neighborhood of Ouges, Burgundy, reduced the number of households from fifty-three to twelve between 1404 and 1423.[88] The combination of war, famine, plague, and their secondary effects reduced the population of the Ile de France by 50 per cent between 1346 and 1470.[89] Between 1437 and 1496 the countryside of Brabant lost almost one-third of its population.[90]

Because all these catastrophes worked selectively, sparing one area and devastating another, attempts at regional cooperation were constantly disrupted, the tendency to evolve larger and larger social groups broke down over and over again, and politicians spent most of their time trying to repair the rents and tears in the political fabric they had inherited— like Charles the Bold, forced to interrupt peace talks with France in order to deal with Liége, or like Louis XI, neutralizing Brittany only to face Burgundy, Burgundy only to face Anjou, Anjou only to face Guyenne, and so on in a never-ending circle.

Secondly, feudal institutions hung on because they still worked to the advantage of the upper classes in most of Europe. Only in the limited areas mentioned above had urbanization gone so far that the upper classes in the towns—merchants, bankers, and industrialists—profited by abolishing feudalism. In the rest of Europe the new urban elites tended to accommodate themselves to the feudal system, acquiring positions of varying privilege in accord with the local balance of power. For the urban upper classes feared insurgence by artisans and industrial workers from below as much as they disliked feudal interference from above. Thus, when guildsmen revolted against the oligarchic regimes of merchants and industrialists, many of the latter called upon nobles, clergy, and prince to thwart them. Even where guildsmen were successful, their new

86. Herman Van der Wee, *The Growth of the Antwerp Market*, III (The Hague, 1963), 16. With the exception of the period from 1478 to 1482, when rye prices rose in two gigantic jumps with no dip between, rye subsided in each case to approximately its former price within two years.

87. See *Cambridge Economic History*, I, ed. Postan (Cambridge, 1966), 675. This work will henceforth be cited in this form: C E H, p. 675.

88. C E H, p. 676.

89. C E H, p. 664. The Ile de France is the province of which Paris is the center.

90. Van der Wee, *op. cit.*, II, 294. Brabant is the province of which Brussels is the center.

government either made its peace with feudalism, by coalition of the guild leaders with the older upper classes inside and outside the city walls, or else it succumbed. Those who revolted against the feudal-manorial system in the countryside had no hope of even a truce; the bloodbaths ending the French *Jacquerie* of 1358, the English Peasants' Revolt of 1381, and the German Peasants' War of 1525 are only the most famous of a host of examples.

The disorder prevailing in fifteenth-century Europe due to all these causes had two contrasting effects, fragmentation and centralization. Pockets of prosperity occurred only a few miles from regions devastated by famine and plague. Organization of villagers and townsmen for local self-government grew, but the lines of authority leading to regional and national levels were broken. Since they were broken, there were always opportunities for gangs of mercenary soldiers with no legitimate employment to move in and then move on before higher authorities could catch up with them, or for a ruthless lord to revise arbitrarily the charters of service owed to him by his peasant tenants, should the village organization in his area be weak. It became easier, too, for the upper classes to monopolize the well-paying offices in church and state. These manifestations of fragmentation only stimulated greater efforts by those at the top of the institutional hierarchy to control the bottom.

The multiplication of church officials, new taxes, and centralizing procedures during the Avignon Papacy (1305–1378) and Great Schism (1378–1415), the very moment of breakdown in the administrative unity of the church, was characteristic of secular governments as well. Inhabitants of some villages in north France, for example, exhausted by the Hundred Years' War, were nevertheless obliged to pay to the state 2 per cent of their total fortune each year in order to help finance national recovery. The end was rendered unattainable by such means, and the manner of tax collection reinforced the contradiction. In the village of Wavrin those exempted from taxpaying (nobles, clergy, and others who had bought exemption) possessed approximately one thousand acres of land; those not exempted possessed one hundred and fifty acres.[91] Attempts to centralize and to augment the means of the prince in order to combat local disorder therefore resulted as often as not in still greater disorder.

Polarization in Politics   What was happening, of course, was a kind of polarization of political behavior. As the old feudal structure was hollowed out by the urban-commercial revolution and by calamities of all

91. C E H, p. 698.

kinds, the only security that could be found was in attachment to the prince at the center or, second best, in local cooperation. Patronage by the prince was the road to power, as Commynes' own career bears witness. Local cooperation, however intense, could not stand when the prince directed his power against it, as Liége discovered in 1468. All intermediate institutions, the old hierarchies laboriously built up through subinfeudation and a growing economy, were fatally disrupted. And the absence of anything stable between prince and subject only augmented the attraction of each for the other. The rise of European absolutism begins in the 1450's; it is built upon the hollowing out of the feudal system and the resulting willingness of the subject to pay any price for security.

Philippe de Commynes in writing his *Memoirs* takes the social situation just described for granted. The character, experience, and method of historical explanation which he brought to his writing led him to concentrate not upon the state of society as such, but upon the kind of politics which resulted from it. Commynes focused his attention upon the filigree of diplomacy and negotiation, and it is precisely the narrowness of his vision which makes the *Memoirs* valuable. He had no idea of cultural growth or institutional change, not even a grasp of the larger aspects of policy-making.[92] Thus, Commynes' frequently praised realism is not only a matter of style; it is also a reflection of the limitations of his outlook. Commynes' supposed Machiavellism, on the other hand, reflects the common practice of his time as much as the peculiarities of his moral vision.[93]

It is not a very personal confession which Commynes makes when he praises craftiness as the most indispensable quality of the prince. We must take it as a sign of the times when Commynes advises us that "matters cannot be carried through without dissimulation."[94] When he reports his own betrayals, lies, and spying with matter-of-fact calmness, and indeed vaunts his special knowledge of the "secret tricks or deceptions which have been carried on . . . in the last twenty years,"[95] his tone should not surprise us. He is not advocating such practices, he tells us;

92. Other historical writers in Commynes' time possessed little more awareness of cultural and institutional factors. Nevertheless, in writers such as Molinet and Basin, a conceptual framework taking account of these factors did exist, as I show with respect to Molinet later in this Introduction.

93. As I point out later in this Introduction, to Commynes the state and its leaders are not independent of the moral standards applied to private persons in any respect, whereas to Machiavelli they are. But of course in many ways Commynes is similar to Machiavelli. See M. Daviso, "Commynes e la ragione di stato," *Occidente,* VIII (1952), 104–11; K. Dreyer, "Commynes and Machiavelli: a study in parallelism," *Symposium,* V (1951), 39 ff.

94. M, p. 214.   95. M, p. 215.

he is simply reporting how things are done and warning future politicians to be on their guard.[96]

Commynes is as aware as any cleric of the corruption of politics from a Christian point of view. He agrees with the clergy, too, in diagnosing corruption's cause: "lack of faith."[97] But Commynes never urges men to purge themselves of faithlessness and corruption. Instead he takes the fatalistic attitude that God will eventually right these wrongs. Indeed, he believes that the process has already begun. Just as "our faith and loyalty to one another" seems weaker to Commynes in his time than it had formerly been,[98] so "the cruel and sudden punishments which Our Lord has laid upon the great in the last thirty years" outnumber all those occurring during the preceding two hundred years.[99]

This pessimism, this sense that the times are decadent and that nothing can be done about it, coupled as it is with reliance on God to right the wrongs in which men fatalistically engage, reflects the polarization of political behavior described earlier. That is, Commynes deals with the gap which had emerged between prince and people, between institutional prescriptions and bureaucratic corruption, by allowing a gap in his own thinking. On one hand, he accepts the corruption here below and offers a series of practical suggestions to princes in which haggling and subterfuge are key methods. On the other hand, he asserts that the perfidy and cruelty which such methods perpetuate must and will be punished by an all-powerful God above. It is as if Commynes were seeking an explanation of the social world in the same terms as those which had worked in his own career: working ruthlessly and alone, he had risen to high favor with his sovereign. To God, as to his king, he left responsibility for the ultimate consequences of his actions.

Politics as Economics   The sense of money which Commynes brought from his life to his writing led him to quantify his observations of events; thereby he gained insights into war, diplomacy, and national power ignored by historians like La Marche and Molinet, who wrote in the chivalric tradition, or by those like Basin and Gaguin, who were influenced by the nascent humanist tradition. The chief difficulty with Charles VIII's invasion of Italy, says Commynes, was the king's failure to provide sufficient money at all stages of the preparation and execution of the campaign.[100] Even at the end, he points out, if the forty

96. M, p. 213.
97. M, p. 362.
98. M, p. 169.

99. Calmette, III, 300.
100. Calmette, III, 3 and 256.

thousand ducats due France's mercenaries had arrived at the right time, the last French footholds south of the Alps could have been preserved.[101] The essence of diplomacy is the art of bribing; in Commynes' opinion the judicious employment of secret pensions and wine to the English army and royal counselors by Louis XI at Picquigny averted the English invasion of France in 1475. Every pensioner is named and the amount of his bribe stated. The memorialist describes how three hundred wagon-loads of the best wines of France were carted into the village and dispensed freely at public tables near the city gates and in nine or ten taverns.[102]

Numbers, time, and place serve to define reality for Commynes to a remarkable extent. The urge to quantify reveals the materialism of his view of life. What struck Commynes most about Charles VIII's death, for example, was not the feelings of the king or those of the bystanders but the fact that "this great and powerful king died . . . in such a miserable place [a part of Amboise castle fallen into disrepair], when he possessed so many magnificent houses; . . . he could not choose anything but a poor chamber to die in at the end."[103]

Commynes reduces politics to economics. I do not mean merely that he sees money and goods, rather than loyalty, social prestige, or law as the instruments by which political affairs are successfully carried through. I mean above all that the ideal prince in Commynes' eyes is the one who carries on state business with a minimum of human as well as monetary expenditure. The most economic way is the best way in Commynes' eyes, and it is reached by those who are "shrewd about how to reach their goals."[104] The ability to calculate, to think clearly from envisaged ends to possible means, is thus the fundamental political art: this insight into the need for rationalization of politics is what leads Commynes to be both a staunch supporter of royal centralization and a critic of Louis XI's tax policy.[105] He believed that a centralized, rationalized policy would cost least, and so reduce the need for taxes. Commynes' derogatory remarks about those who let passions interfere with their handling of state affairs, and his preference for non-military solutions of political disputes derive from this same economical habit

---

101. *Ibid.*, p. 266. 102. M, pp. 274–76.
103. Calmette, III, 307. Commynes' materialism obtrudes again in his description of the funeral, *ibid.*, p. 313, where the total cost, number, and richness of vestments and length of the services are described with wonder.
104. M, p. 144.
105. Cf. Calmette, II, 278, and M, p. 360. See p. 6 and pp. 11–12 above for the personal roots of Commynes' economic habits, which of course supplement his intellectual inclination to rationalize and order affairs.

of mind. Commynes' advice in politics is formally moderate: one should respect treaties, safe-conducts, and the "natural boundaries" of nations. But it is substantively unscrupulous: if need be, anything goes, for "those who win get all the honor."[106]

The commonplace wisdom of this epigram strikes us because it is both knowing and cynical. It suggests in one direction Commynes' suave acceptance of fraud as the common practice of his time and his advocacy of it as the most efficient and rational means available. But it also retains—and from this derives the stylistic thrust of Commynes' phrase—the notion that there is something illicit in the pair, "profit" and "honor." When Commynes speaks of negotiation as "haggling" or "merchandising," he is fully aware that he is describing the process of distributing public power as if it were no different from the marketeering processes of private men of low estate.[107]

Commynes, for all the professionalism of his approach to politics, did not grasp the structure of foreign relations as it was emerging in his time. He reproduces the new atmosphere of diplomatic intrigue marvelously, but he does not see that continuous negotiation on the basis of standing embassies was now becoming the normal means of furthering the state vis-à-vis its neighbors. He emphasizes again and again that kings should not see each other personally, that diplomats should be diligent in hiring spies in foreign capitals and in pursuing every scrap of information about those with whom they share frontiers.[108] Yet he also insists that a wise prince will never allow standing embassy and will permit representatives to remain in his country as little as possible.[109] For Commynes—and for his master, Louis XI, too—negotiation is still an extraordinary means of politics, where no rules of justice are possible, and where immoral practices therefore predominate. Frequent embassies are a sign of bad faith and evil intent. In an ideal state of politics, negotiations would not be necessary, just as taxes would not be. For Commynes, the rationalistic, economy-minded conservative, the

106. M, p. 325. See pp. 33–34 above for a variation of the same phrase.

107. See Karl Bittmann's pamphlet, *Contribution à l'histoire de Louis XI. Un document inédit* (Paris, 1945). In the letter edited by Bittmann in this pamphlet, Louis XI uses *sage* and *marché* just as Commynes does: ". . . Si j'estoye si sage que je sceusse conseiller le Roi, je luy oseroye bien conseiller qu'il ne se fiast point en celuy qui ont prins en leur cuer le parti de ses ennemis . . . et encore quant ilz lui offreroient ung grand marché si n'y devroit il pas entendre, car on dit un commun proverbe pardeça que oncques grand marché ne fut net et qu'il y a tousiours gare derriere." The king speaks of himself in the third person in this letter for reasons of secrecy, as Bittmann shows. (The letter is reproduced by Bittmann on an unnumbered page following p. 31 of his pamphlet.)

108. M, pp. 227–28.   109. M, pp. 226–27.

ideal situation is clearly that where the state is in balance within and without, at peace with foreign powers and in equitable control of affairs at home.

God's System of Just Balances   God has organized the universe as a system of balances, not for economy, but for the sake of justice:

All things considered, it seems to me that God has created neither man nor beast in this world without establishing some counterpart to oppose him, in order to keep him in humility and fear. . . . For to the kingdom of France He has opposed England; to the English He has opposed the Scotch, and to the kingdom of Spain, Portugal. . . . God gave the house of Aragon the house of Anjou as its counterpart; the Visconti, dukes of Milan, have the house of Orleans. . . . The Genoese have their bad government and their lack of faith toward each other, and divisions occur in their very [family] alliances, such as the Fregosi, Adorni, Doria, and others. . . .[110]

This remarkable passage introduces the most detailed exposition of God's government of human affairs in the *Memoirs*. Divine providence sets nation against nation, city against principality, dynasty against dynasty, and faction against faction. It cuts across religious barriers, pitting Moslem against Christian, and across continents, operating in Asia and Africa as well as in Europe.

It may seem, therefore, that these divisions are necessary in all the world. . . . And offhand, speaking as a unlearned man who wants to hold only opinions which we should, it seems to me that this is so, and principally because of the stupidity of many princes, and also because of the wickedness of others, who have enough sense and experience but wish to use it evilly.

Human stupidity is more important than men's wickedness in moving God to set up his system of balances because the evil resulting from stupidity can scarcely be remedied. Stupidity, or lack of wisdom, results either from one's temperament or from improper education, Commynes tells us. If princes are unwise from either of these causes, they will not know how to rule properly, even if they are "good"; and those who do know how to rule well will not offer good advice to the unwise prince "for fear of displeasing them." On the other hand, wicked men, gaining knowledge, may abstain from evil because "they will not wish

110. M, pp. 353–54.

to appear bad." They may also avoid evil "because of fear of God's punishments, of which they are more aware than ignorant persons who have neither seen nor read anything."[111] Thus, if one considers mankind from the point of view of the duality good-evil, one can see that dissent and division might be avoided by both sorts of men. But, if one considers men from the point of view of the duality wise-stupid, there seems to be no remedy for the quarrels caused by stupidity except that set up by God in the form of an opposing faction.

The foundation stone of Commynes' thought, the most frequently invoked psychological quality, the category in terms of which most other categories are judged, is intelligence. The memorialist tends to polarize the possession of this quality—one is either stupid or wise; the only prominent nuances he admits are that youth is an excuse for ignorance and overindulgent education a severe handicap in developing wisdom. Wisdom is practical intelligence, not power of mind; the wise man displays his possession of that quality through activity and increases it through experience.[112] This emphasis on practicality and experience as the measure of mind is the reflection of Commynes' sense of economy and of his preference for what can be quantified. Such practical genius or "good natural sense" shows itself early, Commynes insists; princes who do not possess it "are very dangerous and dreadful, for they are the source of the prosperity or adversity of their territories."[113]

This last quotation indicates the economic basis of the third duality employed by Commynes in his work, princes-subjects, or more generally, "the great" and "the small." This pair, together with the moral and intellectual oppositions just described, almost exhausts Commynes' not-very-subtle notion of human nature and of social distinctions. But surely the lack of subtlety displayed here, and the fact that all three of these descriptions of human behavior, moral, intellectual, and social, are conceived as polar opposites, reflects the hollowing-out of institutions in Commynes' time mentioned earlier. Social disorder led men to think in extremes; fine distinctions of class, culture, and conduct no longer mattered. As a consequence, the quality of life among those with whom

111. M, p. 355.
112. This is why, as mentioned on p. 33, n. 78, the word "wise" in the *Memoirs* usually means "shrewd," "sharp," or "smart."
113. M, p. 356.
114. Commynes was obtuse socially but not psychologically; his perceptions of others' characters are marvelously various and precise, as I have shown elsewhere. But the conceptual molds into which he poured his perceptions were crude; consequently, the more he generalized, the more his distinctions tended to melt into simplifying dichotomies.

Commynes was not habitually in contact was essentially unknown to him. Commynes registers pity at the suffering of "the small," but never empathy.[115] His comment on "quarrels among persons of inferior rank," like his comments on the people of Liége discussed earlier, must be seen in the context of alienation and incommunicability between those at the top and those at the bottom. Commynes tells us that such quarrels may be disregarded, since the weak "have superiors who sometimes give justice to those involved. . . . In the long run he will receive justice if the court (that is to say, the prince under whose authority he [the small man] lives) is not against him."[116] Anyway, says Commynes later on, "The greatest misfortunes generally proceed from the strongest, for the weak seek only to have patience."[117]

Only the quarrels of the great who have no superior, therefore, provoke God to intervene in history. "How would one punish these strong men, who use force to accomplish whatever they please, if God did not put His hand in it?"[118] These men indulge in judicial murder, illegal confiscation of feudal property, and aggression against their neighbors on false pretenses. They replace loyal officers with influential favorites, disregard the counsel of the nobles, crush the common people with taxes, and quarter rapacious mercenaries on the land.[119] Some of the items in this eloquent diatribe, like Commynes' recurring jeremiads against princes who fail to heed wise counselors, seem to reflect personal grievances. One might almost guess, therefore, that the last and greatest of princely sins is the invasion of private property through taxation; Commynes asserts roundly that no king or lord in the world has the right to levy money without counsel, "unless he does it by tyranny and is excommunicated."[120]

115. See, for example, the chilling manner in which he describes the starving survivors of the siege of Novara in Calmette, III, 238: ". . . I saved at least fifty of them with an *écu* . . . [in return for which] they were given soup, and only one died; though on the road back about four died. . . ." The quantities, not the qualities, of suffering are what Commynes is anxious to get straight for the reader. His narration of the events accompanying Charles the Bold's pillage and burning of Liége exposes even more cruelly the absence of any humanitarianism in his thought. The barbarities reported here impressed his ears, in one case at least, as "dreadful," but for the rest they seemed more "peculiar" than pitiful. His only comment on the bestial manner in which Charles's nobles hunted down villagers hiding in the woods near Liége, for example, is to point out that many of them "gained much loot" from such business. See M, pp. 190 and 192–93.

116. M, p. 356.   118. M, p. 357.
117. M, p. 361.   119. M, pp. 357–58.
120. M, p. 361. This is one of the few references in the *Memoirs* to church powers of any kind. See also M, p. 358, where Commynes emphasizes again that taxation without consultation is evil. Note also on p. 354 that violation of this right is the only fault of Italian princes mentioned by Commynes.

Whether by means of clerical sanctions or other punishments, Commynes was certain that God would punish these evil lords:

> The blows that [God] gives to the great are much more cruel and much more weighty and of much longer duration than are those which he gives to the small. And it seems to me that, considering everything, they [the great] have scarcely any advantage in this world over others. . . . For they punish the men who live under them at their pleasure, and Our Lord disposes of them as He wishes, for they have no superior except Him.[121]

Commynes' suggestion that the great suffer as much as the small is based on his conviction that God often—Commynes does not say "always"—punishes men for their sins in this world, rather than deferring it to the after-life. ". . . God has to show His will by means of examples and instances, so that they and everyone else may be convinced that their punishments are the result of their cruel offenses. . . ."[122] The punishment proceeds by stages: "First of all He attacks their understanding. . . ." Commynes gives an example of this when he speaks of how God "troubled the sense" of Charles the Bold, so that he failed to heed warnings that Campobasso, one of his generals, intended to betray him.[123] "Then He troubles their house and allows division and dissension to arise in it. . . . The prince . . . shuns the advice of the wise and raises to high positions persons of little experience. . . ."[124] This brings high taxes, arbitrary court procedures, and dissent among the prince's subjects. "When there is internal dissension, outsiders frequently step in," and so finally ". . . when he [the prince] least suspects it, God will raise an enemy against him" and put an end to his power.[125] Commynes offers a number of proofs of these propositions in the final section of the long disquisition on the power of God in history from which we have been quoting: the kings of England, Spain, and Scotland, he asserts, all received their thrones due to divine retribution.

These proofs of God's power over evil princes do not, in Commynes' description, follow exactly the sequence of steps in punishment earlier outlined by him; in the same way Commynes' notion that the great suffer as much as humble people is not very well substantiated by his accounts of the tribulations of princes like Louis XI and Charles the Bold.[126] But the interesting thing about Commynes' analysis of the ways of God in history is not whether the theory fits the facts he offers but

---

121. Calmette, III, 300.
122. M, p. 364.
123. M, p. 296.
124. M, p. 364.
125. M, p. 365.
126. See, e.g., M, p. 362, where Commynes contradicts the statement that the small get justice in the end.

rather that he felt impelled to resort to such explanation of events, and that in doing so, he felt compelled to try to rationalize and systematize God's action, just as he was trying to do with men's action.

Commynes avoided narration of the past as a tissue of divinely ordained miracles; when God appears in the *Memoirs*, Commynes nearly always offers a rationalization for it. He also avoided narration as the mere logical interweaving of men's selfish interests; the catastrophes of his time were apparently too sudden and too grand to be explained by means of the primitive psychology and scarcely existent sociology available to him. God had to be brought in. But, most importantly, Commynes avoided relating his scattered reflections on God, on the need for economic wisdom, and on human injustices and cataclysms to each other. Each reflection is roughly congruent with the next, yet if compared with others in detail, there are always inconsistencies.

Commynes' moral and religious convictions, like his political principles, are commonplace and conservative; he bases his meditations on the assumptions of divine omnipotence, human sinfulness, and the need for justice in a world gone wrong. But his methods of applying these assumptions are new and remarkable: Commynes demonstrates his propositions in a narration which proceeds with an almost mechanistically conceived rationalism and with an attentiveness to concrete detail and specific example for each of the generalizations asserted. He thus combines new ways of looking at reality with older, commonplace ways of judging reality. This strange mixture is made possible by the gaps in his thought, gaps which we have already observed in citing his political and psychological views, and which we have guessed may reflect or have been absorbed from confronting the hiatuses in his society. The lack of congruence between means used and ends sought, between assumptions and proofs, between the realism of his descriptions and the idealism of his reflections is one reason why Commynes appears to be very medieval and very modern at the same time.

Commynes' Materialistic Christianity   It is impossible to say whether Commynes' rational, factitious method of understanding human behavior was more important to him than the ideals of justice, balanced control, and retribution in accordance with which he thought God governed the world. But one may observe that the habit of collecting facts to demonstrate the truth of his observations invaded every sphere of Commynes' thought, so that even heaven and hell are finally conceivable only in material terms. Consider, for example, Commynes' definition of "lack of faith," to which he attributes the unjust acts of the great.

If a poor man, who has true and good faith in God, and who firmly believes the tortures of hell to be as they really are, and who also has wrongly possessed himself of someone else's property, or whose father took it, or his grandfather, and he possesses it now, whether it is a duchy, county, city, castle, furniture, a field, a pool, [or] a mill, depending on each person's rank, believes firmly, as we all should, that: "I shall never enter paradise if I do not give full satisfaction and if I do not give back what I truly know belongs to others," is it possible that any king, queen, prince, princess, or any other persons of whatever quality or condition they may be in this world, great or small, men or women, living on this earth would in true and good conscience (as I said before) retain anything from his subject, or subjects, or anyone else, whether a close or distant neighbor, or would want to put him to death wrongly and unjustly, or keep him in prison without reason, or rob some to make others rich (which is their most common occupation) or act dishonorably toward their parents or servants to further their own pleasures, as with women, or do anything similar? By my faith, no! It would be incredible. Therefore, if they had firm faith, and believed what God and the church command us under penalty of damnation, knowing that life is so short and the pains of hell so horrible and without end or remission, would they be as they are? One must conclude that they would not, and that all evils come from lack of faith.[127]

The shift in the subject of the first sentence in this quotation from poor man, to possessors of duchies, counties, cities, or less, to kings or queens or anyone, betrays Commynes' excitement and desire to convince—himself as well as his reader, perhaps—even before the expostulating climax. Note once again that the illegitimate seizure of property occurs to Commynes as the paradigm case of injustice, by means of which other unjust acts may be understood.

Apparently Commynes made evil or injustice, as well as the penalty paid for it in hell, most meaningful to himself by materializing it. It followed from this propensity to conceive evil materially rather than spiritually that one's failure to calculate correctly the material consequences of one's actions was in some sense the origin or cause of one's sin. Lack of faith, Commynes seems to say, is what causes man to miscalculate. For the length of suffering to be borne in hell in exchange for earthly gratifications procured through injustice is so disproportionate that a rational man who believes this exchange will take place would never commit injustice. The only reason immoral acts occur, therefore, must be that men do not believe in this exchange; they do not believe that injustice must be paid for in hell.

The proof which Commynes offers for this definition of the world's

127. *Ibid.*

ills illustrates again the materialistic quality of his Christian convictions. Men would give up their evil gains, he asserts, if they truly believed in the horrors of hell, because princes who have been imprisoned give up anything they own for their freedom. When King John of France was captured by the English, for example, he did not hesitate to surrender "a third of his kingdom." Yet if he had surrendered nothing and the English had killed him, "the agony of the execution would not have been equal to the one hundred thousandth part of the least torment of hell."[128]

The external, punitive quality of Commynes' idea of faith is thus intimately connected with the calculating attitudes which he advocates in political life. This materialization of Christian teaching and calculation of its implications is apparently the only way Commynes can conceive of the connection between politics and morality. Commynes sees no way by which expiation can be insured for the tremendous injustice which he saw about him except by using the same weapon with which this injustice was created: power can only be fought with power, and thus God is forced to punish men in ways just as hideous as the crimes they have committed.

To suggest, as Pietro Pompanazzi did some thirty years after Commynes wrote, that sin and virtue are their own reward, that the very quality of one's life constitutes the severest punishment or the highest reward of moral action, was quite beyond the memorialist.[129] To accept the injustice and suffering confronting him as a fact without redress was equally inconceivable. The most eloquent example of the one-dimensional, superstitious, and trivial religious faith which resulted from this is Commynes' discussion of Louis XI's last days.

The details which Commynes reports of Louis' bizarre attempts to prolong his life—his collecting manias, his suspicions, and his frantic pieties[130]—are sufficient in themselves to warn us against considering Commynes' materialistic religiosity unusual.[131] In this as in his amoral political advice, Commynes reflects his age as much as his poor education[132]

128. M, p. 363.

129. See the concluding sections of Pompanazzi's *On the Immortality of the Soul*, translated in E. Cassirer, *et al.*, ed., *Renaissance Philosophy of Man* (Chicago, 1948).

130. Calmette, II, 282–99, 308–24.

131. Johan Huizinga has catalogued dozens of other examples in *The Waning of the Middle Ages* (New York: Anchor Books, 1954). The opposite extreme, a complete immaterialization of religion, occurs in equally striking fashion in the thought of Commynes' contemporary, Nicholas of Cusa.

132. Commynes speaks frequently (e.g., M, p. 92, and Calmette, II, 340) in the *Memoirs* of the deficiencies of his education. He seems to have received the education of a nobleman—horseback-riding, weaponry, and polite manners—without acquiring even a touch of Latin, let alone of theology.

and scrambling, parvenu career. Yet the note on which Commynes concludes this description of the king offers a curious illustration of how close he was to formulating Pompanazzi's insight for himself. Louis fortified his residence at Plessis-lez-Tours, Commynes tells us, in order to discourage anyone from wresting power from the ailing king. The castle was

enclosed with large iron bars in the shape of a thick grating, and at the four corners of the house he had four iron cabins built, which were solid, large and thick. . . . He had many iron spikes put in the wall; each one had three or four points and they were planted very close together. Furthermore he placed ten crossbowmen at each one of the iron cabins, in the ditches, to shoot at anyone who might approach before the opening of the gate. . . . The gate of the castle of Plessis was not opened before eight o'clock in the morning, nor was the bridge lowered before. Then the officers entered and the captains of the guards placed their ordinary gate keepers at their posts and ordered their archers to keep watch at the gate and in the middle of the courtyard, as in a frontier town that is closely guarded. No one was allowed to enter except by the wicket and with the king's knowledge; only major-domos and persons of that sort were not required to be seen by the king.[133]

"Is it possible . . .," exclaims the memorialist,

to confine a king . . . in a closer prison than that in which he kept himself? The cages in which he had kept others were about eight feet square; and he, although he was such a great king, had only a small courtyard of a castle in which to walk. . . . Would anyone say that the king did not suffer, considering that he locked himself up and had himself closely guarded, that he was afraid of his children and of all his close relatives, that he changed and transferred from day to day his servants and those whom he had nourished, who owed all their goods and honors only to him? Yet he did not dare trust any of them but fettered himself in such strange chains and enclosures.[134]

If Commynes had ended his reflection here, we should admire his insight into the psychological consequences of Louis' ruthless pursuit of power, a pursuit which led inexorably to his own isolation at the center of the web of money, men, and iron with which he had successfully held together a disintegrating state.[135] But he does not. Before and after the passages just quoted Commynes points to the heavenly plan behind this suffering of his hero:

133. Calmette, II, 322–23. 134. Calmette, II, 323.
135. Louis was called "the universal spider" by the Burgundian chronicler Georges Chastellain.

... Just as these various evil prisons [e.g., the iron cages] were invented in his time, so he himself, before he died, found himself in comparable prisons, and in even greater ones, and in as great fear as those whom he had kept there. I hold this to have been all the greater grace for him and part of his purgatory. And I say this to show that there is no man, of whatever dignity he may be, who does not suffer either secretly or publicly, especially if he has made others suffer.[136]

... The patience with which he endured his sufferings, which were similar to those which he had inflicted on others, is attributable in my opinion to the punishment which Our Lord sent him in this world, so that he would have less of it in the next.... After so many fears and suspicions and sorrows, Our Lord accomplished a miracle for him and cured his soul as well as his body, as it is always His custom when He performs miracles, for He took him away from this miserable world in excellent health of sense and understanding, and with his memory in good state.[137]

Psychological suffering had no meaning for Commynes until it could be seen as part of a religio-moral economy. God gave Louis this punishment here in exchange for less suffering after death. Every unrighteous act has its exact price in religious torture; this balancing of one kind of suffering with another allows Commynes to demonstrate once again the logic with which God governs the world.

The Government of the World   Although the events confronting Commynes seemed unbearable to him without the thought of God, the memorialist did not revert to the kind of history written by the authors of saints' lives and some early medieval chronicles, who delighted in demonstrating the deity's day-to-day involvement with humanity. Nor is Commynes' God the intimate interlocutor of the soul invoked by his contemporary, Thomas à Kempis, in his *Imitation of Christ*. Kempis' God is immanent, a warm and unfailing presence in the hearts of those men open to Him. Christ is involved in every instant of life, at least potentially; the absorption of that which is temporal into that which is eternal is a constant quest if not a constant fact.

Commynes' God is related to the world in a different manner. He is remote and passionless, like the memorialist's notion of the ideal king. Like a perfect king, too, God knows all and controls all, but He is not usually involved in the day-to-day working-out of events. There is a gulf between men and God something like that between the fifteenth-century king and the mass of his subjects. This leaves the stage of his-

136. Calmette, II, 321–22.   137. Calmette, II, 324.

tory free for the twists and turns of policy-making which Commynes, like Machiavelli, found so fascinating. Behind the scenes, however, Commynes saw the power of the director of history. Machiavelli did not.

Machiavelli in a famous passage divides the forces at play in politics almost evenly between man's will and resources on one hand and Fortune—the diverse circumstances of time, place, and environment—on the other. The outcome of the struggle between man and circumstance is thus left open. Given sufficient *virtu*, suggests Machiavelli, man might nearly always win.[138] Whether his winning be by fair means or foul, however, God cannot be expected to intervene. Machiavelli was no atheist. He reports an occasional miracle in his *History of Florence*, and he seems to have believed that divine providence directs history in some general manner. But the Florentine never suggests that man could or should rely upon God in his efforts to shape events.

I have referred to the differences between Italy and northern Europe in the fifteenth century as that between an area where urban, commercial, and even republican institutions had acquired some permanence and an area where such institutions either did not exist or tended to be engulfed by rural, agrarian, and monarchical ones. The former area was of course beset by many of the same calamities as the latter, and politics were just as venal. But because in much of Italy the institutional structure allowed for continued growth, venality and calamity did not usually provoke the same response in Italian historians and political writers as in Commynes. Machiavelli's confidence in human autonomy and his tacit assumption that this world and the next, while related, are not dependent upon each other for righteousness and stability, seem to reflect this difference between north and south.

Philippe de Commynes' impulse to understand history began with the observation of the apparently haphazard, irrational sequence of events. He was a good observer and a cool one: standing to the side of much that was important, he was involved and yet not involved. Intimacy with the king and the dramatic events of his own rise to power as a refugee diplomat equipped Commynes to perceive and emphasize in his *Memoirs* the centralizing and rationalizing of government. As the personal dependent of the king, Commynes could perceive the new practices of government replacing feudal forms of loyalty from the one point of view from which they seemed something more than cunning: at the center, they could be shown rational as well as devious, centralizing as well as aggrandizing.

Thus the careful study of men's motives from the fulcrum-point of

138. Machiavelli, *The Prince*, Chapter 25.

the new French monarchy emerging from the Hundred Years' War carried Commynes a certain way in bringing order to the jumbled sequence of time—just far enough, we may guess, to satisfy Commynes' sense of the order of day-to-day events. But the larger changes in his time—the fall of Burgundy, the execution of the count of Saint-Pol, the French invasion of Italy, the unfailing success of Louis XI against his many enemies—could not be explained by Commynes' rudimentary notions of historical causation. It was above all death which provoked Commynes' sense of the deeper forces governing history. The death of Charles the Bold of Burgundy, of Richard III of England, of Philip I of Spain, of the young son of Charles VII of France, and above all of Louis XI—each of these produced a meditation on the macabre which led to formulations of the manner in which God controls events.[139]

God's direction of history is a "mystery."[140] But if one reflects upon the course of events in retrospect, God's hand is easy enough to observe in every remarkable turn of events, and even, as we have also seen, in the bizarre psychological behavior of men like Louis XI. The same shrewd calculations which Commynes employs to uncover the tricks of wily negotiators and to suggest an ideal course of political action are used to discover the secret plans of God.

The notion of a rational, manipulating God behind history is the connecting link between Commynes' otherwise disparate thinking about politics and religion. There is only one kind of power demonstrated in the *Memoirs*. It is the kind of power which worked for Commynes in his own life—commonsensical, unwearying pursuit of the practically attainable. This power, which Commynes attributed equally to a God who ruled history like a fifteenth-century monarch and to a king whom he worshipped almost as a god, was in fact the means by which men of the fifteenth, sixteenth, and seventeenth centuries in northern Europe finally overcame the inertia of a thousand years of feudalism. Not the Italian system of a full break with the institutions on which medieval Europe was founded after the fall of Rome, not the rough-and-ready democracy of the communes, destroying feudality root and branch and absorbing whatever aristocracy remained into the precarious oligarchies of a commercial nobility, but the northern monarchical method of an equality

139. The long passage on balance of power and balance of suffering analyzed earlier in this section also grows out of a meditation on death, in this case the judicial murder of Hugonet and Humbercourt by the people of Ghent. This execution leads Commynes to try to explain why God preserves such unjust people as those of Ghent, and from this evolves his theories of balance.

140. M, p. 322.

imposed by those at the top upon all those below was the way in which Europe modernized its politics.[141]

The adjustment of society to new conditions of urban and industrial growth, to new demands for security, and to the civil equality of town and country dwellers, came through centralizing all power in the hands of the prince rather than in the hands of commercial patricians. The disparities between peasant and peddler, knight and burgher, prelate and pastor, humanist and scholastic, were rationalized or eliminated by reference to those at the pinnacle of the social pyramid who, each time they won, separated themselves somewhat more from the lower echelons. The piecemeal practice and rational intent of Commynes' ideal prince and ideal God became norms in European political life for some three hundred years.

4/COMMYNES' SENSIBILITY

The paradoxical aura of thought permeating the *Memoirs*—a cool and often ironic practicality punctuated by outbursts of fervent religious reflection—tends to obscure Commynes' evident conviction that the economics of heaven and earth operate in general with the same even-handed, compensatory logic. Belief in this operational consistency allowed Commynes to retain that association of the temporal with the eternal which, ever since Saint Augustine's time, had afforded a sense of security and stability in a world of flux and frequent catastrophe. Few Christians as yet questioned this fusion of time with non-time, this absorption of the endlessly varied dynamics of European local life into the ideal static unities of goodness and truth. But new institutions in European life which facilitated deviation from the repetitive rhythms of manorial and feudal activity were bound to raise the question. When change ceased to mean flux, the unending round of crop failure or harvest confiscation or soldierly plunder or knightly oppression, when

141. The death or destruction of feudalism referred to here and elsewhere in this Introduction must not be taken to imply the death of aristocracy. Fifteenth-century monarchs and their descendants never intended nor accomplished the destruction of the nobility as a privileged social class. But the gradual transformation of the landed aristocracy from feudal lord into pensioned courtier had egalitarian implications politically. The noble in effect gave up his political independence in return for a guarantee of economic and social privilege from the sovereign. In the long run the noble's new dependency on the monarchy for his privileged position reinforced the tendency of central government officials to regard all the king's subjects as equal politically.

change began to mean progress, the gradual accumulation of lands or money or offices or knowledge, the temporal world acquired form in and of itself; history no longer needed God's constant intervention in order to give it shape and meaning.

The processes stabilizing European life and giving human activities a progressive and developmental rather than cyclic or fluctuating form had been operating for centuries before Commynes' time. Yet the *Memoirs* express a need to apply the sanctions of heaven to earth, to reveal God's work in time, which is far greater than that in the history written one hundred years earlier by Jean Froissart or that in the chronicles of Commynes' contemporaries, Georges Chastellain, Olivier de La Marche, and Jean Molinet. Why?

Commynes' greater emphasis on God is a result of his greater emphasis on "lack of faith" in politics. The cash nexus and instability of promises which he discovered behind each encounter of princes, the injustice which had become a norm, moved him to search for God's hand in anguish. Froissart and the chroniclers who continued his tradition, confronted with similar situations, invoked feudal, chivalric, and ascetic codes which either avoided the evidence of moral failure in complacent praise of their culture's heroes or lamented human frailty without perceiving that that frailty took certain recurring forms.[142]

Commynes' lack of education and checkered career spared him a cultural indoctrination which would probably have rendered him less apt to perceive what was new in politics in his time. Had he brought more ideological preconceptions to his work, he could not have portrayed the gaps between intention, word, and deed so graphically, nor have pursued so relentlessly what appeared to him to be God's secret manipulation of history. All this is reflected in Commynes' style, as compared with that of the chivalric chroniclers.

Style   Take, for example, Jean Molinet's portrayal of the relationship between a general and his soldiers as they prepare for battle. Molinet records a speech, probably fictitious, which Charles the Bold gave to his men during the siege of Neuss in Germany in 1474–1475. It concludes:

142. See the article by Denys Hay, "History and Historians in France and England during the Fifteenth Century," *Bulletin of the Institute of Historical Research*, XXXV (1962), 111–27, which admirably summarizes some of the main characteristics of the historical works of Chastellain, La Marche, and Molinet. Hay asserts correctly, I believe, that Froissart is the founder of this type of historiography and that to speak of a "Burgundian school" of chroniclers obscures their dependency on Froissart in matters of method and world-view.

"Take to yourselves the hearts of lions and, if it pleases Our Lord, in guarding the rights of the Church at the same time as that of our cousin [the archbishop, who had been expelled from Neuss], we shall obtain a glorious victory." Molinet continues:

When the high barons, chivalrous vassals and their subjects heard this very sweet and heartfelt persuasion of their duke and natural lord, emotion overcame them. They began to weep and, due to the singular love and ardent affection with which they were enflamed, they were content to adventure their lives in his good and just cause. The duke never wavered nor faltered in his high intention, always he persisted in his greathearted courage. . . .[143]

Commynes offers no account of the fighting at Neuss, because, he says, "I was not there."[144] But Commynes does describe the interaction between Charles the Bold and his soldiers at an earlier battle in which he took part:

The king's men were near the castle of Montlhéry and had before them a large hedge and a ditch; further away were the fields, full of wheat, beans and other grains in abundance, for the land was good there. All the count's [Charles the Bold's] archers marched on foot before him in loose order. . . . It had been agreed that there would be two rest periods on the road in order to give the infantrymen [and archers] a breathing-spell because the road was long and the fruits of the soil [through which they marched] thick and tall, and this slowed them down. . . . The king's men, all of them men-at-arms, broke through the hedge at both ends. When they were so close that they were about to use their lances, the Burgundian men-at-arms broke through the ranks of their own archers, and passed over them without giving them a chance to draw a single arrow. The archers were the flower and hope of the army, for I believe that out of some twelve hundred soldiers who constituted the corps of men-at-arms not even fifty knew how to lay a lance in rest.[145]

Thus one of the skirmishes began at Montlhéry in 1465.

Whereas Molinet initiates affairs with a conventional picture of a heroic leader inspiring his knightly followers, Commynes begins by indi-

143. Molinet, *Chroniques*, ed. Doutrepont and Jodogne, I (Brussels, 1935), 92. Translation mine.
144. M, p. 252. This is a good example of Commynes' care to inform his reader that his work is a collection of remembrances, not a work of history. The statement should not be taken as referring to historical method: Commynes seems to be unaware of the classical and medieval historiographical rule of preference for eyewitness accounts.
145. M, pp. 107–8.

cating where the French and Burgundian armies were in relation to hedge, castle, ditch, and field. Commynes situates his subject in a natural landscape, Molinet in a moral one.[146] But immediately after locating his subject in space and time ("about seven in the morning"[147]), Commynes makes one of his peculiar and apparently spontaneous leaps from what he has seen to what he feels is generally true. The infantrymen and archers were supposed to have been given a rest.

. . . The opposite was done, however, as if they had made a special effort to lose the battle. Thus God showed that battles are in His hands and that He ordains victories as He sees fit. I do not believe that the mind of one man can bear or give order to such a large number of men, or that things can be carried out in the field as they have been planned in one's chamber.[148]

Exhausted by their march without rest, the footsoldiers were overrun by their own cavalry as they approached the enemy. "Thus they themselves destroyed the flower of their hope."[149] God arranged it that way: the disorder on the field which, Commynes asserts, no man could have prevented, had its secret causes. ". . . God begins sometimes with small steps and movements, granting victory sometimes to one side and sometimes to the other. The mystery is so great that sometimes certain kingdoms and large territories come to their end and desolation and others begin to grow and rule."[150]

God hovers over the battle, determining its course, but His remoteness and stealth allows Commynes to pursue his description in thoroughly tactile, sensory terms:

Our field was now tramped flat, where it had been abundant with tall wheat one half hour before. Soon it was filled with the most terrible dust in the world; the whole field was strewn with dead men and horses, and none of the dead could be identified because of the dust.

146. The speech given by Charles the Bold marks the beginning of the second year's fighting over Neuss. At the beginning of his account of the first year's fighting, he states the juridical basis of the dispute, in contrast to Commynes who, as in the case of Liége, acts as if no legal forms existed in the controversy over Neuss. Molinet's presentation of the affair, on the other hand, is strongly prejudiced in Charles the Bold's favor: moral attitudes obscure the facts as in the passage quoted in the text. Again, although Molinet offers a physical description of the walls and town of Neuss in chapter 1 of his *Chroniques*, the description is curiously generalized. Nothing is precisely located; the force of the description is in its adjectives, not its nouns: ". . . entre lesdis murs y avoit certains fossez assez parfons et, de rechief, estoyent devant lesdittes brayes aultres grans fossez d'extreme profondeur . . . ." See Molinet, *op. cit.*, I, 31.

147. M, p. 105.   149. M, p. 108.
148. M, p. 107.   150. *Ibid.*

Forthwith we saw the count of Saint-Pol emerge from the wood; he was accompanied by about forty men-at-arms and his standard-bearer. He marched straight toward us and his men increased in number as they advanced; yet they seemed very far. Word was sent three or four times that he should hasten but he did not hurry and moved only at a pace. He had his men arm themselves with lances which were lying on the ground; they came in orderly formation and this gave great comfort to our men. They joined together in great numbers and came to the place where we were assembled; and we found ourselves to total some eight hundred men-at-arms. There were few or no infantrymen, however, and this alone prevented the count from achieving complete victory, because a ditch and a thick hedge were between the two camps.[151]

Commynes' locative description was probably part of his method of recall. By replacing himself in the very position in which he had once lived through the events he narrates (Saint-Pol marched "straight toward us"), he is able to remember details which would otherwise have escaped him.

But the functional emphasis which we have noted in his emphasis on quantification also helps materialize the scene. Molinet sees a battle as a series of incidents, succeeding each other like waves upon a shore. Each engagement moves toward the same goal, a victory gained by means of a headlong assault upon the enemy. Just as each wave attacks the shoreline in a slightly different manner, but always with the same thunderous rush, so Charles's knights vary in their precise objective, but never in the valor with which they attempt it:

. . . Those in Neuss were very proud and haughty about the huge and powerful bastion, fortified by trenches, which was by the abbey gate. . . . But my lord Philippe de Poitiers, lord of La Freté, noble in blood and valor, a most valiant war leader, accompanied by a number of strong and hardy knights, gave them an assault so fierce, terrible, and frightening that, by force and power, they [the men of Neuss] were driven from their fort and their trenches. The assault was fierce and marvellous; many glorious feats of arms shone on that occasion. The lord of La Freté conducted himself with honor. . . . Those in Neuss had another large and strong bastion in the Lombard quarter, which was their special refuge, entire hope and final guarantee . . . but it was overthrown, struck down to the ground, destroyed to the very base, reduced to earth and scattered about by robust arms. . . .[152]

The incidents of war which Molinet chooses to narrate are not necessarily those most decisive militarily (the trenches taken by La Freté

151. M, pp. 110–11.   152. Molinet, *op. cit.*, I, 64–65.

were immediately retaken by the besieged, Molinet admits), but rather those most illustrative of the social norms which he took for granted. In another engagement at Neuss, Molinet spends two pages to name and locate the various commanders in Charles's army as they were drawn up for battle, a third page to list new members of the Order of the Golden Fleece which the duke, amid the cannon shots of the enemy, decided to create, and a part of the fourth page to another speech by Charles. Description of the fighting along lines similar to the passage quoted above occurs only on the final two pages of the chapter.[153]

In Molinet's descriptions the body of Charles's army—archers, infantrymen, cannoneers—seems almost inanimate, a tool with no life or force of its own in the hands of the lords who lead. The feudal host, drawn up in hierarchical order to hear their lord orate, consists, as we have seen, of "high barons," "chivalrous vassals," and "their subjects":[154] those without knightly status go through the motions of war unnamed except as the subjects of those socially superior to them.

For Commynes the "flower and hope" of the army are a band of archers, not the knightly men-at-arms. He places the count of Saint-Pol in relation to his men, not in relation to another count. The commandant and his men move as a group toward the narrator. The strategic structure of the scene, the functional force of the corps as it advances, preoccupy Commynes. The memorialist concludes:

On both sides at least two thousand men died and the battle was well fought, for in both camps one could find honorable as well as cowardly men. But it was a great thing, in my estimation, to assemble in the field and to remain three or four hours in this state, one side facing the other. And the two princes had reason to think highly of those who were at their side in this hour of need. But they acted like men and not angels. Some men lost their positions and territories because they had fled, and these things were given to others who had fled ten leagues further. One man from our side lost his powerful position and was banished from his master's presence, but one month later he was reinstated and given more power than he had ever had before.[155]

Commynes does not neglect the importance of those highly placed socially. In paragraphs not quoted here he dwells upon the behavior of various nobles and lists the "men of name" killed on either side. But his emphasis is on material results, the balance of power before and after battle. The ironies of individual fate, revealing as they are of Commynes'

153. *Ibid.*, pp. 100–101. 155. M, p. 112.
154. See the quotation on p. 60 above.

special interest in treachery and princely favor, are reduced to a moral commonplace (men are not angels), which implies that the behavior of these few did not have any significant effect on the outcome.

Massed strength, the technology of supply trains and artillery, the accidents of time and terrain, determined the battle of Montlhéry. To Commynes the feudal formalities in which war procedures were clothed were either disastrous (as in the case of the hasty cavalry charge) or irrelevant (as in the case of the lords who were killed). Reality, as Commynes portrays it, is fragmented, uncontrolled by customs or convictions or justice or anything except—and this, too, only in limited degree —the wit and skill of the various commanders. Commynes is characteristically overgenerous, and even somewhat contradictory in tone, when assessing the role of his future patron: "Our band was stronger than the king's. His presence, however, was very beneficial to his men-at-arms, as were his fine speeches to them. I truly believe that had it not been for him alone, everyone would have fled, and I learned later that this was indeed the case."[156] In spite of its bias in favor of what Commynes "learned later," this statement remains related to the flights, the disruptions, and the balance of power which the memorialist has narrated earlier. In Molinet's account of the siege of Neuss, on the other hand, after Charles's stirring speech to the soldiers which we have examined, the author breaks off his narration to address a long lament to the duke, which begins: "O most powerful duke, with virtuous heart like a lion's, fortitude like Scipio's, an arm like Hercules', a fist like Alexander's, a body hardened to steel, for whom nothing seems impossible, will you carry your swo.d always drawn and ready?"[157]

The siege of Neuss failed. The forces facing the duke outnumbered his by three to one, and Charles was also distracted by the maneuvering of Louis XI and Edward IV on his southern frontier, as Commynes tells us.[158] But Molinet, instead of assessing the situation in terms of the facts, turns away from them by claiming that Charles was simply too valorous. Hero that he was, he exhausted his followers by undertaking too ambitious projects too often. No one, Molinet seems to say, is really to blame for the failure of the siege.

Jean Molinet is the last distinguished historian who writes in the chivalric mode, which was the predominant, although not the only historio-

156. M, p. 111.
157. Molinet, *op. cit.*, I, 92. I was forced to change several words for sense in translating this rhetorical period: "O trés puissant duc, vertueux coer leonique, voloir scipionique, bras herculyen, poing macedonien, corps acheré quasy impossible, à qui riens ne semble impossible, aras tu tousjours l'espée en dextre?"
158. M, pp. 255–262.

graphical tradition in Commynes' time. In Molinet's narration clichés of knightly virtue and obedience to established forms fill up the spaces left vacant by institutional decay—spaces which Commynes' tactile, discontinuous style leaves gaping. All action and movement are muffled by the honorific conventions with which Molinet fills each generalized scene; ideologies so connect and unify his narrative that the men whom he depicts appear to be actors in a static tableau. The stance of each individual is depicted in vivid colors and in a graceful pose, by means of a language rich in historical allusion and emotional subtlety. The details are charming, to be sure, like those in the Flemish paintings which illustrate this edition. But the account as a whole lacks life. The author has abandoned the depiction of historical reality in favor of achieving an almost purely esthetic purpose, the display of his rhetorical art. Commynes' flat and clumsy diction seems charged with life in comparison, endlessly changing and varied in its concerns. Commynes asks us to look at an object separate from himself and his language, an object remarkable in and of itself. Molinet asks us to look at an object through the medium of his language, an object enhanced by the style of the author describing it. Commynes uses words as signs, or pointers; Molinet uses words as symbols, or images.

Modesty and Suspicion   Commynes' sensibility is pragmatic and materialistic. He credits his eyes more than his emotions and the end result more than the means. The pragmatism conditions the materialism: Commynes early observed that the conclusion of a negotiation between two princes was often very different from the movement of diplomacy which could be observed. He came to believe, therefore, that reality lay just below the surface, in the "secret tricks or deceptions" about which he claimed to know more than anyone else "in the last twenty years."[159]

Commynes sees deceptions and trickery everywhere. In Book 1 of the *Memoirs* he tells us how one of the king's chief officers, Pierre de Brézé, betrayed Louis' orders to avoid battle with Charles the Bold at Montlhéry by leading the king's army so close to Charles's host that battle could not be avoided.[160] Karl Bittmann has shown that Louis in fact desired battle and had led the army toward the Burgundians personally on the two days preceding the battle.[161] Although Brézé, not Louis, led the vanguard toward Charles on the day of battle, this initiative was apparently an act of bravery and loyalty rather than betrayal. In Book 5 of

159. M, p. 215.
160. M, p. 104.

161. Bittmann, *op. cit.*, I, 97.

the *Memoirs* Commynes describes the events leading up to Charles the Bold's defeat and death in battle before Nancy, his opponent's stronghold. If the count of Campobasso, one of Charles's mercenary generals, had not betrayed the duke by secretly sending a man into Nancy to urge them to hold out until supplies arrived, asserts Commynes, Nancy would have fallen to Charles without a battle.[162] Campobasso, he continues, beset the duke with assassins. Louis XI, whom Campobasso approached to ask reward for planning the duke's murder, instead sent a message to the duke warning him of Campobasso's plans.[163] Charles refused to believe the warning, and put to death Siffredo di Baschi, one of Campobasso's soldiers, who was caught trying to enter Nancy and who also tried to tell the duke of Campobasso's plots to murder him.[164]

Benedetto Croce has shown that this picture of Campobasso's actions at Nancy is mostly fantasy. After a successful career in Italy, this Neapolitan nobleman had taken service with Charles the Bold in 1473. He quarreled with the duke in 1476 over military policy and over the nonpayment of wages due him and his soldiers, and deserted the Burgundian army four days before the battle of Nancy, after King Louis had made attempts to suborn him. No evidence exists, aside from Commynes' assertions, that Campobasso planned to assassinate Charles. Croce concludes that although Campobasso's action at Nancy cannot be excused —he did desert without warning—his betrayal was a result of legitimate grievances against Charles the Bold, which Louis XI evidently had tried to exploit by encouraging him to desert.[165]

What led Commynes to assert the presence of treachery and plots even where there were none? One reason is Commynes' superstitious sense of catastrophe, which erupted, as we have already seen, in the midst of a vivid, well-ordered description of the cavalry charge at Montlhéry. In the same way, Commynes interrupts his narration of the king's maneuvers before the battle to cite Brézé's words, "I will put them [the two armies] so close together that it will take a very skillful man to separate them," and then adds: "So he did. And the first man to die was himself . . . ,"[166] obviously in recompense for his supposed treachery. Commynes mentions a parallel case in his account of Charles the Bold's war against Liége in 1467. The Liégeois had given the duke hostages at

---

162. M, p. 322.

163. M, p. 319.

164. M, pp. 316–17.

165. Benedetto Croce, "Un condottiere italiano del '400: Cola di Monforte, Conte di Campobasso e la fede storica del Commynes," in his *Vite di aventure di fede e di passione* (Bari, 1935), pp. 136–51.

166. M, p. 104.

the end of the campaign of 1466. When the Liégeois took the field again against the duke in 1467, Charles held a council at which he asked whether the hostages should be executed or not. One lord of Contay urged that they be put to death immediately, since the Liégeois had broken their treaty. Someone standing next to Commynes in the council-room thereupon whispered in the memorialist's ear: "Regard this man well. Although he is quite old, he is very healthy. Yet I would wager a large sum that he will not be alive a year from now. And I say this because of the cruel words he pronounced."[167] Sure enough, the lord of Contay "died a few days later in the town of Huy.... He did not live long after the cruel opinion he had expressed against the hostages from Liége."[168] Charles the Bold meanwhile had refused to follow Contay's advice, had released the hostages, and had won the battle of Brusthem and a subsequent siege against the Liégeois. "He gained great glory and honor ... and it came to him solely by the grace of God, against all human odds.... In the judgment of most people, he received all these honors because of the mercy and kindness which he extended to the hostages...."[169]

Commynes' impulses to record God's control of history seem to be proportionate to the scope of the catastrophic changes he describes. Brézé's sudden death, his recompense for involving France and Burgundy in an indecisive battle, does not provoke the name of God directly. Contay's cruelty and Charles's mercy, which allowed Burgundy to win the campaign of 1467 against Liége, stimulates a brief reflection on God's grace to the duke. The death of Charles the Bold at Nancy, on the other hand, meant the fall of Burgundy and the rise of France: this cataclysmic reversal had so many implications for Commynes, personal as well as conceptual, that he endeavored to show its divinely ordained inevitability not once but several times and from two distinct points of view.

The Burgundians, Commynes tells us in chapter two of his first book, enjoyed great prosperity and tranquillity when he was a boy. But instead of thanking God for such gifts, they acquired increasingly profligate manners, so that "no prince [seemed] magnificent enough to them ...."[170] Therefore "God gave them this duke [Charles], who constantly maintained them in fierce wars, which involved much trouble and expense.... So much so that at the last battle [Nancy], all the strength of his country was used up, and all his men ... were killed, destroyed, or taken prisoners." God "made everything equal.... This loss was equal to their former measure of felicity."[171]

167. M, p. 155.
168. M, p. 157.
169. M, p. 161.

170. M, p. 100.
171. M, p. 326.

Discovering this balance of gains and losses was not enough for Commynes: the personal fate of Charles the Bold had somehow to be rationalized also:

> You have heard earlier in these memoirs of the disloyal trick which the duke had played on the count of Saint-Pol, constable of France. . . . He sent a good and valid safe-conduct to the constable and nevertheless seized him and sold him [to Louis XI] for purely avaricious motives, not merely to obtain the town of Saint-Quentin and other places, as well as inheritances and movable possessions belonging to the constable, but also for fear of not taking Nancy when he besieged it for the first time. . . .
>
> Just as it was precisely during his first siege of Nancy that he had committed this crime, it was right after he had laid the second siege there that he had Siffredo [di Baschi] executed (for he would not hear him, and thus he acted like a person who has his ears stopped and his judgment impaired)—and it was again in the same place that he was deceived and betrayed by the person [Campobasso] in whom he had the most trust.

Commynes concludes: ". . . God established the count of Campobasso to be His instrument to take vengeance in this world for the action taken against the constable by the duke of Burgundy."[172]

Many of the themes of the first five books of the *Memoirs* were interwoven into Commynes' explanation of the death of Duke Charles at Nancy. The immoral reaction of the people of Burgundy to their prosperity is introduced in Book 1, the duplicity of Saint-Pol and Charles the Bold's treachery in return is the subject of much of Books 3 and 4, and the plots of Campobasso are dwelt upon in Book 5. Commynes grew up in Burgundy, and served its fated prince for eight years. He could not be indifferent to the destiny of his homeland. Obsessed with political power as he was, the central decision of his life—his desertion—depended for its justification on the outcome of the duel between his old master and his new. Yet self-justification in this case was a kind of self-denial, for Burgundy's greatness and Charles's greatness were part of Commynes' heritage; to justify their destruction involved destroying part of himself. Every new thrust by one or the other opponent in the duel between France and Burgundy, therefore, was liable to provoke in Commynes a fresh attempt to rationalize a catastrophe which was his own. This personal involvement in Burgundy's fall is the most important reason for Commynes' strained moralizations and his blackening of Campobasso's character. The fall is explained over and over again, in

172. M, pp. 317–18.

an attempt to exorcize the past; yet each time the explanation is made in such a way as to avoid admission of Commynes' own involvement, for to be involved was to be guilty.[173]

Jean Dufournet has suggested that this avoidance of involvement may be the reason for Commynes' extraordinary modesty in the *Memoirs*, the rarity with which he speaks of his own actions in situations where he is an important participant.[174] Commynes' description of the Péronne interview is a striking example of this. In the royal letter bestowing the rich fief of Talmont upon Commynes, Louis XI describes in glowing terms the manner in which Commynes risked his life to "tell us all that he could for our welfare, acting so effectively that, by his means and aid, we were delivered out of the hands of . . . rebellious, disobedient men [Charles the Bold and his adherents]. . . ."[175] The *Memoirs* make no mention of such signal action. We are told only that the king was notified about the duke's angry threats "by some friend, who assured him that he would be safe if he accepted [the duke's demands]. . . ."[176] Were it not for the king's letter, it would be only conjecture to say that Commynes was that friend. The same silence is maintained, of course, concerning Commynes' desertion. Having described the war operations of the duke of Burgundy in north France during the fall of 1472, the memorialist inserts the phrase, "About this time . . . I entered the service of the king. . . ,"[177] and then continues with his description of the war. Commynes mentions his imprisonment at three points: in the Prologue, where he points out that although he has suffered "losses and afflictions" since King Louis' death, such changes are not unusual when a great prince dies;[178] in depicting the greatness of Paris, when he comments that while a prisoner in the tower of the Conciergerie overlooking the Seine, he was astonished at the amount of produce arriving at the city by boat;[179] and in describing Louis XI's use of iron cages to detain noted

173. See, e.g., M, pp. 326–27, and p. 100. Similar disquisitions on Burgundy's rise and fall occur on pp. 137, 294–96, and elsewhere.

174. Jean Dufournet, *La destruction des mythes dans les Mémoires de Ph. de Commynes* (Geneva, 1966), p. 151.

175. Reprinted in Dupont, *op. cit.*, III, 12.

176. M, p. 178. See the discussion of Commynes' actions, pp. 29–30 above. As indicated there, Commynes introduces himself by name in an active role at Péronne only in association with two *valets de chambre*, who try to assuage the duke's anger at news of the surprise attack at Tongres. He does also mention that he slept in Charles's room and walked with the angry duke up and down during the night before "some friend" notified Louis, but he does not say what he said to Charles nor what Charles said to him (M, p. 178).

177. M, p. 238.   179. M, p. 125.
178. M, p. 92.

prisoners, where he states: "The first to invent them was the bishop of Verdun. . . . A number of people have cursed him since for it, including me, for I tried one of them out for a period of eight months under our present king."[180] That is all. Dufournet points out that the effect of such laconic and peripheral reference is to assimilate personal experience into something happening to a number of people in common, and thus to present that experience as external to the personality, caused by circumstances or the actions of others rather than by the self.[181]

Commynes avoids self-portrayal partly because, in common with most of his contemporaries, he had developed little capacity for self-analysis.[182] His importance, as he saw it, was derived from what he had observed about the great men among whom he moved, not from what he had felt and done himself. This tendency to eliminate everything but his eyes from the historical scenes he recorded had important consequences for Commynes' historical method and style, as we have seen. But avoidance of personal details cannot be attributed simply to psychological naiveté. Commynes' silence protects him in the *Memoirs*, as it did in his career as a diplomat. Secrecy helped to disguise the ambiguous consequences of his commitments. Being right was for Commynes a matter of not being found wrong. The artful concealment of his own actions in the *Memoirs* produces in the reader a powerful impression of Commynes' astuteness, of his ability to penetrate beneath the surface of politics to seize the real forces at play and to offer advice on how to deal with these forces. This effect was probably not calculated by the author; it was the natural result of the habits of a lifetime.[183] But when one analyzes where Commynes was and when, and what he has omitted from his accounts of others' treachery, the astuteness begins to disappear and the unconscious self-defense to materialize. "It is not I," Commynes seems to say, "but Campobasso, the villain, who is guilty of deserting the duke. It is not I, but Duke Charles himself, who destroyed the prosperity of his country." Most of all, "It is not the proud, prosperous friends of my youth, not the impetuous, valiant duke whom I served, but God who destroyed this house and this bountiful land." No man could have pre-

180. Calmette, II, 320.   181. Dufournet, *op. cit.*, p. 21.
182. See the remarks about Commynes' psychology on p. 48. Self-analysis, the attempt to find some correlation between feelings, behavior, and ideals, is scarcely found in France before Montaigne. François Villon, for example, describes himself at considerable length in his poems, but always in the external, commonly human, assimilative manner of Commynes.
183. Dufournet, *op. cit.*, *passim*, believes that it was calculated, and this notion of the *Memoirs* as a work filled with hidden intentions (see especially *ibid.*, p. 150) distorts his interpretation of many passages in Commynes' book, as I have tried to show in my review of Dufournet's work in *Renaissance Quarterly*, Winter, 1968.

vented the fall: ". . . When God decides to put His hand to it, man can do nothing."[184]

Personal protectiveness accounts in part for the atmosphere of treachery pervading the *Memoirs*.[185] The character of his professional work was probably equally important in leading Commynes to attribute treacherous designs to nearly everyone involved in politics. Commynes looked upon diplomacy as a form of spying, a craft which would perhaps be unnecessary if the world were not a decaying place in which unexpected changes and "lack of faith" lurked everywhere.[186] But in this "unstable" world Commynes' business was to suspect the presence of spies wherever plausible and to use them whenever he could.[187]

Commynes' opportunistic life, his furtive profession, and the critical social situation of his time are related reciprocally. Each reinforces the others, and each in perhaps equal measure contributes to the strange mixture of beliefs by means of which Commynes sought to order the rich experience he had acquired. Commynes is a materialist, yet he puritanically warns against the dangers of sensuous life.[188] He insists on quantifying and rationalizing power, yet he superstitiously sees God's hand in every catastrophe. Divine Providence directs everything that happens, but not palpably so, for "God no longer speaks directly to people. . . ."[189] God is neither immanent nor transcendent—He is hidden,

---

184. M, p. 165. The longest uninterrupted series of reflections in the *Memoirs*, chapters 18, 19, and 20 of Book Five, discussed on p. 47 ff., was also motivated in part by self-defense. Ostensibly a demonstration of God's system of balances in politics and morality, this long passage reveals at a number of points Commynes' angry feelings about the immoral politicians, as he felt, who had jailed him and stripped him of his property (see M, p. 356, n. 131). Not he, but they were guilty of distorting royal prerogatives and misusing governmental powers. But Commynes in exile had no hope of redress against these men except from God. The fact that he accumulated proofs of divine power in the very chapters in which he expresses most fully his feelings about his imprisonment helps substantiate Liniger's hypothesis about Commynes' religious conversion in prison (see p. 14 above). It also is evidence of Commynes' tendency to depend upon "the great" (see the next section of this Introduction), and thus is related to Commynes' so-called political realism. I have analyzed this crucial section of the *Memoirs* fully in a forthcoming article on political realism in Commynes and Machiavelli.

185. Another signal example of Commynes' tendency to fabricate conspiracies where there were none is the supposed plot of the princes in Book 3. See M, p. 205, n. 72.

186. See M, p. 169, for Commynes' notion of the decadence of the times.

187. Association between the uses of secrecy and the instability and constant change in the world is found in M, pp. 215, 220, and 221.

188. See the passage referred to in note 170 above, where Commynes elaborates a bit upon how the Burgundians indulged their senses instead of giving thanks to God for their prosperity.

189. M, p. 356.

and He orders the world by means of secret calculations, like the good spy, the sly diplomat, the crafty king.

The roots of Commynes' insights into his time are enmeshed in a morass of personal and professional biases. Commynes' peculiar sensibility throws new and unexpected light upon contemporary reality, yet subtly distorts it. It is not strange, therefore, that the greatest of Commynes' biases is also the source of his most valuable perceptions: his admiration for Louis XI.

Dependency   Commynes received from the king many of his misrepresentations of action at Péronne, as we have learned. The same is true of his story of Brézé's whispered treachery. Somehow Brézé's words "to one of his [Brézé's] intimates" were discovered by Louis and "related to me by the king later, for at the time I was in the service of the count of Charolais."[190] As for that marvelously orchestrated superstition, God's stalking of Charles the Bold to his death at Nancy, Commynes received one of the basic elements in that tale, too, from Louis XI. For in order to avoid the consequences of his own unsuccessful attempts to buy Campobasso's desertion from the duke, the king apparently set on foot the story that Campobasso planned to assassinate Charles the Bold.[191]

How can we explain the naïve acceptance of these subterfuges from a man so cynical about the political maneuvers of the great? The answer is obviously that the exaggerated sense of dependency which Commynes felt toward his "master" precluded a critical attitude toward the king's words. Louis was Commynes' master in more than an economic or social sense. He was his teacher in politics, his intellectual mentor as well. It is the social rather than economic or mental dimension of that dependency which concerns us here.

Commynes' use of status to define his characters is noticeable to every reader of the *Memoirs*. Titles, offices, friendships, and family relations are multiplied on every page, and form a formidable barrier to the modern reader's understanding of the movement of events. But to Commynes these class denominations and connections, instead of being a

190. M, pp. 104–5.
191. Cf. M, pp. 295 and 319. This is not to say that Campobasso may not have contemplated assassinating Charles (see, e.g., M, p. 324, where Commynes claims to have known several of the potential assassins). But if so, it is strange that none of Campobasso's foolproof (according to Commynes) plans worked (also according to Commynes), and that none of the Burgundian chroniclers, with all the motivation they would have had for blackening Campobasso's character, says a word about assassins.

barrier, offered clues to the secret patterns of politics. Louis XI, for example, plotting together with the count of Warwick to dethrone Charles the Bold's ally, King Edward IV of England, "negotiated the marriage of the prince of Wales with the count of Warwick's second daughter. The prince was the only son of [former] King Henry VI of England, who was still alive and a prisoner in the tower of London. . . . It was a strange marriage—to have the prince marry the daughter of the man who had overcome and ruined his father."[192] Commynes is warning the reader that this strange marriage of the daughter of Edward IV's former backer, Warwick, with the son of Edward's enemy foretold the *coup d'état* which followed, when Warwick, with Louis XI's help, set the former king, Henry VI, on England's throne once more.

The "great" form a kind of network of power, defined by social privileges of one sort or another. These privileges, however various, have this in common: they are all derived from, or have been adjusted to, feudal institutions. Thus, men from the urban areas of France or Burgundy, where anti-feudal institutions and privileges had long been maturing, do not belong to this network. However powerful locally, they are among the "small," and their political actions are for that reason condemned *a priori* by Commynes to futility.[193] Commynes assumes without thinking that to be effective requires operation within the confines and conventions of feudal privilege.

We have seen, however, that such feudal privilege had been hollowed out by social disaster and by the consequent reliance on those at the top of the feudal hierarchy for security. The titles were there, but the substance was slipping away. The network of power consisted no longer of a king surrounded by his peers, a circle with a center in which policy decisions taken without the agreement of any substantial number of the feudal lords meant that the gap between center and circumference could not be closed, and that king, vassals, and the society below the circle fell into formless disarray. Connections among the powerful few had now rearranged themselves into a kind of irregular web, dotted with little concentrations of lords and their dependents, criss-crossed by lines running in all directions between these nodules of power, and arrayed about a gigantic knot near the center consisting of the king and his servants.

The king, by Commynes' time, was no longer a mere organizational

192. M, p. 214.
193. Note Commynes' attitudes toward the revolutionaries of Liége described in this Introduction, and toward the people of Ghent in Book 2, chapter 4, of the *Memoirs*.

necessity, a coordinator of and rallying-point for the interests of a sovereign class. The king was emerging now as sovereign of a nation; the lords in reaction were forced to pose as sovereigns of their regions. There was more room to maneuver in this situation for both king and lord than in the early days of feudalism. Coalitions formed and dissolved endlessly, but after each confrontation the society below transferred a bit more of its allegiance from the smaller centers of power to the largest of them; after each conflict a bit more initiative lay with the king.

Feudal institutions and the ideologies supporting them were by the late fifteenth century in hopelessly defensive postures. Power was slowly polarizing—politically toward the king, economically toward the urban centers with their bourgeoisie. The traditional upper class nevertheless held on tenaciously to its prerogatives. And so society suffered—but did not die, did not even decay—because of the entrenched power of the feudal elite.

In fifteenth-century Italy artists illustrate the birth of spring; in northern Europe poets depict the dance of death. This is no evidence of the backwardness of the Gothic North, nor of the lugubriousness of their sullen climate. It is a matter of social structure. In the Italian centers of culture the feudal nobility had from the thirteenth century been exterminated or absorbed into the elites in the towns; in the north that class remained distinct, retaining its social privileges and its position as the arbiter of taste even as it was shunted aside politically and economically by urban and national centers. As the feudally-based traditions of northern culture became more and more incapable of reflecting the new reality emerging in the towns and princely courts, the official spokesmen of that culture became more and more obsessed with ceremony—chivalric jousts, extravagant religious exercises, pomp in dress and gesture. What was once content became form; Molinet's depiction of battle at Neuss is an example of this.

The *Memoirs* rarely portray this decorative, futile culture, not because their author lacked reverence for its patrons, but because he—almost alone among the chroniclers of his time—had discovered that a noble's gestures almost never agreed with his secret intent. Commynes' dependency on surrogate fathers—as an orphan living with a rich uncle, as a bankrupt squire serving Charles the Bold, as a fugitive diplomat whose lands and freedom depended upon royal favors—this dependency precluded much questioning of the class roles confronting him. But it also precluded Commynes from adopting a feudal class role successfully himself. Commynes had almost no class position to defend, in spite of his titles, for the vicissitudes of his career had prevented him from forming the social ties and vested interests which would protect him if his protector disappeared. He was irretrievably enmeshed in the network of feudal power, and yet he could never become part of it.

The best that Commynes could do was to try to choose his masters wisely, and to do that he had to look beneath the emblems of class for the secret intentions and tendencies of his superiors. Only the sovereigns at the centers of the various feudal networks must have felt as exposed as he, for they, too, could scarcely rely on their inherited institutional position, surrounded as they were on all sides by bewildering coalitions of feudal lords and clamored to from below by the ever increasing needs of the "small" whom the lords exploited rather than preserved and governed. This exposure, this inability to coordinate a power structure which they were forced either to wield or to be destroyed by, gave Louis XI and Philippe de Commynes a community of interest, a similar need to be wary, which perhaps helped cement their intimacy, combined as it was with Commynes' sense of dependency. Wise princes— like wise servants, Commynes might have added—"are so subtle and so very mistrustful that it is difficult to live at their side, for they always have the impression that they are being duped. . . ." Whether princes are wise and deceitful or foolish and credulous, however, "everyone must serve and obey them in the territories where they rule because one is bound and also forced to do so."[194]

Commynes' analysis of politics ends in resigned acceptance of the polarization of society going on in his day. As in his own life, so in society at large more and more people were being forced into a radical dependency upon "the great." But few among them were able to recognize that dependency, let alone to accept it. Even Commynes could not accept it. Immediately after the iron words quoted above he dissolves the tension they imply in the name of the still more powerful supernatural force of God: ". . . All things considered, our only hope should rest in God because He is the source of all our strength and of all goodness, and this is not to be found in anything in this world. But each of us realizes this late in life, after we have been in need of Him. However, it is better late than never."[195]

Expressiveness   The gaps and inconsistencies in Commynes' thought reflect the lack of cohesion in his life. This fragmented quality, which one senses in the personality behind the writing, is probably rooted in

194. M, pp. 144–45. For another example of how Commynes' feelings of dependency helped him organize (and warp) his material, see M, p. 205, n. 72.
195. M, p. 145. I have discussed the possible biographical implications of these words on pp. 14–16.

the loss of his parents as a very young child. But it was reinforced by the fragmented quality of social life in his time. Tradition crumbled away everywhere at the touch of money and influence; Commynes ran away to serve the king, married for money himself, and married off his daughter for prestige.[196] If there is a split, a mixture of tone in the *Memoirs*, it is a split inherent in the times as much as in the self. Everywhere men proceeded with watchful opportunism toward others, and finding themselves thus alone, they sought refuge in God. Never have men been so devout, nor so hypocritical and superstitious in their religion. Commynes' description of the purgatory of loneliness which Louis XI suffered at the end of his life must stand not only for the experience of one man but also, as Commynes himself emphasizes, for the common fate of the great and powerful—including Commynes himself.

Reading the *Memoirs* is to get to know Commynes, and to know Commynes is to understand the soul of an epoch. The scattered judgments, shrewd observations of character, and seemingly limitless recall of circumstance work together to build an effect of coherence and expressive power which individual passages, analyzed and exposed in their inconsistencies, fail to convey. The very lack of systemization, the slowly accumulative way in which Commynes clarified his feelings about great men and great events by repeating the same ideas in varying circumstances, the gradual discovery as he dictated the *Memoirs* that he was composing, not a collection of source materials for Angelo Cato, but a work of independent value, with distinctive political and moral lessons to offer—all this gives an expressive unity to Commynes' book which may strike the reader more strongly than the kind of unity given by elaborate and well-stated conceptual systems.

The *Memoirs* cannot be read today as they were in the sixteenth and seventeenth centuries, for their nuggets of political wisdom. Detached from its economic and social context, Commynes' advice to princes is either commonplace or no longer relevant. Nor can the *Memoirs* any longer be read as they were in the nineteenth century, for their unbiased reporting of events. Twentieth-century curiosity about intellectual traditions and social movements, too, can scarcely be satisfied by the *Memoirs*. Commynes has no notion of the power of ideas, whether traditional or innovating, whether as ideology or as policy, nor does he show much

---

196. Commynes' marriage to Hélène de Chambes was arranged by Louis XI within five months of his desertion. In 1504 Jeanne, Commynes' only child, married the count of Penthièvre, who was closely related to Anne, duchess of Brittany and Louis XII's wife. The count of Penthièvre was a spendthrift; Commynes, avaricious as he was, loaned large sums to the count for several years preceding the marriage. These loans were canceled after the ceremony. See Mandrot's edition of the *Memoirs*, II (Paris, 1903), lxx, for details.

awareness of the way institutions—religious, economic, political, or cultural—mold behavior. But if Commynes is blind to much that molds public life, trivial in his conclusions about effective public conduct, and
prejudiced in his descriptions of the historical process, he does discern
and depict unerringly the essence of the political impulse, the "restless
desire of power after power, that ceaseth only in death."[197] Commynes'
unblinking description of men's pursuit of power is the main source of
the perennial attraction of the *Memoirs*, and of the interest which his
words still hold for us today.

I have asserted that the beginnings of modern Europe are to be found
in the centralizing activities of northern monarchs from the fifteenth
century onward. The beginnings were very small, almost imperceptible
in the constantly disrupted Europe of Commynes' day. I have emphasized the natural and social causes of this disorder; there was also a cultural cause of the malaise of the fifteenth century. This was the inertia
of European tradition, that medieval heritage of localized, agrarian culture which now lay like an incubus upon all efforts to see clearly the
way ahead.

Europe was entangled in the mesh of its own past. It could emerge
only by patient effort, enlarging a rip here, a weakened thread there,
rather than by thrashing about uselessly in an effort to burst loose of
the whole intricate network at once. It is one of the virtues of Commynes' *Memoirs* that he shows us a whole gallery of men engaged in
just such slow, painful work. Here the essential breakthrough to a new
Europe first came.

No better symbol of this breakthrough could be found than Commynes' description of the interview at Picquigny between Louis XI and
Edward IV of England. Mindful of the murder of John the Fearless in
1419 and of his own semi-imprisonment at Péronne, says Commynes,
Louis erected a barrier across the middle of the bridge upon which the
two kings were to meet. The barrier was "a strong wooden trellis like
those made for the cages of lions;" the holes between the bars were "just
large enough for one to stick his arm through easily."[198] Through these
holes Commynes observed King Edward advance toward the center of
the bridge.

When he had arrived within four or five feet of the barrier, he doffed his
hat and bowed deeply to within a half-foot of the ground. The king [of
France], who was already leaning against the barrier, returned the courtesy
with just as deep a bow, and they began to embrace each other through

197. Thomas Hobbes, *Leviathan*, Part I, chapter 11, paragraph 2.
198. M, pp. 278–79.

the holes; then the king of England made another even deeper bow. The king [of France] began the conversation, saying, "My lord my cousin, you are most welcome. There is not a man in the world whom I so much desired to see as you. And God be praised that we are assembled here for this good purpose."[199]

The contrast between words and action could scarcely be more graphically represented. Louis bought peace from the English, distributing large sums of gold to the king and his officers both before and after this interview.[200] But he and his interlocutor conducted the interview itself in the most elegant and formal manner possible. The presence of the barrier between them bespeaks not only the savage, lawless maneuvering behind the scenes of fifteenth-century politics but also the constriction of discourse, the artificiality of the chivalric forms in terms of which negotiations were conducted. Men regarded each other like wild beasts, yet they pretended as if the good fellowship and trust of King Arthur's court were both the end and means of all their intercourse. In spite of all the distrust, subterfuge, and artificiality, however, peace was made at Picquigny. King Louis and King Edward achieved their goals, breaking through the barriers to discourse and accomplishment.

This, then, is why we read Commynes. No other writer reports the play of politics in this decisive period with quite the freshness of detail which we find in the *Memoirs*. To such intimate glimpses of life gone by Commynes' reflections add piquant and often passionate flavor. They should be taken as exactly that—as part of Commynes' description of his time, rather than as informed political, historical, or moral judgments.

Commynes' greatness has an affinity with that of another strangely unselfconscious fifteenth-century writer, François Villon. Like Commynes, Villon transformed a genre of writing which in the hands of the learned often consisted of little more than cliché and filigree. Like Commynes, Villon accomplished the feat with a minimum of technical virtuosity and a maximum of expressive freshness. And Villon's originality, like Commynes', arose in good part from facing a society which maneuvered him into isolation. Why is it that those to whom we turn for insight and authenticity in fifteenth-century France are *déclassé* poets like François Villon, soldier-bandits like Jean de Bueil, author of that brutal military manual, *Le Jouvencel*, or unofficial chroniclers like "the bourgeois of Paris"[201] and Philippe de Commynes? Court poets, royal

---

199. M, p. 281.
200. See the reference to this on p. 45 above.
201. The anonymous *Journal d'un bourgeois de Paris*, ed. Tuetey (Paris, 1881), is a frighteningly vivid record of the sufferings of the common people during the first half of the fifteenth century.

historians, and military commanders a century after Commynes seem to us to be among the most important representatives of their professions. But if we look for the precursors of Ronsard or de Thou or the duke of Guise we turn not to those whom the world acclaimed as its cultural leaders, but to men in the shadows, close to power but not of it. Surely this reflects a period of cultural breakdown, when those outside official institutions speak for society best.

"I am a poor man . . . who never owned a plate or bowl or sprig of parsley. . . . Justice whacked me on the arse, although I shouted, 'I appeal.' " Villon's appeal, according to his poem, was denied; he was condemned to die. He prays, "Grant me eternal rest."[202]

"Could one have better examples to show what a petty thing man is, how short and miserable his life is, and how empty the differences between the great and the humble are, as soon as they are dead? For everyone is horrified by a corpse and vituperates it, while the soul must immediately go to receive God's judgment. Sentence is given at that very moment, according to the works and merits of the corpse."[203]

Commynes concludes the first part[204] of the *Memoirs*, as Villon ends his poem, by speaking of the common fate of man. The dance of death, uniting tattered priest and mitred bishop, robber baron and thieving merchant, peasant's wife and royal concubine, appealed to northern artists in this period because, like Commynes' picture of Louis and Edward embracing through the trellis on the bridge, it combined high ceremony with radical materialism. It acknowledged life's conventions in such a way as to show their meaninglessness in the same moment. It captured men's sense of life's process and life's end in a single gesture: "great" and "small" link hands, for beneath the conventions of class, of which the formalism of the dance is a shadowy reminder, men are equal in the flesh. They are equal as material beings, not spiritual ones. Death reveals this truth because it is the realm of maggotry, not transcendence. Instead of dissolving the corporeal to reveal the eternal spirit within, death is seen as a sudden unveiling of the material insignificance of man. Class clothes have hidden this fleshly truth; they are deceptions. The real truth lies neither on the inside nor outside of man, but just below the surface which we see.

202. Villon, *Complete Works* (New York: Bantam Paperback, 1964), p. 122. The poem is written in the third person, which I have changed for clarity to first person in my translation. The poem is written in the form of an imagined epitaph.

203. Calmette, II, 341.

204. Books 1 to 6 of the *Memoirs*, dealing with events up to Louis XI's death in 1483, were conceived and written as a separate, self-contained unit between 1489 and 1491. Books 7 and 8 were added to the *Memoirs* between 1495 and 1498, after Commynes' unexpected participation in the Italian invasion of 1494. See pp. 16 and 19 above.

Commynes' moralistic materialism culminates in a vision of human behavior as an absolutely determining factor in heavenly judgment. The soul is judged "according to the works and merits of the corpse." The soul has no existence separate in the slightest degree from the body. Spiritual aspiration, intellectual and emotional awareness, the varying circumstances of education and birth which aid one to choose well or ill in life, count for nothing; man is what he does.

If life for Commynes seemed only a short, miserable voyage toward death, rather than travel from "death" amid the transitory and material toward "life" amid the eternal and spiritual, this perversion of the Christian message reflects only half of his divided sensibility, that portion absorbed from a society whose dominating class and dominating culture were doomed. The other half of Commynes' self pointed to the way in which his society was to tear down and replace feudal-chivalric institutions and ideologies with new ones. The cynical realism and quantifying rationalism which Commynes felt compelled to employ in every portion of his *Memoirs*, though it paradoxically increased his superstitiousness and naïve dependence on a devious master, was a self-curative reaction to a new political world whose usages fatally transcended medieval modes of understanding. That is why, although the paragraph ending with the word "corpse" above is Commynes' last word about the significance of life, the paragraph preceding it describes the solution to the problem of dying feudal institutions which men in his time had already found:

. . . To speak naturally, as a man who has no learning but only a bit of experience, would it not have been better for them and for all other princes, as well as for persons of middle estate who have lived under these great men and who will live under those who reign at present, to have chosen the middle way in these matters? That is to say, should they not have worried less and have been less concerned, and have undertaken fewer things, and have been more fearful of offending God and of persecuting the people and their neighbors in so many cruel ways, which I have sufficiently explained earlier, and should they not have spent more time upon their own comfort and in honest pleasures? Their lives would have been longer, their illnesses would have come upon them later, and their deaths would have been more regretted by more people and less desired by them. And they would have had less reason to fear death.[205]

Commynes, speaking "naturally," talks with the tongue of a bourgeois, an *honnête homme*, whose calculations teach how to stave off death and

205. Calmette, II, 340–41.

unpopularity with God and man, and whose recommendations suggest that a life of calm comfort is most to be preferred. The fact that Commynes placed the two paragraphs in sequence shows that he felt no conflict between them. This strange mixture of tones, of medieval and modern, of the coolly objective and the passionately moral, is the true voice of Commynes. It expresses that moment of hesitancy in time, of false beginnings, and still more of false endings, in which a feudal-Christian past and bourgeois-rationalist future coexisted without visible ideological friction, held in solution, as it were, by the furious churning of day-to-day political action.

That Commynes expressed all this so well was, at least in part, due to his corruption. He was available for a fee; he praised princes who lied or killed with "profit." Many of the reasons for this weakness arose from his background and were shared with others living at the time. But one reason was especially Commynes' own. He worshipped power.

5 / BIBLIOGRAPHY

I. Manuscripts of the Memoirs   No manuscript authorized or written by Philippe de Commynes exists. Six manuscripts written between 1520 and 1550 have been discovered, of which the two most important are the Ms. Polignac (*ca.* 1530) at the Bibliothèque Nationale, Paris, and the Ms. Dobrée (*ca.* 1520) at the Musée Dobrée in Nantes, France. Ms. Polignac is the only manuscript including Books 7 and 8, the second part of the *Memoirs*; in most other respects Ms. Dobrée is more correct. Ms. Dobrée is the only manuscript divided into books and chapters; these subdivisions are not always the same as those found in early printed editions.

II. Editions of the Memoirs   The *Memoirs* have been printed in 8 languages and over 120 editions in the past four centuries.[1] The first edition appeared at Paris in 1524, but it was evidently copied from a poor manuscript or edited very poorly because it omits many passages (including all of Books 7 and 8) and incorrectly prints many others.

---

1. See Ferdinand van der Haeghen, *Bibliotheca belgica*, V (Brussels, 1890), no. 161 ff., for a listing of 123 editions and translations. Only a dozen or so editions and translations have appeared since van der Haeghen wrote.

Denis Sauvage's Paris edition of 1552 was the thirteenth to appear, but it was the first to pretend to any critical accuracy and completeness. Sauvage quoted a manuscript now lost for certain readings which are still adopted by modern editors. Four editions remain useful today:

Mémoires, ed. Lenglet-Dufresnoy, Paris, 1747, 4 volumes. Lenglet, comparing only three of the six manuscripts now known with a number of preceding editions, tallied three thousand variant readings in the text of the *Memoirs*, most of them easily eliminated by reference to the manuscripts he possessed. The documents concerning Commynes' life and times which Lenglet included in his notes must still be consulted by the scholar interested in the *Memoirs*.

Mémoires, ed. Mlle. Dupont, Paris, 1840–1847, 3 volumes. Dupont's Introduction and abundant notes (in which new documents concerning Commynes and the subjects of the *Memoirs* are included) are still invaluable.

Mémoires, ed. B. de Mandrot, Paris, 1901–1903, 2 volumes. Mandrot's edition is the first to collate all the manuscripts known at present. Ms. Polignac is presented in the text, with variants from the other manuscripts included in the apparatus. Introduction and notes are excellent.

Mémoires, ed. J. Calmette with the collaboration of G. Durville, Paris, 1924–1925, 3 volumes. This edition is the only critical text in print at present. Ms. Dobrée is followed in the text for Books 1 to 6, and Ms. Polignac for Books 7 and 8. Variants from other manuscripts are included in the apparatus. Introduction and notes are not as full nor usually as helpful as those of Mandrot, but they include some corrections of Mandrot's notes, and some clarifications of passages which Mandrot passed over.

III. Translations   The first English translation was made in 1596 and the last one before this in 1855. Only two translations are of interest to the student of Commynes at present:

Memoiren, ed. Fritz Ernst, Stuttgart, 1952. This translation includes a good twenty-five-page Introduction. The text is a very faithful rendition of the original French.

Memorie, ed. Maria Daviso di Charvensod, Turin, 1960. This careful Italian translation is prefaced by a forty-page Introduction which reflects especially conscientious and judicious reading of recent scholarship about Commynes.

All of the translations, including the present one, lose much of the charm of Commynes' style for two reasons. First, the language of the *Memoirs* is very simple and repetitive, but the same words take on different meanings in different contexts precisely because of Commynes' limited vocabulary. I have mentioned this problem in the Introduction with regard to the word "wise" (*saige*). Most of these associated meanings of the same words derive from slang expressions, the figurative language of the common man. Because such expressions are associated with a way of life unfamiliar to us, we can scarcely feel—let alone translate—the wit and freshness of such expressions as *courir après son esteuf* (to try to answer one's adversary; literally, "to run after the tennis ball"), *laver la teste* (to reprimand sharply) or *accorder ses vielles* (to calm him down).[2] Secondly, Commynes' style is derived from his conversation, and its ease is more difficult to imitate, especially after five hundred years, than a written, formal style would be.

Some of the deficiencies of Commynes' style have been smoothed over in this translation and in most others. For example, long sentences like that quoted on page 52 of the Introduction have usually been broken into two or three shorter ones. Again, the relation of adverbial clauses of time and place to the main subject and vague pronoun references have been clarified by rearranging the sentence structure and by inserting proper names in brackets. Prepositions and conjunctions have been inserted where Commynes' text indicates only a comma, for the memorialist, who dictated his work, apparently used conversational pauses and the intonations of speech to indicate, in many cases, the connections among his rambling reminiscences.[3]

There is great harmony between the language and the spirit of Commynes' work. Forceful, though not learned or eloquent, terse, yet illumined by humor and punctuated by occasional passages of leisurely rumination, the style conveys what Commynes felt as well as what he

2. I take the second and third of these examples and this point of style from N. Dupire's review of Gerhard Heidel's *La langue et le style de Philippe de Commynes* (Leipzig, 1934), in *Romania* (1937), 268 ff.

3. As an example of the ambiguity which results from Commynes' pronoun references and shifts of subject between subordinate and main clauses, see the first paragraph in this translation of the *Memoirs* on page 358. In this sentence "they" refers to princes, to people, to princes again, and to soldiers in successive clauses. Commynes' ambiguity has been left intact in the translation here, just as the long sentence on p. 52 of the Introduction has, by exception, not been broken up. As an example of the difficulty of relating the sequences of events narrated by Commynes, not merely within a sentence but between whole paragraphs, see n. 118 on p. 324. Note that confusions of time and grammatical reference tend to occur especially when Commynes wishes to moralize.

meant. The *Memoirs* are not a work of literature. Words held no magic in and of themselves for Commynes; language was simply a tool. But the indifferent ease with which the memorialist used his instrument has a power of its own.

IV. Documents   The basic collection of documents on Commynes' life is still *Lettres et négotiations de Philippe de Comines*, ed. Kervyn de Lettenhove, Brussels, 1867–1874, 3 volumes. Documents not in French are given in French translation, indications of the provenance of the documents is not always adequate, and the running commentary which surrounds and almost drowns the original sources included is biased and unfounded in fact in many places.

Lettres de Philippe de Commynes aux archives de Florence, ed. E. Benoist, Lyon, 1863, is better edited, as is Charles Fierville's *Documents inédits sur Philippe de Commynes*, Paris, 1881. The only collection of source materials executed with all the rigor of modern philological scholarship is L. Sozzi's recent "Lettere inedite di Filippo de Commynes a Francesco Gaddi," in *Studi in onore di Tammaro de Marinis*, IV (Verona, 1964), 205–62. These last three collections, however, touch upon only a few episodes in Commynes' life, and the full, careful publication of source materials concerning him (there are almost certainly many letters and diplomatic references about him still unedited in the archives of Europe) thus remains a desideratum.

V. Secondary Works   I have included here only the most recent and most essential scholarship on Commynes, together with several introductory surveys on fifteenth-century Europe for the beginning student. More complete bibliographies may be found in the works of Charlier and Liniger quoted below, and in Daviso's Italian translation mentioned above.

Bittmann, Karl. *Ludwig XI und Karl der Kühne: die Memoiren des Philippe de Commynes als historische Quelle*, Göttingen, 1964 (volume one, published in two parts, of a projected four-volume work on Commynes).

Bouwsma, William. "The Politics of Commynes," *Journal of Modern History*, XXIII (1951), 315–28.

Calmette, Joseph. *The Golden Age of Burgundy*, New York, 1963 (first published in French in 1949 as *Les grands ducs de Bourgogne*).

Charlier, Gustave. *Commynes*, Brussels, 1945.

Bibliography

Dufournet, Jean. *La destruction des mythes dans les Mémoires de Philippe de Commynes*, Geneva, 1966 (the first published volume of a projected five-volume work on Commynes).

Fueter, Eduard. *Geschichte der neueren Historiographie*, Berlin, 1911 (later editions and translations of this work reproduce Fueter's words on Commynes unchanged).

Gilmore, Myron. *The World of Humanism*, New York (Harper Torch-book), 1963 (see chapters 1 to 7).

Hale, John R. *et al.*, ed., *Europe in the Late Middle Ages*, London, 1965 (see chapters 2, 5, 9, 10, and 13).

Huizinga, Johan. *The Waning of the Middle Ages*, Doubleday (Anchor Book), 1954 (a shortened version of the Dutch and German editions).

Liniger, Jean. *Le monde et Dieu selon Philippe de Commynes*, Neuchâtel, 1943.

Sainte-Beuve, Charles de. "Philippe de Commynes," in *Causeries du lundi*, Vol. I, Paris, 1857, pp. 240–59.

Vaughan, Richard. *Philip the Bold*, London, 1963; and *John the Fearless*, London, 1966 (two more volumes on Philip the Good and Charles the Bold will complete these excellent political studies of the development of Burgundy).

Waley, Daniel. *Later Medieval Europe*, London, 1964 (see chapters 7, 9, 12, and 15).

The Memoirs

The inscription on this drawing calls Commynes lord of Argenton, a fief which he acquired in 1473. Commynes was about twenty-six in 1473, and he appears at least this old in the drawing. The bemused wrinkles on his full, round face counterpoint the firm-lipped, direct gaze. Matthew d'Arras, one of Commynes' servants, called his master "handsome and tall." The set of Commynes' head and shoulders in this drawing indicate what Matthew meant.

PROLOGUE

Messire Philippe de Commines, seigneur d'Argenton, historien

N.B.   *Book and chapter divisions in the* Memoirs, *together with their titles, stem apparently from editors or copyists of Commynes' original manuscript (see section I of the Bibliography). Therefore, titles to all except book divisions are omitted in this translation. Book titles were composed by the editor. Book and chapter divisions follow Calmette's edition, as does the text unless stated otherwise in the footnotes (see section II of the Bibliography for full citation of Calmette's work). Alterations in this translation of Commynes' grammar, syntax, and wording are discussed and illustrated in section III of the Bibliography. Rather than using lengthy circumlocutions, we have followed Commynes' practice of referring to areas in France, such as the district of Bar or the area around Laon, as "the Barrois" and "the Laonnois."*

Maps indicating the principal places mentioned in the Memoirs *appear in the front matter in each volume. The index at the end of Volume Two contains cross-references, so that Commynes' use of different titles to indicate the same person can be deciphered. To further facilitate consultation of Commynes' lengthy and involuted work, a résumé of the principal dates of his life appears on page xiv of this volume, and chronological tables referring to the principal men and events described in the* Memoirs *are provided in the front matter of each volume.*

Miss Cazeaux is primarily responsible for the translation. Mr. Kinser provided the Introduction, notes, and other materials in the volume, and revised the translation in cooperation with Miss Cazeaux.

Your Excellence, Archbishop of Vienne,[1] in order to comply with your request that I should commit to writing for you an account of what I have known and heard of the acts of King Louis XI (may he rest in peace), our master and benefactor, and prince most worthy of remembrance, I have kept as close to the truth as I could and as far as my memory would allow.

Of the period of his youth, I can say nothing except what I have heard him relate; but from the time when I came into his service to the hour of his death, at which I was present, I have been at his side more continuously than anyone else, performing the duties of the position in which I served him, which has always been at least that of chamberlain, or attending to his great affairs. In him as in all other princes whom I have known or served, I have discerned some good and some evil, for they are men like us. Perfection belongs to God alone. But when virtue and good qualities exceed vices in a prince, he is worthy of great praise, since princes are more inclined than other men to be willful in their actions, owing to the upbringing and scarce discipline which they receive in their youth; and when they reach manhood, most people take pains to cater to their whims and their rank.

Since I would not wish to lie, it is possible that at some point in this writing some detail might be found which might not entirely reflect credit on the king; but I hope that those who read this will take into account the above-mentioned reasons for it. And I venture to affirm in his praise that, all things considered, I do not believe I have ever known any

1. Angelo Cato or Catone (1430's–1496) was a Neapolitan who entered Louis XI's service about 1476 and was rewarded with the archbishopric of Vienne in 1482. Professor of natural philosophy and astronomy at the University of Naples as early as 1465, he edited the *Pandectae medicinae* of Matteo Silvatico in 1474 and wrote a commentary on Aristotle's ethical writings, now lost, between 1487 and 1493. Commynes must have known Cato for many years at the French court, where Cato was in close attendance upon the king as doctor and astrologer. See Edmondo Cione, "Una lettera poco nota di Angelo Catone sulla congiura dei baroni," *Rivista storica italiana*, LVIII (1941), 235–55, and Benedetto Croce, "Il personaggio italiano che esortò il Commynes a scrivere i 'Memoires,'" in his *Vite di avventure di fede e di passione* (Bari, 1935), p. 161 ff.

prince in whom one could find fewer faults than in him. And I have known as many great princes and have been as frequently in touch with them as any man who has lived in France in my time. I have known sovereigns in this kingdom as well as in Brittany and in these parts of Flanders, in Germany, England, Spain, Portugal and Italy—temporal as well as spiritual rulers. Several I have not seen, but I have known them by means of communications from their embassies, or by means of letters and instructions from them, from which one can have enough information about their nature and character.

However, I do not intend to praise the king here to the detriment of the honor or good reputation of others. I am merely sending you what I could readily call to mind, hoping that you are requesting this in order to make use of it in some writing which you intend to compose in Latin, for you are very well versed in that language; your work will proclaim the greatness of the prince of whom I shall speak to you and will bear witness to your understanding of affairs. Wherever I am lacking, you may consult my lord of Bouchage and others, who will be better able to enlighten you and will couch the information in better style. But due to the obligation of honor and because of the great intimacies and kindnesses which were to be uninterrupted until the death of one or the other of us, no one should be in a position to remember him better than I am. The losses and afflictions which have befallen me since his death also serve to remind me of the graces which I received from him. It is not unusual that after the decease of so great and powerful a prince great changes should take place. Some people lose from this, and others gain. For goods and honors are not divided up according to the desire of those who request them.

In order to inform you about the period when I knew the king, that period you requested me to write about, I must begin before the time when I entered his service; and then, in orderly fashion, I shall pursue my account until the moment when I became his servant, and shall continue to his death.

Roger van der Weyden, in his portraits of the last three great dukes of Burgundy, gave them all a pinch-cornered, self-determined mouth. But in his portrait of Charles at about age twenty-one (1454), the cropped, curly hair, broad chest, and well-fleshed face bespeak the man of action and impulse rather than the careful, reflective willfulness attributed by van der Weyden to Charles's forefathers. In the lost original of which this is a replica, Charles held a scroll, not a sword.

BOOK ONE

The War for the Public Good, 1465

1

Near the end of my boyhood, at the age when horsemanship is first acquired, I was taken to Lille and presented to Duke Charles of Burgundy, at that time called the count of Charolais,[2] who took me into his service. This was in the year fourteen hundred and sixty four.

Some three days later the ambassadors of the king [Louis XI of France (1461–1483)] arrived in Lille; they included the count of Eu, the chancellor of France, named Morvilliers, and the bishop of Narbonne. In the presence of Duke Philip of Burgundy, the count of Charolais, and their entire council, the ambassadors were granted an audience in open court.[3] Morvilliers spoke most arrogantly, maintaining that the count of Charolais, while in Holland, had ordered the seizure of a small war vessel. This ship had left from Dieppe and had on board the bastard of Rubempré, whom the count had imprisoned on the charge that he had come to Holland for the purpose of abducting him.[4] He had this proclaimed far and wide, and particularly in Bruges, haunt of strangers from all nations, by a Burgundian knight named Olivier de la Marche.

Therefore, the king, who was being charged with this offense (falsely, as he put it) demanded of Duke Philip that Olivier de la Marche be sent to him as a prisoner in Paris, to be punished according to the merits of the case. At this point Duke Philip replied to them that Olivier de la Marche, his major-domo, was born in the county of Burgundy [Franche-Comté] and was in no way subject to the crown;[5] however, if he had said

2. Charles the Bold was styled count of Charolais until the death of Philip, his father, duke of Burgundy from 1419 to 1467.

3. This negotiation between Louis XI's ambassadors and the Burgundians was Commynes' first experience in public service. He was seventeen years old.

4. Rubempré was considered by the Burgundians an agent of their enemy, Louis XI. Charles the Bold believed that Rubempré had intended to take him prisoner, and therefore he took Rubempré prisoner instead. Whether Rubempré really hoped to capture Charles has never been ascertained.

5. La Marche, like Commynes, has left us important memoirs about the life and politics which he observed as a Burgundian courtier. Franche-Comté was an imperial fief (see the map, p. xi); therefore its residents owed no allegiance to the French king.

or done anything which might reflect on the king's honor, and if this could be properly ascertained, the duke would inflict a penalty fitting the offense. Concerning the bastard of Rubempré, he had indeed been captured because of certain manifestations and attitudes on his part and that of his men in the vicinity of the Hague in Holland, where the duke's son, the count of Charolais, resided at the time. If the count was mistrustful, he did not take after his father, who had never been of a suspicious nature, but after his mother, the most mistrustful lady her husband had ever known. But although the duke, as was stated, was never given to suspicion, nevertheless, if he had happened to be present instead of his son at the time when the bastard of Rubempré was frequenting the neighborhood, he too would have had the man arrested. If upon investigation the bastard were no longer charged with having plotted to capture his son, as had been claimed, the duke would have him released at once and returned to the king, as his ambassadors had requested.

Then Morvilliers proceeded to make severe and dishonorable accusations against the duke of Brittany, named Francis, asserting that he and the count of Charolais, while the latter was in Tours, paying a visit to the king, had exchanged documents sealed with their arms by which they became brothers-in-arms. These documents were exchanged through the intermediary of Tanneguy du Chastel, who has since become governor of Roussillon, and who has enjoyed a position of authority in this kingdom. Morvilliers built up this case to such enormous and criminal proportions that he spared no conceivable detail in his speech which might put a prince to shame and bring censure upon him.

The count of Charolais, who appeared to be extremely angered by this insult to his friend and ally, attempted to reply several times. But Morvilliers invariably interrupted him, saying: "My lord of Charolais, I have not come to speak to you, but to your honored father." The count begged his father repeatedly to allow him to reply. The duke said to him: "I have spoken in your place, as it seems to me proper that a father should answer for his son. However, if you feel so strongly about the matter, think it over for today, and tomorrow say whatever you please." Moreover, Morvilliers declared that he could not imagine what had moved the count to enter into this alliance with the duke of Brittany, unless it were a pension which the king had given him, together with the governorship of Normandy, and which the king had subsequently taken away from him.

The next day at the assembly and in the presence of the above-named persons, the count of Charolais, kneeling upon a square cushion of velvet which had been placed on the floor, addressed himself first to his father and began to speak of the bastard of Rubempré, asserting that the causes for his seizure were just and reasonable, as would be established in his trial. However, I do not believe anything definite was ascertained, although suspicions were numerous. I saw him freed from a prison where he had been confined for five years. After disposing of this matter, the count proceeded to vindicate the duke of Brittany and himself. He acknowledged that the duke of Brittany and he had indeed entered into an alliance, had made a pact of friendship, and had become brothers-in-arms; however, they intended this alliance to be in no way detrimental to the king and his realm, but rather to be of service and assistance to him, when occasion required. Concerning the pension which had been canceled, he claimed that he had never received more than one quarter of it, amounting to nine thousand francs, and that he had never requested this pension or the administration of Normandy; as long as he might enjoy his father's favor, he could well do without all other benefits. I am convinced that had it not been out of respect for his father, who was present and whom he addressed, he would have spoken much more sharply. Duke Philip's conclusion displayed great humility and wisdom; he beseeched the king not to think unkindly of him and his son, but always to keep him in his good graces.

Wine and sweetmeats were thereupon brought in, and then the ambassadors took leave of father and son. After the count of Eu and the chancellor had taken leave of the count of Charolais, who was standing a certain distance from his father, the count said to the bishop of Narbonne, whom he saw last: "Recommend me most humbly to the good graces of the king, and tell him that he had me given a good dressing down by the chancellor, but before a year has passed, he will have reason to regret it." On his return, the bishop of Narbonne relayed this message to the king, as you will discover shortly.

These words gave rise to great hatred between the count of Charolais and the king. Matters were not improved by the fact that, a short time before, the king had repurchased for 400,000 *écus* the towns on the river Somme—Amiens, Abbeville, Saint-Quentin and others—which had been ceded by King Charles VII to Duke Philip of Burgundy by the treaty of Arras, for his benefit and that of his male heirs. However, in the duke's declining years, all his affairs were administered by the brothers de Croy and Chimay, and others from their household. The duke recovered his money from the king and made restitution of the above-mentioned lands. The count, his son, was greatly perturbed by this turn of events because these areas constituted the boundaries and limits of their territories and represented the loss of many subjects, who could have provided good soldiers in case of war.[6] He held the house of Croy responsible for this state of affairs; and when his father Duke Philip had reached extreme old age, which he had been approaching fast, the count banished all the de Croys from his father's lands, deprived them of their positions, and confiscated all their property.[7]

2

Only a few days after the departure of the above-mentioned ambassadors, John, late duke of Bourbon [1456–1488], came to Lille, ostensibly to visit his uncle, who loved the house of Bourbon more than any other family in the world. The duke of Bourbon was the son of Duke Philip's sister; she was for many years a widow and resided with the duke her brother with several of her children—three daughters and one son. The true reason for the coming of the duke of Bourbon, however, was to convince and persuade the duke of Burgundy to consent to the raising of an army in his territories; similarly, all the other princes of France would then follow his example in order to point out to the king the deplorable state of order and justice which he maintained in his kingdom. They wanted to be strong in order to force him to submit to their will in the event that he should refuse to change his ways. And this war was afterwards known as the War for the Public Good because it was undertaken under the guise of asserting that it was for the public good of the kingdom.

Duke Philip, called Philip the Good after his death, consented to have an army established, but the heart of the matter was never revealed to him and he never expected the situation to come to the point of violence. Presently soldiers began to be enlisted, and the count of Saint-Pol, who later became constable of France [1466],[8] came to confer with the count of Charolais at Cambrai, where Duke Philip was residing at the time. Saint-Pol met him there, together with the marshal of Burgundy, who was of the house of Neufchâtel, and then the count of Charolais summoned a large assembly of counselors and other dignitaries from his

6. The ten cities along the Somme River which were acquired by Louis XI in 1463 were rich not only in men and military supplies. Strategically, their possession was the key to invasion of the Parisian basin, heartland of Louis XI's realm.

7. The disgrace was just: the de Croys were secretly in contact with Louis XI. See Commynes, *Mémoires*, ed. Calmette (Paris, 1924–1925), I, 9, n. 1.

8. The constable (*connétable*) was commander-in-chief of French armed forces, next to the king himself. Commynes' reference to Saint-Pol's future office under Louis XI is confusing because Saint-Pol, when not yet constable, fought together with Charles the Bold and other rebel princes against Louis in the War for the Public Good.

father's court in the residence of the bishop of Cambrai. In their presence he declared all members of the house of Croy mortal enemies of his father and himself, although the count of Saint-Pol had given his daughter in marriage to the lord of Croy many years before; but he maintained that he was forced to do this. In short, all of them were forced to flee from the territories of the duke of Burgundy, and they lost many of their belongings.

All these proceedings greatly displeased Duke Philip. He had had as his first chamberlain a person who later became lord of Chimay, a very worthy young man, the lord of Croy's nephew, and he departed without taking leave of his master because he feared for his life and security; otherwise he would have been killed or seized, for so he had been warned. Duke Philip's old age made him endure this patiently; and all these declarations against his men were enacted owing to the restitution of his territories on the river Somme, which Duke Philip had returned to King Louis for the sum of 400,000 *écus*. The count of Charolais charged the members of the house of Croy with having influenced Duke Philip to consent to this restitution.

The count of Charolais reconciled himself with his father as best he could. And immediately thereafter he took the field with his men-at-arms, and along with him was the count of Saint-Pol, chief administrator of his affairs and principal leader of his army. His forces consisted of some three hundred men-at-arms and four thousand archers under his command, as well as many fine knights and squires from the provinces of Artois, Hainaut, and Flanders, led by the above-mentioned count, by the appointment of the count of Charolais. Similar bands and units of equal size were under the command of my lord of Ravenstein, brother of the duke of Cleves, and Anthony, bastard of Burgundy. Other commanders were present but I shall not name them now, for brevity's sake. Among them were two knights held in high esteem by the count of Charolais. One was the lord of Hautbourdin, a knight for many years, natural brother [*sic*: cousin] of the count of Saint-Pol; he had received his training in the old wars between France and England, when King Henry V of England reigned in France and Duke Philip joined forces with him as his ally. The other was named the lord of Contay, who was of the same generation as Hautbourdin.[9] Both of them were very valiant and wise knights and had principal command of the army.

There was an abundance of young men. Among the others was one of particular renown, named Philippe de Lalaing, whose family was fa-

9. Guillaume Le Jeune, lord of Contay, plays an especially important role at the battle of Brusthem, narrated in Book 2. See section 4 of the Introduction.

mous for its valiant and brave members; almost all of them died on the battlefield in the service of their lord. The army consisted of some fourteen hundred men-at-arms poorly armed and unskilled, owing to the long peace which these territories had enjoyed; for since the treaty of Arras they had seen few wars of significant duration. In my estimation they had been quiet for more than thirty-six years,[10] except for a few minor skirmishes with the people of Ghent, which hardly lasted at all. The men-at-arms were very well mounted and well accompanied, for few could be seen who did not have five or six large horses in their equipage. The archers must have been eight or nine thousand in number, and when the review was held, it took longer to reject them than to accept them, and only the best were chosen.

The subjects of the house of Burgundy were very prosperous at this time because of the long era of peace which they had enjoyed and because of the kindness of the ruling prince, who levied few taxes on his people. It seems to me that at this time his territories more than any others in the world could be called promised lands. They were abundant with riches and in perfect repose, such as they have never been since; things started to change about twenty-three years ago. The expenditures and clothes of men and women were sumptuous and extravagant; the entertainments and banquets were larger and more prodigal than any given elsewhere to my knowledge; the bathing parties and other diversions with women were on a grand scale, disorderly and rather immodest: I refer to women of low estate.[11] In short, it seemed at the time to the subjects of this house that no prince could be magnificent enough to suit them or even to startle them. Today, however, I know of no other house so desolate, and I suspect that the sins which its members committed during the time of its prosperity have contributed to their present adversity, especially since they did not realize that all these benefits were gifts of God, who distributes them according to His pleasure.

The army was instantly ready; it was composed of all the elements which I mentioned previously. The count of Charolais set forth with all his troops. All the men were on horseback except those who led his train of artillery, which was fine and mighty for the time, and he was accompanied by such a large number of carts that with those that belonged to

10. Either Commynes sees a date before the conclusion of the Treaty of Arras as the real beginning of Burgundian tranquillity, or his arithmetic is bad. Between 1435 (Treaty of Arras) and 1465 (War for the Public Good), there were somewhat less than thirty years of peace.
11. Public baths were a usual feature of medieval cities, and in some cases special police regulations supervised their morality.

him only he could enclose most of his army. He proceeded to Noyon and besieged a small castle called Nesle, which had some soldiers within its walls. In a few days he conquered it. Joachim [Rouault], marshal of France, who had left Péronne, was always in his vicinity, but his presence was harmless because he had few men under his command; and he retired to Paris when the count approached.

Along the road the count did not wage war; neither did his men take anything without paying for it. Therefore the towns on the river Somme and all the others let his men enter in small numbers and gave them what they wished for their money; it seems that they had a ready ear for any rumors as to who would be the stronger, the king or the lords. The count advanced so far that he came to Saint-Denis, near Paris, where all the lords of the kingdom were to meet, according to their promise; they did not appear, however.

The duke of Brittany sent as his ambassador to the count the vice-chancellor of Brittany, named Rouville; he carried blank orders signed by his master, and he made use of these for news and various writings as the occasion required. He was a Norman and a very shrewd man; he needed these things, considering all the mutterings that were arising against him.

The count presented himself before Paris and there was much fighting up to its very gates, to the disadvantage of those inside. Few soldiers were there except the above-mentioned Joachim and his men, and the lord of Nantouillet, later grand master of France, who served the king of France that year as well as any subject had ever served him in time of need; he was nevertheless ill-rewarded in the end, owing to the pursuit of his enemies rather than to any default on the part of the king. Neither the one [Louis XI] nor the others [Nantouillet's enemies] was entirely free from blame, however. Some of the common people, as I learned later, became so frightened that day that they exclaimed: "They are inside!" Several people told me about this afterwards. But this fear was without foundation. My lord of Hautbourdin, however, of whom I spoke earlier and who had been raised there when it was not as strong as it is at present, seemed to believe rather firmly that the city should be assailed. The men-at-arms, all of whom despised the people because they had been able to chase them to the very gates of their city, were all for it. It is probable, however, that it could not have been captured. The count returned to Saint-Denis.

The next morning a meeting was held in order to deliberate on the question of going forth to meet the duke of Berry [Charles, brother of Louis XI] and the duke of Brittany [Francis II] who were close by, according to the vice-chancellor of Brittany, who showed letters from them; but he had written them himself on blank orders over their signature and actually did not know any more about the matter than the rest of them. It was concluded that they would pass the Seine, although many proposed to turn back, since the others had failed to keep their appointment and since it had been sufficiently difficult to pass the rivers Somme and Marne without also having to pass the Seine. Many had their doubts about the plan because they had nowhere to retreat if the need should arise.

The whole army complained loudly about the count of Saint-Pol and the vice-chancellor [of Brittany]. The count of Charolais, however, proceeded to pass the river and establish himself at the bridge of Saint-Cloud. The day after he arrived there, he received a message from a lady [Marie de Clèves, duchess of Orleans] of this kingdom, written in her own hand, indicating that the king was leaving the Bourbonnais with forced marches and was advancing toward him.

It would be useful to explain how the king had gone to the Bourbonnais. Since he realized that all the lords of the kingdom were declaring themselves against him, or at least against his government, he decided first to advance against the duke of Bourbon, who seemed to him to be more openly against him than the other princes, and who would willingly have devastated his country, which was in a weak position. He conquered several of his possessions and would have taken the rest if help had not been forthcoming from Burgundy, under the command of the marquis of Rothelin, the lord of Montagu, and others. Also in arms was the present chancellor of France, named my lord Guillaume de Rochefort, a man very much esteemed.

Count [Pierre de] Beaujeu and Cardinal [Charles] of Bourbon, brother of Duke John of Bourbon, had raised these forces in Burgundy and then led the Burgundians inside Moulins. On the other hand, the duke of Nemours, the count of Armagnac, and the lord of Albret came with a great number of men to the aid of the duke of Bourbon; many of the fine men from their lands had left the king's regular army and had passed over to their side. Most of them were in a rather sorry state because they were not being paid and had to depend on the good will of the people for vital necessities.

In spite of their great numbers, the king gave them considerable trouble, and so they began negotiating for peace. The duke of Nemours took an especially important part in the negotiations and swore allegiance to the king, promising him to be loyal to his cause; later, however, he did exactly the opposite. This was the occasion of the hatred which the king retained against him for so long, as he told me several times.

Indeed the king realized that these matters were not to be settled very soon and that the count of Charolais was getting closer to Paris. He feared that the count, along with his brother [Charles, duke of Berry] and the duke of Brittany who were coming from the direction of Brittany, would be let in, because they pretended to be interested in the public good of the kingdom; he also suspected that the other cities would react in the same manner as Paris, and it was decided that by forced marches his men should reach Paris and enter it and prevent these two powerful armies from joining forces. He did not come with the intention of fighting, as he told me several times when discussing these matters.[12]

3

As I explained earlier, when the count of Charolais was informed of the departure of the king, who had left the territory of the Bourbonnais and was going straight to encounter him (or so he believed), he decided to march toward the king. He then made public the contents of the letter he had received, without revealing the name of his correspondent, and urged that everyone should make up his mind to do his best, for he had decided to test fortune. He proceeded to take up quarters at Longjumeau, a village near Paris, and my lord the constable [Saint-Pol] with the whole vanguard went to Montlhéry, three leagues beyond. Spies and horsemen were sent out to discover when the king would arrive and from which direction.

In the presence of the count of Saint-Pol, Longjumeau was chosen as the locality where the combat was to take place, and the participants in the discussion agreed among themselves that the count of Saint-Pol should retire to Longjumeau in case the king should arrive. The lord of Hautbourdin and the lord of Contay were present at these deliberations. One must understand that my lord of Maine with seven or eight hundred men-at-arms was advancing against the dukes of Berry and Brittany, who included in their retinue some wise and distinguished knights whom King Louis had cashiered at his accession to the crown, although they had served his father well at the time of the recovery and pacification of the kingdom; he since regretted his treatment of them many times and

12. Commynes' naïve acceptance of Louis XI's version of the maneuvers leading up to the battle of Montlhéry and the treaty of Conflans which ended the War for the Public Good has been shown by Karl Bittmann to lead to a number of distortions in Commynes' account of these events. See Chapter I of Bittmann's book on the *Memoirs*, cited in section V of the Bibliography.

admitted his error. Among these men were the count of Dunois [called the bastard of Orleans], well-esteemed in all matters, the marshal of Lohéac, the count of Dammartin, the lord of Bueil and many others who had left the regular army of the king, and some five hundred men-at-arms, all of whom had passed over to the duke of Brittany; they were his subjects, were natives of his territories, and they were the flower of that army.

As I said previously, the count of Maine, who did not consider himself strong enough to contend with them, always decamped before them while retreating to the king. They [the troops of the dukes of Berry and Brittany] sought to join the Burgundian forces. Some have insinuated that the count of Maine was in compact with them, but I have never had any knowledge of it and I do not believe it.[13]

While the count of Charolais was posted at Longjumeau, as I explained, and his vanguard was at Montlhéry, he was informed by a prisoner who was brought to him that the count of Maine had joined the king, who had in his army all the standing forces of the kingdom, which consisted of approximately twenty-two hundred men-at-arms, besides the *arrière-ban* of Dauphiné, with forty or fifty gentlemen of Savoy, all of them men of high estate.[14] A council was called [by the king]; the count of Maine and the grand seneschal of Normandy named [Pierre] de Brézé, and the admiral of France, who was of the house of Montauban, and others were present. To summarize, whatever advice may have been offered to him, the king decided not to fight but merely to establish himself in Paris without going near the Burgundian headquarters. In my judgment his opinion was correct.

He was suspicious of the grand seneschal of Normandy and therefore asked him to confess whether or not he had given a document sealed with his arms to the princes who were against him. To which the grand seneschal replied that he had, and that they might keep it, but his body belonged to the king. This he said jokingly, for he was accustomed to speak in such a manner. The king accepted this statement and bade him lead his vanguard and guides because he wanted to avoid the battle, as was said earlier. The grand seneschal, determining to follow his own will, then said to one of his intimates: "I will put them so close together today that it will take a very skillful man to separate them." So he did. And the first man to die was himself, together with his men. These words

13. In fact, the count of Maine was secretly on the Burgundian side.
14. The *compagnies d'ordonnance*, instituted in 1445, formed the French standing army. The *arrière-ban*, in contrast to the standing army, was a convocation for military service of all the vassals of the king in a given region.

were related to me by the king later, for at the time I was in the service of the count of Charolais.[15]

Thus on the twenty-seventh day of July, 1465,[16] the king's vanguard was advancing near Montlhéry, where the count of Saint-Pol was stationed. He immediately signaled this arrival to the count of Charolais, who was encamped three leagues away, at the place which had been selected for the battle, and begged him to come to his aid at once because men-at-arms and archers were dismounted and on foot, and encumbered with their train of artillery. It was not possible for him to join the count of Charolais, as he had been ordered to do, because if he made a move, it would be interpreted as flight and this would be very dangerous for the whole company. The count of Charolais sent in haste the bastard of Burgundy, named Anthony, to join him, together with a large number of men under his command; he debated with himself as to whether he should go or not. Finally he marched after the others and arrived at about seven in the morning. Five or six standards of the king were already posted along the side of a large ditch which separated the two units.

Others in the army of the count of Charolais included the vice-chancellor of Brittany, named Rouville, and an old man-at-arms named Madré, who had surrendered the Sainte-Maxence bridge; and they were fearful because of the hostile comments against them. They realized that a battle was about to begin and that the men on whom they had counted to constitute their strength were not with them, and so, before the combat started, they fled in the direction where they believed they would find the Bretons.

The count of Charolais met the count of Saint-Pol on foot and all the rest ranged themselves in order of battle as they arrived; and we found all the archers unbooted, each with a stake set before him. Several casks of wine had been tapped so that they might drink. From the little I have witnessed, I have never seen any men who were more eager to fight; and this seemed to me a very good sign and a great comfort.

At first we were informed that every man without exception should march on foot, but later this was countermanded and almost all the men-at-arms were mounted again; however, many fine knights and squires including my lord of Cordes and his brother were ordered to remain on foot. Philippe de Lalaing had gone on foot because, among the Burgundians at the time, those who proceeded thus with the archers were the

15. See section 4 of the Introduction for analysis of this passage.
16. The battle of Montlhéry took place on July 16, 1465. Chronological inexactitudes are frequent in Commynes, as we shall have occasion to note.

most honored men. Invariably a great number of persons of high estate marched on foot so that the people would be encouraged and would fight better. This custom was acquired from the English, alongside of whom Duke Philip had made war in France during his youth. At that time hostilities lasted for thirty-two years without any truce, but the brunt of the fighting was borne by the English, who were rich and mighty. They were ruled then by that wise, handsome and valiant king, Henry [V],[17] who commanded wise and valiant men as well as very great military chiefs, such as the count of Salisbury, Talbot, and others whom I shall refrain from naming because their deeds took place before my time, although I have witnessed some of their results; for when God became weary of being kind to them, this wise king died in the wood of Vincennes. His foolish son [Henry VI] was crowned king of France and England in Paris. Thereupon the other men of degree in England began moving and division came among them; this has lasted to this day, or practically. Whether those of the house of York usurped the kingdom[18] or obtained it justly I do not know, because in such mat-ters the distribution is made in Heaven.

To return to the main subject, the fact that the Burgundians marched on foot [for a time] and then mounted their horses again caused them great loss of time and loss of men. The valiant and young knight Philippe de Lalaing was killed there because he was insufficiently armed. The king's men defiled through the forest of Torfou; and there were hardly four hundred men-at-arms when we arrived. It seemed to many of us that if they had marched at once, they would have met with no resistance because those from the rear could get there only by being ranged one abreast, as I said before. Still their number increased steadily. When he saw this, the wise knight, my lord of Contay, came to tell his master, my lord of Charolais, that if he wished to win this battle, it was high time for him to march; he gave his reasons for this and pointed out that if they had proceeded earlier his enemies would already have been discomfited because he had found them to be very few in number; but now they were visibly increasing. This was indeed the truth.

From then on every piece of advice and every order was altered, for everyone proceeded to give his opinion and already an important and

17. King Henry V (1413–22), victor over France at Agincourt (1415), placed longbowmen on either side of a central corps of nobles, who fought on foot like the archers.

18. This refers to Edward IV's imprisonment of Henry VI and eventual seizure of the throne in 1461. The Wars of the Roses divided England into factions following the Lancastrian or Yorkist houses until well into the reign of Henry VII (1485–1509). These events are recapitulated by Commynes in chapter 7 of this book.

strong encounter had started at the end of the village of Montlhéry between the archers on both sides. The king's men were led by Poncet de Rivière and were all archers from the king's regular army; they were outfitted with gold decoration and were in excellent condition. Those from the Burgundian side were without order or commandment, as happens frequently when encounters start; along with them, on foot, were my lord Philippe de Lalaing and Jacques du Mas, of good reputation, later grand equerry to Duke Charles of Burgundy. The manpower of the Burgundians was the greater; they gained control of a house, unhinged two or three doors which they used as shields, and started to advance into the streets and set fire to another house. The wind served them well by driving the fire toward the king's men, who then began to disperse, to mount their horses, and to flee.

On hearing these news and rumors the count of Charolais began to march, disregarding all previous orders, as I said earlier. It had been proposed that the march should be interrupted by two halts because the distance between the two armies was great. The king's men were near the castle of Montlhéry and had before them a large hedge and a ditch; farther away were the fields, full of wheat, beans, and other grains in abundance, for the land was good there.

All the count's archers marched on foot before him in loose order. In my estimation the chief element of strength in battles is the presence of archers, but then they should number in the thousands because in small numbers they are worthless. It is just as well if they are not well equipped; then they will have no regret at losing their horses. And better still, they should have none at all. And for one day of service in this capacity, those who are inexperienced are better than those with training in warfare. This is also the opinion of the English, who are the best archers in the world.

It had been agreed that there would be two rest periods on the road in order to give the infantrymen [and archers] a breathing spell because the road was long and the fruits of the soil [through which they marched] thick and tall, and this slowed them down; the opposite was done, however, as if they had made a special effort to lose the battle. Thus God showed that battles are in His hands and that He ordains victories as He sees fit. I do not believe that the mind of one man can bear or give order to such a large number of men or that things can be carried out in the field as they have been planned in one's chamber. Anyone who might consider himself capable of accomplishing this, assuming he is a man possessing natural reason, would err in his attitude toward God; although everyone should do his best according to his responsibilities, he should realize that the result is one of the accomplishments of God, which He begins sometimes with small steps and movements, by granting victory sometimes to one side and sometimes to the other. The mystery is so great that sometimes certain kingdoms and large territories come to their end and desolation, and others begin to grow and rule.

To return to the matter under discussion, the said count marched without stopping and gave no breathing-spell to his archers and infantry-men. The king's men, all of them men-at-arms, broke through the hedge at both ends. When they were so close that they were about to use their lances, the Burgundian men-at-arms broke through the ranks of their own archers, and passed over them without giving them a chance to draw a single arrow. The archers were the flower and hope of the army, for I believe that out of some twelve hundred soldiers who constituted the corps of men-at-arms not even fifty knew how to lay a lance in rest. Less than four hundred men were armed with breast-plates and not a single servant was armed at all, owing to the long duration of the peace, and because the house of Burgundy did not maintain mercenaries, which relieved the people from paying taxes. And never since that time has the territory enjoyed tranquillity, and today the situation is worse than ever. Thus they themselves destroyed the flower of their hope. But God, who presides over such mysteries, willed that the side where the count commanded, which was at the right toward the castle, should conquer without encountering any defense. I was with him all during that day and experienced less fear than I have ever felt in any place where I have ever been since, owing to my youth and my total ignorance of the peril, but I was amazed that anyone dared defend himself against the prince to whom I belonged; and I believed him to be the greatest ruler of them all. Such are those without experience, and as a result they support many ill-founded and hardly reasonable arguments; which shows that it is a good idea to adopt the opinion of those who claim that a man never repents of speaking little but often of speaking too much.

At the left-hand side were the lord of Ravenstein and Jacques de Saint-Pol[19] and many others to whom it was apparent that they did not have enough men-at-arms to bear up under the overwhelming forces before them, but from then on they were so close that it was useless to alter the order of battle. Indeed they were entirely broken and were driven to their own carts; most of them fled as far as the forest which was about a half-league beyond. A few Burgundian infantrymen

19. Jacques was a brother of the frequently mentioned Louis, the count of Saint-Pol who became constable of France.

gathered at the carts. The main participants in this pursuit were noblemen from Dauphiné and Savoyards, with many men-at-arms; and they had expected to win the battle. On this side, the Burgundians fled in great numbers, and among them were important persons; most of them fled in the direction of the Sainte-Maxence bridge, which they believed was still holding out for them. Many remained in the forest; among them my lord the constable [Saint-Pol] had gone there accompanied by a rather numerous following. The supply carts were fairly close to the forest. The constable soon showed that he did not consider the whole battle lost.

4

The count of Charolais, on the side which he commanded, pursued the enemy a half-league from Montlhéry with a quite small retinue. No resistance was encountered, however, and soldiers gathered in large numbers, so that he was already confident that victory was his. An old nobleman from Luxembourg, called Antoine le Breton, came to him and told him that the French had rallied their forces on the battlefield and that if he followed his pursuit much longer he would be lost. Although this man reiterated his words two or three times, that did not stop the count of Charolais. Forthwith my lord of Contay, of whom I spoke earlier, arrived; he said to him similar things to those which the old nobleman from Luxembourg had expressed, but so boldly that the count listened to his words and their sense and immediately reversed his course. And I believe that if he had proceeded two bow-shots farther he would have been taken prisoner, as befell several others who advanced before him. As he passed through the village he met with a number of men on foot who were fleeing. He pursued them although he had, all told, hardly a hundred horses. Only one man on foot made an about-face and hit him in the stomach with a pike; in the evening he saw its mark on his flesh. Most of the other men escaped through the gardens, but that one was killed.

As he was passing at the edge of the castle, we saw the archers of the king's guard in front of the gate, standing still. He was much amazed at this because he did not think that they had any means of defense left, and he turned aside to march into the field, where about fifteen or sixteen men-at-arms came charging upon him (a portion of his men had already separated themselves from him). At the very charge they killed his squire-carver, who was carrying a small standard bearing the count's coat of arms; his name was Philippe d'Oignies. The count was in great danger and he received many stabs, including a sword wound in the neck, traces of which remained with him throughout his lifetime. This happened because he was without his gorget, which had been too loosely fastened that morning and had fallen off; I saw it fall. Hands were laid on him and he was told: "My lord, surrender. I know you well. Do not allow yourself to be killed!"

He was still defending himself, and at that moment the son of a physician from Paris, called Master Jean Cadet, who belonged to the count's household, a stout, heavy, coarse man mounted on a horse of the same proportions, thrust himself into their midst and separated them. All the king's men withdrew to the edge of the ditch where they had been stationed that morning because they were afraid of another group of soldiers whom they saw marching and advancing toward them; the count, who was very bloody, retired toward them toward the middle of the field. The banner of the bastard of Burgundy was torn to shreds, to such a degree that there remained hardly a foot of it in length, and the same can be said of the banner of the count's archers. There were hardly forty men in all; and we, who were not even thirty, and even that number is doubtful, joined them. Immediately the count changed horses, and the new mount was presented to him by a young man who was his page at the time and whose name was Simon de Quingey; he has since become well known.

The count proceeded to the field to rally the soldiers; but I had seen such a half hour of fighting then that those of us who remained there would have thought of nothing save flight if a hundred men had marched against us. Ten men came to us, perhaps twenty, both on foot and on horseback; the infantrymen were weary and wounded, owing to the injury they had experienced that morning at our hands[20] and at those of the enemy. Men approached little by little. Our field was now tramped flat, where it had been abundant with tall wheat one half hour before. Soon it was filled with the most terrible dust in the world; the whole field was strewn with dead men and horses, and none of the dead could be identified because of the dust.

Forthwith we saw the count of Saint-Pol emerge from the wood; he was accompanied by about forty men-at-arms and his standard-bearer. He marched straight toward us and his men increased in number as they advanced; yet they seemed very far. Word was sent three or four times that he should hasten, but he did not hurry and moved only at a pace. He had his men arm themselves with lances which were lying on

20. Commynes is referring to the manner in which the Burgundian archers were knocked down by the charge of the Burgundian knights, as described on p. 108.

the ground; they came in orderly formation and this gave great comfort to our men. They joined together in great numbers and came to the place where we were assembled; and we found ourselves to total some eight hundred men-at-arms. There were few or no infantrymen, however, and this alone prevented the count from achieving complete victory, because a ditch and a thick hedge were between the two camps.

On the king's side the count of Maine and many others had fled, as well as some eight hundred men-at-arms. It has been insinuated that the count of Maine was in compact with the Burgundians, but I really believe that nothing of the sort ever happened.[21] No greater desertion ever took place on both sides. Owing to special circumstances, however, the two princes remained in the field. On the king's side one man of high estate fled as far as Lusignan without stopping for food, and on the count's side another man of rank went as far as Quesnoy-le-Comte. These two hardly risked running into each other.[22]

Since these two camps were facing each other, many cannonshots were fired and this killed men from both sides, but no one had any desire to fight any more. Our band was stronger than the king's. His presence, however, was very beneficial to his men-at-arms, as were his fine speeches to them. I truly believe that had it not been for him alone, everyone would have fled, and I learned later that this was indeed the case. Some few from our side were anxious to resume the fighting, especially my lord of Hautbourdin, who said he saw a whole file of men fleeing; and if anyone had been able to muster up one hundred archers to shoot through the hedge, all would have been well on our side.

While we were on these subjects and entertaining these thoughts, and while no fighting was going on, night came upon us. The king withdrew to Corbeil and we believed that he encamped there and retired for the night.

By chance a keg of powder was ignited where the king had been, and the fire spread to the carts that were placed along the thick hedge, and we believed this to be fires from their quarters. The count of Saint-Pol, who seemed very much a military leader, and my lord of Hautbourdin, who seemed even more so, commanded that the carts be conveyed to the very place where we were stationed and that we should be surrounded by them. And this was done. As we were there assembled in order of battle, many of the king's men who had been following the pursuit returned, believing that everything had been won for them. And they were forced to pass through our camp. Some of them escaped

21. See p. 104, n. 13.
22. Lusignan is far south of Montlhéry, Quesnoy far north.

but most of them were killed. Among the men of name who died on the king's side were Geoffroi de Saint-Belin, the grand seneschal [Brézé], and Floquet, a captain. On the side of the Burgundians the dead included Philippe de Lalaing and some infantrymen and men of small estate of whom more died than on the side of the king, but among horsemen more of the dead were from the king's side.

The king's men captured the best [most ransomable] prisoners among those who were fleeing. On both sides at least two thousand men died and the battle was well fought, for in both camps one could find honorable as well as cowardly men. But it was a great thing, in my estimation, to assemble in the field and to remain three or four hours in this state, one side facing the other. And the two princes had reason to think highly of those who were at their side in this hour of need. But they acted like men and not like angels. Some men lost their positions and territories because they had fled, and these things were given to others who had fled ten leagues further. One man from our side lost his powerful position and was banished from his master's presence, but one month later he was reinstated and given more power than he had ever had before. When we had surrounded ourselves with our carts, everyone encamped as best he could. We had a large number of wounded men and most of them were very discouraged and terrified; they feared that the Parisians, with two hundred men-at-arms who were with them, as well as Marshal Joachim, the king's lieutenant in the aforementioned city, would come forth and that we would run into trouble from two sides. When it was completely dark, fifty lance-teams[23] were dispatched to find out where the king was quartered. Only about twenty of them went forth. Our field must have been three bow-shots away from the place where we believed the king to be. In the meantime my lord of Charolais drank and ate a little, as did everyone else, each at his station, and the wound which he had in his neck was bandaged.

At the place where he ate, it was first necessary to remove four or five dead bodies to make room for him; and two trusses of straw were set there for him. As we were removing the bodies, one of these poor naked men began to ask for something to drink, and some herb-tea was poured into his mouth; it was the same kind as had been drunk by the count of Charolais. The man rallied and was recognized. He was an

---

23. A lance-team consisted of six men, a horseman equipped with lance, his page, an arms assistant (*coustellier*), and three archers. Very often the lance-teams were incompletely manned, as was the case in 1476 in Charles the Bold's army. The Milanese ambassador reported on May 10, 1476, that the average number of men per lance-team in Charles's army was only two.

archer from that lord's regiment, named Savarot, a renowned man. His wounds were dressed and he was cured.

A meeting was held to decide what should be done; the first to present an opinion was the count of Saint-Pol; he pointed out that we were in danger and advised that we should retreat toward Burgundy by daybreak and that part of our carts should be burned; only the artillery should be saved and no one should take along his cart unless he had more than ten lance-teams under his command. It would not be possible to remain there without provisions, between Paris and the king. Then my lord of Hautbourdin gave substantially the same opinion except that he thought they should first wait and see what news those who were outside would bring back. Three or four others expressed similar views. The last one to speak, my lord of Contay, said that as soon as the rumor reached the army, all would flee and be taken prisoners before they had traveled twenty leagues. And he gave several good reasons for his advice that everyone should do as best he could for this night and that the next morning at dawn the king should be assailed. They should either die there or live. He considered this way much safer than to flee.

Around midnight those who had been sent out returned—and you can well imagine that they had not gone far—and they reported that the king was quartered where they had seen the fires. Immediately more men were sent there, and an hour later everyone was getting ready to fight, although most of them would rather have run away. When day broke those who had been sent out to scout beyond the field met a carter whom we had, who had been taken that morning while he was delivering a cask of wine from the village; he told them that all the enemy had disappeared. They sent this news to the army and sent people [to observe the situation]. They found that his story was correct and came back to report it; and this brought great joy to the company. Many people then said that they should pursue them; these very people had been rather unhappy one hour earlier. I had a very tired old horse who drank a bucketful of wine into which he had for some reason or other put his muzzle. I let him finish it, and I never found him in such fine shape or so refreshed.

When broad daylight arrived, all mounted their horses and mustered their companies, from which many were missing. However, many persons who had been hiding in the wood returned. The lord of Charolais arranged for a friar to arrive who had been ordered by him to say that he came from the army of the Bretons and that they would be with us that very day. This cheered the army to a certain degree, but everyone did not believe him. Shortly after, at about ten in the morning, the vice-chancellor of Brittany named Rouville arrived; with him was Madré, of whom I spoke earlier, and they brought two archers from the duke of Brittany's guard, who wore the tunic of his unit; this greatly comforted the company. He was asked questions and was praised for his escape, in spite of the hostile comments that had formerly been made against him, and he was praised even more for his return. They were given a warm welcome by all.

All this day my lord of Charolais still remained on the field in a very joyful frame of mind because he considered the glory to be his. He since paid very dearly for this because he never afterward heeded the counsel of any other man. Until that day he had had little experience with war and he had not liked anything that had to do with it; but from that time he changed his mind, for he continued to fight until his death. And in that manner his life was ended and his house destroyed; or, if it is not entirely so, it is certainly in a desolate state.

Three great and wise princes, his predecessors,[24] had raised his house to a very high position, and few monarchs except the king of France are more powerful than he was. As for beautiful and large towns no one exceeded him. One should not think too highly of oneself; this is especially true in the case of a great prince. One should recognize that graces and good fortune come from God. I shall mention two other things about him: I do not believe that any other man could endure more fatigue than he in all circumstances where physical exertion is required; and secondly, in my estimation, I have never known a more dauntless man. I never heard him complain of being weary, nor did he ever give the appearance of being fearful. And I was with him in the war for seven consecutive years, during the summer at least; during some years we were there winter and summer. His thoughts and decisions were grand, but no man could have carried them out if God had not lent the assistance of His power.

The next day we encamped in the village of Montlhéry; it was on the third day of the battle. Some of the people had fled to the church steeple and others to the castle. The count of Charolais had them return, and they did not lose a single penny; every soldier paid the fee for his quarters as if he had been [at home] in Flanders. The castle held out and was not assailed. After the third day the above-mentioned lord left, following the advice of the lord of Contay, and made his way to Étampes, which has good and spacious quarters and fertile land, in order

24. Philip the Bold, John the Fearless, and Philip the Good. See the Chronological Table.

to arrive before the Bretons, who were going in the same direction, and also in order to shelter those who were tired or wounded and to send the others to the fields. And it was owing to the good quarters and our sojourn there that the lives of many of his men were saved.

5

Those who arrived at Étampes included Charles of France—at the time duke of Berry, the king's only brother—the duke of Brittany, my lord of Dunois, my lord of Dammartin, my lord of Lohéac, my lord of Bueil, my lord of Chaumont, and Charles d'Amboise, his son, who has since become an important man in this kingdom. All of these men had been cashiered and deprived of their territories by the king upon his accession to the crown, although they had served the king his father and his kingdom well in the conquests of Normandy and in several other wars.

My lord of Charolais and the chief dignitaries of his company went out to meet and receive them and took them to the city of Étampes where quarters had been prepared for them; and the men-at-arms remained in the fields. In their company were eight hundred excellent men-at-arms, of whom a great number were Bretons who had recently left the king's regular army, as I said here and elsewhere, and who were important reinforcements to their army. They had great numbers of archers and other soldiers armed with good tunics and some six thousand mounted men in good condition; and, judging from the aspect of the company, the duke of Brittany appeared to be a very great lord, because all these men lived at his expense.

The king, who had withdrawn to Corbeil, as I said previously, did not forget what remained to be done. He proceeded to Normandy to enlist soldiers, for fear that there might be commotion in the country, and he put some of his men-at-arms in the suburbs of Paris wherever he judged it to be necessary.

The first night, when all the above-mentioned lords had arrived at Étampes, they exchanged news. The Bretons had taken some prisoners among those who were fleeing from the king's camp, and when they had advanced further, they seized and discomfited a third of the army. They had indeed deliberated to send out men, assuming that the armies had drawn closer; however, many blamed them for this. Nevertheless, Charles d'Amboise and a few others placed themselves ahead of their army to see whether they would encounter anything, and they took several prisoners, as I said before, and some artillery. The prisoners told them that the king was surely dead: they believed this was so because they had fled at the very beginning of the battle.

The above-mentioned persons reported the news to the army of the Bretons, who greatly rejoiced, believing that this was true. They entertained great hopes of favors that would come to them if my lord Charles should become king. They deliberated, as has been told to me later by a worthy man who was present, as to how they could chase away the Burgundians and get rid of them. Some, and in matter of fact almost all of them, expressed the opinion that whoever was in a position to rob them should do so. Their joy was of short duration, however, and thereby one can realize how great is the discord in this kingdom whenever anything changes.

To return to the matter of the army at Étampes, when they had all had supper and many people were taking a walk in the streets, my lord Charles of France and my lord of Charolais withdrew to a window and spoke together with very great affection. Among the Bretons was a poor fellow who took great delight in throwing rockets into the air, which spread among the people when they fell and cast up a small flame; his name was Jean Bouttefeu or Master Jean des Serpens, and he threw two or three rockets into the air which spread among the people. He did this from the upper story of a house so that no one noticed him. One of them struck against the sash of the window where the two princes had their heads, and they were so close together that there was hardly a foot between them. Both of them started up and were astonished, and stared at each other and began to suspect that this had been done expressly to harm them. The lord of Contay came to speak to my lord of Charolais, his master, and as soon as he had whispered a word into his ear he went downstairs and had all the men of his household, and the archers of his corps, and others take arms. Thereupon the lord of Charolais told this to the duke of Berry, who similarly had the archers of his corps arm themselves, and immediately two or three hundred men-at-arms and a large number of archers appeared, armed and on foot, in front of the gate, and they searched everywhere to discover the source of that fire. The poor man who had started it threw himself on his knees before them and told them that he was the culprit, and he threw three or four more rockets into the air. By so doing he relieved many people from the mutual suspicion that had been tormenting them, and there was much laughter. Everyone disarmed and went to bed.

The next morning a very great and splendid assembly was held; all the lords and their principal officers were present, and they deliberated as to what course of action should be taken. Since they consisted of several parties and were not all under one leader, as is most advisable in such assemblies, they proposed various resolutions, and among the other speeches which were carefully noted and considered was one by my lord of Berry, [King Louis' brother] who was very young and had never witnessed such exploits. He implied by his words that he was already weary of the proceedings, and he cited the great number of wounded men he had seen from the army of my lord of Charolais; he showed by his utterances that he pitied these men and went on to declare that he would have been happier if these things had never started than to have to witness so many wrongs due to him and his cause.

This discourse was disagreeable to my lord of Charolais and to his men, as I shall explain further. At this meeting, however, it was decided that they would proceed to Paris and try to convince the inhabitants to concern themselves about the public good of the kingdom, on account of which they all claimed to have assembled; and they were confident that if the Parisians lent an ear to their speeches, all the rest of the towns of the kingdom would follow their example.

As I said before, the words of Charles [of France, duke of Berry] at the meeting created doubt in the minds of my lord of Charolais and his men and led them to say: "Have you heard this man speak? He is astounded at the sight of seven or eight hundred wounded men whom he sees being transported through the town; and these men are nothing to him, nor does he even know them. He would be amazed very quickly if the matter concerned him to the least degree and he would be the kind of man to make a settlement very easily and leave us in the lurch. And because of wars which took place in the past between King Charles his father and the duke of Burgundy my father, these two parties would easily turn against us. It is therefore necessary to provide ourselves with friends."

And on the basis of this sole idea Guillaume de Cluny, protonotary, who since has died as bishop of Poitiers, was sent to King Edward [IV] of England, who reigned at the time. My lord of Charolais had always entertained a feud against this king and had supported against him the house of Lancaster, from which my lord was descended on his mother's side. According to the instructions given to Cluny, he was to enter into negotiations concerning a marriage between the count of Charolais and the sister of the king of England, whose name was Margaret, but he was not to conclude the affair. Since the count knew that the king of England had long wished for this marriage, however, he assumed that at least the monarch would do nothing against him, and if he were in need of his help he would gain him as an ally. Although he had not the slightest intention of concluding the affair, and the family he most hated in his heart was the house of York, this matter was so much worked on that several years later the match was concluded. Moreover, he accepted the Order of the Garter and wore it all his life.

Many such acts are carried out in this world in a manner similar to the one I just described, especially among great princes, who are much more mistrustful than other people because of doubts which are sown into their minds and warnings which are given to them very often through flattery rather than through any real need.

6

Thus as had been agreed upon, all these lords left Étampes after having sojourned there a few days and marched to Saint Mathurin de Larchant and Moret-sur-Loing in the Gâtinais. My lord Charles and the Bretons remained in these two small towns. The count of Charolais encamped in a large meadow on the banks of the river Seine and had a proclamation issued that each man should carry a pike to attach his horses. He had seven or eight small boats brought on carts as well as many pieces of stavewood, later to be assembled together to make barrels, and these were to serve to build a bridge on the river Seine, because these lords had no passageway.

My lord of Dunois accompanied him in a litter; on account of his gout he was not able to ride on horseback. His standard was carried behind him. As soon as they came to the river, they had the boats which they had brought placed there and they reached a small island which was about in the middle of the river. The archers descended and skirmished with some horsemen who defended the passage on the other side. Marshal Joachim [Rouault] and [Jean de] Salazar were present.

The spot was most unfavorable to them because they were in a high place and in wine-growing country. On the side of the Burgundians was, among others, a renowned cannoneer called Master Girault [de Samien] who was leading a large artillery. He had been on the king's side and was then taken prisoner at the battle of Montlhéry. Finally Rouault and Salazar had to abandon the passageway; and they withdrew to Paris. That evening a bridge was erected, and it led to this island. Immediately the count of Charolais had a large tent pitched, and he slept there that night in the company of fifty men-at-arms of his household.

At daybreak a great number of coopers were set to work at constructing barrels out of the stavewood which they had brought; and before midday the bridge was finished, and it extended to the other bank of the river. Thereupon the count of Charolais went across to the other side and had his tents pitched there; and there were many of them. He had all his army and artillery pass over the bridge and they encamped on a hill whose slope extended down to the river. His army made a beautiful sight for those who were still at the rear to behold.

All this day his men were the only ones who could pass. The next day at dawn the dukes of Brittany and Berry and all their men crossed over; they found the bridge very beautiful, considering that it had been built in such haste. They went on a little bit farther and encamped on the hill as the others had done.

As soon as night had fallen we began to notice a large number of fires at some distance from where we were, as far out as we could see. Some believed it was the king. Before midnight, however, we were informed that it was Duke John of Calabria, only son of René, king of Sicily [and duke of Anjou], and with him were some nine hundred men-at-arms from the duchy and county of Burgundy; he was well attended by horsemen but as for foot-soldiers he had few. Considering the small number of men in the duke's retinue, I have never seen such a fine company, nor one which seemed to consist of men better trained in the military profession.

There must have been some one hundred and twenty armored men-at-arms, all Italians or trained in the Italian wars. Among them were Giacomo Galeotto, the count of Campobasso,[25] the lord of Baudricourt, at present governor of Burgundy, and others. His men-at-arms were very adroit and indeed they were almost the flower of our army, at least compared to an equal number of others. He had in addition four hundred crossbowmen whom the count palatine [Frederick the Victorious] lent him, all well-mounted soldiers who very much seemed to have the bearing of military men. And there were five hundred Swiss on foot, the first who were ever seen in this kingdom; and they were the ones who made a fine reputation for those who came later, for they conducted themselves most valiantly everywhere they happened to be.

The company of which I am speaking approached in the morning and on that day they passed over our bridge; and one might say that all the power of the kingdom of France, except the men who were with the king, passed over that bridge. I can assure you that this was a fine and great company, consisting of a large number of worthy men in excellent shape. One should wish that the friends and partisans of the kingdom

25. Campobasso was to play a decisive role in the fall of Burgundy, according to Commynes. See section 4 of the Introduction.

might have seen it and have appreciated it as it deserved; and the same holds true for the enemies [of France], for at no time would they have had greater occasion to fear the king and the kingdom.[26]

The leader of the Burgundians was my lord of Neufchâtel, marshal of Burgundy; with him were his brother, the lord of Montagu, the marquis of Rothelin, and a great number of knights and squires, of whom several had been in the Bourbonnais, as I said at the beginning of this discourse. For security's sake all of them had joined forces with my lord of Calabria, as I said, and he seemed as fine a prince and great military leader as anyone else I have seen among the company. A great friendship arose between him and the count of Charolais.

After all this company had passed, and it was estimated at 100,000 horsemen, both good and bad, or so I believe,[27] the lords resolved to leave and to proceed to Paris; and so they joined all their vanguards together. As for the Burgundians, they were led by the count of Saint-Pol; the vanguards of the dukes of Berry and Brittany were led by Odet d'Aydie, later count of Comminges,[28] and the marshal of Lohéac, it seems to me. And thus they set out. All the princes remained with their men. The count of Charolais and the duke of Calabria made great efforts to give commands and to keep order in their ranks, and they rode well armed; they seemed to have good intent to fulfill their responsibilities well.

The dukes of Berry and Brittany rode along on small hackneys, at ease, armed with little tunics which were very light, to say the least; moreover, according to some people, these tunics consisted merely of a few golden nails placed over the satin so that they would weigh less on them. I am not positive about this, however. Thus all these companies rode to the bridge of Charenton, two small leagues away from Paris; they quickly overcame the few free archers who were stationed on the bridge, and the whole army passed over it. The count of Charolais encamped between the bridge of Charenton and his house of Conflans-l'Archevêque nearby along the river, and fenced in a large piece of land with his carts and train of artillery and put all his army inside; and with him the duke of Calabria set up his quarters. The dukes of Berry and

26. This passage forces one to conclude that Commynes in some sense accepted the propaganda of the leaders of the War for the Public Good, and believed that the enemies confronting Louis on the banks of the Seine were really working for the good of France. Commynes wrote these lines while in disgrace for joining a similar feudal coalition directed against the regency of Anne de Beaujeu. See section 1 of the Introduction.

27. This number is more than double the estimate of modern scholars.

28. Odet d'Aydie, lord of Lescun and later count of Comminges, was the most valued counselor of the duke of Brittany. His allegiance was bought by Louis XI in 1472, as Commynes describes at the end of Book 3.

Brittany encamped at Saint-Maur-des-Fossés with a number of their men, and they sent the rest to encamp at Saint-Denis, also two leagues away from Paris. All this company remained there for eleven weeks, and certain things came to pass which I shall relate below.

The next day the encounters began and continued at the very gates of Paris. My lord of Nantouillet, grand-master, who served well there, as I have indicated earlier, and Marshal Joachim were inside. The people were terrified and some from other estates would have wanted the lords to be inside, because in their estimation this enterprise was to be beneficial and profitable to the kingdom. There were others inside from the territories of the rebellious lords who were pursuing their own interests and who hoped through a victory of the lords to obtain certain offices or high positions, for these offices are more in demand in Paris than in any other city in the world. Those who hold them make them yield as much as they can obtain from them and not merely as much as they honestly should. Some unsalaried positions are sold for eight hundred *écus*; others which carry very small emoluments are sold for a greater amount than their income from fifteen years. It is rare that anyone is removed from his office, and the court of Parlement upholds this article, and rightly so; almost everyone, however, is affected by this. Among the lawyers one always finds on the whole fine and notable persons as well as a few of rather evil character. Thus it is in all walks of life.

7

I speak of these offices and office-holders because they made people desire changes, and not only in our time.[29] But during the wars which started from the time of King Charles VI [1380–1422] and lasted until the peace of Arras [1435], the English had conquered so great a part of this kingdom that the negotiations for that peace lasted a full two

29. This sentence and the three sentences preceding it refer to an opinion expressed in the middle of the last paragraph of chapter 6. There were many people in Paris, Commynes says, who favored the party of the feudal lords against the king simply because they wanted to turn out current office-holders and substitute themselves. These offices were bought and sold—a practice which continued down to the French Revolution—and the buyer recouped the price he had paid by various practices, legal and illegal, in the exercise of his office. Once installed, office-holders were hard to remove except through "changes"—that is, revolution—for the Parlement of Paris, the supreme court of France and final authority on points of law, supported irremovability. Commynes is probably referring to royal lawyers (*conseillers*) admitted to practice before the Parlement of Paris in the penultimate sentence of chapter 6.

months. The king's delegates then included four or five princes, dukes or counts, five or six prelates and ten or twelve counselors from the Parlement. They were matched by the representatives of Duke Philip [the Good of Burgundy], persons of high rank and far more numerous than the king's. The pope's legates consisted of two cardinals as mediators. And the English envoys were men of distinction. The duke of Burgundy was very anxious to acquit himself of his obligations to the English before leaving them, because of the alliances and promises they had exchanged; and for these reasons the duchies of Normandy and Guyenne were offered to the king of England for himself and his lords, on condition that he should render homage to the king of France for these territories, as his predecessors had done before, and that he should return to the kingdom all of his French possessions with the exception of these two duchies: and this they refused on the grounds that they did not want to render the required homage. It was unfortunate for them afterwards because they were forsaken by the house of Burgundy, and once having lost their influence in the kingdom, they began to lose power and diminish in stature. At the time of the treaty the regent of France for the English was the duke of Bedford, brother of King Henry V and husband of the sister of Duke Philip of Burgundy. He resided in Paris and the least stipend he ever received in his office was twenty thousand *écus* per month. They lost Paris and little by little the rest of the kingdom.

Having returned to England, no one wanted to diminish his estate. There was not enough wealth in the kingdom of England to satisfy everyone. Wars broke out among them to obtain authority; they lasted for many years, and King Henry VI [1422–1461], who had been crowned king of France and England in Paris, was imprisoned in the castle of London and declared a traitor and criminal of lese majesty. He spent most of his life there and was finally put to death. The duke of York, father of the late King Edward [IV], declared himself king; a few days later he was routed in battle and slain [1460]. He and the late count of Warwick [d. 1471], who enjoyed so much credit in England, both had their heads cut off after they were slain. He [Warwick] conducted the count of March, later called King Edward [IV (1461–1483)], from England to Calais by sea with a few people who were fleeing from the battle. The count of Warwick supported the house of York and the duke of Somerset the house of Lancaster. These wars lasted so long that all those from the houses of Warwick and Somerset were beheaded or died on the battlefield. King Edward had his brother, the duke of Clarence, drowned in a cask of malmsey because he wanted to proclaim himself king, or so it was alleged. Upon Edward's death, his second brother, the duke of Gloucester, had the two sons of Edward murdered, declared the daughters illegitimate, and had himself crowned king [Richard III (1483–1485)].

Immediately after, the count of Richmond, the present king [Henry VII (1485–1509)], who had been a prisoner in Brittany for several years, returned to England where he overthrew and killed in battle the cruel King Richard, who had his nephews killed a short time before. And thus, as far as I can remember, at least eighty men of English royal lineage died in these civil wars of England. I knew several of them and I learned about the rest from the Englishmen who were staying with my lord of Burgundy while I was in his service.

So it is not only in Paris or in France that men fight each other for the goods and honors of this world. Princes and those who rule over large territories should take heed lest division arise in their household; for from there this fire spreads throughout the province. But I believe that nothing is effected save by divine disposition: for when princes or kingdoms have enjoyed great prosperity and wealth and disregard the source of such graces, God unexpectedly sets up an enemy or enemies against them, as you may see from the kings named in the Bible and from the events seen several years ago in England, the house of Burgundy, and other places which you have seen and see every day.

8

I have been lengthy in my digression and it is time that I should return to the main discourse. As soon as these lords had arrived before Paris, all of them began to deal and promise offices and goods and everything which could further their cause. After three days they held a large assembly in the town hall of Paris, and after impressive and lengthy discourses and consideration of the requests and petitions which the lords presented to them in public audience, for the greater good of the kingdom, as they put it, it was decided to send envoys to them to discuss pacification.

Many persons of high standing came to the above-mentioned princes at Saint-Maur and Master Guillaume Chartier, at the time bishop of Paris, a man of great renown, spoke in their name. The lords' spokesman was the count of Dunois. The duke of Berry, the king's brother, presided, seated on a high chair, and all the other lords were standing. On one side were the dukes of Brittany and Calabria, and on the other the lord of Charolais, in full armor, except for helmet and brassart; he wore a rich mantle over his cuirass, for he came from Conflans, and the wood of Vincennes was holding out for the king; and it had strong troops. Thus he had to come with an escort. The requests and aims of the lords were to enter Paris so as to have conversation and understanding with the Parisians on the question of the reform of the kingdom, which they claimed was badly governed and concerning which they made several important charges against the king. The answers were quite mild, although they were made only after some delay. Since that time the king disliked the bishop and those who were with him.

Thus they left, but big deals continued to be discussed, because everyone spoke to them privately. I believe that some of them agreed secretly that the unescorted lords would enter Paris and that their men could pass through if they so desired, a few at a time. This conversation would not only have resulted in gaining the city but would have meant success in the whole enterprise; for several reasons the people would have easily been won over to their side, and consequently all the other cities in the kingdom would have followed their example.

God gave wise counsel to the king and he carried it out successfully. Having been advised of all these things before the envoys to these lords had made their report, he arrived in the city with appropriate bearing to comfort the people: he came with a large company and he placed in the city a good two thousand men-at-arms, all the noblemen from Normandy, a large force of free [archers from the royal militia], gentlemen-at-arms from his household and other high-ranking persons who normally accompany a king of his stature on similar business. And thus this compact was broken and all these people turned back to their own side;[30] no one among those who had previously come to us would have dared speak of the bargain, and some people had a bad time of it.

The king did not use cruelty in this matter, although some lost their offices and others were sent to live elsewhere. I hold it to his credit that he did not take any other revenge, for if what had begun had taken effect the best that could have befallen him would have been to escape from the kingdom. For he told me several times that if he had not been able to gain admission to Paris and if he had found

30. Calmette, I, 56, follows Ms. Polignac ("mué d'essiens") instead of Ms. Dobrée ("mué des siens") in this phrase. J. Podgurski has shown in *Zeitschrift für romanische Philologie*, LXXVII (1961), 82–84, that Ms. Dobrée's reading is more likely. A similar phrase occurs in M, p. 223 ("return to the king's side"): Calmette, I, 213, has emended all manuscript readings in this case without warrant ("se tourna d'essiens" instead of "se tourna des siens" or "se trouva des siens").

the inhabitants rebellious, he would have fled to the Swiss or to the duke of Milan, Francesco [Sforza], whom he considered his great friend; and the duke showed it by the help he sent him—five hundred men-at-arms and three thousand infantrymen led by his eldest son, named Galeazzo, who later became duke. They marched as far as Forez and fought against my lord of Bourbon, but because of the death of Duke Francesco they turned back. The duke also showed his friendship by advising the king, in relation to the peace called the treaty of Conflans, not to refuse any request in order to break up the alliance, but to insist on keeping his own men.[31]

In my estimation we had not stayed more than three days before Paris when the king marched in. Shortly we began to feel the effects of the war very strongly; this was especially true in regard to our foragers, because it was necessary to go far from the camp to forage, and many guards had to be sent along to protect them. One must admit that the Ile-de-France and the city of Paris are well situated since they could provide food for two such powerful armies. For we never lacked supplies, and within Paris they hardly noticed that there were extra men to feed. Prices did not increase except for bread, and that was raised by only one *denier* per loaf. For we did not block the rivers above it, which are three in number—the Marne, Yonne, and Seine—and several small rivers which are tributaries of these.

All things considered, this city of Paris is the one surrounded by the best and most fertile land I have ever seen, and it is almost incredible to consider how many products arrive there. I have been there since that time with King Louis continuously for a half year; I stayed at the hôtel des Tournelles where I habitually ate and slept with him, and after his death I was kept in his palace against my will for twenty months as a prisoner. From my windows I could see what was coming up the Seine from Normandy against the stream. Products from the north arrive in greater quantities than I should have ever thought had I not seen it.

Every day many people sallied forth from Paris and skirmishes were numerous. Our guards consisted of fifty lance-teams who were stationed near the Grange des Merciers, and they kept horsemen as close to Paris as possible; very often the horsemen were driven back to the guards' station and quite often they had to turn back as far as our carts, retiring at a pace, and sometimes fleeing on the trot. We in turn

31. The time sequence is confusing in this sentence and the preceding one. The treaty of Conflans, which ended the War for the Public Good, was made in October, 1465, two months after the events narrated here. Francesco Sforza died still later, on March 8, 1466.

sent fresh troops to reinforce them and very often also drove the
enemy back very close to the gates of Paris. And this took place at
all times, for in the city were more than twenty-five hundred first-
rate and well-housed men-at-arms, a large force of noblemen from
Normandy, and free archers. They saw ladies every day, and this made
them eager to show off.

On our side there was a large number of men, but not too many horsemen because only the Burgundians were left and they consisted of
some two thousand lance-teams—some good and some weak—who were
not as well equipped as those who were inside, owing to the long peace
which they had enjoyed, as I said before. From this number should be
subtracted two hundred men-at-arms who were at Lagny; and the duke
of Calabria was among them. But we had a great number of foot-soldiers
and good ones at that.

The army of the Bretons was at Saint-Denis, making ravages
wherever possible, and the other lords were dispersed, trying to obtain
supplies. Towards the end, the counts of Armagnac, the duke of Nemours, and the lord of Albret arrived. Their men remained at a distance
because they had not been paid and they would have caused our army
to starve if they had taken food without paying for it. And I well know
that the count of Charolais gave them money—as much as five or six
thousand francs—and it was decided that their men would not come
further forward. The force consisted of about six thousand horsemen
who caused a great deal of mischief.

9

To return to the happenings in Paris, it is certain that not a day passed
without some loss or gain on one side or the other; but important things
did not occur, because the king would not suffer that his men should go
forth in large numbers and did not want to leave anything to chance in
battle. He wanted peace and wisely wanted to divide our forces.

One day early in the morning, however, four thousand free archers,
the noblemen from Normandy, and some few men-at-arms took up
quarters facing the house of the count of Charolais at Conflans, along
the river at its very edge. And other men-at-arms from the king's regular
army stayed a quarter of a league away from there in a village. Only
a fertile plain stood between their foot-soldiers and the rest. The river
Seine was between them and us. The king's men started to dig a trench
at Charenton, where they constructed a bulwark of wood and trampled
earth, which led to our army; and this ditch extended in front of Con-

flans with the river separating them and us, as has been said. A large number of pieces of artillery were planted there, and from the very beginning all the men of the duke of Calabria were driven from the village of Charenton, with the result that they had to retreat in great haste and encamp with us. Both men and horses were killed. Duke John took up quarters in the main part of a small building right in front of the one which was occupied by the count of Charolais, facing the river.

This artillery first began to shoot through our army and greatly frightened the company because upon the first firing they killed many of our men; as he was having dinner, they fired two shots across the room where the count of Charolais was staying, and killed a trumpeter on the stairs as he was bringing up a dish of meat. After dinner the count of Charolais went downstairs to the lower floor, decided not to move from there, and had his quarters set up down there as best he could.

The next morning all the lords assembled for a meeting; and it was never held anywhere else but at the count of Charolais' house. They always dined together after the meeting. The dukes of Berry and Brittany always sat on the bench [against the wall, the most honorable place], and the count of Charolais and Duke John of Calabria sat in front. Thus the count honored them all, conducting them to table. Of course, it was fitting that he acted so to some of them and to all, since they were his guests.

It was decided that all the artillery of the army would be matched against the king's. The lord of Charolais was strong in artillery. The duke of Calabria had some fine artillery too, as did the duke of Brittany. Large openings were made in the ramparts along the river behind the count's house at Conflans, and all the best arms were gathered there (except for bombards and other large pieces which were not fired at all), and the rest were placed where they could be of greatest use. Thus there were more of them on the side of the lords than on the side of the king. The trench which the king's men had made was very long and pointed toward Paris; they dug constantly farther and farther and threw the soil over on our side in order to protect themselves from the artillery, because all of them were hidden in the ditch and not one of them would have dared show his face. They were in a place as level as a man's hand, and in a beautiful meadow.

I have never seen so much shooting in such a few days; for our part, we expected to drive them away by dint of artillery. On the other side, reinforcement was being sent to them from Paris every day; these men, for their part, performed their duty with diligence and did not spare the powder. A large number of soldiers from our army dug ditches in the ground on the site of their encampment, even though there were many holes there already, since it was a place where stones had been quarried. Thus everyone had protection and three or four days passed. There was more fear than losses on either side, for no one of stature was killed.

When the lords noticed that the king's men were keeping busy, it shamed them and seemed dangerous, and they considered that this state of affairs would encourage the Parisians; for during a mere day or so of truce so many people appeared that it seemed none were left in the city. It was decided at a meeting that a very large bridge would be improvised by means of large boats; the bow and the stern would be removed, a wooden base would be placed across the widest section, and the last pair of boats would have large anchors which would be cast into the ground. Thereupon several large boats were brought to the Seine; they were capable of transporting a large number of foot-soldiers at one time. It was thus determined to pass the river. The responsibility for this task was given to Master Girault, the cannoneer; it seemed to him that it was to the great advantage of the Burgundians that the others had thrown the soil toward our side because once we passed the river, the king's men would find their trench far below the assailants and would not dare emerge from the ditch for fear of the artillery.

These arguments gave our men great desire to pass the river, and the bridge was completed and ready for use, except for the last pair of boats which were turned to the side, ready to be put in position; all the boats had been brought. As soon as the bridge was erected, one of the king's military officers came to inform them that this was contrary to the terms of the truce. (Since there had been a truce that day and the preceding day, the man had been sent to see what was the matter.) By chance he met my lord of Bueil and several others on the bridge and he spoke to them. That night the truce was over. Three men-at-arms with their lances in rest could easily pass abreast, and there must have been six large boats, each of which could have carried one thousand men at a time, as well as several small boats. The artillery was arranged to serve them at this passage; units were formed and lists were compiled of those who should cross over. Their leaders were the count of Saint-Pol and the lord of Hautbourdin.

After midnight those who belonged to these units began to arm and before dawn they were ready. Many heard Mass as they waited for daybreak, and they acted as good Christians do on such occasions. That night I was in a large tent which was in the middle of the army's encampment, where watch was kept; I was on patrol that night, for no one was excused from duty. The leader of this guard was my lord of Châteauguion, who since died at Morat; and we were waiting for the hour when the frolic was to take place. Suddenly we heard those who were in the trenches cry out: "Farewell, neighbors, farewell!" And immediately they set fire to their camp and withdrew their artillery. Dawn began to come upon us. Those who were to take part in this enterprise, or at least part of them, were already on the river, and they saw the others who were withdrawing to Paris at a great distance. Thus everyone went to disarm and was very happy about their departure.

Indeed the king had placed his men there only to cannonade us and not with the intention of having a combat, because he did not want to leave anything to chance, as I said previously, even though his power was greater than that of the united forces of all the princes. But his intention, as he was to prove later, was to negotiate peace and to divide the forces of the enemy without putting his office, which is so great and fine as to be king of this great and obedient kingdom of France, in danger of such a precarious event as a battle.

Every day minor agreements were being contracted in order to persuade men from one side to pass over to the other, and there were several days of truce during which meetings were held with representatives of both sides to negotiate a peace settlement. The assembly met at the Grange des Merciers rather close to our army. The count of Maine and several others came to represent the king; the count of Saint-Pol and several others were present to represent the lords. They met a great number of times without accomplishing anything significant and during that time the truce was in effect; many men from the two armies had glimpses of each other, separated by a large ditch which was about midway between them; some were on one side and some on the other, and because of the truce, no one was allowed to pass.

Because of these agreements, not a day passed without ten or twelve men, and sometimes even more, turning to the side of the lords. Another day just as many from our side passed over to the other; and for this reason that spot came to be called the Market, since so many bargains were transacted there.

And indeed such meetings and communications are very dangerous when arranged in such a manner, especially for the side that is most likely to lose. Naturally most people are on the lookout for ways to gain advantage or to save themselves, and this makes them lean more readily toward the stronger side. There are others who are so worthy and steadfast that they have no such considerations, but they are very few in number. And this danger is especially apparent when princes try to win people over to their side. If they know how to do it well, it represents a very great grace granted by God to the prince in question, and it is a sign that he is not tainted with the foolish vice of pride, which leads to hatred from all men. Therefore, as I said, when people resort to bargaining for negotiating peace, it should be done by the most faithful servants whom the princes have, and they should be middle-aged, so that their weakness may not lead them to conclude some dishonest bargain or to alarm their master more than necessary on their return. It is better to employ those who have received a favor or benefit from their prince than others, and they should above all be shrewd persons, for no one has ever gained anything from a fool. These treaties are better negotiated at a distance than directly, and when the ambassadors return, they should be heard in private audience or in small committee, so that if their words are of a nature to frighten people the prince may tell them what kind of comments to make to those who ask questions of them. For everyone wants to hear the news from them when they return from such negotiations, and many say: "Such a person will not keep anything from me." But the envoys will keep secrets to themselves if they are of the type I described and if they realize that they have a wise master.

10

I am discussing this matter because I have seen many deceptions in this world, perpetrated by many servants in their relations with their masters; and the proud princes and lords who have no great desire to listen to people are deceived more often than the humble ones who listen willingly. Among all those I have ever known, the most skillful at extricating himself out of a disagreeable predicament in time of adversity was King Louis XI, our master, the most humble person in terms of speech and manner and the prince who worked more than any other to gain to his cause any man who could serve him or who could be in a position to harm him. And he was not discouraged if a man he was trying to win over at first refused to cooperate, but he continued his persuasion by promising him many things and actually giving him money and dignities which he knew the other coveted; as for those he had expelled and dispossessed in time of peace and prosperity, he repurchased their favors at a great price when he needed them, made use of them and held no grudge against them an account of things past.

He was naturally a friend of those of middle rank and an enemy of all the powerful lords who could do without him. No man ever gave ear to people to such an extent or inquired about so many matters as he

did, or wished to make the acquaintance of so many persons. For indeed he knew everyone in a position of authority and of worthy
character who lived in England, Spain, Portugal, Italy, in the territories
of the duke of Burgundy, and in Brittany, as well as he knew his own
subjects. These methods and manners which he had, of which I have
spoken above, saved the crown for him, in view of the enemies he had
acquired for himself at the time of his accession to the throne.

But above all his great liberality served him well. For although he
was a wise leader in time of adversity, as soon as he believed himself to
be secure or at least in a state of truce, he began to antagonize people
by means of petty actions; this was hardly to his advantage, and it was
with great difficulty that he could endure peace. He spoke slightingly
of people in their presence as well as in their absence, except in the case
of those he feared; and they were numerous because he was by nature
rather apprehensive. When as a result of his words some harm came
upon him or if he suspected that it might, he wanted to make amends
and would make the following speech to the person he had offended:
"I well realize that my tongue has brought me great disadvantage, but
it has also occasionally brought me much pleasure. It is reasonable, however, that I should make reparation for my blunder." And he never
said these kind words without granting the person whom he thus addressed a favor, and no small one at that.

Yet God gives infinite grace to a prince when he knows the difference
between good and evil, and especially when his good actions outnumber
his bad ones, as was the case with the king, our above-mentioned
master. In my opinion, the distress he endured in his youth when he
was a fugitive from his father and escaped to Duke Philip of Burgundy,
with whom he resided for six years [1456–1461], was beneficial to him
because he was forced to please those whose help he needed. Adversity
taught him that, and it is no small lesson. After he had grown up and
was crowned king, at the beginning of his reign he had no other thought
but of revenge. The injury that resulted from this came soon, and then
his repentance. He made reparations for his folly and his error by regaining those he had wronged, as you will hear shortly.

If his education had not been different from that of the lords whom I
have seen brought up in this kingdom, I do not believe that he would
ever have regained ground: for they are taught only to act like fools
in dress and speech; of letters they have no knowledge. Not a single
wise man is placed in their entourage. They have tutors to whom one
speaks about matters concerning them, but not a word is said to them
about it, and these tutors manage their affairs. There are some lords

with income of less than thirteen silver livres who are proud to say: "Speak to my servants," and they think that by these words they imitate very important people. I have also very often seen their servants derive profit from them, making it obvious that they take them for fools. And if by chance one of them regains control and inquires about what belongs to him, it is so late that it hardly matters any more; for it should be noted that all men who have ever been famous and have accomplished great deeds have started very young; and that depends on one's education or the grace of God.

11

Now I have discussed this matter for a long time but it is of such a nature that I cannot leave it just when I wish to. And to return to the war, you have heard how those whom the king had entrenched along the river Seine moved out at the moment when they were to be assailed. The truces never lasted longer than a day or two. On the other days the war was fought as fiercely as possible, and the encounters continued from morning to night.

Large units did not go forth from Paris; however, they often destroyed our patrol and then we would reinforce it. I never saw a single day pass without skirmishes, however unimportant they may have been; and I believe that if the king had wished it they would have been much more serious, but he was very mistrustful of many people, although his suspicions were without foundation. He told me once that one night he found the gate of the fortifications of Saint-Antoine open toward the fields. This was at night and he strongly suspected that the culprit was Charles de Melun, because his father was in charge of the stronghold. I shall not add any further comments to those I have already made about Charles but I can only say that the king had no better servant than him that year.[32]

One day it was resolved in Paris that they should come and fight us (and I believe that the king had nothing to do with that decision which was made by the army chiefs) and assail us on three sides: some were to come from Paris, and that was to be the principal column, another unit from the bridge of Charenton (and those would hardly have been able to cause much damage), and two hundred men-at-arms were to

32. Charles de Melun, also referred to by Commynes as the lord of Nantouillet, fell from favor with Louis XI in 1465 and was executed in 1468 for high treason after a highly arbitrary trial in which little certain was proved against him.

come from the wood of Vincennes. The army was informed of this decision toward the middle of the night by a page who cried out from the other side of the river that some good friends of the lords were warning them about the enterprise I have just described; he named a few of them and left instantly.

At early dawn Poncet de Rivière arrived in front of the bridge of Charenton and my lord of Lau and others toward the wood of Vincennes; they came up to our artillery and killed a gunner. There was great alarm because everyone believed that this was the event of which the page had warned them the previous night. My lord of Charolais armed himself hastily, but Duke John of Calabria did so even more rapidly, for in any alarm he was the first man to be armed, and fully so, and his horse was always armored. He was dressed in a suit such as is worn by the condottieri in Italy, and he certainly had the aspect of a prince and a war leader; he always marched directly toward the limits of the enemy camp so as to prevent the soldiers from breaking forth. The men responded to his commands as readily as to those of my lord of Charolais, and all the army obeyed him willingly, for indeed he was most worthy of being honored.

In one moment all the troops were armed and drawn up on foot behind our carts, except for some two hundred horsemen who were outside on patrol. Except for that day, I never observed that anyone expected to fight, but this time everyone expected to do so. And following this report, the dukes of Berry and Brittany arrived; this was the only time I had ever seen them armed. The duke of Berry was armed from head to foot. They had few men with them. Thus they passed along the field and went outside to meet my lords of Charolais and Calabria, and there they had a conference. The horsemen who were reinforced marched closer to Paris, and they saw many horsemen from the enemy who were approaching to discover what all the commotion was about in our army.

Our artillery had been shooting firmly when my lord of Lau's men came so near to them. The king had a large train of artillery mounted on the walls of Paris, and they fired several shots which reached as far as our army; this is no small distance, for it consists of two leagues; but I believe indeed that the muzzles were raised very high. The noise made by the artillery made those on both sides believe that an important undertaking was taking place. The sky was dark and cloudy, and our horsemen, who were very close to Paris, saw many enemy horsemen advancing, and much farther away they saw large quantities of raised lances, or so it seemed to them. And they assumed that all the king's battle corps were in the fields, as well as all the people of Paris; it was the obscurity of the weather which led them to imagine these things.

They withdrew straight toward the lords who were on the outside of our field, told them the news and assured them of the existence of a battle corps. The horsemen who had gone forth from Paris were still approaching because they saw that ours were retreating, and this made their assumption more believable. Thereupon the duke of Calabria came to the place where the standard of the count of Charolais was set, with most of the men of rank of his house ready to accompany it; his banner and the field-colors of his arms were ready to be unfurled also, as was the custom of his house. Duke John said to all of us: "Well! Now we've gained what we all desired! See, there is the king and all those people leaving the city! They are on the march; our horsemen have reported it. Let us all take heart, then: all those who go forth from Paris we will measure up with their Parisian measure, which is the largest measure!"[33] Thus he cheered up the company.

Our horsemen regained a little courage when they saw that the enemy's horsemen were weak. They drew closer to the city and still found these battle-corps in the same place where they had left them; this gave them food for thought. They came as close as possible to them; the sun had risen and there was more light. They discovered that they were large thistles. They proceeded right up close to the gates and did not find any troops outside. They sent word to the lords, who went to hear Mass and then had dinner. Those who had spread the news were ashamed of themselves but they were excusable in view of the bad weather and the page's statement from the previous night.

12

The king and the count of Charolais continued negotiating for peace more closely than the others did because the power lay with them. The demands of the lords were great, especially on the part of the duke of Berry, who wanted Normandy for his share; and this the king would not grant him. The count of Charolais wanted to have the towns on the river Somme, such as Amiens, Abbeville, Saint-Quentin, Péronne, and others, which the king had repurchased from Duke Philip for 400,000

33. A reference to the fact that each region of France had its own set of standard weights and measures.

écus less than three months previously.[34] The duke had obtained these towns at the peace of Arras from Charles VII. The count of Charolais claimed that the king was not entitled to repurchase them during Duke Philip's lifetime. He reminded him of how greatly indebted he was to the house of Burgundy, because when he was a fugitive from his father, King Charles, he was received and taken care of for six years, was supplied with money for his needs, and was escorted by them as far as Reims and Paris for his coronation. Therefore the count of Charolais was greatly vexed at the redemption of the above-mentioned territories.

These peace negotiations went on so well that one morning the king came by water to a spot facing our army; he had many horsemen on the bank of the river. In his boat were only four or five persons, not including the sailors. My lord of Lau, my lord of Montauban, who was admiral at the time, my lord of Nantouillet and others were present. The counts of Charolais and of Saint-Pol were on the bank of the river on their side awaiting the said lord.

The king addressed my lord of Charolais in these terms: "Brother (because the count had formerly married his sister), will you guarantee my safety?"[35] The count replied: "Yes, my lord." I heard it and so did many others. The king landed with the above-named lords who had come with him. The counts treated him with great honor, as was proper, and the king, who was not sparing in politeness, opened the discussion by saying: "Brother, I know that you are a gentleman and that you are from the house of France." The count of Charolais asked: "Why so, my lord?" "Because," he replied, "when I sent my ambassadors to Lille not long ago to my uncle your father and yourself, and that foolish Morvilliers spoke to you so arrogantly, you sent word to me by the archbishop of Narbonne (who proved himself a gentleman, for everyone was pleased with him) that I should repent before the end of the year for the words that Morvilliers had said to you." And the king added: "You kept your promise to me, even much sooner than the end of the year." He said that cheerfully and laughingly, knowing the nature of the man to whom he spoke to be such that he would appreciate those words: and indeed they pleased him. He added: "And I want to deal with the kind of persons who keep their promises." He disavowed Morvilliers' words, claiming he had not instructed him to speak as he had done.

Indeed the king walked for a long time between the two counts; a

34. *Sic*: three years, not three months. See p. 98, n. 6, and p. 142, line 1.
35. Louis XI demands assurance of his safety during the meeting with Charles, basing his demand on the fact that Charles's first wife was Louis' sister Catherine. Charles's marriage to Catherine lasted from 1439 to 1446, when Catherine died.

large number of armed men were present, watching them closely. At
that meeting the duchy of Normandy was demanded, as well as the river
Somme, and several other favors were requested for each one, including some propositions which had been advanced for some time concerning the good of the kingdom. But this was the least important aspect of
the question, for the public good was being converted into the good of
certain individuals. About Normandy the king would hear nothing, but
he granted the count of Charolais his request and offered the count of
Saint-Pol the office of constable of France to please him, and their leave-
taking was very gracious. The king boarded his boat and returned to
Paris; the others returned to Conflans.

Thus the days passed, some in truce and some in war; but all the
promises were broken. I refer to those made at the place where the
representatives from both sides were accustomed to meet, that is to say,
the Grange des Merciers. But the above-mentioned negotiations between
the king and the count of Charolais were being kept up; they continued
to send representatives to each other, although they were at war. One of
them was named Guillaume Bische and another Guyot d'Usie; both were
in the service of the count of Charolais. However, they had formerly
received favors from the king because Duke Philip had banished them
and the king had then received them, at the request of the count of
Charolais.

These procedures did not please everyone and already these lords
were beginning to mistrust one another and split up; and if it had not
been for the happenings which took place a few days later, they would
all have left shamefully. I saw them hold three meetings in a room where
they were all assembled and I noticed one day that the count of Charolais was most displeased by this, for it had already happened twice in his
presence; he considered that the greatest forces of the army were his,
and that to talk over affairs in his chamber without calling on him was
most improper.

The lord of Contay, a very wise man (as I said previously) spoke to
him about it and advised him to bear this patiently, for if he were to provoke them, they might find a more advantageous arrangement than he,
and since he was the strongest of them he should also be the wisest; he
should keep them from being divided and instead do everything in his
power to keep them united. He should conceal his feelings about all these
happenings. But indeed much amazement was expressed, even in his own
household, at the fact that such insignificant persons as the two named
above became involved with such an important affair, and it was considered a dangerous thing, considering that they were dealing with such

a liberal king as Louis XI. The lord of Contay hated Guillaume Bische; however, he was only echoing what many others were also saying, and I believe that he was not speaking so much out of mistrust as because of the urgency of the situation. The lord of Charolais was pleased with this advice and he made merry with the lords more than in the past, treated them better, and communicated with them and their men more than he had been accustomed to do before.

In my opinion, there was great need for better relations between them, because they were in danger of separating. A wise man is extremely useful in such company, but on condition that his advice be heeded; such a man is then invaluable. I have never known any prince capable of recognizing the difference between men until he was in need and in the midst of important affairs; and even when a prince does recognize good counselors, he still neglects their advice. Princes delegate authority to those who are most agreeable to them or whose age is most suitable in relation to theirs, or to those who always agree with their opinions, and sometimes they are managed by those who tolerate their weakness and organize their little pleasures. But those who are sensible soon change their attitude when the need arises.

In such circumstances have I seen the king and the lord of Charolais at the time, as well as King Edward of England and several others. At certain times I have seen these three in critical situations, and they were in need of those whom they had previously scorned. As for the count of Charolais, after he had been duke of Burgundy for a while and fortune had exalted him to a higher position than any man from his house had ever enjoyed, and had made him so great that he considered no other prince capable of being his equal, God allowed him to fall from this position of glory and dimmed his sense so much that he disdained every piece of advice in the world except his own. Shortly after, his life ended sorrowfully, together with the lives of a great number of his servants and subjects; and his house was made desolate, as you see.

13

I have spoken at length about the dangers that are involved in these treaties and how princes should arrange them wisely and be well informed about the persons who are in charge of them, and especially about those who apparently are not taking much part in the game; and the reasons that made me devote so much time to the subject will now be apparent.

While these treaties were being arranged by means of assemblies, and

one side was able to talk with the other, certain envoys instead of negotiating peace were negotiating about how the duchy of Normandy
should be put in the hands of the duke of Berry, the king's only brother,
and that he would consider this his share and leave Berry to the king.
The bargaining was transacted so seriously that the widow of the former
grand seneschal of Normandy and others, including some of her servants
and relatives, established Duke John of Bourbon in the castle of Rouen
with her consent; and thus he entered the city.

The townsmen rapidly consented to this change because they very
much desired to have a prince who would reside in the territory of
Normandy.[36] All the other towns and places in Normandy followed the
example, with very few exceptions. The Normans had always considered, and they still do, that a duchy as large as theirs certainly deserves
a duke [of its own]; and it is indeed a land of great value, and much
money is levied there. I have seen 950,000 francs raised there, and possibly more, according to some accounts.

Since the city of Rouen had been persuaded to support the duke, all
its inhabitants swore allegiance to the duke of Bourbon, who was acting
as proxy for the duke of Berry, with the exception of the bailiff, named
Houaste, who had been in the king's service as his *valet de chambre* when
he was in Flanders and had been in great favor with him, and another
man, named Guillaume Picard, who later became general administrator
of finances in Normandy. In addition, the grand seneschal of Normandy
who still holds the office today refused to take the oath but returned to
the king, against the wishes of his mother, who had had the major role in
this affair, as has been said.

When the king heard of the changes in Normandy, he decided to
make peace, since he could do nothing to remedy the existing situation.
Immediately he sent word to my lord of Charolais, who was in the midst
of his army, that he wished to speak with him and named the hour when
he would meet him in the fields close to his camp near Conflans. He came
forth at the appointed hour with some one hundred horsemen, most of
whom were Scotsmen from his guard; he brought few other men with
him. The count of Charolais had hardly any men with him and went to
the meeting without formality; nonetheless many more men appeared—
so many that they were more numerous than those who had come forth
with the king. He had them remain at a distance and the two walked
together for a while. The king told him how peace had been made and

36. The duchy of Normandy was held by King Louis XI at the time, whose
interests were of course national rather than regional. The townsmen hoped that
if the duke of Berry became the duke of Normandy instead, he would reside in
Normandy and devote himself to Norman interests.

gave him an account of the happenings in Rouen, which the count had not known yet. The king said that he would never have consented to give such a large share to his brother, but since the Normans had of their own volition introduced this new state of affairs he was satisfied and would ratify the treaty in its actual form, as it had been negotiated several days previously. And there were only a few other things to be settled.

The lord of Charolais was very happy about this turn of events because his army was in great need of supplies and principally of money, and if this had not happened, all the lords present would have left shamefully. However, on that day or a few days later, the count received some reinforcements which his father, Duke Philip of Burgundy, was sending him. My lord of Saveuses was bringing it, and it consisted of one hundred and twenty men-at-arms and some fifteen hundred archers, and 120,000 *écus* in cash, carried by six pack animals, and a large quantity of bows and arrows. The Burgundians provided rather well for their army, while suspecting that the rest might make separate agreements among themselves from which they might be excluded.

These words concerning a settlement were extremely agreeable to the king and the count of Charolais. I heard him say later that they spoke in such affectionate terms of putting an end to their differences that they did not look where they were going. And they proceeded straight toward Paris. They went so far ahead that they came into a bulwark of earth and wood which the king had constructed at a fair distance from the city, at the far end of a trench whose other end led to the city. With the count were no more than four or five persons. When they found themselves there, they were very astounded; however, the count maintained as good a countenance as he could. One can believe since no harm resulted for either of them, that the faith[37] of these two lords [in each other] was never greater than this time.

As word was brought to the army that the lord of Charolais had entered the bulwark there was great commotion; the count of Saint-Pol, the marshal of Burgundy, the lords of Contay and Hautbourdin and many others gathered together, strongly blaming the count of Charolais and others in his retinue for this foolish act and referring to what happened to his grandfather at Montereau-Faut-Yonne in the presence of Charles VII.[37a] Immediately they gave orders that all those who were walking in the fields should retreat within the army; and the marshal of

37. We follow Mandrot's edition (see p. 82 for full citation), translating "foy" instead of "joy," even though the latter reading appears in all the manuscripts in which this sentence is included.

37a. See p. 279 for Commynes' account of Duke John's assassination.

Burgundy (whose surname was Neufchâtel) spoke thus: "If that young and foolish or mad prince has gone to his downfall, let us not ruin his house or his father's possessions or ours. Therefore let everyone retire to his quarters and keep himself in readiness without being astonished at any turn of fortune, for we are sufficient in number, if we keep together, to make our retreat to the borders of Hainaut or Picardy, or to Burgundy."

After these words, he and the count of Saint-Pol mounted their horses and rode out of the army camp to see whether anyone was coming from the direction of Paris. After having been stationed there for a long time they saw forty or fifty horses coming and the count of Charolais was there with some of the king's men, archers, and others who were escorting him back. As he saw the marshal and the count approaching, the lord of Charolais sent back his escort and spoke to the marshal of Neufchâtel, whom he feared, for the marshal used very harsh words and was a good and loyal knight to his party, and dared tell him: "I am only on loan to you as long as your father lives." The count said the following words: "Do not rebuke me, for I well realize my great foolishness, but I noticed it so late that I was near the bulwark." The marshal said more to his face than he had said in his absence. The lord of Charolais lowered his head without replying and returned to his army where all were relieved to see him again, and everyone praised the king's good faith. However, the count never again returned within his power.

14

Finally everything was settled, and the next day the count of Charolais held a big review of his troops to discover how many men he still had and how many he might have lost. And, without warning, the king returned with thirty or forty horsemen and proceeded to inspect all the companies in turn, except the one led by the marshal of Burgundy. This officer did not like the king because some time before, in Lorraine, the monarch had given him the administration of Épinal and had then taken it away from him to give it to Duke John of Calabria; and the marshal felt very hurt by this.

Little by little, the king became reconciled with the good and notable knights who had served his father the king and whom he had revoked upon his accession to the crown; it was for this reason that they were assembled there. And the king admitted his error. It was announced that the next day the king would be in the castle of the wood of Vincennes with all the lords who were to render homage to him; for everyone's security, the king would give the castle to the count of Charolais.

Book One

The next day the king was there with all the princes without exception, and the portal of the gate was well filled with men of the count of Charolais in armor. This was the place where the peace treaty was signed. My lord Charles [of France] rendered homage to the king for the duchy of Normandy, the count of Charolais did the same for the territories of Picardy which were mentioned earlier, and others for what they held elsewhere; and the count of Saint-Pol took his oath of office as constable. There was never so fine a feast that someone did not leave hungry. Some obtained whatever they wanted and others obtained nothing. The king gained to his side some good men of middle rank. But most of the nobles stayed with the new duke of Normandy and the duke of Brittany, and they went to Rouen to take possession of that city.

When they departed from the castle of the wood of Vincennes, they all took leave of each other and everyone returned to his lodgings. Letters were written, pardons were given, and all matters serving the cause of peace were attended to. On the same day the duke of Normandy and the duke of Brittany left for the latter's province of Brittany and the count of Charolais left for Flanders. And as the count was ready to leave, the king came to him and escorted him as far as Villiers-le-Bel, which is a village four leagues away from Paris; by this gesture he demonstrated that he was very eager for the count's friendship, and both of them took lodgings there that night. The king had few men with him but he summoned two hundred men-at-arms to escort him home. The count of Charolais was informed of this as he was going to bed; he became very suspicious and had his men arm themselves well. Thus you may see that it is almost impossible for two great lords to have harmonious relations, owing to reports which they receive about each other and the suspicions that are planted in their hearts almost every hour. Two great princes who have great desire for mutual love should never meet but instead they should send good and wise envoys to discuss matters, and these people would keep up friendly negotiations and rectify errors.

The next morning the two lords took leave of each other with some wise and good words. The king returned to Paris in the company of those who had come to fetch him; and this removed any trace of suspicion that may have arisen at their coming. The count of Charolais went in the direction of Compiegne and Noyon—and all the gates were opened for him by orders of the king—and from there to Amiens where he was rendered homage by the townspeople as well as by those of the other towns on the river Somme; and the territories of Picardy had been restituted to him by the peace treaty, although the king had paid

141

400,000 *écus* for them less than nine months previously [*sic*], as I explained earlier.

Immediately he went on and proceeded in the direction of Liége, for the Liégeois had waged war against his father in the provinces of Brabant and Namur for five or six months already, while he was occupied elsewhere; and already the Liégeois had done some plundering. Because of the winter, however, he was not able to accomplish much. A large number of villages were burned and some minor pillagings carried out against the Liégeois, but peace was finally made [at Saint-Trond]. The Liégeois were bound to respect it under penalty of a large sum of money. And the count returned to Brabant.

15

To return to the dukes of Normandy and Brittany, who had gone to take possession of the duchy of Normandy, as soon as they had made their entry into Rouen they began to disagree about sharing the booty. Still with them were the knights whom I named earlier. These men had been accustomed to obtain large estates and great honors from King Charles, and it seemed to them that they had come to the end of their enterprise and that they could not depend on the king; therefore each one aimed for the best place. On the other hand, the duke of Brittany wanted to own part of Normandy because he had the most at stake there and had contributed the most to the manpower and expenses of the war. So violent was their discord that the duke of Brittany, fearing for his life, had to withdraw to Mont-Sainte-Catherine, near Rouen; and things went so far that the soldiers of the duke of Normandy together with those of the city of Rouen held themselves ready to go and assail the duke of Brittany at the above-mentioned place; therefore the duke was forced to retreat directly to Brittany.

On hearing of this conflict the king marched toward this territory. And you may be sure that he understood everything about this division of interests and helped to stir it along, for he was a master of that art. Some of those who had the command of important locations began to give them up to him and became reconciled with him. I know these things only from what he told me later, for I was not present then. He had a meeting with the duke of Brittany, who held a portion of the places in lower Normandy, and hoped to make him abandon the party of the king's brother [the duke of Normandy] altogether. They remained together for a few days in Caen and made a treaty according to which the city of Caen and others were to remain in the hands of my lord of Lescun [the duke of Brittany's counselor] and a number of paid soldiers. But this treaty was so obscure that I do not believe either of them ever understood its terms fully. The duke of Brittany departed, and the king left in the direction of his brother's residence.

The duke of Normandy, realizing that he was not in a position to offer resistance, in view of the fact that the king had already taken Pont de l'Arche and other places from him, decided to flee and to move toward Flanders. The count of Charolais was still at Saint-Trond, a small town in the province of Liége, and he was rather hampered in his actions; the army had been broken up and disbanded, it was winter, and he was still not free of the Liégeois. The count was very unhappy about the conflict between the two dukes, for his greatest desire was to see a duke established in Normandy. It seemed to him that as a result the king was weakened by one-third. He had some troops raised in Picardy with the intention of placing them in Dieppe. Before they were ready, the administrator of the city of Dieppe gave it up and made arrangements about it with the king. Thus the whole duchy of Normandy was returned to the king except for the places which were kept by my lord of Lescun, according to the agreement made in Caen.

16

The duke of Normandy, as I said before, had decided all of a sudden to escape to Flanders; but soon afterwards he and the duke of Brittany were reconciled because they recognized their errors and realized that when dissension occurs, all good things in the world are lost. It is almost impossible for many great personages of similar rank meeting together to maintain good relations for long unless they have a single leader over all the rest. And such a leader should be wise and well respected in order to earn everyone's obedience. I have seen several examples of such a situation with my own eyes and I do not speak from hearsay. We are much inclined to discord among ourselves to our own disadvantage, without giving much thought to the consequences which follow. I have seen such things happen everywhere, and it seems to me that a wise prince who has control over ten thousand men and is able to provide for their upkeep is more to be feared and respected than ten rulers, each of whom might have six thousand men, and operate as allies with their forces pooled, because when matters must be cleared up and agreed upon by them, half the time is lost before anything is concluded or agreed.

Thus the duke of Normandy withdrew to Brittany, poor, dejected, and abandoned by all the knights who had formerly been in the service of Charles VII and then had passed over to Louis XI, and they were better provided with offices by him than they had ever been under his father.

The two dukes were wise, but only after the fact (as people say about the Bretons) and they remained in Brittany. The lord of Lescun, their principal servant, had many embassies coming and going to the king and to the two dukes, and there were others going from the king to them, and from the dukes to the count of Charolais, later duke of Burgundy, and from him to them, and from the king to the duke of Burgundy and from him to the king; the purpose of some was to obtain information and that of others was to win people over and to make all sorts of dishonest bargains under the guise of good faith. Some went there with good intentions, hoping to achieve pacification. But it was great folly on the part of those who considered themselves so good and wise to think that their presence could pacify such great and cunning princes as these, and so shrewd about how to reach their goals, especially since there was no reason on either side to suppose it. But there are some good people who glorify themselves so much as to believe that they are taking the lead in certain affairs when in reality they understand nothing about them, for sometimes their masters do not tell them their secret thoughts at all.

Such persons as I have described are sent to these meetings only to serve as extra adornments for the feast, and they often go at their own expense. And there is also sure to be some humble little fellow who has some business on the side. At least this is what I observed during all the years I am speaking of and in all places. And just as I said that princes should be wise and consider to what sort of persons they entrust their affairs, similarly those who act as their envoys should think twice before proceeding in such matters; and whoever could be excused from such an obligation and free himself of it, unless it is obvious that he is an expert on the question and is eager to work on it, would be very wise. And I have known many worthy people who were very embarrassed and troubled in such situations.

I have seen two types of princes: the first are so subtle and so very mistrustful that it is difficult to live at their side, for they always have the impression that they are being duped; the others trust their servants well enough, but they are so dull and have such a lack of understanding of their tasks that they are incapable of realizing who serves them well and who serves them badly. And the former kind change immediately from love to hate and vice versa. Although not many good ones are to be found of either of the two kinds, nor does one find much firmness of purpose or security among them, when all things are considered, I should always rather serve under wise ones than foolish ones because there are more ways to escape the wrath of the former and to acquire their good graces. With the ignorant, on the other hand, one cannot think of any expedient because one has nothing to do with them directly but has to deal with their servants instead. However, everyone must serve and obey them in the territories where they rule because one is bound and also forced to do so.

But all things considered, our only hope should rest in God because He is the source of all our strength and of all goodness, and this is not to be found in anything in this world. But each of us realizes this late in life, after we have been in need of Him. However, it is better late than never.

Louis XI is shown in this portrait at about age fifty (1473) with the chain of the Order of Saint Michael about his neck, as Charles the Bold is decorated with the chain of the Order of the Golden Fleece in the painting on page 93. Louis' pose in profile, in contrast to Charles's three-quarter face pose, emphasizes the king's stooped shoulders, large nose, and flat, concentrated gaze, and peculiar headgear. These features, together with the disenchanted flat-lidded stare, combine to make the knightly insignia seem incongruous or irrelevant. In Charles the Bold's portrait stance, insignia, and countenance harmonize. Commynes' sharp eyes noted much the same contrasts between the two princes, between appearance and action, and between social attitudes and social power, in his Memoirs.

BOOK TWO

The Wars against Liége
and the Interview at Péronne, 1466-1468

1

Thus several years elapsed during which the duke of Burgundy was at war each year with the Liégeois.[38] When the king saw that he was occupied, he attempted some new action against the Bretons while giving some help to the Liégeois. At one moment, then, the duke of Burgundy would turn against him in order to give help to his allies [the Bretons], while at other times they [king and duke] would negotiate a treaty or a truce.

In the year 1466 Dinant was taken; it is a town in the province of Liége (and it is very strong for its size and very rich because of articles which are manufactured from copper and are called *dinanderie*; these include pots, frying pans and other similar utensils). The town was taken by [Charles] the duke of Burgundy before the death of his father, Duke Philip, which occurred in June, 1467. And Duke Philip of Burgundy had himself carried there in a litter in his extreme old age. He hated them violently owing to the great cruelties which they had inflicted on his subjects in the county of Namur and especially in Bouvignes, a small town situated a quarter-league away from Dinant; and only the river Meuse stood between them. Only a short time before, the inhabitants of Dinant had besieged Bouvignes for eight successive months, the river lying between them, and they perpetrated many cruel acts in the vicinity; and during that time they cannonaded continually with two bombards and other large pieces of artillery, shattering the houses of the town of Bouvignes and forcing the poor people to take refuge in their cellars and to remain there.

It is incredible to think of the hatred that these two towns entertained for each other; and yet their children frequently intermarried, for they were far from any other important town. The year preceding the destruction of Dinant, which was the time when the count of Charolais

---

38. See Section 2 of the Introduction for an analysis of Commynes' narration of the wars with the Liégeois.

returned from Paris, where he had been with the other lords of France, as you have heard, they had made an agreement and peace with this lord and they gave him a certain sum of money. They had separated from the city of Liége and made their own settlement; and when those who should cooperate separate from and abandon each other, it is a sure sign of the destruction of a territory. This applies to princes and lords who are allies as well as to communities; but since I assume that everyone may have seen such examples or read about them, I shall not speak about them. However, it is to be noted that King Louis, our master, was more skillful at the art of separating people than any other prince I have ever known, and he spared neither money nor possessions nor pains, not only with masters, but also with servants.

Thus the townspeople of Dinant soon began to repent about the above-mentioned arrangement and they executed cruelly four of their principal burghers, who had negotiated the said treaty. And they began to fight anew in the county of Namur for these reasons as well as because of solicitation on the part of the inhabitants of Bouvignes. The siege was undertaken by Duke Philip, but the leadership of the army was the responsibility of his son; and the count of Saint-Pol, constable of France, came to their aid; he came in a private capacity and was not acting by the king's authority nor with the assistance of the king's men-at-arms, but he brought troops which he had assembled on the borders of Picardy.

The soldiers of Dinant proudly made a sally from the town, to their great disadvantage. On the eighth day, after they had been severely beaten, they were captured by storm, and their friends were not in a position even to consider whether they could help them or not. The town was burned to the ground; the prisoners, who numbered up to eight hundred, were drowned before Bouvignes, at the specific request of the townspeople of Bouvignes. I do not know whether God allowed this to be done as a punishment for their wickedness, but the vengeance was cruel upon them.

The Liégeois arrived in great numbers on the day after the town was taken to help defend Dinant, although this was contrary to their promise, for they had agreed by treaty to remain separate from them, just as those from Dinant had separated from the Liégeois. Duke Philip withdrew because of his old age, and his son with all his army proceeded against the Liégeois.

We met them earlier than we had expected, for by chance our vanguard became lost through the fault of its guides and we encountered the enemy with the main body of the army, where the principal leaders were. It was already late; however, we were getting ready to assail them. At that moment a delegation sent by them to the count of Charolais requested that in honor of the Virgin Mary, whose feast was the next day, he should take pity on the people; and they apologized for the errors of the people as best they could.

The Liégeois, however, appeared to desire a battle and were not at all as their delegates represented them to be. However, after they had come and gone two or three times, they agreed to maintain the peace that had been negotiated the previous year and to pay a certain sum of money. And to make sure that they would keep their word better than they had done before, they promised to deliver three hundred hostages listed in a roll by the bishop of Liége and some of his officers who were in the army, and to surrender them the next day by eight o'clock. That night the Burgundian army trembled because they were not enclosed by their carts, nor were they strong; they were scattered in a locality which was advantageous for the Liégeois, who were all foot-soldiers and who knew the territory much better than we did. Some of them were anxious to attack us, and if they had done so, I believe they would have had the upper hand. Those who had negotiated the agreement broke up these plans.

At daybreak, all our army assembled and the troops were placed in order of battle; the number of men was great—about three thousand men-at-arms, partly good and partly bad, and twelve or thirteen thousand archers, and many other infantrymen from the neighboring territory. We proceeded directly toward them to receive the hostages or to combat them in case they had not kept their word. We found them already disbanded, and they were going off by small groups and in disorder, in the manner of people with poor leadership. It was already almost mid-day and they had not yet brought the hostages.

The count of Charolais asked the marshal of Burgundy, who was present, whether he should attack them or not. The marshal replied affirmatively, saying that he could conquer them without any danger; he need not have any qualms about this, since it was their fault. Then he asked the lord of Contay, whom I have mentioned several times, and he agreed with the preceding opinion, adding that they might never have another such opportunity; he pointed out that they were already scattered in small groups as they were leaving and gave many arguments for attacking them without further delay. The duke next asked the constable, the count of Saint-Pol, who differed with the other two, claiming that it would be contrary to his honor and his word to proceed in this fashion and that it was not possible for so many people to agree so soon on such a matter as the delivery of hostages and in such great numbers. He proposed that the count of Charolais send someone to them to find out their intentions. The reasoning of these three men with the count was long and intense as they discussed this contention. On the one hand, he visualized his great and confirmed enemies defeated and imagined them offering no resistance. On the other hand, he was reminded of his promise. It was finally decided to send them a trumpeter, and he met the hostages as they were bringing them to him.

Thus no more was said about the matter, and everyone returned to his station. The soldiers were greatly displeased with the constable's advice, for they had seen fine loot before their eyes. An embassy was immediately sent to Liége to confirm the peace. The people, who are fickle, shouted at the ambassadors that they [the Burgundians] had not dared fight them; they shot at their heads with culverins and were very insulting to them.

The count of Charolais returned to Flanders. His father died that season, and he had a very elaborate and solemn church ritual and funeral service celebrated at Bruges for him; and he notified the king of this lord's death.[39]

2

Secret and new transactions were constantly being made by the princes. The king was so incensed against the dukes of Burgundy and Brittany that it was marvelous to observe. The dukes had great difficulty in communicating with each other, for their messengers were often intercepted and in time of war they had to travel by sea. The fastest way they could manage this, under the circumstances, was to cross from Brittany over to England and then to proceed by land to Dover, and from there to Calais; or else, if they took the most direct route, by land, they were in great danger.

In all these years of dissension and others which succeeded and which lasted some twenty years or more, partly spent in war, partly in truces and dissimulations (and each of the princes included his allies in each of the truces), God favored the kingdom of France by allowing the wars and divisions in England to continue; they had started some fifteen years before, and many important and cruel battles took place which resulted in the death of many worthy men. And each faction claimed that the others were traitors, because two houses were pre-

39. Philip the Good died on June 15, 1467. His funeral took place on August 16, 1467.

tenders to the crown of England—the house of Lancaster and the house of York. And there is no doubt that if the English had been in the same condition as they were formerly, this kingdom of France would have been in great trouble.

The king of France was concentrating on achieving his aims in Brittany, for it seemed to him that it would be easier to conquer and would offer less resistance than the house of Burgundy, and, furthermore, the Bretons were the ones who welcomed those who wished him ill such as his brother and others, and who had spies in his kingdom. And because of this reason he negotiated actively with Duke Charles of Burgundy so that he would consent, in exchange for several offers and bargains, to abandon the Bretons; to compensate for this, the king would abandon the Liégeois and Charles's other enemies. This agreement did not materialize. The duke of Burgundy proceeded once more against the Liégeois, who had broken the peace, and he captured a town called Huy. He pursued the men out of the town and pillaged it, although the previous year they had handed over hostages who risked the death penalty if they violated the treaty,[40] and although they were also liable for a large sum of money under the same circumstances. He assembled his army near Louvain, which is in the province of Brabant and on the borders of the province of Liége.

The count of Saint-Pol, constable of France, who was now entirely devoted to the king and had become related to him by marriage, came to the duke. With him were Cardinal Balue and other envoys, and they warned the duke of Burgundy that since the Liégeois were allies of the king and were included in the terms of his truce, he would come to their assistance in case the duke of Burgundy assailed them. However, they proposed that if he would consent to let the king wage war in Brittany, that lord would let him have his way in the matter of the Liégeois. Their audience was of short duration and was held in public; the ambassadors remained only one day.

The duke of Burgundy gave as his excuse that the Liégeois had assailed him and that the breaking of the truce was their fault and not his, and for these reasons he should nòt abandon his allies. The abovementioned ambassadors were allowed to leave. As they were ready to mount their horses, and this was the day after their arrival, he told them out loud that he begged the king not to undertake anything in the territory of Brittany. The constable pressed him and said: "My lord, you are not making a choice, for you are taking everything; you want

40. These are the three hundred hostages of whom it was a question in the preceding chapter.

to wage war against our friends according to your pleasure, but you also want to make us keep quiet without daring to attack our enemies as you attack yours. Those terms are unacceptable and the king will not tolerate them."

The duke took leave of them and said: "The Liégeois are assembled and I expect to have a battle within three days. If I lose, I am sure you will do as you please; but if I win, you will leave the Bretons in peace." Thereupon he mounted on horseback and the ambassadors returned to their lodgings and prepared to leave. The duke left Louvain in full armor and with a very great company, and went to besiege a town called Saint-Trond. His army was very large because all the troops that could be raised in Burgundy had come to join him. And I have never seen him with such a large body of soldiers, by any means.

Shortly before his departure, he held a meeting at which it was deliberated whether the hostages should be executed or not and what should be done with them. Some proposed that he should have them all killed. The lord of Contay, of whom I spoke several times, was particularly insistent on this; and I have never heard him speak so fiercely and cruelly as on that occasion. Therefore it is very necessary for a prince to have the advice of many people, for the wisest of them can occasionally, or even very often, err, owing to their biased interest in the matter under discussion, or to love, or to hatred, or to their tendency to contradict someone else, and sometimes to the way they feel at that particular moment: for one should not heed advice offered after dinner. Some might point out that persons guilty of any of these faults should not belong to a prince's council. To which one might reply that we are all human, and anyone who would like to find men who never fail to speak wisely or who do not show more emotion at certain times than at others would have to look for them in heaven, for they cannot be found among men. But to compensate for this, there is bound to be someone in the council who will speak very wisely and very well, although he is not accustomed to speak thus very often. Thus the one makes up for the other.

To return to our discussion, two or three agreed with Contay, out of respect for his authority and wisdom; for in such councils there are many people (and there are always enough of them) who speak only after others have expressed an opinion, although they themselves understand little about the matter, so as to please a particular speaker who is in a powerful position. After this the question was put to my lord of Humbercourt, who was born near Amiens, one of the wisest and most experienced knights I have ever known; he said that in his opinion, in order to put God entirely on his side and prove to everyone that he was neither cruel nor vindictive, the duke should release all of the three hundred hostages; and since they had given themselves up with good intentions and in the hope that peace would be maintained, they should be reminded upon leaving of the favor the duke was granting them and exhorted to try to persuade the people to make an honorable peace; and if they failed in their mission, they themselves, at least, in recognition for the kindness which was extended to them, should agree never to wage war against him or their bishop, who was in his company. This opinion prevailed and the hostages made the requested promises as they were freed. They were also told that if any of them engaged in the war and were taken, they would be beheaded. And thus they left.

It seems to me worthwhile to add that after the lord of Contay had pronounced this cruel judgment against the unfortunate hostages, as you have heard (and several of these men had offered themselves out of pure goodness), one of those who was present at this council whispered to me: "Regard this man well. Although he is quite old, he is very healthy. Yet I would wager a large sum that he will not be alive a year from now. And I say this because of the cruel words he pronounced." And thus it came to pass, for he did not live much longer; but before he died, he served his master well in a battle about which I shall speak presently.

To return to the matter under discussion, you have heard how, upon his departure from Louvain, the duke besieged Saint-Trond and set up his artillery. Inside the town were some three hundred Liégeois led by a very competent knight; it was he who had negotiated peace when we faced them in battle the previous year. The third day after the town was besieged, a great number of Liégeois—about thirty thousand or more men, both good and bad, all of them foot-soldiers except for about five hundred horsemen, with a large train of artillery, came to raise our siege.[41] At about ten in the morning they were a half-league away from us, in a strong village called Brusthem, which was partly enclosed by marshes. With them was François Royer, bailiff of Lyon, at the time the king's ambassador to the Liégeois. Our army was soon alarmed. To be truthful, one must say that orders had been slack about sending good scouts to the fields, because we were notified of the happenings only by foragers who were fleeing.

I never saw the duke of Burgundy give good military orders entirely on his own except on that day. At once he had all the troops repair to the fields except for a few whom he ordered to remain at the siege.

41. Commynes' estimate of the number of Liége combatants is exaggerated, as is evident from comparing other sources about this battle with Commynes' account. The battle of Brusthem took place on October 28, 1467.

And among others he left five hundred Englishmen there. On both sides of the village he placed some twelve hundred men-at-arms and he stationed himself facing them, farther away than the rest from the village, with some eight hundred men-at-arms. And there were several persons of high rank on foot with the archers, as well as a great number of men-at-arms. My lord of Ravenstein marched at the head of the duke's vanguard, all of them on foot, partly armed soldiers and partly archers, with certain pieces of artillery, to the edge of the ditches, which were wide and deep, and full of water; and, by the use of our arrows and cannons, we forced them to retreat and we overcame their ditches and their artillery. However, when our men shot and missed, the Liégeois took heart again; with their pikes, which were long and therefore made advantageous weapons, they charged upon our archers and those who were leading our ranks. In one group they killed four or five hundred men all at once, and all wavered, as if on the point of rout. Thereupon the duke had the archers from his troop, who were led by Philippe de Crèvecoeur, lord of Cordes, march forth; several other persons of high rank were with them, and with a very great cry they assailed the Liégeois, who were routed in a moment.

The horsemen of whom I spoke, who were on both sides of the village, could not harm the Liégeois; neither could the duke of Burgundy from his position because of the marshes. But they remained there as a precautionary measure so as to be able to encounter the Liégeois in the event that they should break our vanguard, pass their ditches, and reach the plain. The Liégeois began to flee along the marshes, and they were pursued only by foot-soldiers. The duke of Burgundy sent some of the horsemen who were with him to help chase them, but they had to make a detour of two leagues to find a passage. Night came upon them and this saved the lives of many Liégeois. He sent other men before the city, because he had heard noise there and suspected that they might rush forth. Indeed, they made three sallies, but they were repulsed each time. And the English who had remained there conducted themselves most valiantly.

The Liégeois, after having been beaten, rallied a little around their carts. They could not hold out for long. Some six thousand men died, and this seems a large number to people who do not wish to lie; but in my time I have been in many places where for one man who was killed one hundred were reported dead, in order to please the ruler; and with such lies masters are sometimes deceived. If night had not fallen, more than fifteen thousand would have died.[42]

Since his task had been accomplished and it was already very late,

42. Other sources estimate that between three and four thousand died.

the duke of Burgundy retired to his encampment with his whole army, except for one thousand or twelve hundred horsemen who had been sent two leagues from there to pursue those who were fleeing; they could not have reached them otherwise, because of a little river. They were not able to accomplish any great feat, owing to the darkness of the night. However, they killed some men and captured others. The rest of them, which consisted of the greatest part, escaped to the town. The lord of Contay was most helpful in ordering the battle that day, but a few days later he died in the town of Huy. His last hours were relatively easy. He had been a valiant and wise man, but he did not live long after the cruel opinion he had expressed against the hostages from Liége, as you heard earlier.

As soon as the duke had disarmed, he sent for a secretary and had him write letters to the constable and others who had taken leave of him at Louvain; and it was only four days since they had come as ambassadors, as it was reported. He informed them of this victory and requested that nothing be attempted against the Bretons.

Two days after this battle, the pride of this foolish people suffered a severe blow, and it was owing to a relatively small loss. But everyone, whoever he may be, would be wise to refrain from exposing his position to the hazard of battle if he can possibly avoid it. For the loss of a small number of men can lead to an incredible change in the courage of the army of the losing side. They are not only afraid of the enemy, but they begin to despise their master and his close advisers. They begin murmuring and machinating, they make demands more boldly than they were accustomed to before, and they become incensed when their requests are refused. One *écu* would procure more for a general before defeat than three would afterwards. If the commander of the weaker side is wise, then he will take no chances with those who have fled, but will keep his eyes open and try to find an easy victory so that his men cannot avoid doing well; thus their courage will be revived and their fears dispelled.

In any case, a lost battle always has important and unfortunate results for the loser. It is true that conquerors should seek occasion for battle in order to end the business quickly, provided they have better footsoldiers than their neighbors, as is the case with the English and the Swiss today. I do not say this in order to minimize the accomplishments of other nations, but these two have obtained great victories, and their men do not believe in remaining long in the battlefield without action, as would the French and Italians, who have more sense and can be led more easily.

On the other hand, a winning ruler acquires greater reputation and esteem from his men than he had before; he earns increasing obedience from his subjects; because of the greater respect they have for him, they grant him whatever he requests. His men become more courageous and dauntless. Sometimes princes also become so conceited about their good fortune that misfortune comes upon them later. All these arrangements are made by God, who changes things according to people's merit or lack of it.

When those who were within the walls of Saint-Trond saw that the battle was lost for them and that they were enclosed on all sides, they judged the defeat to be worse than it actually was, and so they surrendered the town, abandoned their arms, and yielded ten men—who were to be selected by the duke of Burgundy—to be disposed of as he saw fit. He had them beheaded. Six of them had been among the hostages whom he had released a few days before, under the conditions mentioned earlier.

He broke camp and proceeded to Tongres, where the people expected a siege. However, the town was not too strong, and without waiting for their walls to give out, they made a similar arrangement and gave up ten men, among whom were also five or six of the abovementioned hostages. All ten died like the others.

3

From there the duke proceeded to the city of Liége, in which there was great commotion. Some wanted to hold and defend the city, and claimed that there were enough people to serve the purpose. Especially forceful in expressing that opinion was a knight named Raez [de Heers, lord] of Linter. Others, on the other hand, realizing that the whole territory was being burned or destroyed, wanted peace at any price.

Thus, as the duke approached the city, several overtures were made by persons of low estate, such as prisoners; but these negotiations were carried on more seriously by some of the above-mentioned hostages, who acted altogether differently from the first group[43] of whom I spoke. They acknowledged the favor that had been granted to them and brought with them three hundred of the most prominent men of the town in their shirtsleeves, bare-legged and bare-headed. They presented the keys of the city to the duke and surrendered themselves to him unconditionally, aside from a request that the town should not be burned

43. The "first group" were those hostages who violated their oath to work for peace when released by Charles the Bold. The second group, described here, was true to the oath.

or pillaged. On that same day my lord of Moy, as well as one of the king's secretaries named Master Jean Prevost, arrived as the king's ambassadors to the duke. They came to make the same requests and arrangements as the constable had made several days earlier.

On the day of the capitulation [November 11, 1467], the duke, assuming that he could enter the city, sent my lord of Humbercourt before him, because he knew the city well; he had been its administrator during the years when they were at peace. However, he was refused entrance that day, and so he went to lodge in a small abbey which is near one of the gates; he was accompanied by about fifty men-at-arms. All told, he had about two hundred men capable of fighting, and I was among them. The duke of Burgundy sent word to him that he should not leave the premises if he felt safe there; but if the place was not sufficiently well protected he should return to him, because the passage was too difficult for reinforcements to be sent: the area was full of rocks. Humbercourt decided not to leave the abbey, for the place was very strong, and he kept with him five or six of the worthy townsmen who had come to give up the keys of the city, so that they could help him, as you will hear.

As the clock struck nine at night, we heard their bell ring; at this signal the people assembled, and Humbercourt suspected that they intended to come and assail us, for he had been well informed that my lord Raez of Linter and several others would not consent to have peace. And his suspicion proved to be well founded, because they had indeed assembled for that purpose and were ready to attack us.

The lord of Humbercourt said: "If we can put them off until midnight, we are safe, for they will be tired and will become sleepy, and those who are against us will take flight when they realize that their plans have miscarried." In order to bring this about, he sent out two of the burghers whom he had retained, as I told you, and gave them certain articles written in rather friendly terms. He did this merely to give them an occasion to discuss, and to gain time; for it was the people's custom, and still is, to gather together at the bishop's palace whenever something noteworthy is announced, and they were alerted by a bell which was sounded from within the palace.

Thus our two burghers, who had been hostages, and good ones,[44] came to the gate, which was hardly two bow-shots away from our station, and they found a great number of people in arms. Some were for assailing the enemy and others not. The envoys cried out to the

44. That is, they were among the second group mentioned on p. 158, n. 43.

burgomaster that they brought good tidings in writing from the lord of Humbercourt, the duke of Burgundy's lieutenant in the region, and that it would be a good idea to go to the palace and hear about them. And they did so accordingly. Immediately we heard the bell ring in the palace, and we therefore knew that they were being kept busy.

Our two burghers did not return; but after an hour we heard more noise at the gate than there had been before, and more people gathered there, and they shouted insults at us over the walls. Then Humbercourt realized that the peril was greater for us than before, and he sent out the other four hostages who were with him, bearing a written document to them, which implied that when he was governor of their city by appointment of the duke of Burgundy, he had treated them in a friendly manner and that he would never consent to their destruction; for not long ago he had been made a member of one of their corporations, the guild of blacksmiths, and had worn their official costume. For this reason they could have more faith in his words. To summarize, he told them that if they wished to enjoy the benefits of peace and save their country, they must honor their promises and, after opening the gates of the town, they should do what was indicated in a certain document which he had sent them. When he had given instructions to the four men, they went to the gate, as the others had done before them, and found it wide open. Some people received them with foul language and great menaces; others were pleased to hear the news they were bringing and they returned to the palace. Immediately we heard the palace bell ring, and we rejoiced greatly; and the noise which we had heard at the gate faded away.

Indeed, they stayed a long time at the palace, until two hours after midnight at least. There they agreed that they would honor their promise and that in the morning one of the gates should be given up to the lord of Humbercourt. And everyone retired to have some rest, as the lord of Humbercourt had predicted. Thereupon Raez of Linter fled from the town with all his adherents.

I should not have spoken so long about this matter, considering that it is not very important, if it had not been to point out that sometimes by such expedients and artifices, which come from possessing a great deal of sense, great dangers and disadvantages and losses can be avoided.

The next morning, at daybreak, several of the hostages came to ask the lord of Humbercourt to come with them to the palace, where all the people were assembled; there he would swear to uphold the two points about which the people were uneasy—those concerning the bans on burning and pillaging the city. After this formality they would let him have one of the gates. He sent word about this to the duke of Burgundy and went to the palace. After taking the oath he returned to the gate; those who were on guard were made to come down. They were replaced by twelve men-at-arms and some archers of his, and the duke of Burgundy's standard was set upon the gate. From there he went to another gate, which was walled up, and put it in the hands of the bastard of Burgundy [Anthony, illegitimate son of Philip the Good], who was quartered in the vicinity, and another gate he gave to the marshal of Burgundy. He delivered another to one of the gentlemen who were still with him. Thus these four gates were well protected by the duke of Burgundy's men, and his banners were set upon all of them.

It should be understood that Liége at that time was one of the most powerful cities in the whole area; only four or five surpassed it in strength. It was one of the most populated cities, and people from the vicinity had taken refuge there. Therefore the loss which they had sustained in battle was not apparent in the least. They were not in need of anything. They were in the middle of winter and were having the most abundant rainfall one can imagine, and this had made the soil wonderfully miry and soft. We were in dire necessity of supplies and money, and our army was practically broken; and so the duke of Burgundy was in no mood to besiege the town. Besides, he would not have been in a position to do so if he had wished it. And if they had waited two more days before surrendering, he would have had to leave by the same way he had come.

Therefore I want to point out that he gained great glory and honor in this enterprise; and it came to him solely by the grace of God, against all human odds, for he would never even have ventured to hope for the good fortune which came upon him. In the judgment of most people, he received all these honors because of the mercy and kindness which he extended to the hostages of whom you heard earlier. I say this all the more willingly because princes and others sometimes complain and seem to regret when they have been kind or have granted a favor to someone; they claim that nothing good will come of it and that in the future they will not grant pardons or gifts or other favors so lightly, although such actions are part of their office.

In my estimation such actions and speeches are poorly spoken and proceed from a cowardly heart; for a prince or any other man who has never been deceived is like an animal, has no knowledge of good and evil, and cannot tell the difference between the two. Furthermore, people are not all of one character. Therefore the wickedness of one or two should not prevent us from doing favors to many, when the time and opportunity present themselves. I should like to see everyone capable of judging the character of people; for all are not equally deserving. And indeed it is almost inconceivable to me that a wise person can be ungrateful after receiving a great favor from someone. In this matter princes are often misled, for in the long run it is never profitable to deal with a fool; and it seems to me that one of the best proofs of intelligence that a lord can show is to associate with and attract to his circle worthy and honest men: for he will be judged by others to be of the same character as his closest companions.

To conclude this discourse, it seems to me that one should never be deterred from being benevolent, for a single person, or even the most humble among all those to whom a kindness has been extended, will be of such great service and will be so grateful, should the occasion arise, that he will compensate for all the base and wicked acts which the rest would have carried out in the same situation.

And as you have seen in the case of the hostages, some of them were good and grateful, whereas the rest, which constituted the majority, were evil and ungrateful. But it sufficed that five or six alone carried through this affair in accordance with the goals and intentions of the duke of Burgundy.

4

The day after the gates had been given up, the duke of Burgundy entered the city of Liége in great triumph; twenty arm-spans of the wall were broken down and the ditch was filled up along the main street. With him were some two thousand men-at-arms in full armor and ten thousand archers, and still many remained in the camp. He was on horseback and was accompanied by dignitaries from his household and the chief officers of his army, all of them dressed as lavishly and elegantly as possible; and thus they rode solemnly to the principal church. In short, he remained several days in the city. During that time he had five or six men who had been among the hostages executed; they included the messenger of the town, whom he greatly hated. He imposed new laws and customs. He exacted large sums from them which he claimed were due him because they had broken the peace and had not observed the arrangements made with him some years before.

He took away with him all their artillery and arms and had all the towers and walls of the city razed, whereupon he returned to his own territory, where he was received with great honor and obeisance, particularly by the townspeople of Ghent, who had been in a kind of rebellion against him, along with some other towns, before his march into the territory of Liége. But now [December, 1467] they received him as a victor, and all the banners were carried to him by the chief townspeople, who proceeded as far as Brussels; those who carried them came on foot. This was because immediately following the death of his father, he had made his entry into Ghent before visiting any other town in his territory, in the firm belief that he was more beloved there than in any other one of his towns and that the other towns would follow the example of Ghent and behave similarly.

And he was right: for the day after his entry [July, 1467] they had assembled in armor in the market-place and brought with them the image of a saint called Saint Liévin. They conducted the saint to a little house called La Cuillette, where certain taxes on wheat were levied in order to pay back certain debts which they had incurred to remunerate Duke Philip of Burgundy when they made peace with him, after having been at war with him for two years. Thumping the saint's reliquary against the portal of this house, they had claimed that the saint wished to pass through without bending, and so they had forthwith demolished the house.

The duke had then proceeded to the market-place and had gone up into a house to speak to them. A great number of the high dignitaries had honored him on his passage and offered to accompany him. He had had them remain in front of the town hall and wait for him to return; however, the common people had compelled them to proceed to the market-place. When the duke arrived on the premises, he had ordered them to remove the reliquary and return it to the church. Some had raised it to comply with his request, and others had put it back where it was. Then they had requested justice against certain individuals because of their handling of money. He had promised them that he would take care of the matter. And when he had seen that he could not make them disperse, he had returned to his lodgings. And they had remained in the market-place for eight consecutive days.

The next day they had brought him certain documents by which they demanded restitution of everything Duke Philip had taken away from them by the peace of Gavere [1453], and among other things they had requested that each corporation might have its own banner, as they were accustomed to have, and there were a total of seventy-two guilds. Since he had been in a precarious position, he had been forced to grant them all their requests and any privileges they had asked for. And as soon as he had given his consent, after much commotion, they had set up all of these banners, which had already been prepared, in the market-place; thus they had demonstrated that they would probably have done this against his will if he had not acceded to their request.

He had been right in thinking that if he made his first entry into Ghent the other towns would follow its example, for many towns rebelled as the townspeople of Ghent had done, killed some of their officers, and committed other atrocities. If he had believed his father's saying, that the inhabitants of Ghent were fond of their prince's son but never of their prince, he would not have been so deceived. And to tell the truth, except for the people of Liége, none are so inconstant as those of Ghent. In spite of their wickedness, however, they have one good trait: they never touch a hair of the person of their prince; and the burghers and higher strata of society are good people, and they are much displeased with the foolish acts of the common people.

The duke had been compelled to close his eyes to all these impertinent acts in order not to have a war with his own subjects and the Liégeois at the same time; but he calculated that if his present trip[45] was successful, he would bring them back to reason. And so it happened. For, as I said previously, they brought all the banners to Brussels as they went on foot to meet him, as well as all the privileges and documents which they had made him sign before he left Ghent [in July]. And in a large assembly at the great hall in Brussels, in the presence of many ambassadors, they presented him with all the banners, and similarly all the privileges were handed over to him for him to dispose of as he saw fit.

By his command, his heralds pulled the banners from the lances upon which they were fastened and they were sent to Boulogne-sur-Mer, ten leagues away from Calais; in that town were also kept the banners which had been taken from them in the days of his father, Duke Philip, as a result of the wars that were fought between them, in which he had vanquished and subjugated them. The duke's chancellor also took all their privileges and canceled one of them, which had to do with their aldermen; for in all the other cities of Flanders, the prince renews the terms of office of the aldermen and has their accounts audited. But in Ghent, owing to their privilege, he could appoint only four men, the other twenty-two being selected by the townspeople, for they have a total of twenty-six aldermen. When these officials are on good terms with the count of Flanders,[46] he has peace for that year, and they grant

45. The "present trip" is that made in December, 1467, on Charles's return from Liége (see p. 163). However, Commynes in this chapter mixes together incidents which took place on a later visit of Charles to Ghent in 1469, such as the alteration of the town's privileges, with those which took place in 1467.
46. See n. 84, p. 39.

him his requests willingly; but, on the other hand, when the aldermen do not see eye to eye with him, all sorts of unexpected difficulties are likely to arise. In addition, they paid thirty thousand florins to the duke and six thousand to his retainers, and some of the townspeople were banished. All their other privileges were returned to them. All the other towns made peace by offering money, for they had not undertaken anything against him personally.

Thus you can see the profit in being the conqueror and the damage in being the conquered. Therefore one should be very wary of risking a battle unless it is unavoidable, and, if it becomes absolutely necessary, then all things should be seriously considered before starting. And, most of the time, those who act cautiously and use good foresight obtain better results than those who proceed with great arrogance; yet when God decides to put his hand to it, man can do nothing.

The Liégeois in question were excommunicated for five years, owing to some disagreement between them and their bishop, but they disregarded his pronouncements and continued in their foolish and wicked ways, although they would have been unable to explain what moved them to do this, except too much wealth and too much pride. And King Louis had a saying, and in my opinion a wise one, according to which when pride rode before, shame and destruction were soon to follow closely. And he was certainly not tainted with that sin.

After attending to these matters, the duke retired to Ghent, where he was given a magnificent reception. He entered the city in arms. And the townsmen sallied forth to the fields, so that he could bring people out of or into the town as he pleased. Several of the king's ambassadors came to him and others were sent by him to the king. Similarly, envoys from Brittany were sent to the duke of Burgundy and others from him to Brittany. Thus the winter passed. The king was always trying to persuade the duke to let him have his way in Brittany and made him several advantageous proposals as compensation for this. However, the duke would hear none of it, and the king was greatly displeased, in view of what had happened to his allies, the Liégeois.

5

Finally at the beginning of summer [1468], the king lost patience and entered Brittany, or rather his men did, according to his command, and they captured two small castles; one was called Chantocé and the other Ancenis. The duke of Burgundy was immediately notified of this and was earnestly solicited and begged by the dukes of Normandy and Brittany to come to their assistance. He raised his army in all diligence and wrote to the king, entreating him to desist from that enterprise in view of the fact that they were mentioned in his truce and were his allies. Since the king's answer was not satisfactory, the duke took the field near the town of Péronne with a considerable force. The king was in Compiègne and his army still in Brittany. After the duke had been in Péronne three or four days, Cardinal Balue came as the king's ambassador; he stayed only a short time and made overtures to the duke, telling him that the Bretons might come to terms without him. It was always the king's intention to separate them. The cardinal was honored and feasted and sent back shortly. He was to bring back the message that the duke had not taken the field to do harm to the king or to wage war against him, but only to come to the assistance of his allies. And sweet words were exchanged on both sides.

Immediately after the cardinal's departure, a herald called Bretagne came to the duke and brought him letters from the dukes of Normandy and Brittany informing him that they had made peace with the king and were renouncing all their former alliances and particularly his, and that for his sole share, the duke of Normandy should have a pension of sixty thousand livres a year and should renounce his claims to Normandy, which had recently been given to him. My lord Charles of France was not particularly pleased with this arrangement but he was forced to conceal his true feelings. The duke of Burgundy was astounded at the news, in view of the fact that he had raised his army only to come to the assistance of the two dukes; and the herald was in a very dangerous position. The duke suspected that because he had passed through the king's quarters the letters might have been forged. However, he received similar letters from other sources.

Now the king thought that he had attained his goal and that he would easily persuade the duke of Burgundy to similarly abandon the above-mentioned dukes. Secret messages were exchanged between the king and the duke of Burgundy; finally the king gave him 120,000 gold *écus*, half of which was paid in cash before the duke broke camp, as compensation for the expenses he had had in raising his army.

The duke sent to the above-mentioned lord a *valet de chambre* of his, named Jean de Boschuysen, a close friend of his. The king was encouraged by this move and proposed an interview with the duke, hoping he might gain him over entirely to his will, in view of the mean trick which the two above-mentioned dukes had played on him, as well as in view of the large sum of money he had given him. He suggested this to the duke in a message which he gave to Boschuysen, and with him he dispatched Cardinal Balue a second time, as well as Tanneguy du Chastel, governor of Roussillon, who implied by their words that the king very much desired that this meeting should take place. They found the duke at Péronne, and he was not particularly anxious for this interview; for the Liégeois once more gave indications that they might rebel because of two ambassadors whom the king had sent them to suggest that they do so before the truce, which had been agreed upon by the two dukes and their allies and was to last for a few days. The Liégeois had replied to the ambassadors that they would not dare to do it, since the duke had destroyed them the previous year and had demolished their walls; and if this settlement[47] was made, they would no longer have any desire to fight, if indeed any of them had ever had it at all. Anyway, it was finally concluded that the king should come to Péronne, since that was his pleasure. The duke wrote him a letter in his own hand; it guaranteed him a safe-conduct which would allow him to go and return as he pleased. Thus the ambassadors took leave of him and proceeded toward the king, who was at Noyon. In order to straighten matters out at Liége, the duke had the bishop of Liége retire, since the whole quarrel had taken place on his account; and with him retired the lord of Humbercourt, the duke's lieutenant in that country, and many others.

6

You have heard in what manner it was decided that the king should come to Péronne. And so he did, and he did not bring any guard with him; he wished to entrust himself entirely to the duke and traveled only with his safe-conduct. He asked, however, that the duke's archers, under the command of my lord of Cordes, who was in the duke's service at the time, should come to meet him and escort him. And so it was done. Few of his own retinue came with him. However, he was accompanied by several persons of high rank, including the duke of Bourbon, his brother the cardinal of Bourbon, and the count of Saint-Pol, constable of France, who had had nothing to do with this meeting but was displeased about it; for now his courage had increased, and he was not prepared to humble himself before the duke as he had done on previous occasions, and so there was little affection between them. Along with them were also Cardinal Balue, the governor of Roussillon, and others.

47. That is, the settlement pending between Charles and Louis, prepared by the truce mentioned in the preceding sentence.

As the king approached Péronne, the duke went out to meet him in numerous company, led him into the town, and had him lodge with the collector of taxes, who had a beautiful house not far from the castle; for the accommodations in the castle were inferior and small.

War between two great princes is easily started but difficult to stop because of various things which occur and their consequences; for many intrigues take place on both sides in order to harm the enemy, and they cannot suddenly be recalled. And this is what happened to the two princes, who decided to hold this meeting so suddenly that they failed to notify those who were serving them afar, with the result that these men went on following their masters' previous orders in various parts of the country.

The duke of Burgundy had sent for his army from Burgundy, in which at the time there were many high-ranking noblemen. With them came my lord of Bresse [Philip, later duke of Savoy and brother-in-law of Louis XI], the bishop of Geneva, and the count of Romont, all three of them brothers from the house of Savoy (for Savoyards and Burgundians have always loved each other very dearly), and a few Germans, whose country borders on both Savoy and the county of Burgundy, were also with the group. One should remember that the king had formerly imprisoned the lord of Bresse because of two knights whom he had caused to be killed in Savoy: there was thus no great love between them. With this company was also my lord of Lau (whom the king had similarly kept for a long time as a prisoner, although he had originally been one of his close friends, and who later escaped from prison and fled to Burgundy), Poncet de Rivière, and the lord of Urfé, who later became grand equerry of France.

All this company of whom I spoke arrived before Péronne as the king was making his entry. Bresse and the three I mentioned earlier entered the town, wearing the cross of Saint Andrew;[48] and they had expected to arrive in time to accompany the duke of Burgundy when he went out to receive the king. But they came slightly late. They went directly to the duke's chamber and bowed before him; my lord of Bresse, as their spokesman, begged the duke to grant the three above-mentioned lords his protection, in spite of the king's coming, as he had agreed with them to do in Burgundy and had promised for the time when they arrived there, and assured him that they were ready to serve him against anyone. The duke granted their request orally and thanked them. The rest of the army, under the command of the marshal of Burgundy, went

48. St. Andrew was the patron saint of the Burgundian dukes.

to encamp in the fields by order of the duke. The marshal had no less dislike of the king than the others of whom I spoke, because of the town of Épinal in Lorraine, which he had formerly given to the marshal and had later taken away from him to give to Duke John of Calabria, who has been mentioned frequently in these memoirs.

The king was soon informed of the arrival of all these men and of the outfits with which they arrived. He fell into great fear and sent word to the duke of Burgundy, begging him to let him stay in the castle and telling him that the men just arrived wished him ill. The duke, who was extremely pleased to hear that, had his lodgings prepared and assured him that there was nothing to fear.

It is great folly for a prince to put himself in the power of another, especially when they are at war; and it is also to their advantage if they have studied history in their youth. They can thus realize what happens in such assemblies and how some of the ancients committed great frauds, impostures, and perjuries against each other, capturing and killing those who had confidence in their word. This is not to imply that everyone acts in this manner, but a single example should be sufficient to make many people wiser and to inspire them to guard themselves well.

It seems to me (and I speak on the basis of what I have seen in this world, which includes eighteen years or more experience in close relationship with princes, having had intimate knowledge of the greatest and most secret affairs which have been transacted in this kingdom of France and in neighboring territories) that one of the surest means to make a man wise is to have him read ancient history and learn how to conduct and guard himself and how to manage his affairs wisely, according to histories and examples of our ancestors. For our life is so short that it cannot give us the necessary experience in so many matters.

Besides, our life-span is diminished, and we do not live as long as men did in former times; neither are our bodies as strong, and similarly our faith and loyalty to one another have been weakened. I could not say by what ties one could assure oneself with regard to the great, who are rather inclined to do as they please without regard to any reason that can be offered. And, worst of all, they are usually surrounded by persons who are only interested in pleasing their masters, and they invariably praise all their actions whether they are good or bad. And if someone is found who wants to improve things, every one falls to quarreling.

Again I cannot help but blame lords who are ignorant. Around every lord one is sure to find some lawyers and ecclesiastics, as is proper; and they are indeed valuable when they are good men, but very dangerous otherwise. At every turn they cite a law or story, and even the best story is liable to be given a bad interpretation at their hands. But wise men and those who have read things will never be deceived by them, nor will anyone be so convincing that they [the wise] will accept lies. You may be sure that God did not establish the position of king or prince to have it filled by stupid people or by persons who pride themselves in saying: "I am no scholar; I refer my affairs to my council and I trust them." And without further explanation they proceed to their pleasures. If they had been better educated in their youth they would reason differently and they would want to earn the respect of others for their person and their virtues.

I do not wish to imply that all princes use the services of unworthy persons. But most of those whom I have known have been surrounded by them. I have known some wise princes who, when the necessity arose, knew how to select the advice of the best ministers and followed it without complaining.

Among all the princes whom I was privileged to know, the one who could do this best was the king, our master; and no one knew better how to honor and respect people of worth and excellence. He was rather well-read; he liked to ask questions and to learn about everything and was endowed with good natural sense, which is more important than any science that can be learned in this world. All the books that have been written would be useless if they did not serve to bring to mind past events. And one man can learn more in three months' time from reading a book than twenty men living successively could observe and understand from experience.

Thus, to conclude this digression, it seems to me that God cannot send a greater plague on any country than a prince of little understanding: for that is the source of all other misfortunes. First of all, division and war arise because he delegates his authority to others, although that is the prerogative which he should most want to reserve for himself. And from this division famine and death proceed, as well as the other afflictions which derive from war. Thus one may observe how much the subjects of a prince have reason to lament when they see his children badly educated and in the hands of men of bad temperament.

7

You have already heard about the arrival of the Burgundian army in Péronne almost at the same time as the king. Since they were already in Champagne while the king's visit was being negotiated, the duke was not in a position to countermand the orders he had given them. Their coming caused trouble owing to suspicions which resulted from their presence. However, the two princes summoned some of their counselors to a meeting at which they were to transact their affairs as amicably as possible. And after they were well under way and had been there for three or four days, some very important news arrived from Liége, which I shall relate to you.

In concentrating on coming to Péronne, the king had forgotten that he had sent two ambassadors to the province of Liége to stir up the inhabitants against the duke; and they were so successful in their mission that they had already gathered together a large number of soldiers. And the Liégeois went straight to take the town of Tongres, where the bishop of Liége and the lord of Humbercourt were quartered with some two thousand or more men; they captured the bishop and Humbercourt and killed a few people. They took only these two and some of the bishop's servants. The others fled, leaving their possessions behind them in the manner of people routed by surprise. After this, the Liégeois proceeded toward the city of Liége, which is rather near the town of Tongres. On the way, the lord of Humbercourt made an agreement with a knight called William[49] "de Wilde," which means the wild man. This knight saved Humbercourt from death at the hands of the Liégeois and remained faithful to his word, but not for long, since he was killed a short time later.

The people were exceedingly happy at the capture of their bishop, the lord of Liége. They had caught several cathedral canons that day whom they hated, and they killed five or six of them straight off; among the rest was one of the bishop's close friends, called Master Robert, whom I had often seen attending him in full armor, for such is the custom of the prelates in Germany. They killed Master Robert in the bishop's presence and cut him up into several pieces, which they tossed at each other's heads with great laughter. Before they had marched seven or eight leagues, which they were supposed to cover, they killed as many as sixteen persons, canons or other high-ranking persons, most of them in the service of the bishop. Already they had heard rumors that the peace treaty was being negotiated, and they would have been content to say that they had rebelled only against their bishop, whom they were taking with them as a prisoner into their city.

Those who were fleeing, about whom I spoke, spread the alarm to the localities where they passed; and the duke soon learned the news.

49. *Sic.* His name was John.

Some claimed that everyone was put to death and others said the opposite. In such matters one usually hears more than one version of what happened. Some of those who came had seen how the canons were treated, and they believed that the bishop, the lord of Humbercourt, and all the others were dead. They affirmed that they had seen the king's ambassadors in this company and they named them. All this was reported to the duke, who immediately gave credit to it; he became very angry and said that the king had come to deceive him. Immediately he ordered the gates of the town and the castle to be shut and gave as his reason a rather lame excuse: that it was done in order to recover a lost casket which contained precious rings and money.

When the king saw himself enclosed in this castle, which is small, and saw many archers posted at his door, he hardly felt secure, especially when he realized that he was lodged next to a large tower where a count of Vermandois had ordered one of his predecessors, a king of France, to be put to death.[50]

At that time I was still with the duke in the capacity of chamberlain, and I slept in his room whenever I pleased, as was the custom of his house. When the duke saw that the gates were shut, he had the people leave his room and said to the few of us who remained that the king had come to betray him; he himself had done everything in his power to avoid this interview but had not been able to prevent it. He then gave us an account of the happenings in Liége, insisting that the king had provoked the rebellion through the intrigues of his ambassadors, and he related how all his men had been killed. He was extremely incensed against the king and threatened him in strong terms. I believe indeed that if at the time he had found those he addressed in a mood to confirm his opinions, or if they had advised him to harm the king, he would not have hesitated to do so, or at least would have imprisoned him in the large tower. Besides myself no one was present when these statements were uttered except for two *valets de chambre*, one of whom was named Charles de Visen, born in Dijon, an honest man who was much esteemed by his master. We did not excite the duke, but instead we did our best to calm him.

Shortly after, he spoke in the same manner to many people and the news spread to the whole town and finally reached the king's chamber; and he was terrified. Indeed, so was practically everyone else, because the situation seemed dangerous, considering the variety of factors which

50. King Charles the Simple died in Péronne in 929 after a six-year imprisonment by Herbert, count of Vermandois. There is no proof that the count killed him, although there is also no proof that he did not.

must be taken into account in order to settle differences between princes, especially when they are so powerful, and considering, too, the errors which they both committed in not sending word of the new turn of events to those who were managing their affairs in distant regions, and considering what might suddenly occur as a result.

8

It is very unwise for two great princes of approximately equal power to have an interview unless they are extremely young, at the age when they have nothing on their minds except pleasure. But after they reach the stage when they want to enhance their standing at each other's expense, even though they might not be in danger personally (and that is practically impossible), their malevolence and their jealousy increase. It would therefore be preferable that they settle their differences through the mediation of wise and worthy ministers, as I explained at length elsewhere in these memoirs. However, I should like to give a few examples to support this statement, and I shall select them from my own observations and from what I have learned in my time.

A few years after our king's coronation, and just before the formation of the League for the Public Good, the kings of France and of Castile had an interview; they are the most closely allied princes in Christendom, for they are related king to king, kingdom to kingdom, and man to man, and are strictly bound to observe their alliances under penalty of great maledictions. King Henry of Castile[51] came to this interview well attended, as far as Fuenterrabia; the king stayed at Saint-Jean-de-Luz, which is four leagues beyond. Each of them was on the limits of his kingdom.

I was not present but the king told me about it, and so did my lord of Lau. And it was confirmed to me in Castile by some of the lords who were there with the king of Castile; these included the grand master of [the crusading order of] Santiago and the archbishop of Toledo, two of the most prominent men in Castile at the time. Also present were the count of Ledesma, the king's favorite, in great pomp, and all his guard, consisting of some three hundred horsemen. It is true that King Henry was not very wise, for he gave away all his property or allowed it to be taken by anyone who wanted it or was in a position to obtain it. Our king was also well attended, as you have seen, and as was his custom. His guard was especially impressive. The queen of Aragon was

51. Henry IV (1425–1474). The meeting took place on April 28, 1463.

also present at the meeting, owing to differences between her and the king of Castile concerning Estella and some other localities in Navarre. The king of France was to serve as arbitrator in this matter.

To continue with our thesis that personal interviews between princes are not necessary, one should be reminded that these two had never had any differences or anything to settle; they saw each other once or at most twice on the banks of the river [Bidassoa] which separates the two kingdoms near a small castle called Urtubie, where the king of Castile passed to the other side. They did not appreciate each other. Our king noted especially that the king of Castile was hardly able to make any decisions of his own, unless they were approved by the grand master of Santiago and the archbishop of Toledo, and so he desired to make their acquaintance. They came to him at Saint-Jean-de-Luz. Many arrangements were made between them and they became fast friends, although the king had a poor opinion of their master.

Most of the two kings' men were quartered at Bayonne, where they started fighting right away. Although they are related, nevertheless they [the French and Castilians] speak different languages. The count of Ledesma crossed the river in a boat whose sail was of gold material. His shoes were set with many precious stones. And he presented himself before the king. The French claimed that he had rented the shoes and borrowed the gold cloth from some church; this was not true, however, for he was very wealthy, and I have seen him since he became duke of Albuquerque and the possessor of rich lands in Castile.

These two nations scoffed at each other. The king of Castile was ugly and his clothes seemed ridiculous to the French, who made fun of them. Our king had very short clothes and was so inelegantly dressed that he could hardly have done worse, and most of the time the material he wore was cheap looking. His hat was ugly, different from the others, with a little image made out of lead fastened to it. The Castilians ridiculed his outfit and claimed that it was out of stinginess that he dressed in such a manner. In short, this assembly ended full of mockery and petty arguments. Since that time the two kings never liked each other, and great division arose among the ministers of the king of Castile. It persisted until his death and much later. I saw him become the poorest king in the world and abandoned by all his servants.

The queen of Aragon grieved about the pronouncement which the king of France made in favor of the king of Castile. She and the king of Aragon hated him ever since, although they accepted his help against the townspeople of Barcelona for a time out of necessity. However, this friendship was of short duration and a war broke out between our king and the king of Aragon which lasted more than sixteen years and still remains unsettled.[52]

Let us speak of others. Duke Charles of Burgundy, following his urgent request, was granted an interview with Emperor Frederick, who is still living, and he spared no expenses to show his magnificence.[53] They met at Treves and they discussed several matters including a marriage between their children, which eventually took place. After they had been together for several days, the emperor departed without so much as taking leave, to the duke's great shame and humiliation. Since that time there has no longer been any affection between them or their subjects. The Germans despised the duke's pompous manner and speech, which they attributed to pride. The Burgundians, on the other hand, had contempt for the emperor's mean demeanor and his shabby clothes. This had such important consequences that it resulted in the war of Neuss.[54]

I was also present at an interview at Saint-Pol in Artois between the duke of Burgundy and King Edward of England, whose sister he had married; and they both belonged to the same order.[55] They were together two days. The king's servants were quite stirred up, and both sides complained to the duke. He was more partial to one side than the other, and as a result their hate increased. However, he gave assistance to the king and his kingdom and gave him men, money, and ships, for he had been driven out by the count of Warwick. In spite of this good turn, which resulted in the recovery of the kingdom, they never again liked or spoke well of each other.

I have also witnessed the visit which the count palatine of the Rhine [Frederick the Victorious] made to the duke of Burgundy.[56] He remained several days in Brussels where he was lavishly feasted, well

52. Louis XI sent French soldiers to aid the king and queen of Aragon to repress the Catalan revolt of 1462. But Commynes fails to point out that these soldiers simply seized for France the two northernmost counties of Catalonia, Cerdagne and Roussillon, leaving the Aragonese king to deal with the rest of the revolting province as best he could. After Barcelona was pacified, the Aragonese turned against the French to try to recover Cerdagne and Roussillon, and in 1473 they made an alliance with Charles the Bold and regained Roussillon.

53. Frederick III (1452–1493) met Charles at Treves in September, 1473.

54. This war is discussed at length in Book 4 of Commynes' *Memoirs*. See also the brief discussion of it in section 4 of the Introduction.

55. Charles and Edward IV, who met in January, 1471, made each other members of the Order of the Golden Fleece and the Order of the Garter, chivalric orders sponsored by the sovereigns in their respective countries.

56. Frederick and Charles met at Brussels in February, 1467. See p. 119, where Commynes mentions Frederick's aid to Burgundy during the War for the Public Good.

received, honored, and lodged in richly furnished rooms. The duke's servants, however, complained that the Germans were dirty, that they threw their boots on the richly ornamented beds, and that they were not as considerate as we were. And so they had less esteem for him [Frederick] than before they had met him. The Germans, for their part, spoke ill of the Burgundians as if they had been envious of their great pomp. Indeed, they never again liked each other or helped each other since that time.

I also saw Duke Sigismund of Austria come to the duke of Burgundy to sell him the county of Ferrette, near the county of Burgundy, for 100,000 gold florins, since he was not able to defend it against the Swiss. These two lords made a poor impression on each other. Since then Duke Sigismund made peace with the Swiss, took the county of Ferrette away from the duke, and kept his money. This resulted in great hardships for the duke of Burgundy.[57]

At the same time the count of Warwick also came for a visit, and similarly he was not a friend of the duke of Burgundy nor the duke of Burgundy his.[58]

I was present at the meeting which took place at Picquigny between our king and King Edward of England and shall have more to say about it in its proper context.[59] Few of the promises that were made were kept. They negotiated underhandedly. It is true that they no longer had wars, because they were separated by the sea, but there was never any real friendship between them.

To summarize, I do not think that great princes should ever meet if they wish to remain friends, as I said previously. And these are the occasions which cause trouble: the courtiers cannot refrain from speaking of things past, and one or the other is sure to take it amiss. The retinue and attendants of one of the princes cannot help but make a better appearance than those of the other, and this leads to mockery, which is most offensive to those who are the victims of these jests. When the princes are of two different nationalities, their language and dress are different, and what pleases one does not please the other. Besides, one of the princes is likely to have a more courteous and pleasant per-

57. Sigismund had an interview with Charles at Arras in March, 1469, but Louis XI succeeded in reconciling Sigismund with the Swiss in 1474. The Swiss cities and Sigismund joined in the League of Constance, which led to the war that caused Charles's ruin. Contrary to Commynes' statement, however, Sigismund did pay back to Charles the money which he had received in 1469 for the county of Ferrette.

58. The interview took place near Saint-Omer on April 26, 1469.

59. This interview of August 29, 1475, is described by Commynes in chapter 10 of Book 4.

sonality than the other; this brings him honor and compliments and it gratifies him, but it cannot help but reflect on the other prince. The first few days after they have taken leave of each other, all of these nice estimates are whispered in private; later, by force of habit, they are made at the dinner and supper table and then reported to both parties, for there are few comments which can remain secret in this world, especially those which are conveyed by word of mouth.

These are part of the reasons for my point of view, and they are the result of what I have seen and heard on the subject.

9

I have taken a long time before returning to the subject of the state of arrest in which the king believed himself to be at Péronne, of which I spoke earlier, before I digressed to give my advice to princes concerning such meetings. The gates were shut and guards were stationed there, as I said previously, for two or three days. The duke of Burgundy did not see the king and only a few of the king's men entered the castle, by the wicket. None of the king's men were removed from his presence, but few or none of the duke's men went to speak to him or entered his room, at least those who had any authority with him.

On the first day there was great terror and murmuring in the town. But on the second day the duke had calmed down somewhat. He held a council meeting during most of the day and part of the night. The king had overtures made to all those whom he considered to be in a position to help him; and he did not fail to make generous promises. He gave orders to have fifteen thousand gold *écus* distributed among them; but the person who had been assigned to do this kept part of it for himself and acquitted himself most improperly of this task, as the king was to discover later. The king greatly feared those who had formerly served him and who had come with the Burgundian army, as I said before, and had already openly declared themselves for his brother, the duke of Normandy.

At the council meeting of which I spoke, several opinions were expressed. Most of those present advised that the king's safe-conduct should be valid, in view of the fact that he was more than willing to accept peace in the form in which it had been drawn up in writing. Others proposed to have him taken prisoner right away without any ceremony. Some others wanted to send for his brother, the duke of Normandy, with all haste, and to make a peace advantageous for all the princes of France. Those who made this proposition were of the opinion that if it were accepted, the king should be restrained and given guards, because such a great lord could never be freed, or at least not without danger, after having offended him so greatly. This view was so close to being accepted that I saw a man with his boots on, ready to leave; he already had several messages addressed to the duke of Normandy in Brittany and was waiting only for the duke of Burgundy's letters. However, this project was called off.

The king had overtures made to them and offered to give up as hostages the duke of Bourbon, his brother the cardinal, the constable, and several others on condition that after the conclusion of the peace he might be allowed to return to Compiègne; then he would have the Liégeois make reparation for their rebellion, and if they refused, he would declare himself against them. Those whom the king named as hostages offered themselves most willingly, at least in public. I do not know whether their attitude was the same in private. I doubt it. And to tell you the truth, I believe that the king would have left them there and that he would never have returned for them.

That night, which was the third, the duke did not disrobe. He only lay on his bed two or three times and then got up and walked around, for such was his custom when he was troubled. I slept in his room that night and walked with him several times. The next morning he was angrier than ever, made all sorts of threats, and was ready to put some great plan into execution. However, he relented and resolved that if the king would swear to uphold the peace and was willing to accompany him to Liége and to help him avenge the death of my lord [the bishop] of Liége, who was a close relative of his, he would be satisfied. And immediately he proceeded to the king's chamber to announce this decision to him.

The king had been notified of this by some friend,[60] who assured him that he would be safe if he accepted these two points; but, if he refused, he would place himself in such a dangerous position that nothing worse could happen to him. As the duke arrived before him, his voice trembled, owing to his inner agitation and his readiness to become incensed again. He did his best to assume a humble countenance, but his gestures and his words were sharp as he asked the king whether he would consent to honor the peace treaty which had been drawn up and agreed upon and whether he would swear to do it. The king replied that he would. Actually nothing or very little had been modified in the conditions which had been formulated before Paris, concerning the

60. This "friend" was Commynes himself.

duke of Burgundy. As for the duke of Normandy, many favorable changes were made in the clauses pertaining to his allotment, for it was agreed that he should renounce the duchy of Normandy and would receive instead Champagne, Brie, and other adjacent lands as his share.

Then the duke asked the king whether he would accompany him to Liége to help take vengeance for the treacherous way in which they had acted on his instigation. He pointed out the close family ties which had existed between the king and the bishop of Liége, for he was from the house of Bourbon. To these words the king replied that as long as the peace was sworn, and he was very anxious for that, he would indeed be pleased to accompany him to Liége and to bring men with him, as few or as many as he wished. These words pleased the duke exceedingly. Thereupon the peace treaty was produced, and the relic of the true cross, which Charlemagne had worn, and which is called the cross of victory, was taken from the king's coffer, and the peace was sworn. Presently all the bells in town began to ring and everyone rejoiced greatly. The king once kindly did me the honor of saying that I had served well in bringing about this pacification.

The duke of Burgundy immediately wrote to Brittany about the new turn of events and sent a copy of the treaty, so that they might see that he was not withdrawing from their alliance or severing relations between them. And indeed my lord Charles [of France, Louis XI's brother] had received a favorable share, considering that the treaty which they had negotiated a short time before in Brittany had left him only a pension, as you have heard.[61]

10

The day after the conclusion of the peace, the king and the duke proceeded to Cambrai and from there to the province of Liége. It was the beginning of winter and the weather was very bad. The king had brought with him the Scotsmen of his guard and a few of his men-at-arms; but he had about three hundred men-at-arms come and join him.

The duke's army was divided into two sections. One was led by the marshal of Burgundy, who was mentioned earlier, and with him were all the Burgundians and the lords from Savoy of whom I spoke previously, as well as a great number of men from Hainaut, Luxembourg, Namur and Limbourg. The other section was led by the duke. As they

61. See p. 166, where the treaty of Ancenis, dated September 10, 1468, is mentioned as the peace which detached the dukes of Brittany and Normandy from their alliance with Charles the Bold.

approached the city, a meeting was held at which the duke was present. Some believed that it would be advisable to send back part of the army because that city had its gates and walls demolished the preceding year and it could not hope to obtain help from anyone; furthermore, the king in person had come against them and he had asked for certain terms for them which were almost the same as those which the Burgundians were prepared to grant them.

This proposition did not meet with the duke's approval, and it was well that it did not, for never was any man so close to losing everything. It was his suspicion of the king which made him adopt this sensible opinion, for indeed those who had suggested reducing the forces, out of a notion that they were superior in strength, were mistaken. It was an instance of great pride or folly. I have often heard of such opinions being given; military chiefs sometimes do so in order to be considered fearless or because they do not know enough about what they have to do. But when princes are wise, they do not pay attention to such advice. Our king (may he rest in peace) was an expert in such matters; for he was slow and hesitant in undertaking a project, but once he had begun, he pursued it so well that he could hardly help overcoming his adversaries and gaining the upper hand.

Thus it was ordered that the marshal of Burgundy and all those whom I mentioned earlier under his command[62] should take up quarters in the city; if they were refused entrance, they should force their way in, as far as possible, for already envoys from the city were coming and going to negotiate. The above-mentioned officers arrived at Namur. The next day, the king and the duke reached the city and the others left. As they approached the city, these rash people rushed forth against them but were easily beaten—at least a good part of them. The rest withdrew. Their bishop escaped and came to us.

A legate had been sent by the pope to pacify them and to investigate the controversy between the bishop and the people, because they were still under excommunication for the offenses and reasons mentioned earlier. The legate, overstepping his authority, and hoping to make himself bishop of the city, favored the people and suggested that they take up arms and defend themselves, as well as a number of other ridiculous proposals. When he realized in what a dangerous situation the city found itself, however, the legate prepared to flee; but he was taken with all his men, who were about twenty-five in number and well mounted. As soon as the duke heard of this, he sent word to those who had captured him that they should take him away somewhere without telling

62. That is, the lord of Bresse and the others mentioned on p. 168.

him the name of the place, and obtain as much money as they could for his ransom, as if he had been an ordinary merchant; for if the duke were officially notified of this action, he would not be able to keep him a prisoner and would have to give him up, out of respect for the Apostolic See. They did not know enough to do this, but instead had a discussion about it; and those who claimed to have a part in it came to tell him about it publicly at dinner time. Immediately he had the legate put into his hands, took him away from them, had his liberty and possessions restituted and treated him with honor.

The large body of men who were in the vanguard, led by the marshal of Burgundy and the lord of Humbercourt, proceeded directly to the city in hopes of entering it; and owing to their great cupidity, they preferred to plunder it rather than to accept the agreement which was offered. And they did not consider it necessary to wait for the king and the duke of Burgundy, who were seven or eight leagues behind them. They advanced so far that they arrived at one of the suburbs at nightfall and entered by a passage leading to the gate which the Liégeois had partly repaired. They held an informal meeting but could not agree to anything. The darkness of the night fell upon them by surprise. They had not taken up their quarters and there was no site large enough to accommodate them. They were in great disorder. Some people walked around; others called out for their master or their regiment, and shouted the names of their captains.

John de Wilde and some of the other military chiefs of the Liégeois took note of this senseless act and this disorder and took courage. Their disadvantage at having their walls in ruins turned out to be an advantage, for they made sallies from any direction they pleased. They went forth from breaches in their walls and attacked those who were in front, and then by way of the vineyards and hills they ran down pages and valets who were at the end of the suburbs where they had entered, and where many horses were roaming; and a great number of men were killed. Many fled, for night knows no shame. They attacked us so fiercely that they killed almost eight hundred men, including one hundred men-at-arms.

The most worthy and virtuous men of this vanguard kept together (and almost all of them were men-at-arms and persons of good family) and proceeded with their standards directly to the gate, in case a sally should be made there. The soil was very muddy owing to the continuous rain; the men-at-arms were in it up to above their ankles, and everyone was on foot. All of a sudden the remainder of the townspeople decided to rush forth from the gate with large lanterns and bright light.

Our men, who were close by, had four good pieces of artillery; they fired two or three major shots along the main street and killed many people. As a result, the Liégeois withdrew and shut their gates. While this fighting was taking place in the suburb, those who had sallied forth reached some of the carts which they used to protect themselves, for they were near the town and they stayed outside of it from two to six in the morning. However, when daylight came upon us and we were able to see each other, they were repulsed. John de Wilde was wounded in this action and died two days later in Liége as did one or two of their other leaders.

11

Although sallies are sometimes necessary, they are rather dangerous for those who are within a city, for the loss of ten men has more serious consequences for them than the loss of one hundred for the attackers outside their walls. For their number is relatively smaller and they cannot replace them at will; besides, they may lose one of their chief men or leaders, and this is quite often the reason why the remainder of the comrades and soldiers are perfectly willing to abandon their position.

The frightening news [of these encounters] was brought to the duke, who was quartered four or six leagues away from the city. First of all, he was told that everyone had been routed. However, he mounted his horse and proceeded with all his army; he had given orders that the king should not be told the news. As he approached the city from another angle, he was informed that all was well, that there were not so many dead as had been feared, and that no one of distinction had been killed except a knight from Flanders, named my lord of Sengmeur. However, the persons of quality who were there were in great need and in pitiful condition, for they had spent all the previous night on their feet in the mire at the gates of their enemies. Furthermore, some of the fleeing men had returned (I am speaking of foot-soldiers), but they were so discouraged that they did not seem fit to accomplish great feats, and they begged that for God's sake the others should come to their rescue fast, so that part of those within the town would be forced to use up their means of defense, each in his own quarter. And they also requested that supplies should be sent to them, for they had not one morsel of food left.

The duke sent two or three hundred horsemen to them in all haste, to carry as much as the horses could, so as to comfort and encourage the soldiers, and he had them take the few provisions he could obtain. It was two days and almost a full night since they had last eaten or drunk, except for those who had brought a bottle of wine with them, and they had the foulest weather imaginable. Many were wounded, among them the prince of Orange, whom I failed to mention; he proved himself a valiant man, for he refused to leave his post. My lords of Lau and of Urfé both conducted themselves bravely there, but during the preceding night more than ten thousand men had fled.[63]

It was already close to nightfall when the duke was informed of this; and after sending supplies to his men, he returned to the place where his standard was posted and gave a full report of the happenings to the king, who was very pleased about it, because a different turn of events might have been to his disadvantage. Thereupon they marched toward the suburb, and many worthy men and men-at-arms joined the archers to enter the suburb and take up quarters there. Among those present were the bastard of Burgundy, who had an important commanding position by the duke's appointment, the lord of Ravenstein, the count of Roussy, son of the constable, and several other high-ranking officers. Quarters were easily established in this suburb right up to the gate, which the townspeople had repaired, as they had the other. The duke took up quarters in the middle of the suburb, and the king stayed for that night in a large rural domain kept up by tenant farmers; it was very spacious and well furnished, and was situated a quarter-league away from the town. In the vicinity was a strong guard composed partly of his men and partly of ours.

Liége is situated in a fertile country with hills and valleys; the river Meuse runs through the middle of it. The city is about the same size as Rouen.[64] At the time it was a densely populated city. From the gate where we were posted to the one where the vanguard was placed was only a short distance, provided one went through the town, but by the outside it was at least three leagues, owing to the sloughs and difficult paths; besides, it was the middle of winter. Their walls were all demolished and the townspeople might sally forth from any direction they pleased. There was only a little ditch; there had never been a real moat, for the foundation consists of very hard and firm rock. On the first night of the duke of Burgundy's stay in their suburb, our vanguard was very much relieved, for the forces which were inside were already divided into two sections. At about midnight we had a

63. Most editors of Commynes change "ten thousand" to read "two thousand." Even the latter estimate is probably too high.
64. Rouen was next in size to Paris in France at the time.

serious alarm. Immediately the duke of Burgundy rushed to the street, and shortly afterwards the king and the constable also arrived; they had been quick to come, considering the distance which they had to travel. Some cried out: "They are coming forth from such and such a gate." Others made all sorts of frightened comments, and the weather was so unpleasant and obscure that it contributed to the people's terror. The duke of Burgundy was never lacking in courage but was frequently deficient in organization. And indeed he did not maintain at this time as good a countenance as many of his men would have wished, considering that the king was present. The king then took it upon himself to issue orders and said to my lord the constable: "Proceed to such and such a place with whatever forces you have, for if the enemy should come, it will be from that direction." And to judge from his words and his countenance, the king appeared to be very brave and wise, and to be a person who had been involved in similar affairs previously. However, nothing happened, and the King and the duke of Burgundy returned to their quarters.

The next morning the king moved to the suburbs and took lodgings in a little house adjacent to the one in which the duke of Burgundy was staying. With him were his guard of one hundred Scotsmen; and his men-at-arms took quarters in a village near him.

The duke of Burgundy had strong suspicions that the king might enter the town, or that he might flee before taking it, or even that, being so close to him, he might do him some bodily harm. However, there was a large barn between the two houses, and the duke had three hundred of his very best men-at-arms stationed there. They broke down part of the sides of the barn so that they could sally forth more easily. And they kept an eye on the king's house, which was adjacent. This little party lasted eight days, for on the eighth day the town was taken, and neither the duke nor anyone else disarmed before they had accomplished this.

The night before the surrender a meeting was held, at which it was decided to assail the town the next morning, which was a Sunday, the thirtieth of October, 1468; it was agreed with our vanguard that on a given signal—when they would hear the firing of one bombard shot and two powerful serpentine shots immediately after, without further firing—they should make a strong attack, for the duke would do the same from his side. The signal was to be given at about eight in the morning. The night before, as it had been agreed, the duke of Burgundy disarmed, which he had not done yet, and had all his men also disarm, especially those who were in the barn, so that they would be refreshed. Shortly after, as if they had been warned of our plan, the Liégeois decided to sally forth on this side, as they had done previously on the other side.

12

Observe how a very great and powerful prince can suddenly fall into disadvantage, through the action of very few enemies; that is why all undertakings should be well weighed and discussed before they are put into effect.

Within the whole city there was not a single soldier except those from their territories. They had no longer knights or gentlemen with them, for the few whom they had had formerly had been killed or wounded two or three days before. They had neither gates, nor walls, nor ditches, nor a single piece of usable artillery. Their forces consisted merely of townspeople together with seven or eight hundred foot-soldiers from a small mountain situated at the rear of Liége, called the territory of Franchimont; among the townspeople the natives of that region have always enjoyed the reputation of being very valiant.

They despaired of obtaining help, since the king in person was there against them, and so they decided to make a general sally and to leave everything to chance, for they considered that all was lost for them. It was concluded that six hundred men from Franchimont, all the best they had, should sally forth from two openings in their walls which were behind the duke of Burgundy's quarters. They had as their guides the owners of the two houses in which the king and the duke of Burgundy were lodged. They could come through a large cavity in a rock rather close to the houses of these two princes without attracting attention, provided that they did not make noise. Although there were some scouts along the way, they were confident that they would kill them or that they would arrive at the houses [of the princes] at the same time as the scouts. They assumed that the two hosts would take them directly to their houses, where the two princes were lodged, and that they would not waste time anywhere else. Thus they would surprise them so suddenly that they would be able to kill them or capture them before their men could come to their rescue. Besides, they would not have to retreat very far, and if worse came to worse and they had to die in order to assure the success of the undertaking, they would accept death willingly, for they considered themselves entirely lost in any case, as I said.

In addition, they gave orders that with a loud cry all the townspeople should sally forth from the gate which led straight into the main street of our suburb, hoping to discomfit all who were quartered there. They were confident that they would obtain a great victory, or if worse came to worse, a most glorious death. If they had had one thousand first-rate men-at-arms with them, the success of their enterprise might have been assured. As things were, they almost reached their goal.

According to their plans, the six hundred men from Franchimont came forth from the openings in their walls; and I believe it was not yet ten o'clock at night. They caught most of the scouts and killed them. Among them, three gentlemen from the house of the duke of Burgundy lost their lives in this action. And if they had proceeded directly without making noise until they reached the place where they wanted to be, they would have been able to kill the two princes lying on their beds without any difficulty. Behind the duke's house was a pavilion in which the present duke of Alençon had taken up quarters; and my lord of Craon was with him. They stopped there for a while, thrust their pikes through the tent and killed a valet. The army was alerted, and as a result a few of the men took arms or at least got up. They left their tents and ran directly to the two houses of the king and the duke of Burgundy. The barn I mentioned earlier, in which the duke had placed three hundred men-at-arms, was adjacent to the two houses; the Liégeois amused themselves here by making great thrusts with their pikes through the wall openings which had been made in order to sally forth. All these gentlemen had disarmed less than two hours before, as I said, in order to be refreshed for the next day's assault. Thus they found them all, or almost all, disarmed. However, some of them had fitted themselves with their cuirasses when they heard the noise from my lord of Alençon's pavilion and they attacked the invaders from the doors and the holes which they had made, and this resulted in the two princes being saved, for this delay gave many of the men time to arm themselves and rush forth into the street.

I was lying in the duke of Burgundy's room, which was very small, with two gentlemen of his bedchamber; above us were only twelve archers who were on guard, fully clothed and armed, and who were playing dice. His main guard was at a good distance, toward the gate of the town. Meanwhile the duke's host arrived with a group of Liégeois and came to assail his own house, in which the duke was lodged; and this happened so suddenly that we hardly had time to fit the duke with his cuirass and to put a helmet on his head. We went downstairs quickly with the intention of rushing to the street. We found our archers busy defending the door and the windows against the Liégeois; and there was a terrible noise in the street. Some cried: "Burgundy!" and others: "Long live the king!" and "Kill!" It took longer than the time to say two paternosters before these archers and we were able to make a sally from the house.

We did not know in what condition the king was, or whether he was on our side or not, and this put us in a perplexing situation. As soon as we were out of the house with two or three torches, we found some other torches and we saw people fighting around us; but it did not last long, for people were coming from all directions to the duke's house. The first man to be killed from the enemy's side was the duke's host, but he did not die immediately and I heard him speak. All of his comrades, or at least most of them, were also killed. The king's house was also assailed and his host entered, but he was killed by the Scotsmen, who proved themselves excellent soldiers, for they did not budge from the feet of their master, and shot many arrows, with which they wounded more Burgundians than Liégeois. Those who had been ordered to sally forth from the gate did so, but they found a strong guard already assembled, which repulsed them in a short time because they did not prove to be as fine soldiers as the others.

As soon as these people were thus repelled, the king and the duke had a meeting. Since they saw many dead men about them, they feared that they might be their own soldiers. But upon investigation it was found that they had few dead but many wounded. It is certain that if the Liégeois had not spent time in these two places I mentioned, and especially at the barn, where they met with resistance, and if they had directly followed the two hosts who were their guides, they would have killed the king and the duke of Burgundy, and probably discomfited the rest of the army. Each of these two princes retired to his lodgings, extremely astounded at this daring enterprise, and a council meeting was soon held to discuss what should be done the next day in relation to the assault which had been decided earlier. The king was greatly perplexed. He feared that if the duke failed to take the town by assault he would pay the consequences for it and would be arrested or made a prisoner, for the duke would fear that if he left, he might wage war against him from the other side.

Thus you can see the miserable condition of these princes, who could not by any means have faith in each other. The two of them had made a final peace less than fifteen days earlier and had sworn most solemnly to preserve it loyally. However, trust could not be found here by any means.

13

In order to alleviate his fears, one hour after he had retired to his lodgings, after the sally of which I spoke, the king sent for some of the duke's close advisers, who had attended the meeting, and asked them for the results. They informed him that they had resolved to assail the town the next day in the manner in which had been decided earlier. The king had his doubts about the success of the plan and made some very wise observations which greatly pleased the duke's officers, for everyone was very apprehensive of the assault, owing to the great number of people in the town and the evidence of great courage which they had given less than two hours before; the duke's men would have been happy to postpone the action for a few days or to negotiate an agreement with them. They came to the duke and reported this to him. I was present. They told him of all the king's doubts as well as their own, but they attributed them all to the king, because they feared that the duke might take it amiss, coming from them.

The duke did not take it well and replied that the king was only trying to save the townspeople. Besides, their plan could not miscarry because the Liégeois did not have the means to defend themselves; they had no artillery nor walls, and whatever they had repaired at their stations was already demolished again. There should be no further delay, and the assault should take place in the morning, as it had been decided. If the king wished to go to Namur and stay there until the town was taken, he might do so, but he himself would not leave the premises until the outcome of this undertaking.

This answer did not please any of those present, for everyone feared this sally. The king was informed of this resolution, not bluntly but as gently as possible. He understood the purpose behind these words and said that he did not wish to go to Namur but would be with the others the next day. In my opinion, if he had wished to escape that night, he could have done so successfully, for he had with him one hundred archers of his guard, several gentlemen of his household, and almost three hundred men-at-arms. But in all probability, since his honor was at stake, he did not want to be accused of cowardice.

The men rested a little as they waited for daylight, all of them armed; and several went to confession, for the enterprise seemed very perilous. As soon as it was broad day and the hour of the assault approached, which was eight in the morning, as I said before, the duke had the bombard and the two serpentine shots fired in order to notify the vanguard who were on the other side of town, very far from us if they were to be reached from the outside, as I explained before, although through the town the distance was not very great. They heard the signal and immediately prepared to assail the town. The duke's trumpets began to sound and the standards to move toward the wall, accompanied by those who were to follow them.

The king was in the middle of the street, well attended, for all of his three hundred men-at-arms were with him, as well as his guard, and several lords and gentlemen from his household. As we came so close that we thought our pikes would touch, we encountered no resistance at all. Only two or three men were on guard, for they had all gone to dinner, thinking that since it was Sunday we would not attack them; and in every house we found the table set. The common people are not usually redoubtable unless they are commanded by a leader whom they respect and fear; however, at certain times they can be very dangerous in their fury.

Already before this assault, the Liégeois were very exhausted, owing to the men whom they had lost at their two sallies, in which all their leaders had been killed, as well as the great fatigue which they had endured for eight consecutive days; everyone had to be on guard, for they were enclosed on all sides, as you have heard. In my opinion, they thought that they might have a day of rest because it was Sunday; but things turned out differently, and as I said, hardly anyone was there to defend the city on the side from which we attacked, and even fewer on the side from which the Burgundians of our vanguard made their assault, together with the others whom I mentioned earlier. They entered before us. They killed few persons, for all the people fled by the bridge over the Meuse into the Ardennes, and from there to places where they hoped to be safe. On the side of town where we were, I saw only three men and one woman dead. I believe that less than two hundred persons in all were killed and that all the rest fled or hid in the churches and the houses.

The king marched at his own pace, for he could see that there was no resistance and that the whole army entered the town at both ends. I believe there were forty thousand men. The duke had advanced farther into the city, but he turned back hastily to meet the king, whom he had led as far as the palace. Thereupon the duke returned to the great church of Saint Lambert, which his men were trying to enter by force to take prisoners and loot. Although he had already posted guards from his household, they could not subdue the soldiers who were assailing the two doors. I know that when the duke arrived, he killed a man with his own hands, and I saw it. Thereupon the soldiers withdrew, and the church was not plundered; but eventually the men inside were taken, as well as all the goods.

Of the other churches, and they were numerous (for I have heard my lord of Humbercourt, who knew the city well, claim that there were as many Masses said there every day as in Rome), most were plundered under the pretense of taking prisoners. I did not enter any church except the principal one, but I was told about it and I saw traces of it. For a long time afterwards, the pope issued severe censures against those who possessed anything which belonged to the churches of the city unless they returned it, and the duke delegated several officers to comb the whole region to see that the pope's ordinance was carried out.

After the taking and plundering of the city at about noon, the duke returned to the palace. The king had already eaten; he expressed great joy at this victory and highly lauded the duke's great courage and boldness. He realized that this would be reported to him. His heart desired nothing except to return to his kingdom. After dinner he and the duke had a festive meeting, and if the king had been unsparing in his praise of the duke's deeds in his absence, he was even more generous in his approval in his presence, and the duke took pleasure in it.

I shall digress a little to speak of the poor people who were fleeing from the city, in order to confirm certain statements which I made at the beginning of these memoirs, where I mentioned the hardships which I have seen befall people after a lost battle or even a much less serious loss. These wretched people were escaping through the Ardennes region with their wives and children. A knight who lived there and had been on their side until then discomfited many of them, and in order to obtain the good graces of the conqueror, he wrote the duke of Burgundy about it and reported the number of dead and prisoners greater than it actually was (although it was impressive enough as it stood) and thus made a settlement with him. Others fled to Mézières on the Meuse, which belongs to the kingdom [of France]. Two or three leaders of these bands were taken there; one of them was named Madoulet. They were brought to the duke, who had them executed. Some of these people died of hunger, cold, and lack of sleep.

14

Four or five days after the taking of Liége, the king began to employ the services of those whom he considered his friends and had them try to influence the duke, so that he would let him return home. He himself also mentioned the matter tactfully to the duke, saying that if he could be of any further assistance he would be glad to do anything in his power to help, but that if his presence was no longer necessary, he would like to go to Paris and have their treaty recorded in the court of Parlement; for it is the custom in France to record all of the settlements there; otherwise they are not valid; however, the kings still have much say in the matter.[65]

Furthermore, he asked the duke that they might have another interview the next summer in Burgundy and enjoy each other's company for one month. Finally the duke agreed to his departure, although somewhat reluctantly. He had the peace treaty reread to the king, offering to have it altered in case he regretted anything, and made some mild apology to the king for having brought him there. He further asked the king to allow a new article to be inserted in the treaty in favor of my lords of Lau and of Urfé, and in favor of Poncet de Rivière, to the effect that the territories and positions which they had enjoyed before the war should be returned to them.

This request displeased the king, for these men were not from his side and he did not see why they should be provided for in the peace treaty, since they served my lord Charles, his brother, and not him. So to this request the king replied that he would be delighted to approve it if the duke would make the same provision for my lords of Nevers and Croy. So the duke said nothing further. The king's answer was shrewd; for the duke hated these men to such a degree and held so much of their property that he would never have consented to add such a clause. The king declared that he did not wish to have anything changed in the other points and that he would confirm everything which had been sworn at Péronne. Thus it was agreed that he might depart, and the king took leave of the duke, who escorted him about a half-league farther.

At the moment of their separation, the king asked him: "If by chance my brother, who is in Brittany, should not be content with the share I am giving him for your sake, what would you have me do?" The duke replied immediately, without realizing what he was saying: "If he refuses this appanage but you see to it that he is satisfied, I shall leave it up to the two of you." This question and answer were to have important consequences, as you shall hear shortly. Thus the king left as he had wished it; he was escorted out of the duke's territories by my

65. The Parlement of Paris, by entering or refusing to enter on its register all laws and treaties involving France, determined constitutionality or unconstitutionality of those laws and treaties.

lords of Cordes and of Aimeries, the latter grand bailiff of Hainaut.

The duke remained in Liége. It is true that the city was cruelly treated in all sorts of ways, but the townspeople had likewise resorted to all sorts of abuses against the duke's subjects since his grandfather's time without ever honoring any promises or settlements that had been made between them. This [1468] was the fifth year that the duke had come in person and made peace, and invariably they broke it the following year. They had already been excommunicated for many years, owing to their cruel behavior toward their bishop, but they never respected or obeyed the commandments of the church in relation to this conflict.

As soon as the king had gone, the duke with a few of his men decided to proceed to Franchimont, which is a little beyond Liége; it is rugged country, hilly and full of woods. Their best soldiers come from this region, particularly those who had made the sallies I mentioned earlier. Before he left the city, many of the poor people who had hidden in the houses when the town was taken, and had afterwards been made prisoners, were drowned. Furthermore, it was decided to burn the city, which had always been very populous; orders were given to set fire to it in three different places. Three or four thousand foot-soldiers from the territory of Limbourg, who were their neighbors and were about the same in customs and language, were recruited to effect this desolation and to protect the churches.

First of all, they demolished a large bridge on the river Meuse, and they posted large forces to defend the houses of the canons, which were in the vicinity of the principal church, so that they might keep their lodgings and be able to celebrate the divine office. Similarly, other soldiers were organized to protect the other churches. After giving these orders, the duke left for the territory of Franchimont, of which I spoke. As soon as he was out of the city, he saw many houses on fire on the other side, beyond the river, and he went to take quarters four leagues from there. It was dreadful to hear the noise of the houses falling and crumbling in the town that night, for we heard it as clearly, being four leagues away, as if we had been there on the spot. I do not know whether it was because the wind was blowing in our direction or because we were camping on the banks of the river.

The next day, after the duke was gone, those who had remained in the town continued with their destruction, according to their orders; but all the churches were saved, with a few exceptions, as well as more than three hundred houses belonging to the ecclesiastics. This is the reason why the city was repopulated so soon, for many people came there to take refuge with the priests.

Because of the severe cold and frost, most of the duke's men were forced to proceed on foot to the territory of Franchimont, which consists entirely of villages and has no walled towns. The duke stayed for five or six days in a small valley, at a village called Polleur. His army was divided into two groups, so that they might destroy the country faster. He had all the houses burned, and all the iron-mills of the region (which were their chief means of livelihood) broken. They searched for the people among the large forests where they had hidden with their possessions; and many of them were killed or taken, and the men-at-arms gained much loot.

I saw incredible things resulting from the cold. One gentleman lost the use of his foot and never regained it; two fingers fell off from the hand of a page. I saw a woman who had died of cold, together with her newborn child. For three days the wine which was distributed to those who requested it at the duke's headquarters, was dealt out by chopping it with an axe, for it was frozen in the casks, and it was necessary to cut the block of ice, which was solid, into smaller pieces, which the people put in their hats or in baskets, as they pleased. I could tell of many other strange happenings, but they would take too long to write down. Hunger forced us to flee in great haste after having remained there eight days; and the duke proceeded to Namur and from there to Brabant, where he was well received.

15

After the king had taken leave of the duke, he returned with great joy to his kingdom and did not stir against the duke on account of the way in which he had been treated at Péronne and Liége, and he seemed to bear everything patiently. It is true that since then great wars were fought between them, but not very soon, and the matter I spoke about earlier [Louis' desire to recover the Somme towns] was not the cause of this, although it might have contributed to it, for the peace was just about what it would have been if the king had made it at Paris [instead of at Péronne]. But the duke of Burgundy, by the advice of his officers, wanted to extend his boundaries; and certain shrewd moves were made to re-establish discord, as I shall explain when it is time.

My lord Charles of France, the king's only brother, and formerly duke of Normandy, who was informed of the treaty of Péronne and of the share that was allotted to him, sent a request to the king, begging him to agree to carry out the terms of the treaty and to give to him the lands which he had promised. The king communicated with him about this question, and several messages passed between them. The duke of

Burgundy also sent ambassadors to my lord Charles, requesting him not to accept any other appanage except Champagne and Brie, which were granted to him by his interposition. He reminded him of the great affection which he had shown for him, although Charles had abandoned him; the duke of Burgundy had not wished to retaliate, as he had seen, and had included the duke of Brittany in the peace treaty as his ally. Furthermore, he had the envoys point out to him that the situation of Champagne and Brie was advantageous to both of them, and if the king by chance were inclined to deprive him of his rights, he could count on Burgundy's support at a moment's notice; for the two territories were adjacent.[66] Besides, his share was rather valuable, for he would collect taxes and subsidies, whereas the king would retain only suzerainty and appellate jurisdiction.

My lord Charles [of France] was the kind of person who did nothing or very little on his own initiative; in every affair he was managed and led by others, although he was twenty-five years old or more.

Thus the winter passed; it was well advanced by the time the king left us. Messengers were sent back and forth on the question of the distribution of the land, for the king had no intention of giving up the territory which he had promised. He did not want his brother and the duke of Burgundy to be such close neighbors; and so he negotiated with his brother to try to make him accept Guyenne and La Rochelle, which comprise almost the whole of Aquitaine and which are much more valuable than Brie and Champagne.[67] My lord Charles was afraid of displeasing the duke of Burgundy; he also feared that if he agreed to the proposal and the king failed to keep his word, he would lose his friend as well as his appanage and would find himself in a difficult situation.

The king, who was more skillful at negotiating such treaties than any other prince of his time, saw that he was wasting his time unless he won over to his side those who influenced his brother. He appealed to Odet d'Aydie, lord of Lescun, later count of Comminges, who was born and married in the territory of Guyenne, and requested him to

66. Charles the Bold perhaps calculated as follows. If Louis' brother could obtain Champagne and Brie, then the whole eastern frontier of France would be hostile to the king, from Savoy (Burgundy's ally) and Burgundy in the south to Flanders and the Somme towns in the north. Having the king's brother as a neighbor, the duke of Burgundy could count on powerful aid in case the king tried to move against his territories, for such a move would automatically jeopardize the position of Charles of France, too. Note Charles the Bold's similar calculation in relation to Normandy, mentioned earlier by Commynes.

67. Guyenne and La Rochelle in southwest France posed no strategic threat to Louis, nor would their lord be of much use as an ally to Duke Charles.

persuade his master to accept this share, which was larger than the one he had originally asked for, and to agree that they should be friends, as becomes brothers; he and his servants would find this to their advantage, but especially himself. The king assured them that he would not fail to hand over to him the above-mentioned territory. Thus my lord Charles was won over to the king's point of view and accepted Guyenne as his share, to the great dissatisfaction of the duke of Burgundy and his ambassadors who were on the premises.

And this is the reason why Cardinal Balue, bishop of Angers, and the bishop of Verdun were imprisoned [by Louis XI]. For the cardinal wrote to my lord of Guyenne, exhorting him not to accept any other share than the one which the duke of Burgundy had obtained for him by the peace of Péronne, which the king had sworn and promised to honor. He pointed out several things about this matter which he considered necessary, but which were contrary to the king's wishes and intentions. Thus my lord Charles became duke of Guyenne in the year 1469 and took possession of this territory, together with the government of La Rochelle. The king and he had an interview and they remained together for a long time.

Only when Commynes moralizes do "little people" enter his Memoirs. For the rest, he is concerned with the bargaining and trickery of "the great" and is insensitive to the economic and social conditions influencing political activity. On his own manors in west-central France, Commynes must have frequently figured in scenes like this during lulls in political activity (Louis XI sometimes visited Argenton) and after his fall from favor at court.

BOOK THREE

The War over the Somme River Towns, 1470-1472

1

In the year 1470 a desire to revenge himself upon the duke of Burgundy took hold of the king. It seemed to him that the time had come and so he bargained secretly and listened to proposals for getting the towns on the river Somme, such as Amiens, Saint-Quentin, and Abbeville, to turn against the duke and to call in his men-at-arms and station them in these towns, for great princes, or at least the wise ones, always look for a good pretense and one which is not too obvious. So in order to show how such intrigues are carried on in France, I shall relate how this affair was managed, for both the king and the duke were disappointed as a result, and war started anew; it lasted a full thirteen or fourteen years and was very cruelly and fiercely fought.[68]

It is true that the king was very anxious for these towns to rebel; and he tried to justify his conduct by pretending that the duke of Burgundy had extended the limits of his territories further than the treaty allowed. On this account several ambassadors were sent back and forth from one court to the other; and time and time again they transacted bargains as they passed through these towns which had no garrisons, since the whole kingdom was at peace on the side bordering the duke of Burgundy's territories as well as on the side of the duke of Brittany's domains. And my lord of Guyenne [Louis XI's brother Charles] was apparently on friendly terms with the king. The latter, however, had no intention of starting another war merely to recapture one or two of these towns; but he aimed at stirring up a grand rebellion in all the territories of the duke of Burgundy, and hoped thereby to make himself master of all these lands.

In order to please him, many persons took part in these bargaining transactions and reported them to him as much more advanced than they actually were. One man flattered himself that he had practically gained

68. As indicated on p. 193, Commynes believes that the Franco-Burgundian quarrels between 1470 and Louis XI's death in 1483 were started not because of Louis' desire to regain the Somme towns but because of the intrigues of third parties (see n. 72, p. 205). This interpretation exonerates Louis, Commynes' "master."

a town for the king; another claimed that he would take away some of the most important persons from the duke's household and have them turn against their master. But all this was only partly true. And if the king had only considered what might happen, he would not have broken the peace, nor would he have started another war, although he certainly had reason to complain about the treatment he had received at Péronne; for he had the treaty of peace issued in Paris three months after he had returned to his kingdom. And he began to create this disturbance with some fear, but his desires pushed him on.

Here are some of the shrewd moves that were made. The count of Saint-Pol, constable of France, a very wise man, as well as several of the servants of the duke of Guyenne and a few others, preferred to see these two princes at war rather than at peace with each other for two reasons: first, they were afraid that the great revenues which they enjoyed might be diminished if peace were to last, for the constable had four hundred men-at-arms who were paid at every muster, without further control from the king,[69] and he received more than thirty thousand francs per annum in addition to the salary of his office and the income from many fine places which he possessed; secondly, they wanted to make trouble for the king and said among themselves that his nature was such that if he were not at war with some important ruler outside of his kingdom, he would be likely to find something to quarrel about with his attendants, servants, and officers; for his mind could never be at rest.

And for these reasons which I have explained they did everything in their power to persuade the king to start another war. The constable offered to take Saint-Quentin any time one wished, for his lands were in its vicinity. He also claimed that he possessed many informers in Flanders and in Brabant and that he would induce several towns to rebel against the duke [of Burgundy]. The duke of Guyenne, who was present, and all the principal governors of his lands willingly offered to serve the king in this dispute and to bring with them four or five hundred men-at-arms from the duke of Guyenne's regular army. But their purpose was not what the king believed it to be but quite the opposite, as you will hear.

The king always wanted to proceed with great solemnity on all occasions, and so he convoked the three estates at Tours during March

69. Commynes is suggesting—and his suggestion was, in fact, frequently the case —that Saint-Pol's regiment contained less than four hundred soldiers when mustered, since the king did not have a representative present to check affairs. Saint-Pol would then pocket the pay of the missing soldiers himself.

and April, 1470, which he had never done before nor was to do since, but he only summoned certain given persons whom he thought would not oppose his intentions.[70] There he pointed out several of the duke of Burgundy's enterprises against the crown, and had my lord the count of Eu come forth as plaintiff against the duke for withholding from him Saint-Valéry and other lands which belonged to the jurisdiction of Abbeville and the county of Ponthieu, and for not doing him any justice about this. The duke had done this because a small man-of-war from the town of Eu had taken a vessel from the province of Flanders, although the count of Eu had offered to make reparation for this. Furthermore, the duke wanted to force the count to render homage and swear fealty to him against all persons; and this the count would not do under any circumstances because it would have been against the king's authority. At this assembly several lawyers from the Parlement and elsewhere were present, and it was decided, according to the king's intention, that the duke would be summoned to appear in person before the Parlement in Paris.[71] The king knew perfectly well that he would give an arrogant answer or do something against the authority of that court; and so the occasion for making war against him would be still greater.

The duke was in Ghent, on his way to Mass, when he was summoned by a process-server from the French Parlement, and he was greatly astounded and malcontent. He ordered the process-server to be arrested; the man was kept for several days, and finally set free.

Thus you see the measures which were taken to attack the duke. He was warned of this, however, and enlisted a great number of men at household wages, as they put it; this was a token payment which they received to remain at home, ready to serve at the first notice. However, they appeared in places for the muster once a month and were paid. This situation lasted for three or four months, and the duke grew weary of this state of affairs; and so he disbanded his soldiers and erased all fears from his heart, for the king often sent envoys to him. And then the duke left for Holland. He had no regular soldiers in readiness to serve, nor garrisons in his frontier towns, and it was to his disadvantage.

While he was in Holland, he was warned by the late Duke John of

70. Commynes perhaps confuses here two assemblies held at Tours. The first was an Estates-General held in 1468, but that of 1470 was an Assembly of Notables only. In any case, the assembly of 1470 was not Louis' only convocation of representatives of the nation.

71. Since the Parlement of Paris was the highest court of France, the chief vassals of the crown, like the duke of Burgundy, were responsible to it for adjudication of their feudal duties.

Bourbon that war would soon be waged against him in Burgundy as well as in Picardy, and that the king had many informers there and even in his very household. The duke, who was without soldiers (for he had disbanded his army, of which I spoke earlier, and had sent all his men home), was rather astounded at this news; therefore he immediately crossed the sea and proceeded to the Artois and directly to Hesdin. There he began to suspect some of his servants and also the intrigues being carried on in the towns of which I have spoken. It was some time before he took measures to counteract this because he did not believe everything that was reported to him; but eventually he sent for two of the principal dignitaries of Amiens, whom he suspected of having had a hand in these agreements [with Louis XI's representatives]. They justified themselves so skillfully, however, that he let them go.

Shortly afterwards some of his attendants left his household and passed over to the king's service; these included the bastard Baldwin [son of Philip the Good] and others. This made the duke fear that more would follow their example. He issued a proclamation that all his men should arm, but few took it seriously, because it was the beginning of winter and the duke had arrived from Holland only a few days before.

2

Two days after the duke's servants had deserted him, which was in December, 1470, my lord the constable entered Saint-Quentin and had the townspeople swear allegiance to the king.

By this time the duke realized that his affairs were not working out well, for he was without an army, because he had sent his officers to recruit men in his own territory. However, with the few men he was able to assemble and only four or five hundred horsemen, he proceeded to Doullens, intending to keep Amiens from declaring itself for the opposite side. He had not been there five or six days before the people of Amiens began to negotiate, for the king's army was close by and even showed itself before the town. They at first refused entrance to the army because part of the townspeople held out for the duke, who had sent his artillery sergeant to them; and if he had had enough men with him to be able to enter in person, he would never have lost the town. But he did not dare enter with such a small escort, although many townsmen pressed him to do so. When those who were against him saw his dissimulation and that he was not strong, they executed their plans and put the king's troops in the town. The people of Abbeville intended to follow their example, but my lord of Cordes entered the town on behalf of the duke and saw to it that they did not carry out their design.

Amiens is only five small leagues away from Doullens. Therefore the duke had to withdraw as soon as he learned that the king's men had entered Amiens. He proceeded to Arras in great haste and alarm, fearing that more of the same actions would take place elsewhere, for he realized that he was surrounded by relatives and friends of the constable. On the other hand, since the bastard Baldwin had passed over to the king's side, the duke began to suspect that Anthony, the grand bastard of Burgundy, his brother, might do the same. However, soldiers began arriving where he was little by little. The king believed that he had the upper hand in these affairs because he believed whatever the constable and the rest of them told him concerning the informers whom they were supposed to have in the duke's territories. Had it not been for these hopes, he would have preferred not to undertake anything yet.

It is time for me to finish explaining what moved the constable, the duke of Guyenne, and his principal servants to act as they did (although the duke of Guyenne had benefited from so many good turns, help, and many courtesies from the duke of Burgundy) and what advantages they hoped to obtain by instigating a war between these two great princes, who were living in peace, and between their subjects. I have already said something about it and explained that it was to keep a better hold on their positions and to prevent the king from finding time to quarrel with them, should there be peace. But this was not the principal reason. The duke of Guyenne and his adherents had long hoped for a marriage between him and [Mary] the only daughter and heiress of the duke of Burgundy; for he had no sons. Several overtures had been made to him concerning this marriage, and he had always pretended to agree to it, but he had never wanted to conclude the arrangement and still entertained propositions from other sources.

Now observe what sort of trick these people used to try to arrive at their designs and force the duke to give his daughter [to the duke of Guyenne], for as soon as the two towns were taken and the duke of Burgundy had returned to Arras, where he was raising as many soldiers as he could, the duke of Guyenne secretly sent a man to him, carrying a message of three lines in his own hand, folded as closely as possible, and enclosed in a small ball of wax, which contained these words: "Do your best to satisfy your subjects and do not worry, for you will find friends."

The duke of Burgundy, who at first was greatly alarmed, sent a messenger to the constable, begging him to spare him and not to pursue this war so fiercely, since it was begun without any formal declaration. The constable was extremely pleased with this message and believed he had the duke in his power, since he had recourse to him in this unpleasant situation. The constable sent only a brief answer to the effect that he realized that the duke was in great danger and that he could think of only one solution to escape from it, which was that he should give his daughter in marriage to the duke of Guyenne. If he did this, he would be supplied with a large number of soldiers, and the duke of Guyenne and many other lords would declare themselves for him; the constable himself would return Saint-Quentin to him and pass over to his side. Without this marriage, however, and without the duke of Guyenne's declaration, he would not dare do this, for the king was too powerful, and had his affairs well managed, and had many informers in the duke of Burgundy's territories; he made other similar comments to add to the duke's fears.

I have never known of any man who came to a good end after having tried to frighten his master or any great prince with whom he had dealings and to keep him in subjection, as you will see from what befell the constable. For although the king was his master at the time, most of his possessions and his children were in the duke's territories. However, he always used the method of pitting one against the other and keeping them in mutual fear of each other; and it eventually turned out to his disadvantage. Although everyone tries to free himself from subjection and fear, and hates those who keep him in that state, no one can compare with princes in this respect, for I have never known any who did not have a mortal hatred for those who attempted to maintain them in such a condition.

After the duke of Burgundy had heard the constable's reply, he realized that he could not expect any friendship from him and that he was the principal conductor of this war. Thereupon he conceived an implacable hatred of him, which never left his heart, especially when he considered that the constable had tried to frighten him in order to compel him to give his daughter in marriage. Already he had regained some of his courage and had assembled a considerable army. You can see from the duke of Guyenne's message as well as the constable's that they had discussed the matter beforehand and acted in concert, for shortly afterwards, the duke of Brittany sent him a communication couched in similar or even more frightening language, and then he let my lord of Lescun take one hundred Breton men-at-arms with him to be put at the king's service. Thus one may conclude that the war was undertaken to force the duke of Burgundy to consent to that marriage and that the king was being duped when he was advised to start this war. Furthermore, the informers they claimed to have in the duke's territories were pure invention or practically so.[72]

However, throughout this whole expedition the king was very well served by the constable, who had great hatred for the duke; and he knew that it was reciprocated. Similarly, the duke of Guyenne served the king well in this war, and he brought with him a large body of soldiers; therefore the duke of Burgundy's affairs were in a dangerous state. However, if at the beginning of this quarrel which I have described, he had accepted to give his daughter in marriage to the duke of Guyenne, that duke, as well as the constable and many other of their partisans would have turned against the king and done everything in their power to weaken him. But no matter how wisely men can deliberate on these matters, it is God who concludes things at His own pleasure.

3

You have been sufficiently informed of the reasons for this war, and how the two princes were first deceived into waging war against each other without either of them understanding the motives behind this enterprise, as a result of the marvelous skill of those who were managing the affair; and one could well apply to them the saying that one half of the world does not know how the other half governs itself.

Now all the things which I mentioned in the preceding chapters came to pass in a matter of very few days. Less than fifteen days after

---

72. Karl Bittmann, *op. cit.*, I, 440 ff., has shown that Commynes' "conspiracy theory" of the causes of the war over the Somme towns is false. As in the case of the supposed conspiracies of Brézé and Campobasso discussed in the Introduction, Commynes' belief in conspiracy here grows in part out of his feelings of dependency upon "the great": the constable Saint-Pol, "principal conductor" of this conspiracy, is doomed because he "tried to frighten his master." Commynes saw that Saint-Pol's attempt to play an independent political role, almost forced upon him by the placement of his territories, was a mistake. But he relates this mistake to what he believes is a universal psychological truth rather than to the special social situation of fifteenth-century feudal princes (see pp. 73–75 of the Introduction). By reducing the matter to an attempt by Saint-Pol to manipulate Charles's (and Louis', as we shall see later in the *Memoirs*) emotions, Commynes is in a position to condemn Saint-Pol morally, and thus to explain his catastrophic fall. This fall is in turn related to the fall of Charles the Bold and is thus involved in the larger religio-moral design around which Commynes organizes much of the material in Books 1–5 (see pp. 68 ff. of the Introduction).

the taking of Amiens, the duke took the field near Arras, for he did not withdraw any farther, and then proceeded toward the river Somme and directly to Picquigny. As he was on his way, he received a message from the duke of Brittany, delivered by a common footman, who told him from his master that the king had informed him of many things, including the informers that he had in several large towns, among which he named Antwerp, Bruges, and Brussels. He also warned him that the king had decided to besiege him in any city where he could find him, even if it were Ghent itself; and I am convinced that the duke of Brittany sent this message to further the designs of the duke of Guyenne and to make the duke of Burgundy consent to the marriage in question.

But the duke of Burgundy was greatly displeased with the duke of Brittany's warning, and immediately replied to the messenger that his master was misinformed and that it was some bad servants of his who had wanted to frighten him so that he would not do his duty and come to the assistance of the duke of Burgundy, as he was obliged to do according to his alliances; he was also misled as to Ghent and the other towns where the king was supposedly going to besiege him, for they were too large to be besieged. The messenger was to tell his master how well provided with troops he had found the duke and to inform him of the true state of affairs; for he had decided to pass the river Somme and to fight the king, if he tried to get in his way. The envoy was to ask his master to declare himself on the duke's side against the king and to act in the same manner as the duke of Burgundy had acted toward him when the treaty of Péronne had been formulated.

The next day the duke of Burgundy arrived near a town called Picquigny, strongly situated on the river Somme, and he intended to build a bridge over the river in the vicinity, so that his men could pass the Somme. But by chance four or five hundred free archers and some noblemen were in town. As they saw the duke of Burgundy passing, they marched forth to encounter him on a long road, and they advanced so far that they gave the duke of Burgundy's soldiers an opportunity of pursuing them; they followed them so closely that they killed part of them before they were able to reach the town, and they conquered the suburb at the end of the road. Thereupon four or five large pieces of artillery were brought, although the town was impregnable from that side, owing to the river which was between them. However, the free archers feared that, since a bridge was being built, they might be besieged from the other side, and so they abandoned the town and fled. The castle still held out for two or three days and then all the men fled in their doublets.

Book Three

This little exploit gave courage to the duke of Burgundy, and he took up quarters in the vicinity of Amiens. He moved his forces two or three times, saying that he kept the field to see whether the king wanted to come and fight him. Finally he came so close to the town that his artillery fired, without aiming, over the rampart into the town. He remained there for six weeks. Some fourteen hundred men-at-arms and four thousand free archers from the king's forces were in the town, as well as my lord the constable, and all the principal leaders of the kingdom, such as the grand master, the admiral, the marshals, the seneschals, and a great number of other persons of high rank.

In the meantime the king was at Beauvais, where he was raising a large number of troops. With him were the duke of Guyenne, his brother, and Duke Nicholas of Calabria (eldest son of Duke John of Calabria and of Lorraine, and sole heir of the house of Anjou), as well as the rest of the noblemen of his kingdom, assembled by *arrière-ban*.[73] From what I have heard, one can be sure that those present with the king were already more than willing to fight. But the king was already beginning to realize the malice involved in this enterprise and was aware that the matter was far from settled, and that he was more deeply involved in war than ever.

Those who were inside the town of Amiens had the intention of assailing the duke of Burgundy and his army, provided that the king would send them the army which he had with him in Beauvais. But the king, when he was informed of this intention, sent express orders to forbid it and break it off entirely. For although it seemed advantageous for the king, there was a chance that it might be dangerous, especially for those who would have to sally forth from the town. For they could do this only from two gates, one of which was near the duke of Burgundy's army, and if they were to fail to discomfit them at the first try, and it would be possible, considering that they were on foot, they would be in great danger of losing the battle and having to give up the town.

In the meantime the duke of Burgundy sent to the king one of his pages, named Simon de Quingey, who has since become bailiff of Troyes, with a message of six lines in his own hand. The tone was very humble, and the content expressed sorrow at the fact that the king had invaded his territories at the instigation of others; the duke believed that if he had been well informed of the true situation, he would not have done so.

Meanwhile the army which the king had sent into [the duchy of] Bur-

73. See note 14, p. 104, for the meaning of this term.

gundy discomfited all the forces of Burgundy which had taken the field, and they captured several prisoners. The number of dead was not considerable, but the defeat was real. And at the same time several places had been besieged and taken, so that the duke was somewhat stunned. However, he had a rumor spread in his army that the opposite was true and that his men had had the upper hand.

When the king saw the duke of Burgundy's letter, he was extremely pleased for the reason which I mentioned earlier, and also because he never liked long enterprises. He dispatched an answer to him and sent an authorization to several persons in Amiens to make a truce; and indeed they made two or three, each of which lasted four or five days. Finally they had one which lasted a full year, as far as I can remember.[74] The constable, the count of Saint-Pol, seemed to be very unhappy about this; for regardless of anything people may have thought to the contrary, the count of Saint-Pol was the duke's mortal enemy at the time, and they never again became friends, as you know from the conclusion of this affair. However, many envoys were sent from both sides to contrive all sorts of bargains by intrigue and to obtain the best terms from each other.

The duke's chief objective in everything he did was to recover Saint-Quentin. Similarly, when the constable was afraid of the king, he promised to return it. And indeed things went so far that the soldiers of the duke of Burgundy, with the consent of the constable, approached within two or three leagues of the town, with the intention of entering it. But when they were on the point of being admitted, the constable invariably had a change of heart and countermanded his previous orders. This finally proved to be to his disadvantage. Owing to his important position and the great number of his men, which the king paid for, he was confident that he could maintain both of them in fear of each other, by means of the discord in which they were kept by his machinations; but his enterprise was very dangerous, because the two of them were too great, powerful, and cunning.

After these armies had disbanded, the king left for Touraine and the dukes of Guyenne and Burgundy retired to their respective territories. And for a while things remained at a standstill. The duke of Burgundy called a general assembly of the estates of his territories to remonstrate with them about all the damage which he had suffered as a result of not having had men-at-arms ready, as the king had;[75] if even five hundred

74. A truce of three months was arranged, which was subsequently prolonged.
75. A meeting of representatives from the various territories of the duke of Burgundy was held at Abbeville on July 22, 1471.

soldiers had been ready to guard his frontiers, the king would never have undertaken the war, and they would have remained in peace. He pointed out the dangers to which they were still exposed and pressed them hard so that they would consent to allocate him funds for eight hundred lance-teams. Finally they gave him 120,000 *écus*, over and above their regular dues; and Burgundy was not included in this grant.[76]

But his subjects were apprehensive, and for many reasons, of putting themselves in the same subjection as they saw the kingdom of France to be in, on account of the standing army of France. And indeed their misgivings were not without foundation, for once he had obtained five hundred men-at-arms, he longed for more so that he could make bolder attempts on his neighbors; the 120,000 *écus* were raised to 500,000 and his men-at-arms were increased to such a number that his territories suffered considerably on account of them. I believe that standing armies are usefully employed under the authority of a wise king or prince; however, when this is not the case and the prince dies, leaving young children, the use to which their governors put the armies is not always to the advantage of the king or his subjects.

The hatred between the king and the duke of Burgundy did not diminish, but always continued. And the duke of Guyenne, after returning to his territories, often sent messengers and pursued the negotiations with the duke of Burgundy for the hand of his daughter. The duke of Burgundy entertained his hopes and let the affair drag on; he treated similarly any man who asked for her in marriage. And I believe that he did not want to have a son-in-law nor to have his daughter marry at all during his lifetime; he preferred to keep her to draw on powerful lords to his side and to make use of their assistance. For he had so many great plans in mind that he could never have lived long enough to put all of them into execution; furthermore, they were practically impossible to realize, for half of Europe would not have been sufficient to satisfy him. He was bold enough to undertake the most difficult enterprise; his body could stand all the required fatigue. He was rather powerful in terms of men and money; but he did not have enough wisdom or shrewdness to manage his affairs well. For along with other things which are important for making conquests, if very great good sense is lacking, everything else is worth nothing; and you may be sure that that is God-given. If any man had been able to acquire part of the qualities of the king our master, and part of the duke's, he would have

76. The duchy of Burgundy proper, in eastern France, had held a separate meeting of estates at Dijon in April and May, where separate aid had already been granted to the duke.

made a perfect prince. For it is evident that the king was much superior to the duke in terms of judgment, as his accomplishments have demonstrated in the end.

4

In speaking of the preceding matters, I forgot to mention King Edward of England; for those three lords, our king, the duke of Burgundy, and King Edward, were great during the same era. I am not observing the order of writing used in histories, and I am not mentioning the years or the exact times during which these events took place, nor do I draw examples from history, for you [Angelo Cato] know them well enough, and it would be like speaking Latin before Franciscans. I merely give you a rough account of what I have seen and known or heard of the princes in question. Since you have lived at the time when these events came to pass, you have no need of being told with precision at what hour or season these things took place.

It seems to me that I spoke earlier of the reasons which prompted the duke of Burgundy to marry King Edward's sister;[77] and it was principally to strengthen himself against the king of France. For otherwise he would never have done it, because of the great affection he had for the house of Lancaster, to which he was related through his mother, who was infanta of Portugal. But her mother was the duke of Lancaster's daughter; therefore he loved this house as much as he hated the house of York. Now at the time of the marriage the house of Lancaster was almost destroyed, and of the house of York hardly anyone spoke any more, for King Edward was both king of England and duke of York, and peace prevailed in the kingdom. During the war between these two houses, seven or eight important battles had been fought in England, in which sixty or eighty princes or lords of royal lineage lost their lives cruelly, as I explained earlier in these memoirs. And those who were not killed were fugitives and lived at the court of the duke of Burgundy; all of them were young lords, for their fathers had died in England. And before his marriage, the duke of Burgundy had taken them in his house, as his relatives from the house of Lancaster. I have seen some of them reduced to such extreme poverty, before the duke took care of them, that common beggars could not have been more destitute. For I have seen a duke of Exeter without any hose walking behind the duke's train and begging for his pittance from house to house, without identifying himself. He was the closest in line of succession from the house of

77. Charles married Margaret of York on July 3, 1468.

Lancaster and had married King Edward's sister [Anne]. He was later recognized and was granted a small pension for his subsistence. Some of the Somersets were there, as well as others; all of them were since slain in battle. Their fathers and their relatives had plundered and destroyed the kingdom of France and possessed the greater part of it for many years. All of them killed each other. Those who were still alive in England as well as their children have since perished, as you can see.

Yet there are those who say: "God does not punish people as He used to in the days of the children of Israel, and He endures bad princes and other wicked men." I believe indeed that He does not speak directly to men as He used to, for He has left enough examples in the world to be believed. But you can see from reading about these events and from whatever else you know about them that of these bad princes and others who rule in this world and misuse their authority by being cruel and tyrannical, very few, if any, have remained unpunished. But it is not always on such and such a day nor at the hour that those who suffer would want it.

To return to King Edward of England, the chief nobleman of England to have supported the house of York was the count of Warwick; the duke of Somerset, on the other hand, upheld the house of Lancaster. And the count of Warwick could almost call himself the father of King Edward, owing to all the services which he had done him, including the supervision of his education; and indeed he had become a great man, for in addition to being an important lord in his own right he also held large territories as gifts from the king—partly crown lands and partly confiscated areas. He was made administrator of Calais and enjoyed other important positions; and I have heard his annual income from various alleged holdings estimated at eighty thousand *écus*, exclusive of his patrimony.

The count of Warwick fell out with his master during the year before the duke of Burgundy fought before Amiens; and the duke had actively promoted their dissension, for he did not look favorably upon the count of Warwick's great authority in England. Besides, they were not on very good terms because the lord of Warwick was always in agreement with the king [of France], our master. Moreover, at this time or shortly before, I saw the count of Warwick so powerful that he took the king, his master, into his custody and had the queen's father, Lord Scales, executed as well as two of his children; and the third was in great danger.[78] King Edward was very fond of all these persons. Warwick

---

78. Lord Scales was brother, not father of the queen. The father, Count Rivers, and only one of his children, John, were decapitated in 1469.

also had several English knights put to death. He kept the king guarded, though respectfully, for a time and placed new servants around him to make him forget the old ones; he considered his master to be a bit simple.

The duke of Burgundy was greatly perturbed at this turn of events; he secretly maneuvered to have King Edward escape and managed to communicate with him. The plan succeeded so well that King Edward did escape, assembled men, and put to rout a great part of the count of Warwick's forces. The king was very fortunate in his battles, for he won at least nine important ones, and they were all fought on foot.

The count of Warwick thus found himself the weaker of the two; he instructed his close friends as to what they were to do, and in his own good time he put to sea with the duke of Clarence, who had married his daughter and was one of his partisans, although he was King Edward's brother. They brought along their wives and children and a great number of men; and he arrived before Calais [April, 1470]. Inside were his lieutenant in the town, named my lord Wenlock, and many of his domestic servants who, instead of welcoming him, fired great cannon-shots at him. While they were anchored before the town, the duchess of Clarence, daughter of the count of Warwick, gave birth to a son. It was only after much persuasion that the lord of Wenlock and the others consented to have two flasks of wine brought to her. This was very severe behavior on the part of a servant toward his master; for it is to be presumed that the count of Warwick thought that he had provided well for him by putting him in charge of that place, which is the greatest treasure of England and the nicest frontier post in the world, or at least in Christendom, in my opinion. For I was there several times during these dissensions, and at the time of which I spoke the mayor assured me that the commander of the place gave the king of England fifteen thousand *écus* as a lease for the right to the wool import tax of Calais; for the commander takes all the profit from whatever goes to England from this side of the sea, as well as the profits from selling safe-conducts, and he also controls the hiring of most of the garrison.

The king of England was very pleased with the lord of Wenlock for his refusal to receive his superior officer and sent him a privilege which made him holder of his office as a tenant-in-chief,[79] for he was an old and wise knight and wore the Order of the Garter. My lord of Bur-

---

79. As Commynes has remarked earlier, Wenlock previously held his office as commander of Calais as the vassal of the count of Warwick. By this privilege, Edward made him a royal vassal or tenant-in-chief, holding his office directly from the king rather than indirectly from Warwick.

gundy, who was then at Saint-Omer, was well satisfied with him; he sent me to the lord of Wenlock to give him a pension of one thousand *écus* and to beg him to maintain the affection which he had already shown to the king of England.

I found him firmly resolved to do so; and he swore to me at the customs building in Calais that he would be faithful to the king of England against any and all persons and then all the garrison and the townspeople took the same oath. For two months I was sent back and forth to and from him, to keep him reminded of his allegiance. I was with him most of the time while the duke of Burgundy was at Boulogne raising a large fleet against the count of Warwick, who had taken several ships from the duke of Burgundy's subjects at his departure from Calais. And this seizure was largely instrumental in getting us into war again, for these people were selling their booty in Normandy. By way of reprisal the duke of Burgundy captured all the French merchants who had come to the fair at Antwerp.

Since it is necessary to be informed of the deceit and the wickedness of this world as well as the goodness, not in order to make use of them but to protect ourselves against them, I shall reveal an example of deceit, or a shrewd piece of business, whatever you wish to call it, for it was wisely managed. I also want you to understand our neighbors' tricks as well as ours, and to realize that there is good and bad everywhere.

When the count of Warwick appeared before Calais, hoping to enter the town which he considered his principal haven, my lord of Wenlock, who was very wise, sent word to him that if he entered he would be lost; for the whole of England as well as the duke of Burgundy were against him; moreover, the townspeople of Calais would oppose him and also several men from the garrison, such as my lord of Duras, who was the king of England's marshal, and many others, all of whom had agents in the town; therefore it would be best for him to retire to France and not to worry about Calais. When the time came, he would give him a good account of it. By giving him this piece of advice he did a good turn to his superior officer but certainly not to the king. As for the count of Warwick, no man was more loyal to him than Wenlock, considering that the king of England had made him chief administrator and that the duke of Burgundy had given him so much.

5

The count of Warwick followed this advice and went to land in Normandy where he was extremely well received by the king [of France], who provided him with large sums of money for his soldiers' expenses. He ordered the bastard of Bourbon, admiral of France, who had strong forces with him, to give assistance to these Englishmen against the duke of Burgundy's naval forces, which were very large and so powerful that no one would have dared face them at sea. The duke fought the king's subjects by land and by sea, and both sides threatened each other. All this took place during the season before the king took Saint-Quentin and Amiens, as I said previously; and these two places were taken in the year 1470.[80]

The duke of Burgundy's naval forces were stronger than those of the king and the count combined, for at the port of Sluis he had seized many large ships from Spain and Portugal, two vessels from Genoa, and several hulks from Germany. King Edward was not very orderly, but he was the most handsome prince whom I have ever seen in his time, and he was extremely valiant. He was not so perturbed about the count of Warwick's landing as was the duke of Burgundy, who sensed that there were movements afoot in England which supported the count of Warwick; and he frequently warned King Edward about it. But the king feared nothing; and I consider it most unwise on his part not to have feared his enemy and not to have wanted to believe any reports, in view of the preparations which he could have observed.

For the king came there with all the ships he had and could muster, and he had them well manned and equipped. He had negotiated the marriage of the prince of Wales with the count of Warwick's second daughter. The prince was the only son of King Henry of England, who himself was still alive and a prisoner in the tower of London; and all these people were ready to descend upon England. It was a strange marriage—to have the prince marry the daughter of the man who had overcome and ruined his father. Strangely, too, the duke of Clarence, brother of the enemy king, was negotiated with, although he should have been the last to wish for the house of Lancaster to get back on its feet. Thus, matters cannot be carried through without dissimulation.

I was in Calais during these preparations to confer with my lord of Wenlock, but until that time I had not been aware of his dissimulations, which had already been going on for three months; for I requested, in view of the news that came to his ears, that he should eject from the town the twenty or thirty servants of the count of Warwick. I added that I was assured that the king's army and the count were ready to leave Normandy, where they were already stationed; if they should land suddenly in England, there might be some commotion in Calais,

80. Saint-Quentin was taken in December, 1470, and Amiens in January, 1471, as described in chapter 2 of this book.

owing to the presence of the count of Warwick's servants, and he might perhaps not be able to control them. And I earnestly entreated him to put them out immediately. He had always agreed that he would do so until then, but at that moment he took me aside and told me that he was sure he could remain in control of the town, but that he wished to tell me something else that I should communicate to my lord of Burgundy: that he advised him, if he wished to be a friend of England, to put his efforts in the promotion of peace rather than of war. And he said this in relation to the forces that he had set up against my lord of Warwick. He told me further that it would be very easy to make an arrangement, for on that very day a lady had passed through Calais on her way to France, where she was to meet the duchess of Clarence and to bring peace overtures from King Edward.

He was speaking the truth, but just as he was dealing underhandedly with others, he was deceived by this lady; for she was involved with the transaction of an important bargain, and it turned out to be to the disadvantage of the count of Warwick and of all his followers. No one can tell you so truly as I can about these secret tricks or deceptions which have been carried on in our countries on this side of the water [the English Channel], or at least about those which have happened in the last twenty years. The secret message which this woman was carrying was to remonstrate to my lord of Clarence that he should not be the cause of the destruction of his own lineage by helping to restore the house of Lancaster and to beg him to consider their former hatred and offenses. He could well imagine that since the count had arranged for the prince of Wales to marry his daughter, he would do everything in his power to make him king of England; and he had already sworn allegiance to him. This woman maneuvered so well that she convinced the lord of Clarence, and he promised to pass over to the side of the king, his brother, provided that he arrive in England.

This woman was not a fool, nor did she speak lightly. She was at liberty to visit her mistress. It was for this reason that she was chosen for the mission rather than a man. And although my lord of Wenlock was a cunning man, this woman deceived him and managed this mystery so skillfully that as a result the count of Warwick and all his followers were defeated and died. For such reasons it is not shameful to be suspicious and to keep an eye on those who come and go, but it is a great disgrace to be deceived and to lose ground through one's own fault. However, our suspicions should be treated with moderation, for to be too mistrustful is not good.

I explained earlier that the count of Warwick's fleet and the ships which the king [of France] had set up to convoy him were ready to sail, and that the duke of Burgundy's naval forces, which were anchored facing them, were ready to fight with them. God arranged things in such a way that on this very night a great storm arose, and it was so severe that the duke of Burgundy's fleet had to escape; some of the ships went to Scotland and others to Holland. And a few hours later the wind was favorable for the count, who sailed safely to England.

The duke of Burgundy had informed the king precisely of the port where the count was to land, and he placed persons constantly about him to remind him that he should arrange things for his own advantage; but it did not matter to the king and he spent all his time hunting. His closest companions were the archbishop of York and the marquess of Montagu, brothers of the count of Warwick, who had taken a great and solemn oath to serve him against their own brother and any other enemy. And he trusted them.

As soon as the count of Warwick had landed, a great number of people joined him and he found himself in a strong position. When he heard of it King Edward began to look after his affairs, although it was rather late to do so, and he sent word to the duke of Burgundy, begging him to have his fleet ready at sea, in order to prevent the count from returning to France, for on land things were sure to turn out well. These words were not appreciated by the duke, for it seemed to him that it would have been better to have prevented the count from landing in England than to have to resort to a battle now.

Five or six days after the count of Warwick had landed, he found himself in a very powerful position, and took up quarters three leagues away from King Edward, who had greater forces than the count, and it would have been well if they had all been good men; and he was ready to contend against the count. King Edward had taken lodgings in a fortified village or at least in a house which could only be reached by a bridge, as he himself told me, and this proved to be to his advantage. The rest of his men were quartered in neighboring villages. As he was having dinner, he was suddenly notified that the marquess of Montagu, the count's brother, and a few others had mounted their horses and had had all their men shout: "Hail King Henry!"

At first he did not believe it, but he immediately dispatched several messengers, armed himself, and had soldiers posted at the limits of his house to defend it. With him was a wise knight named my lord Hastings, grand chamberlain of England, who enjoyed great authority with the king. His wife was the count of Warwick's sister. However, he was loyal to the king and he had in his army some three thousand horsemen, as he himself told me. Also with him was another man, named my lord Scales, brother of King Edward's wife, as well as several excellent knights and squires, all of whom realized that things were not going well; for the messengers reported that what the king had previously been told was true and that the enemy had assembled to come and march against him.

God favored that king so much that He allowed him to be quartered near the sea, and several ships followed with supplies, as well as two hulks from Holland, which were merchant vessels. He had just enough time to take refuge in one of them. His chamberlain stayed behind for a while longer, and told the chief officer of his men and several others from the army to go out and meet the enemy, but he entreated them to maintain their loyalty to the king and to himself. And he went on board the ship with the others who were ready to sail.

It is customary in England that those who have the upper hand in a battle do not ·kill anyone, and especially not common people, for everyone wants to please them, since they determine which side is the stronger; and hardly any soldiers are ransomed. Therefore none of the king's men were harmed after he had left. King Edward also told me that in every battle which he had won, as soon as he realized that he had conquered, he mounted on horseback and proclaimed that the common people should be saved and the lords killed; and indeed few or none of them escaped.

Thus King Edward made his escape in the year 1470, with the help of two hulks and a small vessel of his own; he had some seven or eight hundred persons with him, and they had no other clothes except their war outfits. And they had not a coin in their pockets, and they hardly knew where they were going.

It seemed very strange for this poor king (and indeed the term was appropriate) to run away in this manner and to be persecuted by his own servants. He had already been accustomed to comfort and pleasure for twelve or thirteen years, and more than any prince in his time, for he had nothing on his mind except the ladies (and more than would have been reasonable), the hunt, and the good care of his person. In the hunting season he had several pavilions set up for the ladies where he feasted them lavishly. Indeed, he was better suited for these activities than any other man I have ever seen; for he was young and the most handsome man of his time. I am speaking of the time of this adversity, for later he became very stout.

See how this king came to have his share of the hardships of this world. He fled directly toward Holland. At that time the Hanseatic

League was the enemy of both the English and the French; they had many men-of-war at sea. They were greatly feared by the English, and not without reason, for they are good fighters. They had done them much harm that year and had taken several of their ships. At a great distance the Hanseatic ships spotted the ships in which the king was fleeing, and seven or eight of their ships began to pursue them. He was far ahead of them, however, and reached the coast of Holland or even further, for he arrived in Friesland, near a small town called Alkmaar. They anchored his vessel, and because it was low tide they could not enter the harbor, but they got as near to the town as they could. The Hanseatic ships similarly set their anchor rather close to him, with the intention of boarding his ship at the next tide.

Adversity and danger never come singly. The king's good fortune as well as his way of thinking had changed radically. Only two weeks earlier he would have been rather astounded at anyone who would have said to him: "The count of Warwick will drive you out of England and in eleven days he will be its master." For indeed in that short time he reduced everyone to obedience. Furthermore, the king scoffed at the duke of Burgundy, who was spending his money to retain control of the sea, saying that he wished Warwick were already in England. And what excuse could he have found for such a loss which had come about through his own fault, unless to say: "I did not think that such a thing could ever happen." A prince of mature age should blush to give such an excuse, for it is not valid.

This is a fine example for princes who never fear nor suspect their enemies and who would consider it beneath their dignity to do so. Most of their servants agree with them in order to flatter them. And they believe that they will be more respected and esteemed for it, and that people will say that they have spoken with courage. I do not know what people will say to their face, but wise persons will surely consider such words very foolish. It is all to one's credit to have well-grounded fears and to protect oneself well against danger. It is invaluable for a prince to have a wise and trusted man in his entourage; he should be allowed to speak the truth and the prince should believe him.

By chance, my lord of Gruthuse, governor for the duke of Burgundy in Holland, was at the time in the place where King Edward intended to land. Some of the men who were sent ashore informed him of this state of affairs as well as the danger he was in because of the Hanseatic ships. Thereupon the governor sent word to the Hanseatics forbidding them to do him any harm. Then he went on board the king's vessel to welcome him. Thereupon the king landed with about fifteen hundred men, including the duke of Gloucester, his brother, who later came to be called King Richard.

The king had no money with him, and so he gave the master of the ship a robe lined with beautiful marten skins, and promised to do better for him in the future. Such a destitute company was never seen before. But the lord of Gruthuse acted most honorably, for he gave them several robes and paid all their expenses until they reached The Hague, in Holland, where he conducted them. He then informed my lord of Burgundy of the happenings.

The duke was perfectly aghast at the news. He would have much preferred to hear of the king's death, for he greatly dreaded the count of Warwick, who was his enemy and in control of England, for soon after his landing he found that he had an infinite number of partisans. For the army which King Edward had left behind joined the count of Warwick's side, either through love or through fear, and every day he gained new adherents. Thus he proceeded to London. A great number of fine knights and squires escaped to the sanctuaries in London, and they served King Edward well afterward. The queen his wife took refuge there also, and in the most abject state of poverty, she gave birth to a son.

6

Immediately upon his arrival in the city of London, the count proceeded to the tower, which is the castle, and released King Henry, whom he had committed there a long time before, shouting to his face that he was a traitor and guilty of lese majesty. But now he proclaimed him king, led him to his palace at Westminster, and set him up in his royal estate in the presence of the duke of Clarence, who was not pleased with this act [October 6, 1470]. Thereupon, he sent three or four hundred men to Calais, and they overran the Boulonnais region. They were well received by the lord of Wenlock, of whom I spoke earlier. It then became obvious that he had always had affection for his master, the count of Warwick.

On the day that the duke of Burgundy learned of King Edward's arrival in Holland, I had come from Calais to meet him. I found him in Boulogne-sur-Mer and knew nothing yet about this state of affairs, nor about the king's flight. The duke of Burgundy was first informed that he was dead. He was not overly disturbed at the news, for he had more affection for the house of Lancaster than for the house of York. Besides, he had as guests in his house the dukes of Exeter and of Somerset, as well as many other partisans of King Henry; therefore it seemed to him that he could easily make peace with that family. But he greatly dreaded the count of Warwick; and he did not know how he would be able to satisfy the one who had taken asylum in his territories—that is to say, King Edward, whose sister he had married. Besides, they were brothers of the same orders, for he wore the Golden Fleece and the duke wore the Garter.

The duke sent me immediately back to Calais with a gentleman or two from King Henry's new party. He gave me instructions as to how he wanted me to deal with this new group, and he strongly entreated me to go there, assuring me that he needed my services in this affair. I went as far as Tournehem, which was a castle near Guines, but did not venture to proceed farther, because I found the people fleeing from the English, who were ravaging and overrunning the region. I immediately sent word to Calais to ask my lord of Wenlock for a safe-conduct; I used to go there freely without clearance and was always well received, for the English are most honorable.

All this was rather new to me, for I had never witnessed so closely the changes in this world. That night I informed the duke of the fears which I had that I might not be able to pass, but without letting him know that I had sent for a safe-conduct, for I had a fair idea of the kind of answer I should receive. He sent me a seal ring which he wore on his finger and ordered me to proceed, even if I should be taken prisoner, for he would ransom me. He had no qualms about exposing any of his servants to danger, if it could be of use to him in time of necessity; but I had protected myself by asking for a safe-conduct, and I received it with very gracious letters from my lord of Wenlock, who assured me that I might come and go as I did formerly.

I went on to Guines and found the commander outside the castle; he offered me a drink but he did not invite me to stay in the castle, as he used to do, although he welcomed us warmly and was most courteous to the two gentlemen, partisans of King Henry, who were with me. I proceeded to Calais. No one came to meet me, as they used to do. All the men wore the count of Warwick's livery. At the door of my lodgings and my room, the people made more than one hundred white crosses for me, with rhymed verses to the effect that the king of France and the count of Warwick were all as one.[81]

I found all this rather strange, and by chance I sent a message to Gravelines, which is five leagues away from Calais, with the order to

81. White was the color of the Lancaster and Valois dynasties.

seize all merchants from England and their merchandise, because of the way in which they [the English] were overrunning the area. The lord of Wenlock invited me to dinner; he was well attended and wore the ragged staff of gold on his bonnet, for the ragged staff was the count's emblem. And all the rest wore the same symbol; those who could not afford a gold one had one of woolen cloth. I was told at that dinner that less than a quarter of an hour after the messenger had arrived from England, bringing them the news, everyone was wearing this livery, so hasty and sudden was the change: this was the first time that I ever recognized that the affairs of this world are not very stable. Wenlock was very courteous to me, and he made some excuses in favor of the count, his master, and his various kindnesses to him. But as for the others who were with him, they had never been so excited. Those whom I had considered to be the staunchest supporters of the king were those who made the worst threats against him; and I believe that some did this out of fear and others willingly. Those whom I had formerly tried to have expelled from the town because they were domestic servants of the count were now held in great esteem. However, they never knew that I had spoken against them to Wenlock.

I told them at every occasion that King Edward was dead and that I was sure of it, although I well knew that it was not true; and I added that even if he were not dead it would not make any difference, for the alliances which my lord of Burgundy had made with the king of England and his kingdom were so strong that they could not be broken on account of what happened. And whomever they chose as king we would also accept, for in consideration of past changes the words "with the king and the kingdom" had been inserted [in the Anglo-Burgundian treaties]. And we had been promised the four principal cities of England as security for the maintenance of these alliances.

The merchants insisted that I should be arrested because many of their wares had been taken at Gravelines, and by my orders, as they claimed. The negotiations between them and myself were pursued so earnestly that we agreed that they should either pay for the cattle which they had taken or else return them; for they had made an agreement with the house of Burgundy which allowed them to have access to certain specified grazing grounds and to take the cattle from there for the provision of the town, on condition that they paid a certain fixed price, which indeed they paid; and they did not take any prisoners. Thus it was concluded between us that the alliances which we had made with the kingdom of England would remain as they were, except that we would substitute Henry's name for Edward's.

This arrangement was most satisfactory to the duke of Burgundy, for the count of Warwick was sending four thousand Englishmen to Calais with the express intention of waging war against him, and no way could be found to pacify him. However, the rich merchants of London (many of whom were then in Calais) dissuaded him from carrying out that plan, for in this town was their warehouse of woolens; and the amount of money which comes out of this twice a year is almost incredible. Their goods are kept there until the merchants come for them; and their principal outlet is in Flanders and Holland. Thus these merchants were instrumental in negotiating this agreement and in restraining the forces which the count of Warwick was sending over.

These things occurred at a propitious time for the duke of Burgundy, for it was practically at that precise moment that the king [of France] had taken Amiens and Saint-Quentin. And if the duke had had a war on his hands with two kingdoms simultaneously, he would have been ruined. He was doing his best to pacify my lord of Warwick, assuring him that he had no intention of doing anything against King Henry, especially since he himself was from the house of Lancaster; and he said many other things which he thought would serve his purpose.

To return to King Edward, he came to the duke of Burgundy at Saint-Pol and urgently begged him to give him assistance so that he could return to his country; he assured him that he had many interests in the kingdom of England and beseeched him for God's sake not to abandon him, since he had married his sister, and besides they were brothers of the same orders. The dukes of Somerset and Exeter, on the other hand, put pressure on him so that he would support King Henry. The duke was torn between the two parties and did not know whom to please; and he was afraid of offending either side, especially since he faced a newly begun, fiercely fought war at home. Finally he let himself be influenced for the time being by the duke of Somerset and the others mentioned above and accepted certain promises which they made in the name of the count of Warwick, who had formerly been their enemy. When King Edward, who was on the premises, saw this, he hardly felt secure. He was handed all the best speeches possible, however, and was assured that these were only pretenses which were made in order not to have a war with two kingdoms at the same time; for, if the duke were ruined, he would not be in a position to help him freely afterwards.

However, the duke, realizing that he could not prevent King Edward any longer from returning to England (and for several reasons he did not dare displease him on all points), pretended publicly that he would give him no assistance and issued a proclamation forbidding his subjects to help him. But privately and secretly he had him given fifty thousand florins marked with the cross of Saint Andrew, and he furnished him with four or five large ships, which he had equipped for him at Veere, in Holland, a free port where everyone is received; in addition he secretly hired fourteen well-armed vessels from the Hanseatic League for him. And they promised to be at his service until he had returned to England and for fifteen days after. This assistance was very great, considering the times.

7

King Edward left in the year 1471, at the same time as the duke of Burgundy marched against the king [of France] toward Amiens. It seemed to the duke that the turn of events in England could not be to his disadvantage and that he had friends on both sides. As soon as King Edward had landed, he proceeded directly to London, for he had more than two thousand men of his party in sanctuary; among them were three or four hundred knights and squires who were very useful to him, for he had not brought many men with him.

The count of Warwick was in the north with large forces, but as soon as he heard the news, he hastened back toward London, hoping to be the first to arrive. In any case he was confident that the city would hold out for him; things turned out differently, however, for King Edward was received there on Holy Thursday [April 11, 1471] with great rejoicing on the part of all the townspeople, contrary to most people's expectations, for he had generally been presumed lost. And indeed if they had refused to open the gates for him, he would have been entirely ruined, for the count of Warwick was only within a day's journey from him.

According to what I have been told, three things caused the townspeople's return to the king's side: firstly, he had partisans in sanctuary, including the queen his wife, who had given birth to a son; secondly, he had important debts which he owed throughout the town, and it was therefore to the merchants' interests that they should want him back; thirdly, many ladies of quality and rich townswomen of middle rank, with whom he had been on excellent terms and whom he had known intimately, gained their husbands and relatives for him.

He stayed only two days in the town, for he left on Holy Saturday with all the forces which he could raise, and he proceeded to meet the count of Warwick, whom he encountered the next morning [at Barnet on April 14, 1471], which was Easter Sunday. And as they found themselves facing each other, the duke of Clarence passed over to the side of the king his brother, accompanied by some twelve thousand men; this caused great consternation to the count of Warwick and great comfort to the king, whose forces were not very strong.

You have heard earlier how the bargain with the duke of Clarence was conducted; the battle was nevertheless very fierce and very cruel. Both sides fought on foot. The king's vanguard was hurt and the count of Warwick's troops advanced against his, and they came so close that the king of England fought in person as well, if not better, than any man on either side.

It was not the count of Warwick's habit to fight on foot. After sending his men into battle he was accustomed to mounting on horseback, and, if everything went well for his side, he would join in the fighting; however, if things went badly, he would get away early. But this time he was compelled by his brother, the marquess of Montagu, a very valiant knight, to fight on foot and to send away his horses. The battle was so intense that day that the count was killed, as well as his brother the marquess of Montagu, and many other persons of distinction. The losses were very great, for King Edward had resolved, when he left Flanders, that he would do away with his custom of proclaiming that the common people should be saved and the high ranking noblemen should be killed, as he used to do in his preceding battles; for he had conceived a very great hatred against the common people of England on account of the preference which they had shown for the count of Warwick, and also for other reasons. Therefore they were not spared this time. Fifteen hundred men from King Edward's side were killed, and the battle was bravely fought.

On the day of this battle the duke of Burgundy was stationed before Amiens, where he received letters from the duchess his wife informing him that King Edward had written to her about the happenings. He did not know whether to be happy or sad, for it seemed to him that King Edward was not pleased with him and considered that the help he had received from him had been given somewhat reluctantly and regretfully, and that he would probably have abandoned him under the slightest pretense. And to be truthful, there was never much friendship between them since. However, the duke made use of the news for his advantage and had it announced everywhere.

I have forgotten to mention how King Henry was brought to this battle; for King Edward found him in London. King Henry was a very ignorant man, and almost without any sense; and if what I heard is not a lie, immediately after the battle, King Edward's brother, the duke of Gloucester, who later became King Richard, killed this good man, King Henry, with his own hands, or had him taken to some secret place and had him killed while he looked on.

The prince of Wales, of whom I spoke earlier, had already landed in England when this battle took place; he had joined forces with the dukes of Exeter and Somerset and many others from his family, as well as old partisans. All told, there were more than forty thousand persons, as I was told by those who were present. If the count of Warwick had been willing to wait for these forces to join him, it seems very likely that they would have been the victors. But the fear which he had of the duke of Somerset, whose father and brother he had put to death, and of the prince's mother, Queen Margaret, led him to fight the battle alone, without waiting for them. Observe how long old animosities last and how they should be feared, and how great are the disadvantages which result from them.

As soon as King Edward had won this battle, he marched to encounter the prince of Wales; and a very important battle took place there [at Tewkesbury on May 4, 1471], for the prince had greater forces than King Edward. However, the king was the victor; and the prince of Wales was killed on the spot, as well as several other great lords and a great number of common people. The duke of Somerset was taken and was beheaded the next day.

In eleven days the count of Warwick had gained the whole kingdom of England, or at least had control of it. King Edward conquered it in twenty-one days; but it cost him two great and fierce battles. Thus you can see the great changes that took place in England. King Edward had many people killed in many places, particularly those who had plotted against him. Of all the people in the world, the English are most inclined to such battles. After this day King Edward enjoyed continuous peace in England until his death, but not without much turmoil of spirit and many grave thoughts.

8

I shall refrain from telling you more about the situation in England until it becomes relevant somewhere else. The place where I broke off my account of our affairs on this side of the water was at the duke of Burgundy's departure from Amiens and the king's retreat into Touraine, as well as his brother the duke of Guyenne's return to his territory of

Guyenne. The latter never ceased to pursue his negotiations for his marriage with the daughter of the duke of Burgundy, as I explained earlier.

The duke of Burgundy had always appeared to be willing to grant his request, but he really never intended to do so. He was constantly entertaining every suitor's hopes, as I said before. He could never forget the dishonest terms which they had resorted to in order to force him to accept this marriage. The count of Saint-Pol, constable of France, had always wanted to be the mediator of this marriage; the duke of Brittany also wanted the match to be arranged, but with himself as the principal agent. On the other hand, the king was doing his best to have it broken off; however, he could have spared his pains, for the two reasons explained elsewhere. Furthermore, the duke of Burgundy did not want such a powerful son-in-law as the duke of Guyenne, for he wanted to use this marriage to make bargains with everyone, as I said before. Therefore the king was making efforts for nothing; but of course he could not know what someone else's thoughts were. If this project had come to fruition and the marriage had taken place, his fears would have been justified, for his brother would have become extremely powerful, and with the duke of Brittany joining forces with the two dukes, the king's situation and that of his children would have been in danger. In the meantime a good number of ambassadors were sent back and forth, from the ones to the others, both privately and publicly.

It is not too safe to have so many goings and comings of embassies, for quite often dishonest bargains are transacted. However, it is necessary to employ the services of these men and to receive them. Those who read this may well ask what remedies I should propose for such a situation and may point out that it is impossible to do anything about it. I realize that there are many persons better qualified to speak about it than myself, but at any rate this is what I would do.

Those who are sent by true friends and who do not offer grounds for suspicion should, in my opinion, be warmly welcomed and be allowed to confer with the prince fairly often, depending on the kind of person the prince is. I should wish him to be wise and worthy, for, if he is not, the less he is seen, the better. And when he grants an audience, he should be well dressed and well prepared as to what he should say; he should be made to leave early, for the friendship between princes never lasts forever.

If ambassadors are sent on private or public missions by princes whose mutual hatred is of the type which I have seen continually among all

Book Three

the lords of whom I spoke, and whom I have known and lived with, then they are not to be trusted at any time. In my opinion, they should be entertained well and received honorably; for example, they should be met, they should be lodged in adequate quarters, and they should be provided with trustworthy and wise men to attend them; this is the proper as well as the safe thing to do. For by such means one can find out which persons they generally speak with, and one can prevent malcontents from bringing news to them. For no house is without some dissatisfied people. Furthermore, I should have them granted an audience right away and sent back soon after, for it seems to me a bad idea to keep one's enemies under one's roof. But to feast them, pay for their expenses, and give them presents is simply the courteous thing to do.

Moreover, it seems to me that even if war has started, one should not interrupt any peace negotiation or overture, for one never knows what use one can make of them later; therefore one should maintain all the transactions and hear all the messengers who arrange these things, while keeping a strict eye on people who speak with them or are sent to them either by day or by night; but of course this must be done as discreetly as possible. And for one messenger or ambassador whom they would send me, I should send them two in return. Even if they grew weary of such missions and requested that no more be sent, I still should send people to them if I had the opportunity and the means. For there is no better nor safer way to send a spy, nor could he be in any better position to see and hear everything. And if you send two or three men together, it is hardly possible that the enemy could be so cautious as to prevent one or the other from obtaining some useful information, secretly or otherwise. This is assuming that they will treat the ambassadors worthily, as they should do. One should expect a wise prince to see to it that one or more friends are constantly about the enemy, and he should protect himself against them as best he can. For in such matters one cannot at all do as one wishes.

It may be objected that as a result of this treatment your enemy will become all the more proud. It does not matter to me if he does. In this manner I shall know more about his designs. For when all is said and done, he who collects the profit from such affairs will also have the honor. And although my adversaries might use the same tactics in my house, I should still keep on sending messengers to them and would consider and maintain any and all negotiations without rejecting any offers, so that I could have occasion to send more ambassadors to them. Besides, some men are not as skillful as others; neither have they had

227

as much experience in such affairs, nor is it so necessary that they should. Yet in cases such as these, the wisest men are sure to gain the upper hand.

I shall give you a clear example of this. There was never a treaty between the French and the English in which the French did not prove themselves superior to the English in terms of sense and cunning. The English have a common saying, which they told me formerly when I negotiated with them, that in the battles which they fought against the French, the English always or most often beat them; in all the treaties which they negotiated with them, however, they were always outwitted and put at a disadvantage by the French. And surely, at least in my estimation, I have known men in this kingdom as worthy of negotiating an important agreement as anyone I have ever seen anywhere, especially those who were formed by our king; for in these matters it is necessary to have obliging men, who will overlook any unpleasant acts and words in order to achieve their aims, and such he wanted them to be, as I said.

I have been rather lengthy in speaking of these ambassadors and how one must keep an eye on them, but it was not without cause, for I have seen so many deceits and wicked acts carried on under the color of friendly embassies that I could not refrain from mentioning these things, nor treat the subject more shortly.

The proposed marriage between the duke of Guyenne and the duke of Burgundy's daughter, of which I spoke earlier, was negotiated so seriously that certain oral and even written promises were exchanged. However, I had seen the same thing happen with Duke Nicholas of Calabria and Lorraine, son of Duke John of Calabria, who has been mentioned before, and with the late Duke Philibert of Savoy, as well as with Duke Maximilian of Austria, now king of the Romans, the only son of Emperor Frederick [III]. Maximilian received a letter in the daughter's own hand, written by her father's command, as well as a diamond. All these promises were made in less than three years' time; and I am sure that not one of them would have been kept during his lifetime, at least with his consent. But Duke Maximilian, now king of the Romans, used this promise to his advantage, as I shall explain later. I do not mention these things to reflect on the person or persons I am speaking of, but only to describe the events as I saw them happen. Besides, I assume that stupid or simple people will not amuse themselves by reading these memoirs; but princes or courtiers will find some good advice in them, I think.

As this marriage was being negotiated, new enterprises were being planned against the king. With the duke of Burgundy were the lord of

Urfé, Poncet de Rivière, and several other persons of minor importance, who acted as ambassadors for the duke of Guyenne. Representing the duke of Brittany was the abbot of Bégar, later bishop of Saint-Pol-de-Léon, and he pointed out to the duke of Burgundy that the king was trying to bribe the duke of Guyenne's servants and wanted to attract them to his side, some by love, others by force. Already a place which belonged to my lord of Estissac, one of the duke of Guyenne's servants, had been demolished by royal orders, and several other acts of violence had been started. The king had enticed certain servants from his house, and therefore it was concluded that he wanted to recover Guyenne as he had formerly retaken Normandy, after he had given it to his brother as an appanage, as you have heard.

The duke of Burgundy frequently sent ambassadors to the king to discuss these matters. The king replied that it was the duke of Guyenne, his brother, who wanted to extend his territories and who had started all these intrigues, but that he himself had no intention of interfering with his brother's appanage.

Thus you may see how the affairs or quarrels in this kingdom are great (in fact this term could be applied at any time) when it is in a state of discord, and how cumbersome and difficult they are to conduct, and how far from the goal they are when they are begun; for although at first only two or three princes or persons of lesser condition are involved, by the time the game has lasted for two years, all the neighbors are invited to join in. However, when these affairs are started, everyone believes that they will be of short duration. But they are to be feared for the reasons you will see as you read further.

At the time in question, the duke of Guyenne or his envoys and those of the duke of Brittany begged the duke of Burgundy not under any circumstances to use the services of the English, who were enemies of the kingdom; for everything they [Guyenne and Brittany] did was for the good and the relief of the kingdom, and when he would have his forces ready, they were confident of being strong enough themselves, for they had secret negotiations with many commanders and others.

I was once present when the lord of Urfé was urging the duke of Burgundy to set up his army as soon as possible, and the duke called me aside to a window and said: "Now the lord of Urfé is pressing me to make my army as large as I can, and he tells me that we will contribute to the welfare of the kingdom. Do you think that if I enter France with the forces I shall lead there, I shall do them much good?" I laughed and answered that I did not think so. And he added: "I take the kingdom of France's interest to heart more than my lord of Urfé thinks; for in place of the one king they have, I should like to see six."

At the time we are speaking of, King Edward of England, who firmly believed that the marriage in question would materialize (but he was deceived about this), worked as hard as the king our master to break it off, and pointed out to the duke of Burgundy that the king our master had no son,[82] and that if he should die, the duke of Guyenne could expect to reign. Thus if this marriage should take place, all of England would be in danger of destruction, by reason of so many territories being annexed to the crown. King Edward took this matter very much to heart, as did the entire council of England, although their apprehensions were without foundation. Regardless of all the excuses which the duke of Burgundy made to them, the English refused to believe him.

In spite of the requests which the dukes of Guyenne and Brittany had made that he should not call for foreign help, the duke of Burgundy nevertheless wanted the king of England to become involved in the war to some extent, and in that case he would have pretended not to know anything about it and to have nothing to do with it. As for the English, they would never have done it. They would have rather assisted the king of France at that time because they were so afraid that by this marriage the house of Burgundy might be joined to the crown of France.

You can see from my relation that all these lords were well occupied. They were surrounded by so many shrewd men, who saw so far ahead that their lives were not sufficient to see half of what they foresaw. And this became evident afterward, for all of them died in the midst of their anxieties and their worries, and within a short time of each other. Each of them rejoiced at the death of the other ruler when it occurred, as something he had greatly wished for, and shortly afterwards those who remained died also, leaving their successors involved with many troubles; the exception was our present king [Charles VIII, son of Louis XI], who found his kingdom at peace with all his neighbors and subjects. His father provided for him better than he ever wished or was able to do for himself; for in my time I never saw him out of a war, except very shortly before his death.

At the time of which I am speaking, the duke of Guyenne was a little bit ill; some claimed that he was in danger of dying, and others said that it was nothing serious. His men urged the duke of Burgundy to take the field, for the season was propitious. They said that the king had assembled an army and that his soldiers were stationed before Saint-Jean-d'Angély, or Saintes, or in the vicinity. They persuaded him

82. In fact Louis' son, the future Charles VIII, was born on June 30, 1470, some two years before the events narrated here.

so well that the duke of Burgundy proceeded to Arras, where he assembled his army and marched from there toward Péronne, Roye, and Montdidier. The army was the most powerful and handsome he had ever led, for he had twelve hundred ordinance lance-teams; and they had three archers for one man-at-arms, all of them well armed and well mounted. In each company they had ten extra men-at-arms, not including the lieutenant and the standard bearers. The noblemen of his territories were in excellent condition, for they were well paid and were commanded by notable knights and squires; and his lands were very rich at the time.

9

As the duke was ready to leave Arras, two pieces of news were brought to him. The first was that Duke Nicholas of Calabria and Lorraine, heir of the house of Anjou and son of Duke John of Calabria, was coming to speak to him in relation to a possible marriage between him and the duke of Burgundy's daughter. The duke received him very courteously and gave him great hopes that the marriage would be concluded.

The next day, which was May 15, 1472, I believe, letters were received from Simon de Quingey, who was the duke of Burgundy's ambassador to the king. The message informed him that the duke of Guyenne had died and that the king had already recovered a large portion of his lands. Soon after, confirmation was received from various sources, but each gave a different version of his death.

The duke was driven to despair at this death, and exhorted by others who grieved about it, he sent letters to several towns, blaming the king; however, no profit resulted.[83] But I believe that if the duke of Guyenne had not died, the king would have had much to worry about, because the Bretons were ready to fight, and they had more informers in the kingdom than ever before; but this death put a stop to all these projects.

The duke took the field in anger and proceeded to Nesle in the Vermandois, where he began to wage war with foul and evil means which he had never used before: wherever he went, he had the locality burned. His vanguard proceeded to besiege Nesle, which was hardly worth the trouble, for it had only a small number of free archers. The duke had taken up quarters three leagues from there. A herald who was

83. Modern scholars generally agree that the duke of Guyenne died of natural causes. The circumstances of his death, however, made it easy to suspect Louis XI's hand in it.

coming to the town with a summons [from the duke] was killed by the inhabitants. Their commander came forth with a safe-conduct, with the intention of coming to terms. However, they were not able to make an agreement, and as he returned to the town, which was in a state of truce, owing to his mission, the soldiers stood exposed on the walls without being fired upon [by the duke's men]. Still they killed two more men [from the duke's army]. For this reason the truce was called off, and my lady of Nesle, who was in the town, was sent word that she might leave the premises with her servants and her possessions. And so she did; and thereupon the town was assailed and taken, and most of the men were killed. Those who were taken alive were hanged, except for a few whom the men-at-arms out of pity allowed to escape; and a large number had their hands cut off.

I am reluctant to speak of these cruel acts, but I was present when they were performed and I am obliged to mention them. One must say that the duke of Burgundy was under the influence of passion to act so cruelly or that some very great cause provoked him to do it. Two were alleged: first, there were strange rumors concerning the death of the duke of Guyenne; secondly, there was another grievance which you have learned about: the duke of Burgundy deeply resented the loss of Amiens and Saint-Quentin, as you have heard before.

At this time, while the duke was forming the army of which I spoke, the lord of Craon and the chancellor of France, named Pierre d'Oriole, came to him two or three times, and shortly before this affair and the duke of Guyenne's death, they secretly discussed the possibility of a lasting peace; this could never have been done before because the duke of Burgundy insisted on the restitution of the two above-mentioned towns and the king refused to return them. But now he changed his mind and agreed to give them up, since he realized that the duke was in a strong position and since he hoped that this would serve him well in certain plans of his which I shall explain.

The conditions of the peace were that the king would return to the duke Amiens and Saint-Quentin, of which it was question, and that he would give up to him the counts of Nevers and Saint-Pol, the latter constable of France, with all their territories, to be disposed of as he saw fit, and to be taken as his own, if he could manage to do so; similarly, the duke was to abandon the dukes of Brittany and Guyenne to the king, as well as their territories, for him to do as he pleased with them.

The duke of Burgundy swore to keep this peace; I was present when he did. The lord of Craon and the chancellor of France took the same oath, as representatives of the king, and then took their leave of the duke after advising him not to disband his army, but to march forward with his men, in order to make the king, their master, more inclined to quickly give up the two above-mentioned places. They took with them Simon de Quingey, to see the king take his oath and confirm what his ambassadors had done. The ratification of the treaty was delayed for several days; and in the meantime the duke of Guyenne died. Thereupon the king sent Simon back to the duke with rather insignificant words, without having taken any oath. This the duke deeply resented, considering himself mocked and scorned. While the war lasted, the duke's men, for this reason and others which you have had occasion to hear about, spoke most vulgar and incredible words about the king, and the king's own men scarcely hesitated to do the same.

In days to come, it may seem to those who read this that these two princes were not very trustworthy or that I speak badly of them. I should not like to speak ill of either one, and furthermore I am bound to our king, as everyone knows. But to continue my narration according to what you have requested of me, your Excellence, archbishop of Vienne, I must give an account of what I know, regardless of how it happened. But when they are compared with other princes, these two will appear great and notable; our prince will especially be considered very wise, for he left his kingdom increased and at peace with all his enemies.

Therefore, let us see which of these two lords wanted to deceive the other, in the event that at some future date this account should fall into the hands of some young prince who might have to manage the same kind of affairs. By having seen this he may gain a better understanding of these things and guard himself against deceit. For, although enemies and princes are not always alike, their affairs are often of a similar nature, and therefore it is useful to be well informed of things past. To give you my honest opinion, I am reasonably certain that these two princes had the same intention of deceiving each other and that their ends were about the same, as you shall see.

Each of them had his army assembled and ready to fight. The king had already taken many places, and while he was negotiating peace, he pressed his brother very hard. Several men, including the lord of Curton, Patrick Folcart, and others, had already left the duke of Guyenne and passed over to the king's side. The king's army was near La Rochelle and had many informers in the town; and they intrigued persistently with the inhabitants because of the rumors of peace and of the duke of Guyenne's illness. I believe that the king's intention, if he were to succeed in his enterprise, or almost succeed, or if his brother were to die, was to abstain from swearing to the peace. On the other hand, if the enemy proved themselves strong, he would swear to it and carry out his promises in order to keep out of danger. He measured his time wisely and managed his affairs with marvelous diligence. You have heard how he concealed his true intentions from Simon de Quingey for some eight days, and in the meantime this death occurred. He well knew that the duke was so intent on regaining these two towns that he would not dare do anything to make him angry, and so he was confident that he could easily keep him waiting for fifteen or twenty days, as he did; this would give him ample time to decide on the most advantageous course to take.

Since we have spoken of the king and of the schemes he had in mind to deceive the duke of Burgundy, we must now speak about the duke's plans concerning the king and how he intended to treat him if this death had not taken place. At the king's request Simon de Quingey received orders from the duke to go to Brittany, after witnessing the king's oath of peace and receiving letters to confirm what the king's ambassadors had done, and to inform the duke of Brittany of the contents of the peace treaty, and also to inform the duke of Guyenne's ambassadors, who were there, so that they might report it to their master, who was in Bordeaux. The king was anxious to have this done in order to have the Bretons greatly frightened at seeing themselves abandoned by the one in whom their principal hopes rested.

In the company of Simon de Quingey was one of the duke's equerries, named Henry, a Parisian and a wise and prudent man, who had a letter of credence written in the duke's own hand, addressed to Simon. But he had instructions not to deliver it to Simon until he had left the king and arrived at Nantes to speak with the duke of Brittany. Only then was he to hand him the letter and deliver his instructions, which were that he [Simon] was to tell the duke of Brittany that he should have no suspicion or fear that his master would abandon him or the duke of Guyenne; he would still help them with his person and his fortune. The agreement he had negotiated with the king was accepted simply in order to recover the two towns, Amiens and Saint-Quentin, which the king had taken away from him in time of peace and contrary to his promise.

Simon was also to tell him how the duke his master would send notable ambassadors to the king, as soon as he would repossess the places he had demanded—and this would be done without difficulty—to beseech him to desist from the war and enterprises he had undertaken against the two dukes, and not to adhere too strictly to the oaths which he had taken; for he himself had no more intention of observing them than the king had kept the promises which he had made before Paris, in what is called the treaty of Conflans, or the articles which he had sworn to uphold at Péronne, and which he confirmed a long time later.[84] He well knew that he had taken these two towns contrary to his promise, and in time of peace; therefore he should accept the fact that the duke had taken similar measures to recover them. As for the counts of Nevers and Saint-Pol (the latter constable of France), whom the king had abandoned to him, he was ready to declare that although he hated them, and with good reason, he would remit their offenses and let them enjoy all their possessions, provided that the king would accept to do the same for the two dukes whom the duke of Burgundy had put in his hands, and allow everyone to live in peace and security, in the manner that had been approved at Conflans, where all of them had assembled; if the king should refuse these terms, then he would give help to his allies. And the duke should already have been in the field by the time this message was delivered.

However, things turned out differently. Thus man proposes and God disposes: for death, which disrupts all things and changes all conclusions, caused something else to occur as you have heard and will hear further. For the king did not give up the two towns, and he obtained the duchy of Guyenne as a result of his brother's death, as was reasonable.

10

To return to the war of which I spoke earlier, I told of the cruel treatment which was inflicted upon a great number of unfortunate free archers who had been taken in Nesle. When he left the town, the duke went to take up quarters before Roye, which had a garrison of fifteen hundred free archers, besides a number of men-at-arms of the *arrière-ban*. The duke of Burgundy had never had such a fine army. The day after his arrival, the free archers began to fear; many of them jumped over the walls and gave themselves up to him. On the following day the whole town surrendered; the soldiers left behind them horses and harnesses, except the men-at-arms, each of whom took with him one *courtault* [a horse whose ears and tail have been cut]. The duke left some of his men in the town and proceeded to Montdidier with the intention of demolishing its fortifications; but when he realized the great affection that the people from these territories had for him, he had the walls repaired and left soldiers in the town.

84. See chapter 14 in Book 1 and chapter 9 in Book 2 for these treaties.

From there he planned to proceed to Normandy, but as he marched near Beauvais, he attacked the inhabitants with my lord of Cordes leading the way as commander of the vanguard. At the first attempt they took the suburb which faces the bishop's house; it was captured by a very avaricious Burgundian named Jacques de Montmartin, who led one hundred lance-teams and three hundred archers from the duke's regular army. My lord of Cordes assailed them from another side, but his ladders were short, and, besides, he had very few of them. He had two cannons which were fired only twice through the gate and made a large hole in it. If he had had more stones to continue with the firing, he would certainly have taken the town. However, he had not come with the intention of performing such an exploit and was therefore not well provided.

At first there were only the inhabitants in the town, except for Loiset de Balagny, the commander of the town, with a few soldiers from the *arrière-ban*. Nevertheless, these forces were not sufficient to save the town. But God did not wish it to be destroyed and gave definite proof of it. For my lord of Cordes' soldiers fought hand to hand at the breach which had been made in the gate; and thereupon my lord of Cordes sent word to the duke of Burgundy by several messengers that he should come, and that he could rest assured that the town would be his. While the duke was on his way, some of the inhabitants decided to bring ignited faggots to throw at the faces of those who were trying to break the gate. They threw so many at them that the portal was set on fire and the assailants had to withdraw until the fire was quenched.

The duke arrived and considered the town practically taken, or he thought that it would be as soon as the fire would be over; and indeed it was a great fire, for the whole portal was ablaze. And if the duke had decided to quarter part of his army on the side toward Paris, the town could not have avoided being captured by his men, for no one could have entered. But God willed that he should be alarmed, although there was no reason to fear; for it was only on account of a little stream that had to be crossed that he objected so strongly. Later, when the town had been well reinforced with soldiers, he wanted to pass the stream, although it would have put his whole army in a dangerous position; and it was very hard to dissuade him from doing it. It was the twenty-seventh day of June, 1472.

The fire to which I referred lasted the whole day; toward evening no more than ten lance-teams from the standing army entered the town, as I have been told, for at the time I was still in the service of the duke of Burgundy. But they were not seen because everyone was occupied in taking up his quarters, and no one was present on that side. At dawn the duke's artillery drew near, and soon afterward we saw a large number of soldiers entering the town; there were at least two hundred men-at-arms, and I believe that if they had not come the town would have soon begun to negotiate. But the duke of Burgundy was so angry, as you have gathered from what I have said, that he wanted to assail the town immediately; and there is little doubt that if he had taken it, he would have burned it to the ground, which would have been most unfortunate. I believe that it was saved by a true miracle and in no other way.

From the time these soldiers entered the town, the duke's artillery fired continually, for fifteen consecutive days or so. The town was as severely battered as any place ever was, until it was fit to be assaulted. However, there was water in the ditches, and it was necessary to build two bridges on one side of the burned gate; on the other side of the gate it was possible to reach the walls without danger, except for one cannon-hole which was so low that it could not be hit.

It is very dangerous and utterly foolish to assail such a strong place. In addition the constable was in the town, as I believe, or in the vicinity (I am not sure which), with Marshal Joachim, the marshal of Lohéac, my lord of Crussol, Guillaume de Vallée, Méri de Couhé, Salazar, and Estevenot de Vignolles; all of them had at least one hundred lance-teams, men-at-arms from the standing army, many infantrymen, and other worthy men who came with these officers.

Still the duke was resolved to make an assault; but he was alone in his decision, for no one shared his opinion. That night, as he lay on his cot, fully or almost fully clothed, as was his custom, he asked several persons whether they believed that the townsmen expected to be assaulted. They replied that indeed they did since they had so many soldiers within their walls, and even if they had been fortified only with a hedge, they were still strong enough to defend their town. He took it in jest and said: "You will not find a soul there tomorrow."

At daybreak the town was very well and very boldly attacked, but even better defended. Many soldiers passed the bridge, and in the crowd my lord of Épiry was stifled to death; he was an old Burgundian knight and the highest-ranking man to be killed that day. On the other side there were some who got as far as the top of the wall, but not all of them returned. They fought hand to hand for a long time and the assault was rather long. Other troops had been ordered to attack after the first ones had made the initial push; but when the duke realized that they were wasting their time, he ordered them to retreat. The soldiers inside the town made no sally, for they could see that if they had made one, a large force was ready to receive them outside. In this assault we lost about one hundred and twenty men. The most notable was my lord of Épiry. Some estimated the number of dead to be greater. At least one thousand men were wounded.

The following night the enemy sallied forth, but they were not numerous; most of them were mounted and their horses had their legs entangled in the ropes of our tents. They did not gain anything and lost two or three gentlemen. They wounded a very worthy man, named Jacques d'Orsans, master of the duke's artillery, who died several days later.

Seven or eight days after this assault, the duke proposed to take up quarters before the gate toward Paris and to divide his army into two sections. But he found no one to agree with him because it was estimated that the great number of soldiers inside the town made it too strong to be taken. He should have done this at the beginning, for now it was too late. Realizing that there was no remedy, the duke raised the siege and marched off in good order. He had expected the enemy to sally forth fiercely and was ready to do them some damage by this means. However, they stayed inside.

From there he proceeded to Normandy because he and the duke of Brittany had agreed to meet before Rouen, but the latter changed his mind upon the death of the duke of Guyenne and did not budge from his territories.

The duke of Burgundy arrived before Eu and took the town as well as Saint-Valéry-en-Caux; he had the whole region set on fire to the very gates of Dieppe. He also took Neufchâtel-en-Bray and had all the territory of Caux burned, or at least the greater part of it, up to the gates of Rouen, and he proceeded in person before that city. He often lost his foragers, and therefore his army suffered greatly from hunger. He then retired, since winter had come. No sooner was his back turned that the king's men recaptured Eu and Saint-Valéry, and took as prisoners seven or eight men who were stationed in these towns by virtue of the acts of surrender.

11

About this time (which was in the year 1472) I entered the service of the king, who had taken in most of the servants of his brother, the duke of Guyenne.[85] He was at Ponts-de-Cé, where he had assembled his troops against the duke of Brittany, with whom he was at war.

85. This is Commynes' only mention of his desertion. See the discussion of Commynes' "modesty" in section 4 of the Introduction.

Book Three

Several ambassadors from the duke of Brittany came to him there, and others from him were sent to Brittany. Among those who came were Philippe des Essars, an attendant of the duke, and Guillaume de Souplainville, an attendant of my lord of Lescun, who had retired to Brittany when he saw his master, the duke of Guyenne, near death. He left Bordeaux by sea, fearing that he might fall into the hands of the king; therefore he embarked very early. He brought with him the duke of Guyenne's confessor and an equerry of his stable, both of whom were suspects in the death of the duke of Guyenne and were prisoners in Brittany for several years.

These embassies to and from Brittany lasted a short while; and finally the king made up his mind to have peace on that side and to grant so many favors to the lord of Lescun that he would gain him as his servant and would make him abandon any intention which he might have had of doing him any harm; for there was no sense or excellence in Brittany which did not come from him. Such a powerful duke managed by such a man was certainly a menace; however, if the king could contrive to come to terms with him, the Bretons would do their best to live in peace. Indeed, most people of the region never wish for anything else. There have always been well-treated and honored Bretons in this kingdom, and they have always served the country well in former times. Therefore I consider the treaty which the king arranged a very wise move, although he was blamed by some people who were not as far-sighted as he was. He had a high opinion of Lescun personally, and he said that he did not see any danger in putting him in charge of certain affairs; he considered him an honorable man because during these past dissensions he had never tried to negotiate with the English, nor had he ever consented to let them have any place in Normandy. He was solely responsible for this, and this was the reason for all the benefits he received.

For all these reasons the king asked Souplainville to put down in writing everything that the lord of Lescun, his master, requested for both the duke and himself. He did so and the king granted everything. The requests were the following: a pension of eighty thousand francs for the duke; for his master [Lescun] a pension of six thousand francs, the government of Guyenne, the two seneschalsies of the Landes and the Bordelais, the command of one of the castles of Bordeaux, the command of Blaye, of the two castles of Bayonne, of Dax and of Saint-Sever, and twenty-four thousand *écus* in cash, the king's Order, and the county of Comminges. Everything was agreed upon and accomplished except that the duke's pension was decreased by one half and was paid only for two years. In addition the king gave Souplainville six thousand *écus*; the money was paid in ready cash to him and his master, but it took four years for the transaction to be completed. Furthermore, Souplainville obtained twelve hundred francs of pension, the mayoralty of Bayonne, the bailiwick of Montargis, and several other minor estates in Guyenne. All this was kept by him and his master until the king's death. Philippe des Essars[86] became bailiff of Meaux, and master of the waters and forests of France, and received a pension of twelve hundred francs as well as four thousand *écus*. From that time until the death of the king our master, they kept these positions; and my lord of Comminges remained his good and loyal servant.

Soon after the king had made peace in this part of Brittany, he proceeded toward Picardy. As soon as winter came, it was always the custom of the king and the duke of Burgundy to have a truce for six months or a year or more. Thus, according to their custom, they decided to have one, and the chancellor of Burgundy and several other persons came to negotiate it. There the king produced the final peace treaty which he had negotiated with the duke of Brittany, by which the duke renounced his alliance with the English and the duke of Burgundy; and therefore the king did not want the duke of Burgundy's ambassadors to include him among their allies. But they would hear nothing of it and insisted that it was up to the duke of Brittany to declare himself on the king's side or on theirs by the accustomed time. They pointed out that formerly the duke of Brittany had abandoned them according to his letters but nevertheless had not really given up their alliance and friendship. They considered the duke of Brittany to have been influenced by others rather than by his own judgment. But in the end he always returned to whatever was best for his own interests. This was in the year 1473.[87]

While this treaty was being negotiated, both sides murmured against the count of Saint-Pol, constable of France; the king and his closest advisers had taken a violent dislike to him. The duke of Burgundy hated him even more, and with better cause; for I have been well informed of the true reasons on both sides. The duke had not forgotten that the constable was responsible for the taking of Amiens and Saint-Quentin, and it seemed to him that he was the cause of the war between the king and himself, and that he was its real instigator; for in time of truce he made him the finest speeches in the world, but as soon as hos-

86. Another of the duke of Brittany's counselors who passed to Louis XI's service at this time.

87. Commynes is mistaken. The Peace of Compiègne was agreed upon between Charles the Bold and Louis XI on November 3, 1472.

tilities resumed he was his mortal enemy. He had wanted to force him
to give his daughter in marriage, as you have seen before. There was still
another reason for the resentment. While the duke was besieging
Amiens, the constable made an expedition to Hainaut; and among his
many exploits, he burned a castle called Solre, which belonged to a
knight named Baudoin de Lannoy. At the time it was not customary to
burn places on either side; and the duke used this as his reason for setting
fires and having set fire to so many places that season.

Thus they began to conspire to destroy the constable. On the king's
side some persons broached the subject in their conversations with
some of the constable's enemies in the duke's service. They had no
better opinion of the constable than the duke had, and everyone agreed
that he was the instigator of the war. They began to uncover all the
bargains and negotiations which he had transacted on either side, and
they began to advance his destruction.

Someone might wonder whether the king could not have achieved the
constable's ruin by himself. I should think not; for his territories were
situated between the king's and the duke's. He held Saint-Quentin, a
large and strong town in the Vermandois; he had Ham and Bohain as
well as other very strong towns, all of them near Saint-Quentin, and
he could always place soldiers there from whatever side he wished. The
king allotted him four hundred well-paid men-at-arms; he himself was
their commissary and he made his own reviews, thereby gaining much
money, for he did not maintain as many soldiers as he declared. Furthermore, his regular income amounted to at least forty-five thousand francs,
and he exacted one *écu* for each cask of wine which passed through his
territories on its way to Flanders or Hainaut. He possessed very rich
domains and had many informers in France as well as in the duke's lands,
where he had many relatives.

During the full year that this truce lasted, the project of ruining the
constable was actively negotiated. The king's courtiers discussed the
matter with one of the duke's knights, named my lord of Humbercourt,
whom we mentioned earlier in these memoirs, and who had always
strongly hated the constable, but lately even more so; for at a meeting
held at Roye, where the constable and several others represented the
king and the chancellor of Burgundy, the lord of Humbercourt, and
others represented the duke, the constable twice gave the lord of
Humbercourt the lie in the course of their discussions, and in a most
unbecoming way. To this Humbercourt replied simply that if he put
up with this insult, the constable should not attribute this honor to
himself but to the king, under whose security he had come as an am-

bassador, and also to Humbercourt's master, the duke, whom he was representing and to whom he would make a report of this.

This single offense and this affront so suddenly committed were eventually to cost the constable his life, and his possessions were lost as well, as you shall see. Therefore persons in important positions, including princes, should be on their guard against committing or saying anything so offensive and should consider to whom they are speaking. For in just the degree that they are of higher rank, by so much do offenses produce the greater displeasure and sorrow. For they think that they will be dishonored according to the importance and authority of the person who offends them, and if he happens to be their master or their lord, they lose all hope of obtaining future honors or favors from him. And more people serve with an eye on further benefits than in appreciation for those which they have already received.

To return to the matter under discussion, consultations were always taking place with the lord of Humbercourt and with the chancellor, for he had been present when the offensive language was spoken at Roye, and, besides, he was a good friend of the lord of Humbercourt. They proceeded so far in this matter that they had a special meeting at Bouvignes, near Namur, for further discussion of the subject. The king was represented by the lord of Curton, governor of the Limousin, and Master Jean Héberge, later bishop of Evreux, and the duke was represented by the above-mentioned chancellor and the lord of Humbercourt. It was the year 1474.

The constable had been warned that bargaining was going on at his expense, and he immediately sent envoys to the two princes. He let each of them know that he was aware of their intrigues; and he maneuvered so well this time that he led the king to suspect that the duke of Burgundy wanted to deceive him and was trying to lure the constable away from his side. Therefore the king hastily sent a message to his ambassadors at Bouvignes, requesting them not to conclude anything against the constable for the reasons he told them, but to prolong the truce according to their instructions; and it was for six months or a year, I do not remember which.

When the messenger arrived, he found that everything had been concluded and that documents had already been sealed with the lords' arms the night before. But the ambassadors were on such good terms with each other and were such good friends that they returned the sealed documents, which said that, for the reasons given, the constable was declared a criminal and an enemy of both princes; and they mutually promised and swore that the first of the two who could lay hands on him would have him executed within eight days or would turn him over to the other to dispose of him as he saw fit; by the sound of a trumpet he was to be declared an enemy of both sides, together with all those who might serve him, do him favors, or otherwise help him. Furthermore, the king promised to let the duke have the town of Saint-Quentin, which has been mentioned so often, as well as all the constable's money and movable possessions which might be found in the kingdom, together with all the territories which he held from the duke. Among others he gave him Ham and Bohain, which are very strong places; and it was agreed that on a certain day the king and the duke were to have their men-at-arms assembled before Ham and to besiege the constable. However, owing to the reasons I mentioned, all these plans were called off and a time and place were appointed for the constable to come and speak with the king in all security; for the constable feared for the safety of his person, like one who knew everything that had been decided at Bouvignes.

The place chosen was three leagues away from Noyon, in the direction of La Fère, upon a little river. On the constable's side they had made the fords impassable. On one of the roads they erected a strong barrier. The constable was the first to arrive at the meeting-place; he had taken with him all or most of his men, for he had more than three hundred men-at-arms, and he wore his cuirass under a robe without a belt. Accompanying the king were some six hundred men-at-arms, among them my lord of Dammartin, grand major-domo of France, who was a mortal enemy of the constable.

The king sent me to present his apologies to the constable for having kept him waiting for so long. Thereupon he came and they spoke together in the presence of five or six men from both sides. The constable begged the king to excuse him for having come in his armor, and claimed to have done it because he feared that the count of Dammartin might do him harm. To summarize, it was agreed that all things past would be forgotten and never mentioned again. Thereupon the constable passed over to the king's side, and he and the count of Dammartin came to terms. The constable took lodgings with the king at Noyon, and the next day he returned to Saint-Quentin, well reconciled, as he put it.

When the king had reflected on these things and heard the murmurs of his men, he came to think that he had been unwise to grant an audience to his servant, and then to tolerate that a closed barrier should be placed before him and that the constable should have come accompanied by men-at-arms who were all royal subjects and paid out of his own pocket. And if his hatred had been great before this, it was even more violent now; and as for the constable, his spirit was certainly not diminished.

12

When one considers the king's position, one must realize that his action resulted from good judgment, for I believe that the constable would have regained the good graces of the duke of Burgundy by giving him Saint-Quentin, regardless of all his promises to the contrary.

But for such a wise man as the constable to come in such a garb to speak with his king and master, and to be accompanied by so many men-at-arms who were in the king's pay was a mistaken calculation, or else God deprived him of understanding of what this business was about. Indeed, he himself seemed amazed and astounded, judging from his expression. And when he found himself in the king's presence, although there was only a small barrier between them, he immediately ordered it to be opened and passed over to the king's side. He was in great danger that day.

I assume that he and some of his close friends congratulated themselves on this action and were proud of the fact that the king seemed to fear them, for they considered the king a timorous man. And indeed he was, but never without good reason. He had extricated himself from important wars which he had fought against the lords of his kingdom by giving generously and promising even more; and he did not want to leave anything to chance which he could resolve otherwise.

It seemed to many people that he acted in this manner through fear and dread; and many of them found themselves to be greatly mistaken in their notions after they tried to undertake anything against him, as, for example, the count of Armagnac and others who paid dearly for the king always knew whether it was time to fear or not. I am proud to say in his praise (and if I have said it elsewhere, it is well worth saying two times) that I have never known a man so wise in adverse situations.

To return to my lord the constable, by chance he may have wished that the king should fear him—or at least I believe so, for I should not want to accuse him or even talk about it if it were not to inform those who are in the service of great princes and who do not all understand equally well the affairs of the world. I would counsel a friend of mine, if I had one, to take pains to have his master love him, not fear him. For I have never seen any man gain any authority in the eyes of his lord by keeping him in fear; sooner or later misfortune overtook him and it was with the consent of his master himself.

Book Three

Many such examples have been seen in this kingdom in our time or shortly before. My lord of La Trémoïlle comes to mind, as well as others in this country;[88] in England we may cite the count of Warwick and all his followers; and I could name others in Spain and elsewhere. But by chance those who will see this passage may know them better than I do. This boldness often proceeds from the knowledge that one has served well; and it seems to many of those who use these tactics that their merit is such that one ought to endure a good deal from them and that one could not do without them. But princes on the contrary, are of the opinion that everyone is duty-bound to serve them well; they like those who say so and desire nothing better than to get rid of those who rebuke them.

In this context I must cite our master concerning two things which he once told me in relation to those who perform great services (and he told me who told him these sayings). First, he said that to have served too well sometimes leads to one's ruin; and, secondly, great services are often repaid by great ingratitude. But this can happen through the fault of those who have performed these services and are too arrogant in their good fortune, and behave insolently toward their masters and their colleagues, as well as through lack of gratitude on the part of the prince. Furthermore, the king told me that in his opinion, in order to be in a good position at court, it is to a man's advantage if his prince has granted him a favor in return for very little, for in that case he remains the prince's debtor; the opposite is true if he has performed such a great service that it is the prince who is very obligated to him. And princes naturally like their debtors more than their creditors. Therefore in all walks of life it is difficult to manage one's affairs well in this world, and God gives a great grace to those whom he has endowed with good natural sense.

The interview between the king and the constable took place in the year 1474.

88. Georges de la Trémoïlle, the favorite of Charles VII, was murdered in 1433 after dominating the king for years.

Charles the Bold's father is seated at table in the center of this tableau of courtly pastimes. The extravagant costumes and idyllic landscape illustrate Commynes' notion of the recent Burgundian past: peace, prosperity, and moral indifference (see, for example, Book 1, chapter 2). They also illustrate King Edward IV's dream of life, a dream adroitly used by Louis XI, Edward's political opponent in the actions depicted by Commynes in Book 4.

BOOK FOUR

The Franco-English War of 1475 and the Betrayal of the Count of Saint-Pol

1

At this time the duke of Burgundy went to take the territory of Gelderland, owing to a quarrel which is worthy of being related, in order to show the works and the power of God.

There was a young duke of Gelderland, named Adolf, whose wife was one of the daughters of the house of Bourbon, the sister of my lord Peter of Bourbon, the present duke, and he had married her at the court of Burgundy; for this reason he was on good terms with the house of Burgundy.

Duke Adolf had committed a most horrible act, for he took his father prisoner one night as he was about to go to bed, and led him five German leagues bare-legged, in very cold weather, and he put him at the bottom of a tower, where he had no light except what came through a tiny window; and he kept him there for five years [1465–1470]. This led to a fierce war between the duke of Cleves, whose sister the imprisoned duke had married, and young Duke Adolf. The duke of Burgundy had tried several times to have them settle their differences, but he did not succeed. Finally the pope and the emperor intervened energetically, and the duke of Burgundy was ordered under severe penalty to release Duke Arnold from prison.

And so he did, for the young duke did not dare refuse to give his father up to him, since he saw that so many important people were becoming interested in this affair, and, besides, he feared the duke of Burgundy, who was so strong. I saw both of them several times in the grand council meeting where they pleaded their cases, and I saw the good old man challenge his son to a combat. The duke of Burgundy wanted very much to reconcile them, and he favored the younger man. The young duke was offered the title of governor or administrator of the province, together with its revenues, except for a small town near Brabant called Grave, which was to remain in the father's possession; the latter was also to enjoy its revenues and in addition a pension of three thousand florins. Thus the whole proposition amounted to six

249

thousand florins and the title of duke, which was reasonable. Along with wiser men than myself, I was delegated to make this offer to the young duke, and he answered that he would rather throw his father head first into a well and follow him there than make such an agreement; besides, his father had been a duke for forty-four years, and it was high time that he should become one himself. However, he would willingly let his father have three thousand florins a year, on condition that he would never set foot in his duchy again. And he made several other most unwise comments.

This happened precisely at the time when the king took Amiens from the duke of Burgundy [February, 1470], who was with the above-mentioned dukes in Doullens. He found himself thus in a difficult situation, and left Doullens suddenly to retire to Hesdin, and probably forgot about the affair [between father and son]. The young duke disguised himself as a Frenchman and left with only one attendant, in order to return to his own territory. As he came to a river-port near Namur, he paid one florin for his passage. A priest saw him and became suspicious; he said a word to the ferryman, scrutinized the face of the man who had paid the florin, and recognized him. There he was seized and brought to Namur, where he was made a prisoner and remained confined until the death of the duke of Burgundy, at which time the townspeople of Ghent took him out of prison. They wanted to force the lady who has since become duchess of Austria [Mary of Burgundy] to marry him. Then they took him with them before Tournai, where he was slain in an evil way and in evil company, as if God was not yet satisfied with the retribution to be exacted for the outrage committed against the duke's father.

The father had died before the duke of Burgundy, and while his son was still in prison. At his death the old duke had left his succession to the duke of Burgundy because of the ingratitude of his own son. And, taking advantage of the above-mentioned dissension, the duke of Burgundy conquered the duchy of Gelderland, where he found some resistance at the time. But he was powerful and at peace with the king, and he enjoyed the possession of Gelderland until his death; and his descendants enjoy it to this day and will continue to do so as long as it pleases God. Now, as I said in the beginning, I related this only to show that such cruel acts and such wickedness never remain unpunished.[89]

89. Commynes' moral tale neglects the duke's father's debaucheries as well as some attenuating circumstances in the son's life mentioned by other chroniclers, as Jean Dufournet shows in *La destruction des mythes dans les Mémoires de Ph. de Commynes* (Geneva, 1966), pp. 441–42.

Book Four

The duke of Burgundy had returned home and was very proud of himself on account of this duchy which he had added to his territories. He began to take a great interest in the affairs of Germany, because the emperor was a man of small courage who would have endured anything rather than spend money. And indeed by himself, without the help of the other German lords, he could do very little. Therefore the duke prolonged his truce with the king, although it seemed to some of the king's servants that he should not agree to it because it might make the duke too powerful. It was their good sense which made them say this; nevertheless, due to their lack of experience and observation of the world, they did not really understand the matter at all. Others who understood the case better and who had more knowledge from having been on the spot advised the king our master to accept this truce boldly and to let the duke go and exhaust himself in Germany (which is an area so large and so powerful that it is almost incredible). They said: "After the duke will have taken a place or settled a dispute, he will start something else; for he is not the kind of man who is ever satisfied with one enterprise" (and in this respect he was the king's opposite, for the more involved he got in an affair, the more he entangled himself), "and the best way to take revenge on him would be to let him have his way and even to give him some slight assistance. Above all, he must not have reason to suspect that the truce might be broken. For, being faced with the greatness of Germany and its power, it will not be possible for him to avoid being destroyed and lost on all counts. Although the emperor is hardly a valiant man, the princes of his empire will see to it that the duke is ruined." And this is exactly what happened in the end.

At the time of the contention of two candidates for the bishopric of Cologne, one of whom was the brother of the landgrave of Hesse and the other a relative of the count palatine of the Rhine [Frederick the Victorious], the duke of Burgundy took the part of the count palatine's kinsman and attempted to establish him by force in that dignity, in the hope of gaining some towns for himself as a result. He besieged Neuss near Cologne in the year 1474. The landgrave of Hesse was there with a number of soldiers. The duke had so many things in his imagination, and so many great ones, that he was overwhelmed. For at this time he wanted King Edward to come from England with a large army which he had raised at the duke's urgent request. He made great haste to try to achieve his goals in Germany, which were as follows: if he should take Neuss, he planned to put a strong garrison there, as well as in one or two other towns above Cologne, so that the city of Cologne would have to capitulate. Then he would proceed up

251

the Rhine to the county of Ferrette, which belonged to him at the time, and thus all the Rhine would be his as far as Holland, where one finds stronger towns and castles than in any other kingdom in Christendom except France.

The truce which he had made with the king had been prolonged for six months, and the greater part of it was already past. The king requested another prolongation, so that the duke would be free to do as he pleased in Germany, but the duke did not accept because of the promise which he had made to the English.

I could well do without speaking of that affair of Neuss, which does not fit with the character of our material, since I was not there, but I must make mention of it because of certain matters which are related to it. The landgrave of Hesse had withdrawn to the town of Neuss; with him were many of his relatives and friends, as well as at least eighteen hundred horsemen, as I was told, all of whom proved themselves to be very fine soldiers; there were also as many infantrymen as were considered necessary. The landgrave was the brother of the bishop who had been elected and who was the opponent of the person supported by the duke of Burgundy. And thus the duke besieged Neuss in the year 1474.

He led the most handsome army which he had ever had; this was especially true of the horsemen. For, with a view to certain ends to which he pretended in Italy, he had assembled some one thousand Italian men-at-arms, partly good and partly bad; and their commander was a certain count of Campobasso from the kingdom of Naples, a very false and dangerous man.[90] There was also Giacomo Galeotto, a Neapolitan gentleman and a very worthy man, as well as many others whom I shall not name for brevity's sake. Similarly, the duke had with him some three thousand Englishmen, all very brave, and a great number of his own subjects, well mounted and well armed, and having had a long experience in warfare; and he had a very large and powerful artillery. He was keeping all these forces in readiness to join the English, who were hastily being assembled in England.

But such things take time for the king cannot undertake such an important affair without convoking his parliament, which is the equivalent of our three estates; it is a just and holy institution, and the kings are stronger and better served as a result of consulting with this body on such occasions. When these estates are assembled, he declares his intention and requests aid from his subjects, for no money is raised in

90. Commynes' biases have blackened Campobasso's name falsely. See section 4 of the Introduction.

England unless it is for an expedition to France or Scotland, or for something similar to that. They grant the requests most willingly and liberally, especially if it is a question of passing into France. As a matter of fact, when the kings of England want to raise money, they have the habit of pretending to need an army to go to Scotland. And in order to raise large sums of money, they pay the army for three months and then disband it and return home, although they have received enough money for a year. King Edward IV understood this procedure very well and often resorted to it.

It was a full year before this army was ready; when it was finally set up, word was sent to my lord of Burgundy, who had gone to the very gates of Neuss at the beginning of the summer. He had expected to establish his candidate as bishop in the matter of a few days and to obtain several towns, such as Neuss and others, in order to arrive at his ends, as I explained before.

I believe that what happened was the work of God, who took pity on this kingdom, for the duke had a well-trained army of soldiers who were accustomed to invade the kingdom of France for many years without finding anyone to fight against them in the open field, except when an army was found guarding a town. But it is true that this was according to the will of the king, who did not want to leave anything to chance. He did not do this merely out of fear of the duke of Burgundy, but because he foresaw that rebellion might take place in his kingdom if he should happen to lose a battle. For he did not consider himself well regarded by all his subjects, and particularly not by the great nobles. And if I may speak freely, he often told me that he knew his subjects well and that they would make life difficult for him if his affairs turned out badly. And therefore whenever the duke of Burgundy invaded France, he did no more than put strong garrisons into the towns by which he was likely to pass. Thus in a short time the duke's army deteriorated on its own without any need for the king to endanger his country, which seems to me to be a result of using great good judgment.

However, considering that the duke of Burgundy had such a strong army, as I told you, if the army of the king of England had arrived at the beginning of the season for campaigning, as it surely would have done if the duke had not committed the error of besieging Neuss so obstinately, one can be certain that this kingdom would have suffered greatly. For never before had a king of England come to France with such a powerful army as the one of which I am speaking at a single crossing, nor one in such fine form for fighting. All the great lords of

England were there, without any exception. There must have been some fifteen hundred men-at-arms, which was an unusually large number for the English, all of them in excellent condition and well attended, and fourteen thousand archers carrying bows and arrows, and all of them on horseback; in addition there were numerous men on foot employed as army servants. And in the whole army there was not a single page. Furthermore, the king of England was able to send three thousand men to land in Brittany and join the duke's army. I have seen two letters written in the hand of my lord of Urfé, grand equerry of France, who was at the time in the service of the duke of Brittany. One was addressed to the king of England and the other to my lord Hastings, grand chamberlain of England; among other things they stated that the duke of Brittany would accomplish more in one month by means of intrigues than the combined armies of the English and the duke of Burgundy could do in six, regardless of how strong they might be. And I believe that they would have been right if the enterprise had proceeded further. But God, who has always loved this kingdom, managed things as I shall explain later. And the letters which I mentioned were bought from an English secretary for sixty silver marks by our master the king, may God absolve him.

2

The duke of Burgundy was indeed extremely busy before Neuss, as I told you earlier, and he met with greater difficulties than he had anticipated. The people of Cologne, who were located four leagues further up the Rhine, spent 100,000 gold florins a month because of the fear which they had of the duke of Burgundy; together with the other cities beyond them on the Rhine, they had already put into the field fifteen or sixteen thousand foot-soldiers; and they were posted with a large train of artillery on the bank of the river Rhine on the side opposite the duke of Burgundy's forces. And they tried to intercept his provisions, which came by water from Gelderland up the river, as well as to destroy his ships by means of cannon-shot.

The emperor and the electoral princes of the empire had a meeting about this matter and decided to raise an army. The king had already sent several messengers to them to solicit them to do this. And so they sent him a canon of Cologne, from the house of Bavaria, and another ambassador along with him; they brought the king a detailed list of the army which the emperor had the intention of forming, provided that the king, for his part, would be willing to help. They did not fail to obtain a favorable answer, and they were promised everything which they requested. In addition the king promised the emperor, as well as several among the princes and towns, by means of documents sealed with his arms, that as soon as the emperor would be at Cologne and would take the field, he would send twenty thousand men to join him, under the command of my lords of Craon and of Salazar. And thus this army was raised from Germany; it was fabulously large, and so much so that it was almost incredible. For all the princes of Germany, temporal as well as spiritual, the bishops, and all the communities sent men there, and in great numbers. I was told that the bishop of Münster, who is not among the great ones, led six thousand foot-soldiers there, as well as fourteen hundred horsemen, all dressed in green, and twelve hundred carts. It is true that his bishopric is near Neuss.

It took the emperor approximately seven months to raise the army, and at the end of that time it took up quarters within a half league of the duke of Burgundy's headquarters. And according to what I have been told by several of the duke's men, the king of England's army and that of the duke of Burgundy put together did not amount to more than a third of the army which I am speaking about, including men and pavilions. In addition to the emperor's army, there was the army which I mentioned to you, on the other side of the river, facing the duke of Burgundy, which caused great torment to his troops and intercepted his provisions.

As soon as the emperor and the princes of the empire arrived before Neuss, they sent the king a doctor who enjoyed great authority among them; he was named Dr. Hesler and has since become a cardinal. He came to solicit the king to keep his promise and to send the twenty thousand men, as he had pledged to do; otherwise the Germans would negotiate [with the duke]. The king led him to hope for the best, had four hundred *écus* given to him, and sent him back to the emperor with a person named Jean Tiercelin, lord of Brosse. The doctor, however, was not pleased when he left.

Marvelous bargaining was carried on during this siege, for the king was taking measures to make peace with the duke of Burgundy, or at least to prolong the truce, so that the English would not come. The king of England, on the other hand, did everything in his power to persuade the duke to leave Neuss and instead to keep his promise and help him to wage war in this kingdom, asserting that the season was beginning to be unfavorable. Lord Scales, nephew of the constable and a very fine knight, was sent twice as an ambassador to discuss these matters, along with several other persons.

The duke of Burgundy was in an obstinate mood; and God had obviously troubled his sense and understanding, because for all his life he had tried to get the English to pass over [into France], and at this time, when they were ready to do so and when everything seemed favorable to them, in Brittany as well as elsewhere, he remained obstinate in pursuing an impossible enterprise.

With the emperor was an apostolic legate who used to go from one camp to the other every day to negotiate peace; and similarly the king of Denmark [Christian I, 1448–1483], who was quartered in a small town near the two armies, was working for peace. And thus the duke of Burgundy might well have obtained honorable terms and gone to join the king of England. He could not bring himself to do this, however, and he justified himself to the English, claiming that his honor would be trampled underfoot if he left, and offering other lame excuses. For they were not the English who had lived in his father's time and who had taken part in the old wars with France, but these were all inexperienced men and ignorant as far as French warfare was concerned. Therefore the duke made an unwise move if he intended to make use of their services in the future, because it would have been necessary for him to guide them step by step for the first campaign.

While the duke was in this obstinate frame of mind, wars broke out upon him from two or three directions. One resulted from the fact that the duke of Lorraine, who had been at peace with him, bade him defiance before Neuss, by means of my lord of Craon, who wanted to use this for the advantage of the king's affairs and who did not fail to promise the duke of Lorraine that he would be made powerful as a result. And thereupon they took the field, made great ravages in the duchy of Luxembourg, and razed a place called Pierrefort, in the duchy of Luxembourg, situated within a distance of two leagues from Nancy.

Furthermore, it was arranged by the king and some of his representatives to whom he entrusted this affair that an alliance be concluded for ten years between the Swiss and the towns upon the Rhine, such as Basel, Strasbourg, and others, which had formerly been on hostile terms with them. In addition a peace settlement was made between Duke Sigismund of Austria and the Swiss, in order to make it possible for Duke Sigismund to recover the county of Ferrette, which he had pledged to the duke of Burgundy for the price of 100,000 Rhenish florins. And thus it was agreed, except that one thing remained in dispute between Duke Sigismund and the Swiss, who wanted to have the right of passage through four towns of the county of Ferrette, with as many arms and men, and as often, as they pleased. This question was referred to the king, who decided in favor of the Swiss. And from what is related here, you may realize the extent of the disputes which the king secretly provoked against the duke of Burgundy.

All this was executed just as it was planned; for one fine night Pierre de Hagenbach, governor of the territory of Ferrette for the duke of Burgundy, was captured, along with eight hundred soldiers of his. All of them were unconditionally freed except the governor, who was taken to Basel, where he was brought to trial because of certain excesses and violent acts which he had committed in the territory of Ferrette. In the end they cut off his head; and all the territory of Ferrette was put into the hands of Duke Sigismund of Austria. The Swiss began to wage war in Burgundy, and they took Blamont, which belonged to the marshal of Burgundy, who was from the house of Neufchâtel. The Burgundians went forth to help him, but they were put to rout. The Swiss made great ravages in the region and then they retired for the moment.

3

The truce between the king and the duke of Burgundy had expired, to the king's very great regret, for he would have preferred to have a prolongation of the truce. Since he realized that he could not obtain it, however, he proceeded to besiege a paltry little castle called Tronchoy; and this was early in the year 1475, at the beginning and most beautiful period of the season for campaigning. It was taken by assault in a few hours. The next day the king sent me to speak to those who were in Montdidier. They left with their bags intact and abandoned the place. The next day I went to speak to those who were before Roye, together with my lord the admiral, bastard of Bourbon, and similarly the place was given up to me, because they had lost hope of obtaining help. They would not have surrendered it if the duke had been in the territory. In any case, contrary to our promise, these two towns were burned.

From there the king went to lay siege before Corbie, and everyone waited; very fine approaches were made, and the king's artillery fired for three days. Inside the town were my lord of Contay and several others, who surrendered it and left with their bags intact. Two days later the unfortunate town was plundered and then it was set on fire, as had been done in the case of the other two. At this time the king thought of withdrawing his army, and he hoped to convince the duke of Burgundy of the desirability of a truce, owing to the state of need in which he found himself. But a woman whom I know well—and I shall not name her because she is still living—wrote to the king, advis-

257

ing him to have his men proceed to Arras and the surrounding region, and the king believed what she said, because she was a woman of honorable estate. I do not praise her action because she was not bound to do what she did. The king sent there my lord the admiral, bastard of Bourbon, accompanied by a good number of men, who burned a large quantity of their towns, beginning near Abbeville and proceeding as far as Arras. The people of the town of Arras, who had experienced no adversity for a long time and were filled with great pride, forced the soldiers who were in their town to make a sally against the king's men. Their number was not sufficient to hold their own against the king's forces, and therefore they were beaten so severely that many of them were either killed or taken, including all of their leaders, among whom were Jacques de Saint-Pol, brother of the constable, the lord of Contay,[91] the lord of Carency, and others; several of them were close relatives of the lady who had been the occasion of that exploit. And the lady suffered great loss because of it. But the king in time made reparation to her for everything.

At this time the king had sent to the emperor Jean Tiercelin, lord of Brosse, in order to see to it that he should not come to terms with the duke of Burgundy and to make excuses for not having sent his men-at-arms, as he had promised. The ambassador was to give assurance that the king was going to do so and that he would continue and increase his exploits and ravages against the duke's territories, on the frontiers of Picardy as well as Burgundy. In addition he made a new proposition, which was that they should mutually pledge to each other not to make a separate peace or truce; the emperor should take all the lands which the duke held [as fiefs] from the empire and which should by right be held by him, and he should have them declared confiscated into his hands; the king would take the territories which the duke held from the crown, such as Flanders, Artois, Burgundy, and several others.

Although the emperor had hardly been a valiant man during his lifetime, he nevertheless had good judgment; and because of his long life, he was able to accumulate much experience. And these discussions between us and him had lasted for a long time. Besides, he became weary of the war, although it was not costing him anything; for all the lords of Germany participated at their own expense, as it is customary whenever the interest of the empire is at stake.

The emperor replied that near a German city there was once a large bear, which was doing much damage. Three fellows from the town,

91. This is Louis le Jeune, who became lord of Contay after Guillaume le Jeune, the other lord of Contay mentioned in the *Memoirs*, died at Huy in 1467.

who used to frequent the taverns, came to a tavern-keeper to whom they owed money, and begged him to give them credit one more time; in two days' time they would pay off their full debt, for they would catch that bear which was so harmful and whose pelt was worth so much money, not to speak of the presents which would be forthcoming and offered to them by everyone. The host granted their request, and after they had had their dinner they proceeded to the bear's lair. And as they approached the cavern they found the animal closer to them than they had expected. They were frightened and fled. One of them climbed up a tree; the other ran toward the town; as for the third, the bear overtook him and trampled him strongly underfoot, bringing its muzzle near his ear. The poor man was lying flat on the ground and played dead. Now it is the nature of that animal that whatever it holds, be it man or beast, if it sees that it no longer moves, it leaves it alone, believing it to be dead. And so the bear left the poor man without having done him much harm and withdrew to its cavern. As soon as the poor man realized that he was free, he got up and fled toward the town. His companion, who was in the tree and had witnessed this strange affair, came down, ran, and cried out to the other man who was going ahead that he should wait for him; and so he turned around and waited for him. When they had rejoined each other, the one who had been in the tree asked his companion to tell him truly what advice he had been given by the bear, which had held its snout against his ear for so long. To which question the other replied: "He told me never to sell a bear-skin until the animal is dead."

And with this fable the emperor gave a lesson to our king, without giving any other answer to our man, as if he had meant to say: "Come here as you have promised to do and let us kill this man if we can, and then let us divide his possessions."

4

You have heard how Jacques de Saint-Pol and others had been taken prisoners before Arras; this seizure greatly displeased the constable, for Jacques had been a good brother to him. This unfortunate happening was not the only one to befall him, for at the same time the count of Roussy, his son, governor of Burgundy for the duke, was also captured. Furthermore, the constable's wife [Mary of Savoy, sister-in-law of Louis XI], died. She was a worthy lady and the sister of the queen [Charlotte], who protected and favored her. For the bargaining which had been started against him was still in full force, as you have heard, and it almost succeeded at the meeting which took place in Bouvignes about the matter [in May, 1474]. Never again was the constable safe; he was held in suspicion by both sides, but he was especially mistrusted by the king. And it did indeed seem to him that the king repented of having withdrawn the agreement sealed with his arms at Bouvignes. The count of Dammartin and others were quartered with the men-at-arms near Saint-Quentin; the constable feared them as if they had been his enemies and kept himself inside Saint-Quentin, where he had put some three hundred foot-soldiers from his own lands, because he had no confidence whatsoever in the men-at-arms [of the king, who had been placed under his command].

He lived under constant stress, for the king solicited him, by means of several messengers, to take the field and to serve him in the direction of Hainaut, and to besiege Avesne-sur-Helpe at the time when my lord the admiral and the other men were going to burn places in the Artois, as I have told you, which he did with great apprehension, for he was greatly afraid. He stayed before the town only a few days, and he had himself closely guarded; then he withdrew to his territories and sent word to the king (for I heard his messenger, by the king's command) that he had raised the siege because he had unquestionable information that there were two men in the army who had been charged by the king to kill him. And he gave so many apparent proofs of this that people almost believed him, and they almost suspected one of the two of having told the constable something which he ought to have kept to himself. I do not wish to name any of these persons or to make any further mention of this matter.

The constable often sent messengers to the duke of Burgundy's camp. I believe that his aim was to persuade him to withdraw from this foolish adventure. And when his men had returned, he sent some message or other to the king, which he thought would greatly please him, and informed him about certain incidents, and particularly the occasion that he claimed had led him to send envoys [to the duke]; and he hoped by these means to keep the king preoccupied. At other times he also sent word to the king that the affairs of the duke were prospering, so as to instill some fear into him. For he was so afraid of being attacked that he requested the duke to send him his brother, Jacques de Saint-Pol (before his capture, for he was at the siege of Neuss), and also the lord of Fiennes and other relatives of his, and that he should be allowed to put them inside Saint-Quentin with their men, but without their having to wear the cross of Saint Andrew [the symbol of the house of Burgundy]. He promised the duke that he would hold Saint-Quentin for him and return it to him shortly thereafter; and he would give him a solemn engagement, sealed with his arms to this effect. The duke acceded to his request.

And when Jacques, the lord of Fiennes, and his other relatives came twice within one or two leagues of the town of Saint-Quentin and were ready to enter, it so happened that his fears had left him; and so he repented and sent them away. He did this three times, so much did he wish to remain in this state, navigating between the two; for he feared both of them extraordinarily. I have known these things from several persons, and especially from the mouth of Jacques de Saint-Pol, who told this to the king in this manner when he was brought as a prisoner; and I was the only person present. And it was greatly in his favor that he gave frank answers to the questions which the king asked him.

The king asked him how many people he had had ready to enter the town. He replied that the third time he had three thousand men. The king asked him also whether, had he happened to be the stronger [in arms than his brother], he would have held the town for the king [as ultimate sovereign] or for the constable. Jacques de Saint-Pol answered that on the first two trips he came only to help his brother, but on the third, since the constable had twice before deceived both his master [the king of France] and him, if he had found himself in the stronger position, he would have held the place for his master, but without doing violence to the constable or doing anything which might have been prejudicial to him, except that he would not have left the town even if his brother had ordered him to do so. Since that meeting and shortly thereafter, the king released Jacques de Saint-Pol from prison and gave him men-at-arms as well as a fine and large estate; and he made use of his services until his death: and it was all because of his answers.

Since I began to speak of Neuss I have touched upon many happenings, one after the other. And they all took place during this time, for the siege lasted for a year. Two things greatly tempted the duke of Burgundy to raise the siege: one was the war which the king was waging against him in Picardy, which had resulted in the burning of three little towns and a section of the plains of Artois and Ponthieu; the other was the fine and powerful army which the king of England was raising at his request and instigation. He had tried all his life to have the king cross the water [and invade France], and he had never managed to accomplish this until now.

The king of England and all the lords of his kingdom were exceedingly displeased at the duke of Burgundy's long delay; and in addition to the earnest supplications which he made of him, they resorted to threats, owing to the great expense which they had incurred, and to the fact that the favorable season was coming to an end. The duke took great pride in opposing the powerful German army, which was composed of contingents of princes as well as of prelates and of towns, and which was the largest force that had ever been assembled as far as any living man could remember and for a long time before. And all of these troops put together were not able to make him raise the siege. But he paid dearly for his glory, for he who collects the profit from a war will also have the honor.

The legate whom I mentioned earlier was constantly going back and forth from one camp to the other, and finally the emperor and the duke made peace, and the town of Neuss was put into the hands of the legate to be disposed of as the Apostolic See should order.

In what extremity must the duke have found himself, seeing himself thus pressed by the war which the king was waging against him, as well as pressed and menaced by his friend the king of England on the one hand, and, on the other hand, seeing the town of Neuss in such a state that in fifteen days' time he could have it reduced to utter ruin because of famine (and he might even have achieved the same result in ten days, according to what I was told by one of the military leaders who was inside the town and whom the king took into his service). And so it was for these reasons that the duke of Burgundy raised the siege in the year 1475.

5

Now we should speak of the king of England, who kept his army in Dover in order to cross the sea and to land in Calais; and this army was the largest that any king of England had brought [across the water]; it consisted entirely of horsemen, the best mounted and the best armed who had ever invaded France, and it included all the lords of England, or almost all of them. There were fifteen hundred well-mounted men-at-arms, most of them armed and richly attired according to the French fashion, and each had a large retinue of men on horseback. Their forces included at least fifteen thousand archers, all of them on horseback and carrying bows and arrows, as well as a large number of foot-soldiers and others to pitch their tents and pavilions, of which they had great quantities, and to take care of their artillery and enclose their camp. There was not a single page in the whole army; and the English had mustered three thousand men to send into Brittany.

I have mentioned this earlier, but it is pertinent to the point I wish to make, which is that if God had not wanted to trouble the duke of Burgundy's sense and to preserve this kingdom, to which He has granted more favors, up to now, than to any other, would there be reason to believe that the duke would have proceeded so obstinately to besiege the strongly fortified town of Neuss, which was so well defended? Would he not have considered that all his life he had been unable to prevail upon the kingdom of England to form an army and to send it on this side of the sea, especially since he definitely knew that these forces were, so to speak, useless in his wars with France? For if he had wanted to make use of them, it would have been essential that for one whole season he not let them out of his sight, so as to train them in setting up and conducting an army according to the methods of our wars on this side of the water. For when they first come over they could not be more awkward nor clumsy; but after a very short time they become excellent and brave soldiers.

He did exactly the opposite; among other troubles [which he caused them], he almost made them lose their reason. And compared with the king of England's, his army was so broken and in such bad shape, and so poor, that he did not dare present it before the English: for at the siege of Neuss he had lost four thousand mercenaries, among whom some of his finest men had died. And thus you may see that God disposed him in all ways to act contrary to what the situation required him reasonably to do, and contrary to what he had known and understood better than anyone else ten years earlier.

While King Edward was in Dover, ready to sail, the duke of Burgundy sent him five hundred boats or so from Holland and Zeeland. They are flat and low at the sides, and they are very useful for the transportation of horses; they are called *schuiten* [barges] and they came from Holland. And in spite of this large number [of boats] and everything that the king of England was able to provide, it took them more than three weeks to pass from Dover to Calais.

Now consider how difficult it is for a king of England to cross over into France; and if the king our master had understood naval strategy as well as he understood land maneuvers, King Edward would never have landed, at least that season. But he was not an expert in naval matters, and neither were those to whom he gave authority in the management of his war, for they knew even less about them than he did. It took the king of England three weeks to cross over. A single ship from Eu captured two or three of these little boats.

Before the king of England embarked and left Dover, he sent the king just one herald, called Jarretière, who was a native of Normandy.

He brought the king a letter of defiance from the king of England, written in such fine language and elegant style that I believe no Englishman ever had a hand in it. The king of England requested our king to return to him the kingdom of France, which belonged to him, so that he could restore the church, the nobility, and the people to their former state of liberty, and so that he could relieve them from the great burdens and oppressions in which they were held by the king; in case of refusal he predicted that all sorts of evils would follow, in the form and wording which it is customary to use on such occasions.

The king read the letter to himself; he then withdrew alone to a private room, and he had the herald summoned. He told him that he fully realized that the king of England was not acting on his own initiative in coming to France, but that he was being forced to do so by the duke of Burgundy as well as by the commons of England. He could clearly see that the season [for making war] was almost over and that the duke of Burgundy was returning from Neuss like a defeated man, bereft of everything. As for the constable, he well knew that he had had some transactions with the king of England because the latter had married the constable's niece, but he would deceive him. He told him about all the favors which he had done him and added: "He does not want to live in any other manner except in dissimulation, having intrigues with everyone and managing affairs to his own advantage." And he gave the herald several other reasons for admonishing King Edward of England to make peace with him. He gave the herald three hundred *écus* in cash with his own hand, and promised him a thousand if the peace should materialize. And in public the king had him presented with a beautiful piece of crimson velvet, thirty ells long.

The herald replied that he would do his best to bring about this agreement, and that he believed his master would not be adverse to it, but that no word should be said until the king of England had arrived on this side of the sea. But when he should be there, a herald should be dispatched to request a safe-conduct for the purpose of sending ambassadors to him. My lord Howard or my lord Stanley should be approached, as well as himself, so that he might help in presenting the herald.

Many people were in the [outer] room while the king was speaking to the herald. They were waiting and were very anxious to hear what the king would say and to see what sort of expression he would have on his face when he came out of the inner room. When he had terminated his interview, he called me and told me to keep conversing with the herald until an escort was assigned to lead him away, so that no one might be able to talk to him, and to have a thirty-ell piece of crimson velvet delivered to him. And so I did. The king began to speak to several persons and told them about this letter of defiance; and he called seven or eight of them aside and had the letter read. His face appeared to reflect great confidence and he showed no trace of fear, for he was very happy about the reception which his propositions had found with the herald.

6

Concerning this passage [of the king of England into France], another word is in order about my lord the constable, who was rather perturbed because of the trick which he had played on the duke of Burgundy in relation to Saint-Quentin. He already considered himself as deprived of the king's confidence, for his principal servants, such as my lord of Genlis and my lord of Moy, had left him. The king had already taken them into his service, although my lord of Moy had not yet severed relations with the constable. And the king strongly urged the constable to come to him, and he offered him certain recompenses which he had requested for the county of Guise, and which the king had formerly promised him.

The constable would have been very happy to come, provided that the king would swear upon the cross of Saint-Laud in Angers not to do any harm to his person nor to allow anyone else to do so. And he alleged that the king might as well take this oath to him now, since he had formerly taken it to the lord of Lescun. To this the king replied that he would never take this particular oath again, but that any other oath which the constable might wish to request he would be glad to take. You can easily imagine in what uneasy frame of mind the king was, and the constable too, for not a day passed, during a span of time, without envoys being sent from one side to the other to discuss the question of this oath. And to reflect upon it seriously, ours is indeed a miserable life, when we take such trouble and pains to shorten it by saying and writing so many things which are almost the opposite of what we really think.

And if these two persons of whom I am speaking had many worries, the king of England and the duke of Burgundy, for their part, had no fewer. The passage of the king of England to Calais and the departure of the duke of Burgundy from outside Neuss took place more or less at the same time, or certainly within a very few days of each other. The duke, by forced marches, with a very small escort, proceeded straight to Calais in order to meet the king of England. He sent his army, which was all shattered, as you have heard, to plunder the territories of Barrois and Lorraine and to obtain provisions and refresh themselves. And he did this because the duke of Lorraine had started a war against him and had defied him when he was besieging Neuss: this was a major error on his part, along with others which he had already committed in relation to the English, who had expected to find him at their landing, with at least twenty-five hundred men-at-arms in good condition, as well as a large number of other horsemen and foot-soldiers; for the duke had promised them all these things in order to persuade them to come, and he had said that he would start the war in France three months before their landing, so that they would find the king more weary and more crushed. But God took care of everything, as you have heard.

The king of England left Calais, accompanied by the duke of Burgundy; they passed through the Boulonnais and proceeded to Péronne, where the duke received them rather badly, for he had the gates guarded and he allowed only a few people to enter the town. And so they encamped in the fields: they certainly were equipped to do so because they were well provided with the necessary things for camping.

As soon as they had arrived at Péronne, the constable sent the duke of Burgundy one of his men, named Louis de Sainville, to apologize to the duke of Burgundy for not having delivered Saint-Quentin to him. Had he done so, he said, he would no longer have been in a position to be of any service to him in the kingdom of France; for he would have lost all his credit and his power to influence people there. But now, since he realized that the king of England was so close, he would do everything that the duke of Burgundy should require. And for greater assurance, he gave the duke some letters of credence addressed to the king of England in which the constable listed the duke of Burgundy as the guarantor [of the proposals in the letters]. Over and above this, he sent the duke of Burgundy a document sealed with his arms, by which he promised to serve and help him, as well as all his friends and allies, including the king of England and others, against any and all persons who might live or die, with no exception whatsoever.

The duke of Burgundy handed his letter to the king of England and explained the purpose. He padded his claims a bit, for he assured the king of England that the constable would establish him in Saint-Quentin and in all his other towns. The king of England believed it readily, for he had married the constable's niece, and he considered him to be in such great fear of the king that he would not dare fail to keep his promise to the duke of Burgundy. But neither the frame of mind of the constable, nor the fear which he had of the king led him that far yet; he still planned to use dissimulation, as was his custom, in order to satisfy them, and he would present such plausible reasons to them that they would still have patience and they would not force him to declare himself openly.

King Edward and his men were not accustomed to the practices in use in the affairs of this kingdom, and they proceeded more bluntly; therefore they were not so quick to perceive the deceptions which are used on this side of the water and elsewhere. For naturally the English who have never left England are very choleric: so are all the natives of cold countries. Ours, as you see, is situated between both kinds of countries, being bounded, as you know, by Italy, Spain, and Catalonia on the east [*sic*], and England and these parts of Flanders and Holland on the west; and in addition Germany touches us all along the area of Champagne. Thus we take after the warm region and also the cold one, and therefore we have people of two complexions. But my opinion is that in the whole world there is no region better situated than France.

The king of England, who rejoiced greatly at this piece of news from my lord the constable (although he might have had an inkling of it earlier, but not to such a degree as now), left Péronne in the company of the duke of Burgundy, who had no men with him, for all of them had marched into Barrois and Lorraine, as I told you. They approached Saint-Quentin, and a large body of Englishmen ran forward; I heard them speak about it several days later. They had expected that the bells would be rung at their arrival and that the cross and holy water would be brought forth by those who would meet them. As they came near the town, the artillery began to be fired and skirmishers on foot and on horseback sallied forth, and two or three Englishmen were killed and a few were taken prisoners. They had a very unpleasant, rainy day, and they returned to their camp in a pitiful state, very disappointed, muttering against the constable and calling him a traitor.

The next morning the duke of Burgundy wanted to take his leave of the king of England; this was a rather strange thing to do since he was the one who had made them come over to France. He wanted to join his army in Barrois, and he claimed that he would perform great feats to the advantage of the English. The English, who are suspicious, and who were all new to this side of the water, and astounded at all this, could not content themselves about his departure, nor could they believe that he had no troops in the field. Besides, the duke was not able to minimize the constable's actions, although he told them that all that he had done in this affair would turn out well in the long run; they were annoyed at the approach of winter, and to hear them speak it seemed indeed that they had their heart set on making peace rather than war.

7

As these words were uttered and the duke started to leave, a valet in the service of a gentleman of the king's household named Jacques de Grassay was taken by the English; Grassay was among those who [belonged to a company in the standing army whose members] receive twenty *écus* a month. This valet was immediately brought before the king of England and the duke of Burgundy, who were together, and then he was put into a tent. After they had questioned him, the duke of Burgundy took his leave of the king of England and proceeded to Brabant, on his way to Mézières, where part of his men were located. The king of England ordered that the valet should be released, since he was their first prisoner. And upon his departure my lord Howard and my lord Stanley gave him [an English coin called] a noble and said to him: "Recommend us to the good graces of the king your master, if you have occasion to speak to him." The valet came with all speed before the king, who was at Compiègne, to report these words to him. The king became very mistrustful of him, suspecting him to be a spy, because Gilbert de Grassay, brother of the valet's master, was at the time in Brittany, where he was extremely well treated by the duke. The valet was shackled with irons and closely guarded that night. Many people spoke to him by the king's command, however, and reported that he seemed to speak quite sincerely, and that they thought the king should hear him.

The next day, early in the morning, the king spoke to him. After he had heard him, he ordered his irons to be removed; but he still remained in custody. Then the king went to dinner, thinking over several plans, as to whether or not he should send ambassadors to the English. And before he sat down at the table, he said a few words to me about this; for as you know, my lord of Vienne [Angelo Cato], our king used to speak very intimately and often to those who were closest to him, as I was at the time, and as others have been since, and he liked to whisper into people's ears. He called to mind the words which the herald from England had told him, which were that he should not fail to send for a safe-conduct for ambassadors to be dispatched to the king of England, as soon as he had crossed the sea, and that the request should be addressed to Lords Howard and Stanley.

268

Book Four

After he had sat down at the table and had reflected a little, as you know that he used to do, and which seemed rather strange to those who did not know him (for without being acquainted with him people might have judged him to be unwise, but his actions show quite the contrary), he whispered in my ear that I should rise and should send for a valet who was in the service of my lord of Halles, son of [Jean] Mérichon, of La Rochelle, that I should go and have dinner with him in my room, and that I should ask him secretly whether he would have the courage to attempt to enter the camp of the king of England, equipped as a herald.

I immediately did as he had ordered me to do, and I was much amazed when I saw the servant in question, for it did not seem to me that he was fit for such a mission in terms of stature or demeanor. He had good sense, however, as I found out since, and he spoke gently and amiably. The king had never spoken to him except once. The servant was extremely surprised when he heard me speak, and he fell down upon both knees before me, as one who considers himself already dead. I reassured him as best I could and promised him a position as tax-collector in the Île de Ré, as well as money. And to encourage him even more, I told him that all this had been initiated by the English, and I invited him to have dinner with me; only the two of us were present, except for a servant, and little by little, I gave him instructions as to what he was to do.

I had not been there long when the king sent for me. I told him about our man and I suggested others who would have been better qualified to undertake this affair in my opinion; but he would hear of no one else. He went and spoke to him himself, and he reassured him more with one word than I had done with a hundred. Along with the king only my lord of Villiers entered the room; he was at the time grand equerry, and he is now bailiff of Caen. And when it seemed to the king that our man was in good spirits, he had the grand equerry send for the banner of a trumpeter, to make him a tunic embroidered with the royal arms, for the king was not ceremonious, and he did not have a herald or a trumpeter in his retinue, as many other princes do; and so the grand equerry and one of my servants made this tunic as best they could, and the grand equerry went to fetch an emblazoned escutcheon from a little herald called Plain Chemin, who was in the admiral's service; and the escutcheon was fastened on our man. His boots and his equipment were secretly brought to him, his horse was prepared for him, and he was put on it without anyone knowing anything about it. And to the arch of his saddle was attached a fine leather bag in which he was to put his tunic. He was well instructed as to what he was to say, and he proceeded directly to the English camp.

As soon as our man had arrived in the camp of the king of England, with his royal tunic on his back, he was stopped and brought before the king of England's tent. He was asked what he was doing there. He replied that he had been sent by the king of France to speak to the king of England and that he had orders to address himself to my lords Howard and Stanley. He was taken to a tent for dinner and he was warmly welcomed. After the king of England, who was having dinner when the herald arrived, had left the table, the herald was brought before him and he granted him an audience. His coming [he said] was based on the desire which the king had always entertained that he might have friendly relations with him and that the two kingdoms might live in peace with each other, and on the fact that since his accession to the crown of France he had never made war or undertaken anything against the king or the kingdom of England; he apologized for having received my lord of Warwick formerly, and said that the measure had been taken only against the duke of Burgundy and not against him.

The herald also pointed out that the duke of Burgundy had not called him over for any reason except to try to make a more advantageous bargain with the king [of France], once the English had arrived; and if others were taking such pains to further this cause, it was only to put their own affairs in better order and to work for their particular advantage. And the king of England's interest was of no importance to them, however things might turn out, as long as they could advance their own ends. He also emphasized the inclement weather to him, and the fact that winter was approaching; he added that he well knew that he had had considerable expenses and that there were many in England, noblemen as well as merchants, who wanted to have a war on this side of the water. And in the event that the king of England should come to consider a treaty, the king, for his part, would agree to such favorable terms that he and his kingdom would surely be satisfied. In order that he might be better informed of all these things, if he would give a safe-conduct for a total of one hundred horsemen, the king would send him ambassadors who would be well acquainted with his intentions; or if the king of England would rather have the meeting at some village midway between the two armies, where representatives of both sides could be present, the king would be most agreeable to such an arrangement and, for his part, would send the necessary safe-conduct.

Book Four

The king of England and part of his close advisers found these over-tures very advantageous. A safe-conduct was given to our man, accord-ing to his request, and he was presented with four nobles as well; and a herald left with him in order to obtain a safe-conduct from the king, similar to the one which had been issued by the English. And the next day at [Lihons-en-Santerre], a village near Amiens, the ambassadors gathered together. Representing the king were [Louis], bastard of Bourbon and admiral [of France], my lord of Saint-Pierre, and the bishop of Evreux, named Héberge. The king of England sent my lord Howard, someone named [Thomas] Saint-Léger, and a doctor named [John] Morton, who is today chancellor of England and archbishop of Canterbury.

I believe that it might seem to some people that the king humbled himself too much. But the wise might well judge from my preceding account that this kingdom would have been in great danger if God had not lent a helping hand. And He disposed the king's mind to select a wise course of action, whereas he troubled the sense of the duke of Burgundy, who committed so many errors in this affair as you have seen, although he had so often desired what he lost through his own fault. At the time we had many secret intrigues among ourselves, which would have resulted in great hardships in this kingdom, and in a short time (if this agreement had not taken place, and very soon), from the direction of Brittany as well as elsewhere; and I truly believe, from the things which I have seen in my time, that God takes a special interest in this kingdom.

8

As you have heard, our ambassadors met on the very next day after the return of our herald, for we were within about four leagues or less of each other. Our herald was warmly received and he obtained his po-sition on the Île de Ré, of which he was a native, as well as money. Many overtures were exchanged between our ambassadors. The English demanded the crown, as usual, or at least Normandy and Guyenne. Well attacked, well defended. From the very first day the negotiations were well managed, for both sides were very anxious to see this treaty materialize. Our envoys came back and the others returned to their camp. The king heard their requests and the latest conclusions: they consisted of seventy-two thousand *écus* in cash to be paid to the English before they left, the marriage of our present king [Charles VIII] with [Elizabeth], the eldest daughter of King Edward, who is now queen of England, and the duchy of Guyenne for her maintenance, or else fifty thousand *écus* to be paid for a period of nine years at the castle of London and not to be returned; at the end of this term the present king and his wife were to enjoy peacefully the revenues from Guyenne, and our king would then be finished with these payments to the king of England. There were many other minor articles on the subject of merchants, but I shall not mention them. And this peace between the two kingdoms was to last for nine years.[92] All the allies of both sides were included, and principally, on the side of the king of England, the dukes of Burgundy and Brittany were comprehended, if they wished to adhere to the treaty. The king of England offered, strangely enough, to name certain persons whom he claimed were traitors to the king and his crown, and to furnish written proof of this treason.

The king was extremely pleased with the news that his envoys brought him. He held a council meeting about this matter, and I was present at it. Some were of the opinion that it was only an imposture and a deceit on the part of the English. The king thought otherwise, and he pointed out that the weather and the season were not in their favor, and that they had not a single place which they could call their own; besides, they were disappointed by the mean tricks of the duke of Burgundy, who had already abandoned them. He felt quite sure that the constable would not deliver any of his towns, for every hour the king sent people to him to speak with him, to appease him, and to prevent him from doing any harm. Furthermore, the king was well informed of the personality of the king of England, who dearly loved his pleasures and comfort. Therefore it seemed that he spoke more wisely than any other man in this company, and that he had a better understanding of the matters which he was discussing. And he concluded that this money should be sought in all haste; ways of finding it were suggested, and it was proposed that everyone should lend something in order to help raise it in a hurry. In addition the king said that there was nothing in the world which he would not do in order to throw them out of the kingdom, except that he would never consent for anything that they should obtain any land; and before he would suffer that, he would risk and hazard everything.

My lord the constable began to be aware of these intrigues and to be afraid of being attacked from all sides, for he was still in dread of the arrangement which had almost been concluded against him at Bouvignes; and for this reason he often sent messengers to the king.

92. *Sic*. The peace was to last seven years.

And at the very hour of which I am speaking, a gentleman arrived before the king; he was named Louis de Sainville and was a servant of the constable. With him was one of his secretaries, named Richer. Both of them are still alive. And they delivered their message to my lord of Bouchage and to me before giving it to the king, for thus the king wished it done.

The message which they brought was most gratifying to the king, when he was told about it, because he had the intention of using it, as you shall hear. The lord of Contay, the duke of Burgundy's servant, who had recently been captured before Arras, as you have heard, wavered in his loyalty to the duke; the king had promised to take charge of his ransom and to give him a large sum of money if he could arrange to bring about a peace settlement. By chance he had arrived at the king's quarters on the same day as the above-mentioned servants of the constable. The king had Contay hide behind a large old screen that was in his room, and had me stay there with him, so that he could hear and report to his master in what terms the constable and his men spoke of the duke. And the king came to sit on a stool, touching the screen, so that we could hear what Louis de Sainville was saying. With this lord only my lord of Bouchage was present in addition. Louis de Sainville and his companion began to speak, saying that their master had sent them to the duke of Burgundy and that they had made him several remonstrances to persuade him to give up the friendship of the English; they had found him so bitter against the king of England that they almost had him decided not only to abandon the English but also to help destroy them by chasing them back to their retreat.

As he said these words, and because he thought that he would please the king, Louis de Sainville began to mimic the duke of Burgundy by stamping his foot against the floor, swearing by Saint George, calling the king of England Blayborgne, son of an archer who bore his name, and by uttering all the mockeries which it was possible for anyone in this world to use against any man. The king laughed heartily and asked him to speak louder and to repeat what he had said, because he was becoming slightly deaf. The other made no show of reluctance and willingly started over again. My lord of Contay, who was with me behind the screen, was the most surprised person in the world; he never would have believed this, regardless of anything he might have been told, had he not heard it himself.

The conclusion of the [message brought to Louis XI by the] constable's envoys was that in order to avoid all these great perils, which he could see lined up against him, he was advised to make a truce; the constable would undertake to help him bring it about. In order to satisfy the English, it was suggested that they be given only a small town or two for their winter quarters. Whichever towns he would select would be good enough, and the English would accept them willingly. And although they did not name these towns, it seemed that they had in mind Eu and Saint-Valéry. By these means the constable assumed that the English would be pleased with him and would forgive him for his refusal to let them have his towns.

The king, who was satisfied that he had played his role well and that he had made the lord of Contay hear the words which the constable used, and had his men use, gave them no discourteous answer, but only said to them: "I shall send envoys to my brother and he will hear from me." And he gave them leave. One of them swore to me that if he learned of anything which might concern the king, he would reveal it.

It was hard for the king to conceal his feelings when he was advised to give lands to the English; but fearing that the constable might do worse, he did not want to reply in a manner that might lead them to realize that he took it ill; and so he sent an envoy to the constable. It was a short distance: a man took hardly any time at all to go and to return.

The lord of Contay and I came out from behind the screen after the others had left; and the king laughed and made merry. But Contay seemed to have lost patience after having heard this kind of people thus make fun of his master, especially considering the intrigues which the constable was maintaining with him; and he was anxious to be on horseback already, in order to go to report this to his master the duke of Burgundy. He was sent off immediately with his instructions written in his own hand; and he brought with him a letter of credence from the king's hand, and he took his leave.

Our business with England had already been settled, as you have heard, and all these intrigues were being transacted at the same time and all at once. Those who had been sent by the king to confer with the English had made their report, as you have heard, and the king of England's envoys had returned to him. On both sides it was agreed upon and decided by those who had gone back and forth that the two kings should have an interview, and that after they had seen each other and sworn to uphold the treaties which had been drawn up, the king of England should return to England, upon receiving the seventy-two thousand *écus*, and that he should leave Lord Howard and his grand equerry, John Cheyne, as hostages until he had crossed the sea. By a special act, pensions amounting to sixteen thousand *écus* were promised to the king of England's close advisers: to my lord Hastings, two thousand *écus* a year (and he never would give a receipt for it); to the chancellor [Thomas Scot] two thousand *écus*; to my lord Howard, the grand equerry [John Cheyne], Saint-Léger, my lord of Montgomery, and others, the rest. In addition much ready cash and tableware were given to the servants of King Edward of England.

When he heard of this new turn of events, the duke of Burgundy came in very great haste from Luxembourg, where he had been staying, in order to see the king of England; and he had only sixteen horsemen with him when he arrived before him. The king of England was much amazed at this very sudden arrival and asked him what brought him here; and he well realized that he was angry. The duke replied that he had come to speak to him. The king asked him whether he wished to speak to him privately or in public. The duke then asked him whether he had made peace. The king of England answered that he had made a truce for nine years, in which both he and the duke of Brittany were included, and he begged him to agree to the terms of the truce. The duke became incensed; he spoke English (for he knew the language) and he referred to several brave deeds of former kings of England who had invaded France and the pains which they had taken to acquire honor there. He severely condemned this truce and insisted that he had not tried to persuade the English to come over because he needed their help but in order that they might recover what belonged to them; and so that they might realize that he had no need of their presence, he would not accept the truce with our king until the king of England had returned to the other side of the sea and had been there for three months. After saying these words, he took his leave and went back to where he came from. The king of England and the members of his council took great offense at these words; others, who were not happy about this peace, praised the duke's words.

9

In order to conclude this peace, the king of England came to take up quarters half a league away from Amiens; the king was at the gate and he could see them arrive at a distance. To be truthful, it seemed that they were inexperienced at the business of taking the field; and they rode in rather poor order. The king sent the king of England three hundred carts filled with the best wines that it was possible to find. And this train seemed almost like an army, as big as that of the English. Since the truce was in force, a large number of Englishmen came into the town; they behaved somewhat unwisely, and they showed little reverence for their king. They entered all armed and in large bodies, and if our king had wished to act in bad faith, it would have been the easiest thing in the world to put this large company to rout. But the king had no other thought but to feast them well and to make a firm peace with them that would last for the rest of his time.

He had ordered two large tables to be placed at the entrance of the town gate, one on each side; they were covered with all sorts of fine foods which make one thirsty, and with the best wines that one could imagine. And people were stationed there to serve them. Water was out of the question. The king had five or six men of good estate who were rather big and fat sit at each of these two tables, the better to entertain those who wished to drink; and among them were the lord of Craon, the lord of Bricquebec, the lord of Bressuire, the lord of Villiers, and others. As soon as the English approached the gate, they saw this installation; and there were people who took them by their horses' bridles and told them to go ahead and try a little attack on the food. They led them to the table and they were treated handsomely according to their position, and they were well pleased with their reception.

Once they had entered the town, wherever they stayed they paid nothing; and there were nine or ten taverns well provided with whatever they needed, where they went to eat and drink. They asked for whatever they wished and they paid nothing. And this lasted for three or four days.

You have heard how this truce was displeasing to the duke of Burgundy; but it was even more distasteful to the constable, who saw himself in a difficult situation in all respects and realized that he had made a mistake. Therefore he sent his confessor to the king of England with a letter of credence in which he begged him, for the love of God, not to put any trust in the promises and pledges of the king, but only to accept Eu and Saint-Valéry for his living quarters during part of the winter; for before the end of two months he would have managed things in such a way that he would be well lodged. He did not give him any other assurance, but he gave him great hopes. And in order that he might not have cause to make a mean arrangement for lack of sufficient funds, he offered to lend him fifty thousand *écus* and made him many other proposals. The king [Louis] had already ordered the two towns of which he spoke to be set on fire, because the constable had advised him to deliver them to the English, and the king of England was informed of it. And so he [Edward] sent word to the constable that his truce had already been concluded and that he would not alter anything in relation to this matter, and that if he had kept his promise to him, he would never have made this arrangement. When he heard this our constable became utterly desperate.

You have heard how these Englishmen were having a feast in the town of Amiens. One night my lord of Torcy came to tell the king that they were so numerous that it was very dangerous. The king became very angry with him; and so everyone was silent about the matter. The next morning was the day of the week which corresponded to that on which the Feast of the Holy Innocents had fallen that year and on such a day he did not discuss any of his state affairs, nor did he want to; he considered it very bad luck if anyone spoke to him about business and he became very angry with those who were his familiars and who knew about his custom.[93]

On the morning of which I am speaking, however, as the king was rising and saying his hours, someone came and told me that there were at least nine thousand Englishmen in the town. I decided to run the risk [of displeasing him] and to tell him about it, and so I entered the room in which he had withdrawn. And I said to him: "Sire, although it is the [anniversary of the] Feast of the Holy Innocents, it is necessary that I should inform you of what I was told." And I reported to him at length about the number of men present, which was ever increasing, and I mentioned that all of them were armed and that no one dared refuse them entrance for fear of displeasing them.

That lord was not obstinate; he soon left his hours and told me that the ceremony of the Innocents should not be observed that day, and that I should mount my horse and try to speak to the leaders of the English to see whether we could have them withdraw. I was to tell their commanders, if I should meet any, that they should come to speak to him, for he would come to the gate immediately after me. I followed his orders and I spoke to three or four of the English leaders, whom I knew, telling them what would serve the purpose of my mission. But for one soldier whom they sent away, twenty came in. The king sent my lord of Gié after me; he is now marshal of France. In order to discuss this matter, we went into a tavern, in which they had already served one hundred and eleven courses, although it was not yet nine o'clock in

93. The talismanic belief of the least innocent of monarchs that it would be unlucky to transact any business on the day of the week on which the Feast had last occurred was shared by many people in his time. The same belief in the special virtue of the "Innocents" is evident in the extraordinary popularity of burial in the cemetery of the cloister of the Innocents in Paris. The vogue for burial here was so great that cadavers had to be quickly disinterred and transferred to the charnelhouse above the cloister around the cemetery to make way for new burials.

the morning. The house was filled to capacity: some of the men were singing, the rest were asleep, and all were drunk. When I realized this, it seemed to me indeed that there was no danger, and I sent word to this effect to the king, who immediately came to the gate, with a large retinue. He gave secret orders that two or three hundred men-at-arms should be armed in the houses of their commanders, and he stationed some of them at the gate through which they entered. The king had his dinner brought to him at the house of the gatekeepers and he invited several persons of quality among the English to dine with him.

The king of England was informed of this disorder and was ashamed about it; and he sent word to the king asking him to command that no more soldiers be allowed to enter. The king replied that he would never do such a thing, but that if it pleased the king of England, he might send some of his archers and have them guard the gate and admit those of whom they approved. And so it was done. And many of the English left the town by the command of the king of England.

It was then decided that in order to put an end to this whole affair, a place should be selected where the two kings would meet, and certain persons would be ordered to visit the locality. My lord of Bouchage and I went there to represent the king, and my lord Howard, a person named Saint-Léger, and a herald were there on behalf of the king of England. After having surveyed and inspected the river, we agreed that the most beautiful place and the safest was Picquigny, within three leagues of Amiens, a strong castle which belonged to the lieutenant of the bishop of Amiens, and which had been burned by the duke of Burgundy. The town lies low and the Somme flows through it, and the river is not fordable nor is it wide at this point.

On the side from which the king was to come, the country was beautiful and spacious; on the other side, from which the king of England would arrive, the country was very fine too, except that when he was to approach the river there was an embankment at least two large bow-shots long, which had marshes on both sides; and for one who would have ventured to go through there without being assured of the adversary's good faith, it was a very dangerous path. And without a doubt, as I said elsewhere, the English are not so subtle in matters of intrigues and arrangements as are the French; and, whatever one says, they do go about their business rather clumsily. But one must have a little patience and not argue angrily with them.

After we had agreed upon a locality for the meeting, a very strong and rather large bridge was ordered to be erected; we provided the carpenters and the materials; and in the middle of the bridge was constructed a strong wooden lattice like those made for the cages of lions.

The holes between the bars were just large enough for one to stick his arm through easily. The top was covered with boards only to give protection against the rain, and it was large enough to contain ten or twelve persons under it on each side. The trellis extended to the edges of the bridge, so that it would be impossible to pass from one side to the other. In the river there was only a little boat with two men to row across those who wished to go from one side to the other.

I wish to explain the reason which moved the king to have this obstacle set up in such a way that no one could go from one side to the other. It might by chance be useful in the future to someone who might find himself in a similar situation. In the days when King Charles VII was rather young, the kingdom was greatly persecuted by the English, and King Henry V was besieging Rouen and was putting it in a difficult position. Most of those who were inside were those of the party of Duke John of Burgundy, who was reigning at the time. There had indeed been an important dissension between Duke John of Burgundy and the duke of Orleans; most of this kingdom was divided by these two parties, and the king's affairs certainly did not benefit from it. For parties are never started in a country without causing damage in the end and being difficult to stop.

As for this question about which I am speaking, the duke of Orléans had already been killed in Paris eleven years before. Duke John had a large body of troops and proceeded with the intention of raising the siege of Rouen; and in order to manage this better and to make sure that the king would be on his side, it had been arranged that the king and he should have a meeting at Montereau-Faut-Yonne. A bridge was erected there, with several barriers. In the middle of these barriers was a little wicket, which was locked on both sides and through which it was possible to pass from one side to the other, provided that those on both sides so desired. Thus the king was on one side of the bridge, and Duke John on the other, accompanied by a considerable number of men-at-arms; this was particularly true in the case of the duke. They began to confer on the bridge; and at the spot where they were speaking there were only three or four persons with the duke. After their discussion had begun, the duke of Burgundy, either because he had been especially invited to do so, or because he wished to humble himself before the king, unlocked the wicket on his side, and they opened it for him on the other, and he passed to the other side with three companions. He was immediately killed, along with those who were accompanying him. This resulted in a multitude of hardships, as everyone knows.

This does not pertain to my subject, and therefore I shall say nothing more about it. But the king related this to me, exactly as I am passing it on to you, when he ordered me to visit the proposed meeting place. And he said that if there had been no door at this interview of which I am speaking, there would have been no occasion to summon the duke to pass to the other side, and this great misfortune would not have occurred. Its principal instigators were some of the servants of the duke of Orleans, who had been killed, as I told you, and they had authority under King Charles VII.

10

The day after our barriers were thus erected, as you have heard, the two kings came. It was the twenty-ninth of August, 1475. The king was the first to arrive, with about eight hundred men-at-arms in his retinue. On the king of England's side, his whole army was drawn up in order of battle; and although we did not think that we were seeing all of it, it did seem to us that an incredibly large number of horsemen were assembled there. The forces which we had on our side seemed like nothing in comparison with theirs. But of course one-fourth of the king's army was not there. It had been decided that with each of the kings would be twelve of their greatest and most trusted men, who had already been ordered to stand at the barriers. On our side we had four of the king of England's men to observe what was being done among us, and we had as many of our men on the king of England's side. As I told you, the king was the first to arrive, and he was already at the barriers; and twelve of us were with him, including the late Duke John of Bourbon and his brother the cardinal. It was the king's pleasure that I should be dressed like him on that day. It had been his custom for a long time often to have someone dress like him.[94]

The king of England came from along the embankment which I mentioned; he was well attended and had a regal bearing. With him were his brother the duke of Clarence, the count of Northumberland, and several other lords, his chamberlain, named my lord Hastings, his chancellor, and others, and only three or four were dressed in cloth of gold like their master. The king wore a black velvet hat on his head, decorated with a large fleur-de-lis of precious stones. He was a very handsome prince, and tall, but he was beginning to put on weight, and I

94. As Commynes implies, this custom was used by princes of this period and later to designate their favorites. See Johan Huizinga, *The Waning of the Middle Ages* (New York: Anchor Book, 1954), chapter 2, for this habit and the usages associated with it.

had seen him looking more elegant formerly, for I do not remember ever having seen a more handsome man than he was when my lord of Warwick forced him to flee from England.

When he had arrived within four or five feet of the barrier, he doffed his hat and bowed deeply to within a half-foot of the ground. The king, who was already leaning against the barrier, returned the courtesy with just as deep a bow, and they began to embrace each other through the holes; then the king of England made another even deeper bow. The king began the conversation, saying: "My lord my cousin, you are most welcome. There is not a man in the world whom I so much desired to see as you. And God be praised that we are assembled here for this good purpose." The king of England replied to his salutation in rather good French.

Then the chancellor of England began to speak. He was a prelate called the Bishop of Ely[95] and he began with a prophecy, in which the English are never lacking, according to which an important peace treaty was to be concluded between France and England in this town of Picquigny. After this they opened the letters which the king had sent to the king of England concerning the treaty which had been made. And the chancellor asked the king whether they had been drawn up according to his intention and whether they were agreeable to him. To which the king replied that they were, as well as those which had been presented to him on behalf of the king of England.

Thereupon the missal was brought, and the two kings each placed one hand on it and the other on the Holy and True Cross; and they both swore to uphold what had been mutually promised: that is to say, they would observe the truce for nine years,[96] and this would include the allies on both sides, and they would carry out the marriage of their children, as was stipulated by the treaty.

After the oath had been sworn, our king, who was never at a loss for words, began to tell the king of England, laughingly, that he ought to come to Paris; he would have him feasted with the ladies, and he would offer him as his confessor my lord the cardinal of Bourbon, who would very willingly absolve him of sins, should he have committed any, for he well knew that the cardinal was a good fellow.

After some conversation on this subject and similar ones, the king, who showed his authority in this company, had us withdraw and told us that he wished to speak to the king of England privately. The king of England's men left as we did, without waiting to be asked. After the

95. *Sic.* The chancellor of England, Thomas Scot, was bishop of Lincoln.
96. *Sic.* See p. 272, n. 92.

two kings had spoken for a while, the king called me and asked the king of England whether he knew me. He replied that he did and mentioned the places where he had seen me; and he said that formerly I had done my best to be of help to him at Calais, in the days when I was in the duke of Burgundy's service.

The king asked him what he would have him do in the event that the duke of Burgundy should refuse to observe the truce, since he had reacted in such a proud manner in relation to this matter, as you have heard. The king of England replied that he should offer it to him again, and if he did not wish to accept it, he would leave it up to the two of them. After this the king mentioned the duke of Brittany, who was the real object of his previous remark, and he asked the same question about him. The king of England answered that he begged him not to wage war against the duke of Brittany, because in time of need he had never found so faithful a friend. The king did not insist, and in the most gracious and friendly terms which he could think of, he recalled the others and took his leave of the king of England, saying a few kind words to each of his men. And so both of them withdrew from the barrier at the same time, or almost so, and they mounted their horses. The king proceeded to Amiens and the king of England went to his camp; he was provided with everything he needed from the king's household, even including torches and candles.

The king of England's brother, the duke of Gloucester, and several others who were adverse to this peace did not attend this conference. But later on they changed their minds, and, soon after, the duke of Gloucester came as far as Amiens to present his respects to the king, and our master gave him some very beautiful gifts, such as tableware and well-equipped horses.

As the king returned from this interview, he spoke to me along the way about two points. He had found the king of England so very willing to come to Paris that he was not pleased about it; and he said: "He is a very handsome king and he likes women very much. He might meet someone artful in Paris who would give him such fine words that she would make him want to come back." His predecessors had been too often in Paris and in Normandy, and the king did not care for his company on this side of the sea; on the other side of the sea, however, he would be pleased to have him as a good friend and brother.

Moreover, the king was suspicious, insofar as he had found it some-what difficult to accept his statements about the duke of Brittany, and he would have been very happy to obtain from the king of England that he should allow him the privilege of waging war against Brittany.

And he had him sounded out again about this problem by my lord of Bouchage and my lord of Saint-Pierre. But when the king of England saw himself pressed, he said that if war were waged in Brittany, he would cross the water another time to defend it. After this response nothing more was said to him about the matter.

When the king had arrived at Amiens and was intending to have supper, three or four of the king of England's advisers, who had helped to bring about and negotiate the peace, came to have supper with him. And my lord Howard began to whisper in the king's ear that if he wished, he would find a way of persuading the king his master to come to Amiens, and by chance even to Paris, where he could feast with the king. Although this offer was hardly to his liking, the king nevertheless pretended to be very pleased and began washing [his hands] without responding very much to the proposal.[97] But he whispered in my ear that what he had suspected had actually materialized: it was this offer. They still talked about it after supper, but this plan was put off as shrewdly as possible, with the excuse that the king had to leave in all haste to march against the duke of Burgundy.

Although these matters were very serious and great pains were taken on both sides to carry them out wisely, still certain pleasant things came up, which are worthy of being remembered. And no one should be surprised, considering the great hardships which the English have brought on this kingdom, and not very long ago, if the king spared no pains and expenses to put them out amiably, so that he could still maintain friendly relations with them for the future, or at least so that they would not make war against him.

On the day after our interview a large body of Englishmen entered Amiens, and we were told by some of them that the Holy Ghost had made this peace, for they all based their statements on prophecies. What made them say this was that a white pigeon had perched on the king of England's tent on the day of the interview, and regardless of the noise which had been made in the army, he had refused to budge. But others were of a different opinion; there had been a little rain, followed by a bright sunshine, and so the pigeon had planted itself on that tent, which was the highest of all, in order to get itself dry. And this reason was given to me by a gentleman of Gascony, named Louis de Bretelles, who was in the king of England's service; he was most displeased at this peace. And since he had known me for a long time, he spoke to me familiarly and said that we were making fun of the

97. Calmette's emendation of this passage (Calmette, II, 69: "laver" is changed to "louer") is unnecessary. It was the custom to wash hands before meals.

king of England. I asked him how many battles the king of England had won. He told me that there had been nine, and that he had been there in person. Then I asked him how many he had lost. He replied that he had lost only one, and that it was the one which we were causing him to lose; and he considered that the shame at his being sent back in such a state was greater than the honor which he had acquired by winning the other nine battles.

I related this to the king, who told me that he was a very troublesome lout, and that he should be kept from talking. He invited him to dinner and had him dine with him; he made him some very advantageous and fine proposals if he would remain on this side of the water. And when he realized that he did not want to stay here, he gave him a thousand *écus* in cash and promised to help some of his brothers, who were living in France; and I whispered a few words in his ear, so that he would take pains to foster the love which had now begun between the two kings.

There was nothing in the world which the king feared more than to drop some word or other which might make the English think that we were making fun of them. And by chance, the day after this interview, when the king was in his private room, with only three or four of us in attendance, he let escape a few words of jest concerning the wines and the presents which he had sent to the English camp.[98] And as he turned around he noticed a Gascon merchant, who lived in England and had come to request his permission to export a certain quantity of wines from Gascony without paying any duty on them; this could be very profitable to the merchant, if it was granted to him. The king was much amazed when he saw him and he wondered how he had managed to enter. He asked him from what town in Guyenne he came and whether he was married in England. The merchant replied that he was, but that he did not own anything of much value there. Thereupon, before he left, the king assigned a man to take him to Bordeaux. I spoke to him by the king's command; and he was given a very important position in his native town, as well as the privilege which he had requested of exporting wines duty-free, and one thousand francs in cash to have his wife come over; and the king sent one of his brothers to England, so that he would not go himself. And thus the king condemned himself to pay this fine, realizing that he had talked too much.

98. The king's joke has been preserved by Jean de Roye in the so-called *Chronique scandaleuse*, ed. B. de Mandrot, II (Paris, 1896), 344: "And the king said that he had chased out the English more easily . . . than his father [Charles VII, in Joan of Arc's time] had, for he had chased them out simply by having them eat meat and drink good wine."

Book Four

11

On the day of which I am speaking, which was the day after our meeting, my lord the constable sent one of his servants, named Rapine, to whom the king has since granted many favors; he was his master's loyal servant and he brought letters to the king. The king wished my lord of Lude and myself to hear his credence.

Now my lord of Contay had already returned from his journey in relation to the intrigues against the constable, which you have heard mentioned before. The constable did not know which way to turn and considered himself as lost. Rapine's speech to us was very humble; he said that his master well realized that many accusations had been made against him, but that the king might have known from experience that his intentions had not been bad. And in order that the king might be better assured of his good will, he proposed, if he so desired, to enter into an intrigue and to put pressure on my lord of Burgundy, so that he would help to ruin the king of England and all his men. And, judging from his manner of speaking, it seemed indeed that his master had lost all hope. We told him that we were on good terms with the English and that we did not want to have quarrels with them; and my lord of Lude, who was with me, went so far as to ask him whether he did not know what had become of his master's ready cash. I was amazed that these words (since Rapine was a very loyal servant [and was sure to report them to his master]) did not make the constable realize what his situation was and what sort of fate was in store for him, and that they did not lead him to flee, especially considering the danger in which he had found himself only a year before. But I have seen few people in my life, either here or elsewhere, who knew how to flee at the right time; some have no hope of obtaining asylum and safety from neighboring countries; others are too attached to their possessions, their wives, and their children. And these reasons have caused the destruction of many persons of high estate.

After we had made our report to the king, he called in a secretary. The only persons present with him were my lord Howard, servant of the king of England, who knew nothing of what we had in store for the constable, my lord of Contay, who had returned from his interview with the duke of Burgundy, and the two of us, who had spoken with Rapine. The king dictated a letter to be sent to the constable; he informed him of what had been accomplished the day before in relation to the truce. He said that he was busy with many important affairs and that he was in great need of a head such as his. Then, turning to the

Englishman and my lord of Contay, he told them: "I do not mean that we should have his body; I mean that we should have his head and that his body should remain elsewhere." This letter was then delivered to Rapine, who was well pleased with it; and it seemed to him that these were very friendly words on the part of the king to say that he was in great need of a head such as his master's; but he did not realize to what end these words were directed.

The king of England sent the king the letters of credence which the constable had written him, and reported all the propositions which he had ever made to him. Thus you may see in what position he had placed himself among these three great men [i.e., the king of France, the king of England, and the duke of Burgundy], all of whom desired his death.

The king of England, after having received his money, proceeded directly to Calais by forced marches, because he feared the hatred of the duke of Burgundy and of the country people. And as a matter of fact, when any of his men strayed, one of them invariably remained among the bushes. According to his promise, he left behind his hostages, my lord Howard and John Cheyne, grand equerry of England, until he had crossed the sea.

You have heard at the beginning of our relation of the English affair how the king of England was not particularly enthusiastic about the matter. For as soon as he arrived in Dover in England, and before embarking to cross over, he entered into discussions with us. And the reasons that made him pass to this side of the water were twofold: first, all his kingdom desired him to do so, as it has always been their custom in the past, and the duke of Burgundy was pressing them to this end; and secondly, the king intended to reserve for himself a nice fat sum of money from the amount which he had levied in England for this crossing. For as you have heard, the kings of England raise no money except from their own domain, unless they request it for waging war against France.

The king of England had used another skillful maneuver in order to satisfy his subjects. He had brought with him ten or twelve big, fat men from London as well as from other towns in England; they were the principal leaders of the English commons and they were the ones who had done most to bring about this crossing and to set up this powerful army. The king had them take up quarters in elegant tents; it was not the sort of life to which they were accustomed, however, and they soon grew weary of it. And they expected to have to fight a battle three days after landing on the other side of the sea. The king of England did his best to instill doubts and fears in their minds and to make them yearn for peace, so that they would help him, upon their return to

England, to quench the murmurs which might arise on the occasion of his return. For never since the days of King Arthur had any king of England taken so many men at once to the other side of the sea. He returned very speedily, as you have heard; and he kept a large part of the money that had been levied in England for the payment of his men-at-arms. Thus he realized most of his ambitions. It was not in his nature to endure all the pains which would be unavoidable for a king of England who intended to make conquests in France. And at the time our king was well prepared for defense, although he could not have provided against all of his enemies, for he had too many.

The king of England had another great desire: the accomplishment of the marriage between King Charles VIII, who reigns today, and his daughter; and this marriage caused him to close his eyes to many things which have since turned out to the [French] king's great advantage.

After the English had returned to England, except for the hostages who were with the king, this lord withdrew toward Laon, to a little town called Vervins, on the border of Hainaut; and the chancellor of Burgundy and other ambassadors were at Avesnes with the lord of Contay to represent the duke of Burgundy. And this time the king wished to arrange a total peace. He had been frightened by the great number of Englishmen, for in his time he had seen some of their actions in this kingdom, and he did not want them to return.

The king heard from the chancellor, who requested that he send his ambassadors to a bridge halfway between Avesnes and Vervins; he and his companions would be there. The king sent word to him that he would come in person, although several persons whom he consulted about this were against it. He went there, at any rate, and took the English hostages with him; and they were present when the king received the ambassadors, who came with a large retinue of archers and other soldiers. At this time they exchanged no other words with the king, and they were taken to dinner.

One of these Englishmen began to regret this treaty, and he told me at a window that if they had seen many such men with the duke of Burgundy, perhaps they might not have made peace. My lord of Narbonne, who is now called my lord of Foix, heard these words and said to him: "Were you so simple as to suppose that the duke of Burgundy did not have a great number of such men? He had only sent them to refresh themselves. But you were so eager to return home that six hundred casks of wine and a pension which our king gave you sent you very soon back to England."

The Englishman was furious and said: "Just as everyone told us, you have been making fun of us. Do you call the money which your king gives us a pension? It is a tribute. And by Saint George, you might talk so much about it that we may come back." I interrupted this argument and turned it into a joke, but the Englishman remained dissatisfied. I mentioned it to the king, who became exceedingly angry with the lord of Narbonne.

The king did not have a long conversation with the above-mentioned chancellor at this time, and it was arranged that they should come to Vervins, and so they did; and they came with the king. After they had arrived at Vervins, the king appointed Tanneguy du Chastel and Pierre d'Oriole, chancellor of France, and others to take care of the business with them. From each side great remonstrances were made, and everyone tried to work for the good of his own party. The above-mentioned ambassadors came to make their report to the king, saying that those Burgundians were arrogant in their language, but that they had put them in their place; and they repeated the answers which they had given them, but the king was not pleased with them. He said that all these answers had been given many times already and that it was not a question of a lasting peace but only of a truce. He did not want them to be spoken to in those terms again and he wished to speak with them himself. He called the chancellor and the other ambassadors to his room; only my late lord the admiral, bastard of Bourbon, my lord of Bouchage, and I remained with him. And he concluded a truce between them, good for nine years, with each of the two parties returning to its point of departure. But the ambassadors begged the king not to have the truce proclaimed yet, in order to save the oath which had been taken by the duke, who had sworn not to take advantage of the general truce until the king of England had been out of this kingdom for a certain time, and in order that it might not appear as if the duke had now accepted his [England's] truce.

The king of England, who was very much annoyed because the duke had refused to accept his truce and who was informed that the king was arranging a separate one with the duke, sent a knight named Thomas of Montgomery, one of his close advisers, to the king at Vervins at the time when the king was negotiating this truce of which I spoke with the representatives of the duke of Burgundy. Sir Thomas requested the king not to arrange any other truce with the duke except the one which he had already made. He also begged him not to deliver Saint-Quentin to the duke, and he proposed to the king that if he wished to continue the war against the duke, he would be glad to return to France to help him and to fight on his side in the next season, provided that the king would compensate him for the prejudice he would incur, because the duties on the woolens at Calais would be worth nothing to him. (These duties can amount to some fifty thousand *écus*.) He also proposed that the king should pay half of his army, and the king of England would pay the other half. The king thanked the king of England profusely and gave tableware to Sir Thomas. On the question of the war, he made excuses, saying that the truce had already been agreed upon, and that it was no different from the one which the two kings had made for the same duration of nine years,[99] except that the duke wanted separate documents to this effect. He excused himself as best he could in relation to this matter, in order to satisfy the ambassador, who returned to his country along with those who had remained in France as hostages.

The king marveled greatly at the offers which had been made to him by the king of England; and I was the only person present to hear them. And it seemed that it would have been a rather dangerous thing to have the king of England return to France; and, besides, it does not take much prodding to provoke a quarrel between the French and the English when they happen to be together. As a result, they might have once more reconciled their differences with the Burgundians. And he became increasingly anxious to conclude the truce with these Burgundians.

12

After the truce was concluded, the question of the constable came up once more, and to put it succinctly, the proposals made at Bouvignes, of which I spoke earlier, were taken up again. Documents relating to this matter were sent under official seals from one side to the other. And by this agreement the duke was promised Saint-Quentin, Ham, and Bohain, as well as any lands which the constable held from the duke, and all his movable possessions, wherever they could be found. They deliberated and concluded as to how he should be besieged in Ham, where he resided; and they decided that the first of the two [the king or the duke] who could take him should have him executed within eight days or should turn him over to the other.

People soon became aware of this intrigue, and the constable's highest-ranking friends, such as my lord of Genlis and several others, gradually abandoned him. The constable, who knew how the king of England had handed over his letters and discovered his machinations, and who realized that it was his enemies who had negotiated the truce, began to experience great fear; therefore he sent a message to the duke of Bur-

99. *Sic.* The English truce was for seven years, the Burgundian for nine.

gundy, beseeching him to let him have a safe-conduct so that he might call on him and discuss several matters of importance concerning the duke. At first the duke hesitated, but he finally sent him one.

This powerful man was undecided about where he should flee for security; for he was informed of the measures which had been taken at the meeting and had seen copies of the documents which had been drawn up against him at Bouvignes. At one time he consulted with some of his servants, who were from Lorraine; and he resolved to flee with them to Germany, for the road was perfectly safe, and to bring with him a large sum of money so that he could buy a place on the Rhine, where he would remain until he might have a reconciliation with one or the other. Another time he decided to stay on in his strong castle of Ham, which had cost him so much, for he had built it for the purpose of protecting himself in such a necessity; and he had it provided with everything, as well as any castle I have ever seen. Yet he could not find enough men to defend him, for all his servants were subjects of either the king or the duke of Burgundy. And perhaps his fear was so great that he did not dare confide sufficiently in them; for I believe that he would certainly have found a goodly number who would not have abandoned him. He did not need to be afraid of being besieged by both princes as much as by one, because it would have been impossible for both armies to agree.

As a last resort, he put himself into the duke of Burgundy's hands on the strength of this safe-conduct; and he took only fifteen or twenty horses. He proceeded to Mons in Hainaut, where the lord of Aimeries resided; this man was grand bailiff of Hainaut and the truest friend whom the constable ever had. He stayed there with him as he awaited word from the duke of Burgundy, who had begun a war against the duke of Lorraine, because the latter had defied him while he was at the siege of Neuss and had made great ravages in his territory of Luxembourg.

As soon as the king heard of the constable's departure, he resolved to see to it that he would not regain the duke of Burgundy's friendship; thereupon he proceeded in all haste toward Saint-Quentin with seven or eight hundred men-at-arms whom he had assembled. And he was well informed of the state of the troops who were inside. As he arrived near the town, several persons came out to meet him and to present their respects. The king ordered me to enter the town and have quarters assigned to each of the men, which I did. First the men-at-arms entered, and then the king; and he was well received by the townspeople. Some of the constable's men withdrew to Hainaut.

Book Four

The duke of Burgundy was soon informed by the king himself of the taking of Saint-Quentin, so that he would lose all hope of recovering it through the constable. As soon as the duke heard the news, he sent word to the lord of Aimeries, his grand bailiff in Hainaut, that he should have the town of Mons well guarded, so as to make it impossible for the constable to escape, and that he should be forbidden to leave his house. The bailiff did not dare refuse, and so he obeyed the duke's orders. The guard, however, was not so watchful that a man might not have fled if he had wanted to.

What can we say here about Fortune? This man's territories were situated between those of two enemy princes; he held several well-fortified places; he had four hundred well-paid men-at-arms; he was their commissary and chose whomever he pleased for his army; he had managed them for twelve years already; he was a very wise and valiant knight of great experience; and he was very rich. And to think that he found himself in this dangerous position without having the courage or the means to extricate himself from his predicament! One might say that fickle Fortune had turned against him. However, to be more correct, one should say that such mysteries do not derive from Fortune; besides, Fortune is nothing but a poetic fiction, and it must have been God who abandoned him, considering all the things which I spoke about earlier, as well as others which I did not mention. If it were up to man to judge,—and it is not, especially to me—I should say that what reasonably should have been the cause of his punishment was that he had always done everything in his power to prolong the war between the king and the duke. This was the source of his authority and his high position; and it was not very difficult to keep them in a state of dissension, because their dispositions were naturally very different.

It would take a very ignorant man to believe that Fortune or the like would have known how to lead such a wise man into the bad graces of these two princes at the same time, although they had never in their lives agreed on anything except this affair, and, even more, into the enmity of the king of England, who had married his niece and had great affection for all of his wife's relatives, especially those from the house of Saint-Pol.[100] It is probable and even certain that he had alienated himself from the grace of God, since he had made enemies of these three princes and had not a single friend left who would have

100. Calmette's reading of this sentence, taken from Ms. Dobrée (" . . . eust sceü garder ung si saige homme à estre mal de ces deux . . . ,") makes less sense than Ms. Polignac (" . . . eust sceü guider . . .), a reading given in Calmette's apparatus and followed by Mandrot in his edition of the *Memoirs*.

dared give him hospitality even for one night. No Fortune had a hand in this, except God. And so it happened and will happen to many who, after an era of great prosperity, fall into great adversity.

After the constable was arrested, the king sent word to the duke requesting that he should either deliver the constable to him or that he should treat him according to his written agreement. The duke said that he would do so and had the constable taken to Péronne, where he was closely guarded.

The duke of Burgundy had already taken several places in Lorraine and Barrois, and was already besieging Nancy, which resisted valiantly. The king had many soldiers in Champagne, and this perturbed the duke greatly, because the terms of the truce did not entitle him to harm the duke of Lorraine, who had retired to where the king was. My lord of Bouchage and other ambassadors strongly pressed the duke to honor his agreement. He always claimed that he would, but the period of eight days during which the constable was either to be handed over to the king or be executed was extended to more than a month. The duke was hard pressed, and he was afraid that the king might prevent him from succeeding in his conquest of Lorraine, which he very much wanted to conclude, in order to be able to pass freely from Luxembourg into Burgundy and to have all his territories joined together (for if he obtained this little duchy, he could go from Holland almost as far as Lyon without leaving his own lands). For these reasons he wrote to his chancellor and to the lord of Humbercourt, of whom I have often spoken, both of them being the constable's foes and enemies, that they should proceed to Péronne, and that on a given day, which he selected, they should hand over the constable to the king's representatives; for the two above-mentioned men had the power to act for the duke in his absence. And he ordered the lord of Aimeries to deliver the constable to them.

In the meantime the duke vigorously battered the town [of Nancy]. The garrison inside defended it bravely. One of the duke's commanders, named the count of Campobasso, a native of the kingdom of Naples, but banished from there because he had sided with the house of Anjou, had already made secret negotiations with the duke of Lorraine. (For my lord of Lorraine, who was a close relative and heir to the house of Anjou, had managed to gain his support. Besides, the count had great affection for the house of Anjou, whose partisan he had been in Naples, and he became a fugitive from that kingdom as a result; all this made him deceive his master to serve better the interests of the duke of Lorraine.) He promised to prolong the siege and to see that the ammunition necessary for taking the town would be lacking. He was certainly in a position to do this, for at the time he was the most powerful man in the army, and was very disloyal to his master, as I shall explain later. But all this was just a foretaste of the calamities which later befell the duke of Burgundy.

I believe that the duke had expected to take the town before the appointed day for surrendering the constable, and then he would not have given him up. On the other hand, it is possible that if the king had had him in his power, he would have done more for the duke of Lorraine than he was already doing. For he was informed of his intrigue with the count of Campobasso, but he was not helping it along. He was not obliged to let the duke of Burgundy have his way in Lorraine if he had not wished to, for several reasons.[101] He had a number of men stationed near Lorraine.

The duke was not able to take Nancy before the day on which the constable was to be handed over by his commissioners to the king. Therefore on the appointed day these men followed their master's orders most willingly, for they greatly hated the constable, and they delivered him at the gate of Péronne into the hands of the bastard of Bourbon, admiral of France, and my lord of Saint-Pierre, who took him to Paris. Several people told me that three hours later messengers were sent in all diligence by the duke to order his men not to give up the constable; but it was too late.

Upon his arrival in Paris, the constable's trial began. The king pressed the court strongly. Officials were appointed to conduct the trial. They gave consideration to the charges which the king of England had made against him, as you have heard before. And finally the constable was condemned to death [and decapitated on December 19, 1475] and his possessions were confiscated.

13

This surrender was very strange. I do not say this to excuse his faults or to blame the duke of Burgundy, for the constable had done him considerable injury. But there was no necessity for the duke of Burgundy, who was such a great prince, and from such a renowned and honorable house, to have given him a safe-conduct in order to seize him, and it was most cruel to give him up to a person who was sure to put him to

---

101. The semi-independence of the duke of Lorraine presented difficulties for Louis XI, so that he was not entirely discontent to see Charles the Bold attack Lorraine.

death, because of avarice. After this most shameful act it was not long before the duke began to suffer. Judging from the things which God has done in our time and is still doing, it seems that He does not wish to let any wrongs go unpunished; and it is evident that these strange happenings proceed from His will, for they are more than works of nature and are His sudden punishments, mainly against those who have committed violence or cruelty; these persons are usually not of mean condition but instead are very great, such as lords or those with the authority of a prince.

The house of Burgundy had flourished for many years, during the hundred years or so when four of that family ruled, and the family enjoyed as great a reputation as any house in Christendom. Others may have been more powerful, but they had experienced affliction and adversity, whereas this house had enjoyed continuous felicity and prosperity.

The first great ruler of this house was Philip the Bold, brother of Charles V [of France], and he had married [Margaret] the daughter of the house of Flanders, countess of that province and of Artois, Burgundy, Nevers, and Rethel. The second was John [the Fearless]. The third was good Duke Philip, who annexed to his territories the duchies of Brabant, Luxembourg, Limbourg, Holland, Zeeland, Hainaut, and Namur. The fourth was Duke Charles, who became, after his father's death, one of the richest princes in Christendom, and possessed finer jewelry, dishes, tapestries, books, and linens than could be found in the three greatest houses of Europe. Other houses have had more ready cash, for Duke Philip had not raised taxes for a long time; [at his death], however, Duke Charles found more than 300,000 *écus* in cash. And he enjoyed peace with all his neighbors, although it was of short duration. But I do not wish to hold him solely responsible for starting the wars, because enough other people had a hand in them too.

Immediately after his father's death his subjects granted him a certain sum of money, willingly and without being pressed too much, and this was to be continued for ten years, in each territory separately. This could have amounted to some 350,000 *écus* per year, not including the contributions of Burgundy. At the time when he delivered the constable to the king, he was receiving more than 300,000 *écus*. Furthermore, he had more than 300,000 *écus* in ready cash, while all the movable possessions which he obtained from the constable were not worth eighty thousand *écus*, for he had only seventy-six thousand *écus* worth of money. Thus the occasion for committing such a great fault was quite insignificant.

God set up against him a new enemy (the duke of Lorraine), who was rather weak, very young, and inexperienced in everything. And God was the cause that one of his servants, whom he trusted above all at the time, became false and wicked; and this led him to suspect his subjects and most loyal servants. Are not these truly the kinds of measures which God took in the Old Testament against those whose fortune He intended to change from good to bad, and from prosperity to adversity? The duke's heart never softened, and until his death he considered that all his good fortune came from his own good sense and virtues.

Already before he had delivered the constable he had become very mistrustful of his subjects and had held them in great contempt, for he had sent for one thousand Italian lance-teams and had many of them with him in his army before Neuss.

The count of Campobasso had four hundred armed men or more under his command; but he owned no lands, for he had lost them and had been banished from the kingdom of Naples, owing to the wars which were fought there by the house of Anjou, whose partisan he was.[102] As a result he had always been in Provence with King René of Sicily or with Duke Nicholas, son of Duke John [of Calabria], after whose death the duke of Burgundy took in many of his servants, and particularly all the Italians, such as the above-named count, Giacomo Galeotto, a very valiant, honorable and loyal gentleman, and many others.[103]

When the count of Campobasso went to Italy to raise an army, he received from the duke a subsidy of forty thousand ducats for the purpose. As he passed through Lyon he made the acquaintance of a physician called Master Simon of Pavia, and he sent word to the king by this intermediary that if the king would grant certain requests of his, he would on his return from Italy put the duke of Burgundy into

---

102. Since the thirteenth century the southern part of Italy and the island of Sicily, called the kingdom of Naples from the chief city of the region, had been disputed between the French house of Anjou and the Spanish house of Aragon. The Aragonese claimants to the kingdom held the throne successfully during most of the fifteenth century. However, this did not prevent René of Anjou from taking the title of king of Sicily. René's son John and grandson Nicholas were given the title of duke of Calabria, a southern Italian province. They tried unsuccessfully to dethrone the Aragonese king of Naples with the aid of Neapolitan partisans like Campobasso and Galeotto.

103. Unfortunately, we know nothing of the relations between Galeotto and Campobasso, and we also do not know how much of the biased picture of Campobasso Commynes took from conversations with Galeotto. For what he probably took from conversations with Louis XI about Campobasso, see section 4 of the Introduction.

his hands. He made the same proposition to my lord of Saint-Pierre, who was at the time the king's ambassador in Piedmont. When he returned and his men-at-arms were quartered in the county of Marle, he made a further offer to the king, that as soon as he joined his master in his camp, he would not fail to kill him or to imprison him, and he explained how he would accomplish this. It was true that the duke often rode around his camp on a small horse, attended by very few men; therefore he could not fail to kill him or capture him. The count made still another overture: if the king and the duke should happen to face each other on the battlefield, he would pass over to the king's side with his men-at-arms under certain conditions which he stated.

The king had nothing but contempt for this man's evil character; he decided to be perfectly open with the duke of Burgundy and sent the lord of Contay, of whom I spoke earlier, to inform him of all this. The duke, however, did not believe a word of it; he assumed that the king had an ulterior motive in mind, and he showed the count greater affection than before. Thus you may see that God momentarily troubled his sense, as far as this matter was concerned, and prevented him from taking note of the clear indications which the king was sending him.

Giacomo Galeotto was as good and loyal as Campobasso was evil and faithless; and after having lived a long time he died with great honor and reputation.

The stalwart, confident athlete of the painting on page 93 became a bludgeoning, power-mad maniac by the end of his life. This anonymous portrait catches the disarray of mind and will as well as the emotional self-indulgence of Charles the Bold's last days.

BOOK FIVE

The Fall of Burgundy, 1476–1477

1

After the duke of Burgundy had conquered all of Lorraine and had received from the king Saint-Quentin, Ham, and Bohain, as well as the constable's movable possessions, he made an appointment with the king to meet him at Auxerre; they were to have an interview on a river with a bridge built over it, such as had been done at Picquigny for the meeting of our king and King Edward of England. Envoys were sent back and forth to negotiate this affair, and the duke wanted to allow [part of] his army to have a rest, because the men were very weary as a result of the siege of Neuss as well as of the war of Lorraine. The remainder he wanted to send as garrisons to several places near Berne and Fribourg which belonged to the count of Romont and others with the intention of waging war against these towns in retaliation for similar action on their part when he was besieging Neuss, and for having contributed to his losing the county of Ferrette, as you have heard, as well as for having taken part of his territories from the count of Romont.[104] The king was very anxious to have this interview and begged the duke to let his army have a rest and to leave the poor Swiss in peace.

When the Swiss realized that the duke was so close to them, they sent ambassadors to him and offered to restitute whatever they had taken from the count of Romont. On the other hand the count of Romont was beseeching him to come in person to help him. The duke disregarded the wisest counsel and the one which could have been considered the best in all respects, in view of the time of the year and the pitiful state of his army, and he decided to march against them. It was agreed by the king and him, by means of letters which they exchanged, that they would not argue about the question of Lorraine.[105]

104. The Swiss declared war on the duke of Burgundy in October, 1474, invaded Franche-Comté, and defeated the counts of Blamont and Romont, Charles's local commanders, at Héricourt on November 13. On October 14, 1475, Berne invaded and quickly occupied most of the Vaud area which belonged to the count of Romont.

105. Louis offered Charles the option of retaining either Saint-Pol's possessions or his conquests in Lorraine without interference from the king. Charles chose the latter alternative.

The duke left Lorraine with his army and entered Burgundy, where the ambassadors of these old German leagues called the Swiss came to him and made him new offers more advantageous for him than the preceding ones. In addition to the restitution they proposed to abandon all alliances of which he should disapprove, and particularly the one with the king; they would become his allies and would furnish him with six thousand men, in return for a rather small payment, and they would fight against the king whenever he requested it of them. The duke would hear nothing of it, for his unhappy future led him on.

The towns of Basel, Strasbourg, and other imperial cities along the river Rhine are called the New Alliances in this region; they had formerly been enemies of the Swiss and on the side of Duke Sigismund of Austria, whose allies they were when he was at war with the Swiss. But since then they had joined the Swiss and had made an alliance with them for ten years, and Duke Sigismund had done the same [March, 1474]. This alliance was negotiated by the king and was concluded at his request and at his expense, as you have seen elsewhere, at the time when the county of Ferrette was taken away from the duke of Burgundy and when his governor in that territory, Pierre de Hagenbach, was put to death in Basel. Indeed, Hagenbach was the cause of all this misfortune, which was very significant for the duke, for all his other adversities derived from this. A prince should carefully consider what kind of governor he appoints as head of a newly annexed territory. For instead of treating the people with great gentleness and good justice and better than they had been treated in the past, Hagenbach did exactly the opposite; he subjected them to great violence and extortion, and this turned out to be to the disadvantage of himself, his master, and many a worthy man.

This alliance, which was managed by the king, as I explained, proved to be very profitable to the monarch, and more so than most people believe. And I think it was one of the wisest things which he ever did in his time, and the most prejudicial to his enemies. For after the duke of Burgundy had been defeated, there was no man left who dared contradict the king or oppose himself to his will; I refer to those who were his subjects and lived in his kingdom, for all the rest trailed in the duke's footsteps. Therefore it was a masterly stroke to have brought about an alliance of Duke Sigismund of Austria and the New Alliance with the Swiss, who had been their enemies for so long.[106] But

106. Commynes seems to mean that by getting Duke Sigismund and the New Alliance to merge interests with the older allied Swiss cantons, the king's alliance with the latter placed them all on his side at once. See p. 176, n. 57.

this was not accomplished without much expense and without much traveling [on the part of ambassadors].

After the duke of Burgundy had left the Swiss without any hope of coming to terms with him, they returned to inform their masters of this and to make preparations for their defense. He proceeded with his army in the direction of the canton of Vaud in Savoy, which the Swiss had taken from my lord of Romont, as I said before, and he captured three or four places belonging to my lord of Châteauguion, which the Swiss held but defended badly. From there he went on to besiege a place called Granson, which also belonged to the lord of Châteauguion. The Swiss had placed there seven or eight hundred of their best soldiers, because the town was near their territories, and they wanted to defend it well.

The duke had a very large army, for soldiers came to him constantly from Lombardy as well as from the house of Savoy, and he favored over his own subjects foreign mercenaries, whom he could afford to hire in great numbers; and they were indeed excellent. But the death of the constable led him to mistrust his subjects and to suspect them of all sorts of intentions. He had a large and fine artillery and he lived in great pomp in the midst of his army, in order to make a good impression on the ambassadors from Italy and Germany. He displayed his most beautiful jewelry and dishes as well as other ornaments. And he had all sorts of extravagant plans in mind concerning the duchy of Milan, where he expected to find many partisans.

After he had besieged Granson and had battered it for several days, those who were inside surrendered unconditionally and he had all of them killed. The Swiss had assembled [to defend Granson] but they were not very numerous, as several of them have told me. For not so many soldiers are raised from their territories as one would think; and this was even more true then than now, for since that time many of them have abandoned the plow to become soldiers. Few of their allies were with them because they had tried to hurry to the assistance of Granson. And just as they were ordering themselves in the field, they learned of the death of their comrades.

The duke of Burgundy, against the advice of those whom he consulted, decided to advance and encounter the enemy at the foot of the mountains where they were still, and it was to his great disadvantage, for his army was already in a favorable spot to await them; it was enclosed by his artillery on one side and on the other by a lake, and it did not look as if the enemy could have done him any harm.

He had sent a hundred archers to secure a certain path facing this mountain when they encountered the Swiss. The duke marched forward while the greater part of his army was still in the plain. The troops who were in front wanted to turn back to join the rest. The common soldiers who were behind them thought that they were fleeing, and so they themselves began to flee; and little by little the army withdrew toward the field, with some people performing their duty very well. However, when they finally reached their camp, they did not even try to defend themselves, and all of them fled. And the Germans took over this field with his artillery and all the numerous tents and pavilions belonging to him and his men, as well as many other possessions, for nothing was saved except their lives. The duke lost all his most beautiful jewelry, but as for men, he only lost seven men-at-arms this time. All the rest fled, and the duke with them. It was more appropriate to say about him that he lost honor and possessions that day [March 2, 1476], than to say it of King John of France, who fought valiantly before being taken at the battle of Poitiers [in 1356].

This was the first calamity and misfortune which the duke had ever had in his life. In all his other enterprises he had acquired honor or profit. What damage was done that day, as a result of having been stubborn and having disdained advice! What damage his house suffered, and in what pitiful condition it still is and is likely to be for a long time to come! So many people suddenly declared themselves his enemies, although they had negotiated with him and had pretended to be his friends only the day before! And on account of what sort of dispute was this war started? It was for a cart of lambskins which my lord of Romont took from a Swiss who was passing through his territories.[107]

If God had not forsaken the duke, it is not very understandable that he would have exposed himself to such great danger on account of such a small matter, considering the offers which the Swiss had made, and considering that by conquering such people he could not gain any profit or glory. For at the time the Swiss were not held in such high esteem as they are now, and they could not have been poorer. And I heard one of their knights, who had been one of their first ambassadors to the duke of Burgundy, relate that he had told him, as an argument to dissuade him from waging war, that there was nothing for him to gain from them; their country was very barren and poor, and they would

---

107. Commynes' notion of why the war between Charles and the Swiss began has about the same historical value as Pascal's comment on the fall of the Roman Republic and the length of Cleopatra's nose. The oversimplification in Commynes' case has a moral overtone and stylistic thrust illustrated by a similar phrase analyzed on p. 46 of the Introduction.

not make worthwhile prisoners, for he believed that the spurs and bridles of his army's horses would be worth more than the money his countrymen would be able to raise for their ransom, if they were taken.

To return to the battle, the king was soon informed of the event, for he had many spies and messengers in the region, most of them sent out by my orders, and he rejoiced greatly. And the only thing which displeased him was that few men were lost [by the duke]. In order to be better informed and to be better able to act against the duke, the king stayed in Lyon. For he was wise, and therefore he feared that the duke might annex the territories of the Swiss to his own lands by force. For the duke disposed of the house of Savoy as if it were his own house; the duke of Milan was his ally; King René of Sicily wanted to put his territory of Provence into his hands. And if he had been successful in his enterprises, he would have possessed lands from the North Sea to the Mediterranean, and those of our kingdom could not have left the realm except by sea unless the duke had granted them permission, since he would have owned Savoy, Provence, and Lorraine.

The king sent ambassadors to everyone. One was my lady of Savoy, his sister, who was a partisan of the duke. Another was his uncle, King René of Sicily, who hardly listened to his messengers but reported everything to the duke. The king sent envoys to the German leagues, but it was difficult for them to reach their destination on account of the roads. Therefore he had to employ beggars, pilgrims, and similar persons. The towns gave proud answers, saying: "Tell the king that if he does not declare himself, we will make an agreement with the duke of Burgundy and declare ourselves against him," and he feared that they might do so. He had no intention of declaring himself against the duke, and so he was afraid the duke would learn of the spies he was sending about the country.

2

Let us now observe how the world changed after this battle, and how people altered their talk, and how the king conducted everything wisely. It will be a fine example for young lords who foolishly undertake projects without realizing what the outcome will be, because they do not have experience of such matters and refuse to accept the advice of those whom they should consult.

First the duke himself sent the lord of Contay to the king with humble and gracious words, which he was not accustomed to use. See how he changed within a single hour! He begged the king to respect and honor their truce, and he apologized for not having kept their appointment near Auxerre; and he assured the king that he would meet him there or elsewhere shortly, according to his wishes. The king gave the lord of Contay a very warm welcome and assured him that he would grant his requests; for he did not consider the time opportune yet to do otherwise. The king well knew the loyalty of the duke's subjects and he realized that they would soon repair matters; besides, he wanted to see the end of this affair without giving occasion to either side for an agreement with the other. But however splendidly the lord of Contay was entertained by the king, he could not help but hear himself ridiculed by the townspeople; for songs were sung publicly, praising the conquerors and shaming the conquered.

As soon as Duke Galeazzo [Sforza] of Milan, who was still alive at the time [d. December, 1476], learned of the happenings, he was extremely pleased, even though he was the duke's ally; he had made this alliance only out of fear because he was aware of the duke of Burgundy's great popularity in Italy. The duke of Milan immediately sent a messenger to the king; he was a townsman of Milan, a man of mean appearance, and through a mediator he was directed to me and brought me letters from the duke. I informed the king of the man's arrival, and he ordered me to hear what he had to say, for the king was displeased with the duke of Milan, who had left his alliance [with France] to make one with the duke of Burgundy, although his wife [Bona of Savoy] was the queen's sister. The ambassador reported that his master, the duke of Milan, was informed of the interview which was to take place between the king and the duke of Burgundy, for the purpose of making a lasting peace and alliance; this would be very distasteful to the duke, his master, and he gave several reasons why the king should not do this. At the end of his remarks, he said that if the king would consent to abstain from making peace or any truce with the duke of Burgundy, the duke of Milan would give him 100,000 ducats in cash.

After the king had heard the substance of the ambassador's message, he granted him an audience at which I was the only other person present, and told him briefly: "Here is my lord of Argenton, who has told me your business. Tell your master that I want none of his money, and that once a year I raise three times more money than he does; as for the question of war and peace, I will do as I please. However, if he repents of having left my alliance in order to make one with the duke of Burgundy, I shall be content to return to our former relationship."

The ambassador thanked the king most humbly and concluded that he was not avaricious; he beseeched the king to have the alliances pro-

claimed in the same form as they were established before, and said that
he had the authority to promise that his master would honor them. The
king agreed to this; and after dinner the alliances were proclaimed, and
an ambassador was immediately sent to Milan, where they were announced with great solemnity.[108] Here was already one of the evidences
of adversity, the change [in alliances] of a great man who only three
weeks previously had sent such a grand and solemn delegation to the
duke of Burgundy in order to obtain his alliance.

King René of Sicily had intended to make the duke of Burgundy his
heir and to put Provence into his hands. My lord of Châteauguion, who
is now in Piedmont, and others were to take possession of that territory on behalf of the duke of Burgundy and to raise an army; they
were given some twenty thousand *écus* in cash. But as soon as the news
came, it was only with difficulty that they could escape and avoid being
taken; and my lord of Bresse, who was in the region, took their money.
As soon as she heard the news of this battle, the duchess of Savoy sent
word to King René, minimizing the matter and reassuring him about
this. The messengers who were from Provence were taken, and thereby
the treaty between the king of Sicily and the duke of Burgundy was
discovered.

The king of France immediately sent men-at-arms toward Provence
and ambassadors to the king of Sicily to ask him to come, and to assure
him that he would be well received. If he refused, the king would have
to resort to force. The king of Sicily was persuaded so skillfully that
he came to the king at Lyon [April 7, 1476] and he was received with
very great honor and was warmly welcomed.

I was present when they exchanged their first words of greeting at
his arrival, and Giovanni di Cossa, seneschal of Provence, a worthy man
of good family from the kingdom of Naples, said: "My lord, do not
wonder if my master the king, your uncle, has offered to make the
duke of Burgundy his heir, for he was advised to do it by his servants,
and especially by me, because although you are his sister's son and his
nephew, you behaved so badly toward him that you took his castles
of Angers and Bar, and otherwise treated him ill. We therefore negotiated this agreement with the duke, so that you would hear of it and
would thereby be influenced to do us justice and be reminded that the
king my master is your uncle; but we never intended to conclude this

108. Commynes muddles together the events of some six months in this sentence
(March–August, 1476). The Milanese were not so easily swayed by Louis XI as
Commynes implies; they temporized, in order to be certain of Charles's fate, before
renewing their alliance with Louis XI on August 9, 1476. The alliance was published
in Milan only on August 25, 1476.

bargain." The king took these words very wisely and well, and he realized that Giovanni di Cossa was speaking the truth, for it was he who had managed this affair. A few days later, all these differences were ironed out; the king of Sicily and all his servants were given money, and the king feasted him among the ladies and had him entertained and treated in every respect, so far as he could, according to his tastes. They became good friends and no further mention was made of the duke of Burgundy, who was abandoned by King René and renounced by everyone else. This was another misfortune which resulted from his adversity.

My lady of Savoy, who had held her brother the king [Louis XI] in hatred for a long time, sent a secret messenger named the lord of Montagny, who addressed himself to me, to try to effect a reconciliation between her and the king; he alleged certain reasons why she had parted ways with the king her brother, and stated the suspicions which she had of the king's motives. However, she was a very wise lady and a true sister of the king our master. She did not entirely accept the idea of making a complete break with the duke and with his friendship, but she seemed to want to temporize and to begin to resume her former relationship with her brother. The king had me write favorable replies and try to persuade her to come to him. And her emissary was sent back to her. Thus another one of the duke's allies was making bargains to abandon him.

Everywhere in Germany people began to declare themselves against the duke; imperial towns, such as Nuremberg, Frankfurt, and several others joined the Old and New Alliances against the duke, and it seemed that one gained many pardons by doing him harm.

The loot from his camp greatly enriched the poor Swiss. At first they did not realize the value of the treasures which they had in their hands, especially the ignorant ones. One of the most beautiful and richest pavilions was cut into several pieces. Some of these people sold great quantities of silver plates and bowls for two silver coins apiece, believing that they were pewter. The duke's great diamond, which was one of the largest in Christendom, and was ornamented with a pearl, was taken by a Swiss, put back into its case, and thrown under a cart. The man then came back and looked for it again, and offered it to a priest for one florin. The latter sent it back to their lords, who gave him three francs for it. They also took three similar diamonds called the three brothers, another large one called the hood, and still another called the ball of Flanders, which were the largest and most beautiful that one could find, as well as a great quantity of other treasures, which have since taught them the value of money. For their victories and the esteem in which the king held them and the favors which he granted them have made them very rich.

Each of their ambassadors who came to the king for the first time obtained great gifts of money from him. And by these means he made up for not having declared himself for them openly, and he sent them back with their purses well filled and their persons clothed in silk. And he promised them a pension, which he eventually paid (but not before the advent of a second battle): he promised them forty thousand Rhenish florins each year—twenty thousand for the towns, and another twenty thousand for the individuals who were in charge of the government of these towns. And I believe I am correct in saying that from this first battle of Granson until the death of our king, these Swiss towns and their governors have benefited from the king our master and have received the sum of one million Rhenish florins; and I am speaking of only four towns —Berne, Lucerne, Fribourg, Zurich, and the cantons, which consist of mountains. Schwyz is one of them, and it is only a village. I have seen its mayor, who was with the others, and he was in very humble dress.

3

To return to the duke of Burgundy, he assembled soldiers on all sides, and within three weeks he had a great number of men—more than had fled on the day of the battle. He took up quarters at Lausanne in Savoy [during April and May, 1476], where you, my lord of Vienne, helped him with your good counsel, during a serious illness which he contracted as a result of the grief and sorrow which he experienced at the great shame he had sustained; and to tell you the truth, I do not think that he ever again had his mind so sound as he had before this battle.[109]

I speak of this great new army which he had assembled from what I have heard reported by my lord the prince of Taranto [Frederick of Aragon, second son of Ferrante, king of Naples], who told the king about it in my presence. About one year earlier the prince had come with an impressive escort to the duke's court in the hope of obtaining the hand of his daughter and sole heiress; and he very much seemed like a king's son, by his bearing as well as by his clothing and his retinue. And his father, the king of Naples, well showed that he had spared no cost in the matter. However, the duke [of Burgundy] was not being

109. Cato had come to Charles's court with Frederick of Aragon, whose arrival is described in the next paragraph. See also p. 91, n. 1.

perfectly open in this affair, for at the same time he was negotiating with the duchess of Savoy for her son, and with other persons besides. As a result, the prince of Taranto, called Don Frederick of Aragon, and his council, being dissatisfied with so many delays, sent a shrewd officer to the king of France, begging him to grant a safe-conduct to the prince, so that he might pass through his kingdom and return to the king his father, who had sent for him. The king granted it very willingly because he believed that it would reflect against the duke of Burgundy's credit and reputation.

Before the messenger had returned, however, all the German leagues had already assembled and were quartered near the duke of Burgundy. The prince took his leave of the duke on the night before the battle [of Morat] in order to comply with his father's orders, for in the first battle [at Granson] he had proved himself an honorable man. Many people say that he was also guided by your counsel, my lord of Vienne. For when he arrived at the court of France, I heard him say and affirm to the duke of Ascoli, called count Giulio, and to others, that you had written in Italy about the first and second battles and had predicted the outcome several days before it occurred.[110]

As I said before, at the prince's departure all the allies were quartered near the duke and had come to fight him and to make him raise the siege which he had begun of Morat, a small town near Berne, which belonged to my lord of Romont. The army of the allies, as was told to me by those who were there, must have consisted of thirty thousand infantrymen, well selected and well armed, eleven thousand pike-bearers, ten thousand halberdiers, ten thousand musketeers, and four thousand horsemen. The allies were not even all assembled yet; only those which I have listed were at the battle, but they were entirely sufficient.[111] My lord of Lorraine came there with a small force, and it turned out to be to his advantage later, for the duke of Burgundy held all of his lands at the time.

The duke of Lorraine acted graciously, although our court was beginning to grow weary of him; for a great man who has lost his possessions is usually a source of annoyance to those who support him. The king had given him a small sum of money and had him escorted

110. This is a reference to Angelo Cato's supposed power to foretell the future, for which he was greatly esteemed by Louis XI.

111. Commynes' figures are vastly exaggerated. About twenty-four thousand men fought for the allies at Morat. See the illustration of this battle reproduced on the endpapers of this volume.

by a goodly number of men-at-arms through Lorraine; they led him to Germany and then returned. The duke of Lorraine had not only lost his duchy of Lorraine, but also the county of Vaudémont and most of Barrois; and the rest was held by the king. Therefore he was left with nothing. And worse, all his subjects, including the servants of his household, had sworn allegiance to the duke of Burgundy of their own accord. Therefore it seemed to him that there was little he could do to remedy the situation. However, God always remains the final judge in such affairs, if He wishes to be.

When the duke of Lorraine had passed through his duchy, as I said before, after having marched on horseback for several days, he arrived at the camp of the Alliances a few hours before the battle [on June 22, 1476] with a small company of soldiers. This journey brought him great honor and great profit, for if he had acted otherwise, he would have found little welcome. Just as he arrived the troops marched forth on both sides, for the Alliances had already been quartered three days in a strong place at a small distance from the duke of Burgundy. After some minor resistance the Burgundian army was discomfited and put to flight. Nor did the duke come out of it so well as in the last battle, where he had lost only seven men-at-arms. This was because the Swiss had no horsemen then, but at the time I am speaking of, when they were near Morat, the Germans had four thousand well-mounted horsemen who pursued the Burgundians very far; and their infantrymen battled with the duke's foot-soldiers, who were numerous. For without counting his subjects and a great number of Englishmen who were with his army, he had many soldiers newly arrived from Piedmont, and other subjects of the duke of Milan, as I said previously. After he arrived at the king's court, the prince of Taranto told me that he had never seen such a fine army, and that as they were passing a bridge, he counted them himself and also had them counted, and found that they numbered twenty-three thousand mercenaries, besides the others who followed the army and belonged to the train of artillery. I consider this number very great, although some people speak in terms of thousands and lightly represent armies as much greater than they really are.

The lord of Contay, who came to the king shortly after the battle, confessed to him in my presence that eight thousand of the duke's mercenaries had been killed in this battle, as well as a large number of common people; and, judging from what I have heard, I believe that the total number of dead came to about eighteen thousand. And that number should not be hard to accept, considering the great forces of horsemen which had been sent there by several German lords, besides those who were still at the siege before Morat.[112]

The duke fled as far as Burgundy in great despair, as he had reason to be, and he stayed in a place called La Rivière, where he raised whatever troops he could. The Germans pursued him only that night, and then they retired without following him any further.

4

The outcome of this enterprise drove the duke to desperation, and he realized that all his friends were forsaking him, judging from the signs which he had seen since his first loss at Granson, which had occurred only three weeks before the most recent one, which I mentioned. And owing to his apprehensions and by the advice of some persons, he ordered the duchess of Savoy and one of her sons [Charles], who is now duke of Savoy, to be brought by force into Burgundy. Her eldest son [Philibert] was saved by some of the servants of the house of Savoy, for those who seized that family did it with fear, and they had to act fast. The reason behind the duke's exploit was fear that the duchess might retire to her brother's court; and he claimed that all his misfortunes had resulted from the help which he had given to the house of Savoy.

The duke had the lady taken to the castle of Rouvres, near Dijon, and placed a small guard about her. However, everyone was free to call on her. Among her visitors were the present lord of Châteauguion and the present marquis of Rothelin. The duke had negotiated the marriages between these two lords and two of the duchess's daughters; at the time they were not yet concluded, but they have been since.

Her eldest son, named Philibert, at the time duke of Savoy, was taken to Chambéry by those who had saved him. There he found the bishop of Geneva, who was a son of the house of Savoy, a very willful man who was governed by a so-called Commander de Ranvers. Thus they put into the hands of the bishop the duke of Savoy and a younger brother of his [Jacques-Louis de Savoie], called the protonotary, along with the castles of Chambéry and Montmélian; and he kept another castle, which contained all the jewels belonging to my lady of Savoy.

112. Joseph Calmette, basing himself on the research of Ferdinand Lot, corrects Commynes' figures here and in preceding paragraphs in his book, *The Golden Age of Burgundy* (New York, 1963), pp. 274–76 and note 7, pp. 340–41: Probably some thousand men were lost at Granson; Charles had less than ten thousand men in his army at Morat, of which some eight thousand, mostly infantrymen, lost their lives.

Book Five

As soon as the duchess found herself in Rouvres, as I said before, accompanied by all her ladies-in-waiting and many servants, she saw that the duke was very busy raising an army and that her guards did not fear their master as much as they used to; therefore she decided to send a messenger to the king her brother with the intention of making a treaty with him and asking him to take her under his protection. If it had not been for her present predicament, she would have greatly feared falling into his hands, for there had been great hatred between them for a long time.

The lady sent a gentleman from Piedmont named Rivarola, her major-domo. Someone directed him to me. After I had heard him and reported to the king what he had told me, our master granted him an audience. And when he had taken note of his message, the king told him that he would not abandon his sister in this necessity, their past differences notwithstanding, and that if she would make an alliance with him, he would have the governor of Champagne, who was at the time Charles d'Amboise, lord of Chaumont, go and fetch her. Rivarola took his leave of the king and hastened back to his mistress. She was very happy with the report. However, as soon as she had heard the messenger, she sent another man to the king, begging him to assure her that he would let her return to Savoy, that he would give her back her son, the duke, and his younger brother, as well as the castles which belonged to her, and that he would help her maintain her authority in Savoy; in that case she would be glad to renounce all her former alliances and make one with him. The king granted everything she requested and immediately sent a man to the lord of Chaumont for the express purpose of taking care of the matter. The enterprise was well organized and well executed. The lord of Chaumont proceeded to Rouvres with a large number of men, without making any ravage in the territory, and led my lady of Savoy and all her retinue to the closest stronghold belonging to the king.

When the king dispatched the last message to the lady, he had already left Lyon, where he had stayed six months in order to shrewdly thwart the duke's enterprises without violating the terms of the truce. But in view of the situation of the duke, the king was doing him more harm by letting him have his way and secretly inciting others to become his enemies than if he had openly declared war against him. For as soon as the duke would have seen such a declaration, he would have desisted from his enterprise, and as a result the misfortunes which befell him would not have taken place.

After leaving Lyon the king continued on his way; he embarked on

311

the river Loire at Roanne and came to Tours. When he arrived there, he learned of his sister's deliverance and this pleased him greatly. He sent word to her in all haste that she should come to him and saw to it that the expenses of her trip should be paid. Upon her arrival he sent several people to meet her, and he himself went to receive her at the gate of Plessis-du-Parc [i.e., Plessis-lez-Tours]. He was very cordial and said: "Welcome, Madam the Burgundian." But she could tell from the expression on his face that he was only joking, and she answered wisely that she was a loyal Frenchwoman and that she was ready to obey the king in whatever he wished to command.

The king conducted her to her room and had her well treated. It is true that he was very anxious to get rid of her. She was very shrewd and both of them were well aware of each other's intentions. The lady was even more desirous of leaving [than he was of seeing her go]. I was delegated by the king to take care of this matter: first to provide money to defray her expenses at court and on her return journey, and to furnish her with silk cloth; then to put in writing the terms of their alliance and the form of their relations for the time to come.

The king tried to make her change her mind about the proposed marriages of her daughters, which I mentioned earlier, but she shifted the responsibility on the young ladies, saying that they had their hearts set on it. As a matter of fact they really were obstinate about it. When the king realized that it was their will, he consented. After the lady had been at Plessis for seven or eight days, she and the king mutually swore to be good friends in the future, and they exchanged documents to that effect. The lady then took her leave of the king, and he had her escorted home; her children, her castles, her jewels, and other possessions were returned to her by his command. Both of them were very happy to leave each other, and they remained on good terms until death.

5

To continue with the main subject, I should speak of the duke of Burgundy, who after his flight from the battle of Morat in the year 1476 had gone to the Burgundian border and had taken up quarters in a town called La Rivière, where he stayed more than six weeks; and he still had the courage to try to raise an army. However, he proceeded slowly and kept to himself like a hermit. And he seemed to act out of obstination more than anything else, as you will see. For the grief he experienced at the loss of the first battle of Granson was so great and affected his spirits to such an extent that he became seriously ill. His choleric disposition and his natural heat used to be so great that he did not take any wine, but in the morning he usually drank herb tea and ate rose-hip syrup to refresh himself. This sorrow altered his disposition so radically, however, that he had to be made to drink strong wine without water; and in order to draw back the blood, some people put burning tow in cupping containers and applied this heat to the region around his heart. But you, my lord of Vienne, know more about this than I do, because you helped heal him during this illness, and you made him have his beard shaved, because he had let it grow. And, in my opinion, ever since this illness he was no longer as wise as before and his sense was much diminished. Such are the passions of those who have never experienced adversity and who do not know how to find a remedy for their misfortunes, especially proud princes.

For in this and similar cases, one's first refuge is to return to God and consider whether one has offended Him in any way, to humble oneself before Him, and to acknowledge one's misdeeds; for He determines the course of such affairs, and no one can say that He makes a single error. After that it is helpful to open one's heart to some close friend and to complain freely about one's fate; one should not be ashamed to show one's grief in the presence of a special friend, for it relieves one's heart and comforts it, and it revives one's spirits. It is unavoidable, since we are men, that such suffering should be accompanied by great emotion expressed either in public or in private, and therefore one should not follow the example of the duke, who chose to hide and remain alone. Besides, he treated his men so terribly that no one could have ventured to offer him comfort or counsel, but they let him do as he pleased, fearing that if they made any observations to him, it would be taken badly.

During the six weeks or so that he stayed [at La Rivière] his men were very few in number, and this was not surprising, after he had lost two such important battles, as you have heard. Many new enemies had declared themselves against him, his friends had cooled toward him, his subjects were beaten and defeated, and they began to make unfavorable comments about their master and to despise him, as usually happens after such adversities, as I have said.

Many small places were taken from him in Lorraine, such as Vaudé-mont, which was already lost, Épinal, and others after these. From all sides people began to prepare to attack him; and the most insignificant of them became the boldest. And upon hearing this report, the duke of Lorraine raised a few troops and came to take up quarters before Nancy. He already held most of the small neighboring towns.

However, the duke of Burgundy still held Pont-à-Mousson, four leagues or so away from Nancy.

Among those who were besieged [at Nancy] was a man from the house of Croy, named my lord of Bièvres, a fine and honorable knight. He had excellent soldiers, including one named Colpin, a very valiant man, although of low lineage, and my lord of Bièvres brought him along with others from the garrison of Guines into the service of the duke. Colpin had about three hundred Englishmen under his command in the town, and although they were not very pressed by the siege or by batteries, they were annoyed that the duke of Burgundy was taking such a long time to give them assistance; and, to be truthful, he was much to blame for not arriving sooner, for the place where he was staying was far from Lorraine, and he could not be of any use to them there. It would have been more important to defend what remained of his possessions than to try to invade the Swiss to take revenge for his losses; but his stubbornness in following no advice except his own turned greatly to his disadvantage. For no matter how urgently he was solicited to come to save that place, he lingered at La Rivière without any necessity, for six weeks or so. If he had acted differently, he might easily have brought relief to Nancy, for the duke of Lorraine did not have any men before it at all. And by holding on to Lorraine, the duke of Burgundy would always have had a free passage to proceed from his other territories, through Luxembourg and Lorraine to Burgundy. Therefore if his judgment had been as keen as formerly, he would have joined the others with greater haste.

While the soldiers of Nancy awaited their help, Colpin, the leader of the English troops of whom I spoke, was killed by a cannon shot; and this was most unfortunate for the duke of Burgundy, for the presence of a single man, even if he is not of high estate or lineage provided he has good sense and courage, can sometimes save his master from great inconveniences. And in this respect, I have observed that our king was very wise, for no prince was ever more fearful of losing his men than he was.

As soon as Colpin was killed, the English who had been under his command began to murmur and to despair of ever obtaining assistance. They did not know how small the forces of the duke of Lorraine were, nor how great the means of the duke of Burgundy were to recruit soldiers. But the English had not had a war outside their kingdom for a long time, and they did not understand much about siege techniques. And indeed they began to clamor for a negotiation, and they told the lord of Bièvres, who was governor of that city, that if he would not make an agreement with the enemy, they would make one without him. Although he was a good knight, he was not of powerful virtue. He begged them and remonstrated with them, but I believe that if he had spoken with more authority, he would have been more successful, unless God had willed it otherwise; and that I well believe was the case, for if they had held out for another three days, they would have received the necessary assistance. In short, the governor yielded to the English and surrendered the town to the duke of Lorraine, on condition that they might save their lives and their possessions.

The next day, or at most two days after the capitulation of the town, the duke of Burgundy arrived with a good-sized army, considering his situation, for several people from his other territories had come to join him by way of Luxembourg.[113] He and the duke of Lorraine faced each other. However, no action of importance took place, because the duke of Lorraine was not strong enough.

6

The duke of Burgundy tried to retrieve the ball[114] and once again laid siege to Nancy. It would have been better for him if he had not been so obstinate and if he had not delayed so long. But God makes princes extraordinarily willful when He decides to change their fortunes. If the duke had been willing to follow good advice and to put garrisons in the small places near Nancy, he would have been able to recover the town in a short time, for it was not well supplied with food, and there were enough people and more to reduce it to great straits; he would have had time to have his soldiers take refreshment and to rebuild his army, but he went at it in another way.

While he persisted in this siege, which was unfortunate for him, as well as for all his subjects and many others who were not at all involved in this quarrel, several of his men began intrigues. And already, as I said, enemies had appeared from all sides. They included count Nicola di Campobasso, of the kingdom of Naples, from which he had been banished on account of his support of the house of Anjou, and whom the duke had taken in after the death of Duke Nicholas of Calabria, his master, as well as several other servants of the duke of Calabria.

The count was very poor, as I said before, in terms of land and

113. The Burgundian garrison at Nancy capitulated on October 5, 1476. Charles the Bold did not arrive at Toul, en route to Nancy, until October 11.
114. See the comment on this phrase on p. 83 of the Introduction.

money. The duke of Burgundy immediately [after he arrived from Italy] gave him forty thousand ducats to go to Italy and recruit four hundred lance-teams, to be paid by Campobasso. And from that very moment he began to plot his master's death, as I said before, and he continued his intrigues up to the time I have mentioned. And once again, when he saw that his master was in an unfavorable position, he began to negotiate with my lord of Lorraine, as well as with certain commanders and servants whom the king had placed in Champagne, near the duke's army.

He promised the duke of Lorraine that the siege would not progress and that he would see to it that the necessary equipment and battery would be lacking. And he was in a position to do this, for he was the principal officer in charge of this, and he had great authority with the duke of Burgundy. With our men he bargained more openly, for he always offered to kill or capture his master in return for the upkeep of his four hundred lance-teams, twenty thousand *écus* in ready cash, and a good county.

While he was transacting this business, several gentlemen from the duke of Lorraine's army made an attempt to enter the town. Some of them succeeded. Others were taken, among them a gentleman from Provence, named Siffredo [di Baschi], who managed all the bargains between the count and the duke of Lorraine. The duke of Burgundy ordered that Siffredo be hanged immediately, saying that once a prince has besieged a town and has his artillery batter it, if anyone enters and gives assistance to the garrison inside to fight against him, he is liable to death, according to the rules of war. However, this was not observed in our wars, which otherwise are more cruel than those of Italy or Spain, where this custom is in force. Still the duke insisted that this gentleman should die. When Siffredo realized that he could not escape his punishment and that his death was inevitable, he sent word to the duke of Burgundy, begging him to grant him an audience, so that he might tell him something which concerned his person.

Some gentlemen to whom he said this came to report it to the duke, and the count of Campobasso, whom I mentioned before, happened to be with him when they brought the message; he may have been there by chance, or perhaps on purpose, knowing that Siffredo had been taken and fearing that he might tell all he knew about his intrigues. For Siffredo understood the count's maneuvers, both on one side and on the other, and everything had been communicated to him, and that was what he wanted to say.

The duke replied to those who made this report that he was just trying to save his life, and that he should talk to them. The count strongly supported this answer.[115] He was the only person present with the duke, aside from a secretary who was writing; and the count was in charge of all this army. The prisoner said that he would tell the secret only to the duke of Burgundy. Once more the duke ordered that he be sent to hang, and it was done. As he was on his way to the gallows, Siffredo begged several persons to entreat their master that he should hear him, and he would relate something so important that the duke would not want to have been unaware of it for a whole duchy. Some of his acquaintances took pity on him and decided to try to get a word in with their master and beg him to grant him an audience. But that evil count stood at the door of the chamber [decorated with] wood where the duke was staying, and prevented anyone from entering, especially these men; and he said to them: "My lord wants him to be hanged immediately." And messengers were sent to tell the provost to hurry. And finally Siffredo was hanged, much to the prejudice of the duke of Burgundy, who would have done better if he had not been so cruel and if he had humanely heard what the gentleman had to say. Perhaps if he had done it he might still be alive, and his house prosperous and greatly increased, considering what has happened in this kingdom since his day. But one must believe that God had ordered differently.

You have heard earlier in these memoirs of the disloyal trick which the duke had played on the count of Saint-Pol, constable of France, only a short time before. He captured him in spite of the safe-conduct which he had given him, handed him over to the king to be put to death, and turned over to him [Louis XI] all the sealed acts and letters which he had from the constable, to serve as evidence against him at his trial. And although the duke had just cause to hate the constable to the point of having him put to death, and the many reasons would be too long to write down, he should have done this only if it had been possible without first giving him his word that he would be safe. However, all the excuses which I could muster up in this case could not extenuate the disloyal and dishonorable act which the duke committed when he sent a good and valid safe-conduct to the constable and nevertheless seized him and sold him for purely avaricious motives, not merely to obtain the town of Saint-Quentin and other places, as well as

115. According to another contemporary source, Campobasso interceded with Charles the Bold in order to save Siffredo's life rather than in order to insure his death. Instead of replying, Charles cuffed Campobasso across the cheek with his mailed fist and this, according to Benedetto Croce, moved Campobasso to desert the duke four days before the battle of Nancy. See Introduction, p. 66.

inheritances and movable possessions belonging to the constable, but also for fear of not taking Nancy when he besieged it for the first time.

And after several dissimulations he gave up the constable at this time for fear that the king's army, which was in Champagne, might prevent him from succeeding in his enterprise against Nancy. For the king threatened him by his ambassadors, who pointed out that according to their agreement, the first of the two who could seize the constable should deliver him to the other within eight days, or should put him to death himself. But the duke had exceeded this term by many days, and it was only this fear [of the king's army] and the great desire he had to obtain Nancy which prevailed upon him to make him surrender the constable, as you have heard. Just as it was precisely during his first siege of Nancy that he had committed this crime, it was right after he had laid the second siege there that he had Siffredo executed (for he would not hear him, and thus he acted like a person who has his ears stopped and his judgment impaired)—and it was again in the same place that he was deceived and betrayed by the person in whom he had the most trust. He was perhaps justly punished by this treason because of his cruelty to the constable and his cupidity in relation to Nancy. But such a judgment belongs to God alone, and I do not mention it merely to make my narration clearer, but to show how a good prince should avoid such base and disloyal acts, regardless of any advice which he may be given to the contrary. Besides, it frequently happens that those who give them such counsel do so because they want to please them or because they are afraid of contradicting them, although they come to regret their action once their advice has been followed; for they realize that they may be punished for this by God and men. Therefore such advisers are better far than near.

You have heard how God established the count of Campobasso to be His instrument to take vengeance in this world for the action taken against the constable by the duke of Burgundy, in the same place and in the same manner, but even more cruelly. For just as the duke had delivered the constable to be put to death in spite of the safe-conduct which he had granted him and the faith which the constable had put in him, he himself was betrayed by the most loyal person of his army, or I should say the one whom he most trusted, whom he had taken in when he was old, poor, and friendless, and whom he was paying 100,000 ducats a year, besides maintaining his men-at-arms out of his own pocket and granting him many other favors. And when he first began these intrigues, he was on his way to Italy with forty thousand ducats in cash, which he had received for recruiting, as they say, that is, for raising an army of men-at-arms.

And to manage this treason, he had recourse to persons in two localities. The first was a physician in Lyon, called Master Simon of Pavia, and the second, whom I mentioned before, was in Savoy. And upon his return, his men-at-arms were quartered in several small places in the county of Marle in the Laonnois. There he resumed his bargaining and offered to give up all the places which he held and, if the king were to face the duke in battle, upon a signal to be arranged by the king and him, he would turn against his master and pass over to the king's side with all his troops. The king would not have been very pleased with the second proposition. Campobasso offered further that the first time his master would encamp, he would capture him or kill him as he inspected his army. And indeed he might well have succeeded in this third project, for the duke, as soon as he dismounted at the place where he was to take up quarters, invariably used to remove most of his armor and keep only his cuirass; thus he mounted a small horse and took with him only eight or ten archers on foot. Occasionally he was followed by two or three gentlemen of his bedchamber, and he rode outside his camp to see whether his army was securely enclosed. And therefore the count could have put his plan into execution with ten horsemen without any difficulty.

After the king had seen the constant intrigues of this man to betray his master, the last one being made in time of truce, and after he had realized that he did not know the reason for these overtures, he decided to show perfect sincerity to the duke of Burgundy, and he sent him word of the count's maneuvers by the count of Contay, who has been mentioned several times in these memoirs; I was present when the message was given to him, and I am sure that the lord of Contay acquitted himself faithfully to his master. The duke, however, took everything amiss and said that if it had been true, the king would never have let him know. And this took place long before he came to Nancy. And I well believe that the duke did not say a word about this to the count.

7

We must return to our main subject and to Nancy, which the duke was besieging. It was in the middle of winter and he had few soldiers with him. They were insufficiently armed and badly paid; and many of them were ill. Some of the highest-ranking officers were conspiring against him, as you have heard. In general all of them complained about him and despised his actions, as is customary in time of adversity, as I have said at length earlier. But no one except the count of Campobasso intended any harm against his person or his estate, and there was no disloyalty to be found among his subjects.

While he was making his initial preparations, the duke of Lorraine treated with the Old and New Alliances, whom I mentioned before, so as to obtain soldiers to fight the duke of Burgundy, who was besieging Nancy. All these towns were most willing to provide them. All he needed now was to find money. The king comforted him by means of ambassadors which he had sent to the Swiss, and he let him have forty thousand francs to help pay for his German soldiers. My lord of Craon, who was his lieutenant in Champagne, had taken up quarters in the Barrois area with seven or eight hundred lance-teams and free archers, commanded by excellent officers.

The duke of Lorraine accomplished so much with the king's favor and money that he assembled a great number of Germans, both foot-soldiers and horsemen; for in addition to the troops who were in his pay, they provided him with some at their own expense. He also had with him many gentlemen from this kingdom; and the king's army was quartered in the Barrois, as I said, and for the moment they were not fighting, but merely waiting to see who would have the upper hand. The duke of Lorraine came to take up quarters at Saint-Nicolas, near Nancy, with the above-mentioned Germans.

The king of Portugal had been in this kingdom for nine months or so.[116] Our king had made an alliance with him against the present king of Spain [Ferdinand the Catholic]. The king of Portugal had come with hopes that King Louis would give him a large army to wage war against Castile, from the side of Biscay or the side of Navarre; for he held many places in Castile on the frontier of Portugal as well as near our borders, such as the castle of Burgos and others, and I believe that if the king had helped him, as he sometimes intended to, the king of Portugal might have succeeded in his enterprise. But now our king had changed his mind, although the hopes of the king of Portugal had been entertained for a year or more. In the meantime, his affairs in Castile were beginning to worsen; for when he first came [to France], almost all the lords of the kingdom of Castile were on his side, but when they saw that he stayed so long,

116. Alfonso V (1438–1481) arrived in France in mid-September, 1476. Perhaps Commynes' secretary mistook "deux" (two) for "neuf" (nine) months, when the memorialist dictated this chapter. The total duration of the Portuguese king's stay was about a year, as Commynes tells us later on.

they gradually changed their attitude and compromised with King Ferdinand and Queen Isabella, who still reign today.

The king made excuses for the assistance which he had agreed to give, and claimed it was because of the war in Lorraine and the fear which he had that the duke of Burgundy might rise up again and then come to attack him. The poor king of Portugal, who was a good and just man, took it into his head to visit the duke of Burgundy, who was his first cousin, and to try to iron out the differences between him and the king, so that the king would be in a position to help him; for he was ashamed to return to Castile or Portugal without the aid which he had requested and without having accomplished anything at the French court. For his decision to come there had been made lightly and contrary to the opinion of his council.

Thus the king of Portugal set out in the very heart of winter and went to visit the duke of Burgundy, his cousin, at his camp before Nancy [December 29, 1476]; he immediately pointed out to him what the king had said concerning a possible reconciliation. But he found out that it would be no easy matter to have them make peace, and that they were different in everything. Therefore he stayed only two days, and then took his leave of the duke, his cousin, and returned to Paris, from where he had left. The duke begged him to stay a while longer and to proceed to Pont-à-Mousson, which is rather near Nancy, where he would be in charge of the troops who would guard the passage; for the duke already knew that the Germans had arrived and were posted at Saint-Nicolas. The king of Portugal excused himself, claiming that he was neither armed nor attended sufficiently for such an exploit, and he returned to Paris, where he had already stayed for so long.

Finally the king of Portugal began to suspect that the king of France had the intention of seizing him and handing him over to his enemy, the king of Castile. Therefore he put on a disguise and decided to go to Rome with two other men, and then to enter religious orders. As he proceeded in this costume, he was taken by a person named Le Beuf, who was a Norman. The king our master was sorry about this turn of events and was somewhat ashamed of himself for having allowed this to happen. Therefore he ordered several ships to be armed on the coast of Normandy and put under the command of George the Greek, who was to take the king of Portugal back to his kingdom.

The cause of his war against the king of Castile was the interest of his niece [Juana], daughter of his sister, who had been the wife of the late King Henry of Castile [1425–1474]. Her daughter was very beautiful, and she still lives, unmarried, in Portugal. Queen Isabella, King Henry's sister, had her [Juana's] claim of succession to the throne of Castile dismissed on the grounds that her mother had conceived her in adultery. A large number of people shared this opinion and said that King Henry had been impotent, for a reason which I shall be silent about.

Whatever the case may be, and although the girl was born under the cloak of marriage, the crown of Castile was nevertheless enjoyed by Queen Isabella and her husband, king of Aragon and Sicily, who reign today. The king of Portugal tried to arrange a marriage between his niece and our present king, Charles VIII, and this was the reason for his visit to France, which turned out to his great prejudice and displeasure; for soon after his return to Portugal, he died.

Therefore, as I said at the beginning of these memoirs, a prince should consider carefully what ambassadors he sends to various countries. For if those who came to negotiate the alliance between the king of Portugal and our king (at which I was present as one of the king's deputies) had been very wise, they would have informed themselves better of the affairs of our kingdom before advising their master to make this visit which proved so disadvantageous to him.

8

I could well have omitted the above passage, if it had not been to show that a prince should think twice before putting himself into the hands of another, and that he should not come in person to solicit aid. And to return to the principal subject, the king of Portugal had not been gone for a day, after taking leave of the duke of Burgundy, before the duke of Lorraine and the Germans who were with him moved out of Saint-Nicolas and proceeded to fight the duke of Burgundy. And on that very day the count of Campobasso came forth to meet them and concluded his enterprise by joining them with about 160 men-at-arms; and he was much annoyed that he was not able to do greater harm to his master.

Those in the garrison inside Nancy were aware of the count of Campobasso's intrigues, and this encouraged them to hold out. In addition, a man who had entered by throwing himself into the moat assured them of help; for otherwise they were on the point of capitulation. And if it had not been for the count's dissimulation, they would not have held out until then. But God wanted to finish this mystery.

The duke of Burgundy, who was informed of the army's coming, held a sort of council, although it was not customary for him to do so, for he usually followed his own judgment. There many of them expressed the opinion that it would be best for him to retire to Pont-à-Mousson, which was close by, and to leave troops in the places which he held near Nancy, because the Germans would leave as soon as they had brought supplies to Nancy, and the duke of Lorraine, being without funds, would not be able to assemble such a great army for a long time; and their provisions could not be so large but that before half the winter was over, they would be as hard pressed as they were then. And in the meantime the duke of Burgundy could raise more troops.

For I have heard from well-informed people that the army consisted of less than four thousand men, of whom only twelve hundred were fit to fight.[117] The duke was not lacking in money, for he had about 450,000 *écus* in the castle of Luxembourg, which was not far off, and with this amount he could have assembled a fair number of men. But God did not grant him the grace of accepting this wise counsel or of realizing how great was the number of enemies who surrounded him on all sides; and so he chose the poorer alternative, and with the words of one who had lost all sense he decided to wait for the enemy there, in spite of all the observations which had been made to him concerning the great number of Germans who were with the duke of Lorraine as well as with the king's army, which was quartered near him. And he resolved to go to battle with this small number of disheartened soldiers.

As soon as the count of Campobasso came to the duke of Lorraine, the Germans sent word to him that he should leave at once, because they did not want to have any traitors with them. And so he retired to Condé, a castle and a by-road near there, which he fortified as well as he could, hoping that if the duke of Burgundy and his men fled, he would have a good occasion to share in the loot, which he eventually did.

The count's negotiation with the duke of Lorraine was not his principal intrigue; for he had spoken with others shortly before his departure and had concluded with them that since he did not see how he could put his hands on the duke of Burgundy, he would pass over to the other side when the hour of battle came.

The count did not want to leave sooner, so that he could give that much greater fright to the duke's army, but he was sure that if the duke should flee, he could never escape alive, for he would post twelve or fourteen persons who were loyal to him, some to begin fleeing as soon as they saw the Germans approaching, and the others to keep an eye on the duke, in case he should run away, and to kill him as he fled. And this was a foolproof plan; for I have known two or three of those who re-

117. Olivier de la Marche, an eyewitness, states "on his conscience" that Charles had fewer than two thousand soldiers at the battle of Nancy. The combined Swiss and Lorraine forces numbered twelve to fourteen thousand, not counting Campobasso's men. See F. Lot, *L'art militaire et les armées*, II (Paris, 1946), 128 and 134.

mained behind to kill the duke. After the count had concluded this treacherous project, he retired in the midst of the army and turned against his master when he saw the Germans approach, as I said. And when he realized that the Germans did not want him in their company, he proceeded to Condé, as was said.

The Germans marched forth. With them were many horsemen from France, who had been allowed to participate in this action. Many others lay in ambush near the place to see whether the duke would be discomfited, and in order to capture prisoners or loot. And thus you may see in what a state the poor duke had put himself because he disregarded the advice which was offered to him.[118]

The two enemy armies met, and his army, which had already been routed twice, and which consisted of only a few badly equipped soldiers, was quickly defeated; all the men either died or fled. Many escaped. The rest were killed or taken prisoners. Among them the duke of Burgundy was killed on the spot. I shall not say how because I was not there; but his death was related to me by those who saw him pulled to the ground; and they could not come to his aid because they were prisoners. Yet he was not killed while they saw him, but by a great crowd of people who came afterward and stripped him with many others, without recognizing him. This battle took place on the fifth day of January, 1477, on the eve of Epiphany.

9

After his death I saw a seal in Milan, which I had often observed hanging from his doublet; it represented a lamb and a flint, carved on a cameo with his arms; and it was sold in Milan for two ducats. The person who took it from him was a mean *valet de chambre*. I have often seen

118. The sequence of events in the preceding eight paragraphs is confusing because Commynes interrupts his narration (paragraph 1: beginning of the battle of Nancy) by referring to earlier events (paragraphs 2–4: situation in Nancy and in duke's army before battle), and then returns to where he left off (paragraph 5: German reaction to Campobasso's desertion), only to interrupt the narration of the battle a second time (paragraphs 6–7: more intrigues and projects of Campobasso before the battle), and finally a third time (paragraph 8: completion of the outline in paragraphs 2–4 of the situation just before battle). The cause of this temporal disorganization is Commynes' desire to point the finger of guilt over and over again at Campobasso. I have discussed the psychological significance of that desire in section 4 of the Introduction. The fact that, according to other sources, Campobasso abandoned the duke of Burgundy four days before the battle rather than during it probably accounts for such incongruous details in Commynes' narrative as the fortification of Condé by Campobasso after his desertion and after he had supposedly been rejected by the Germans, but still before the battle was over, so that he was able to collect loot from fleeing soldiers.

the duke dressed and undressed with great reverence and by high-rank-ing persons. But at his last hour all these honors were gone.[119] And he perished, with his house, as I said before, at the very place where, out of avarice, he had consented to give up the constable, and this was only a short time after the event. May God forgive him for his sins.

I have seen him as a great and honorable prince, and as esteemed and sought out by his neighbors, for a time, as any prince in Christendom, and perhaps more so. I have not seen any reason why he should have in-curred the wrath of God, unless it was because he considered all the graces and honors which he had received in this world to have been the result of his own judgment and valor, instead of attributing them to God, as he should have. For indeed he was endowed with many good qualities and virtues. No prince ever surpassed him in eagerness to act as patron to great men and to give them a well-regulated way of life. His gifts were not very grand, for he wanted everyone to feel the effects of his liberality. No lord ever granted audience more freely to his servants and his subjects. At the time when I knew him, he was not cruel; but he became so before his death, and this was a sign that his life would be short. He was very ostentatious in his dress and in everything else—a little too much. He was very courteous to ambassadors and foreigners; they were well received and lavishly entertained in his own places of resi-dence. He desired great glory, and it was that more than anything else which made him engage in these wars. He would have liked to resemble those princes of antiquity who remained so famous after their death. And he was as daring as any man who ruled in his time.

But all his projects are over, and they all turned to his prejudice and shame; for those who win get all the honor. I do not know toward whom Our Lord showed the greatest anger: toward him, who died suddenly on the battlefield, without lingering for long, or toward his subjects, who have never since enjoyed prosperity or peace, but have been con-tinually involved in wars in which they have not been able to resist sufficiently, or in civil strifes and cruel and fierce fighting among them-selves. The hardest burden to bear has been the fact that their de-fenders have been foreigners who had formerly been their enemies—the Germans.[120]

119. The signet seal to which Commynes refers in these ironic phrases about how the duke was stripped after death bore the emblems of the Burgundian order of knighthood, the Order of the Golden Fleece. The necklace worn by Charles the Bold in the portrait introducing Book 1 is composed of these two emblems, plus a flame-like symbol representing sparks struck from flint and the glint of golden fleece.
120. A reference to Maximilian of Austria, who by marrying Charles the Bold's daughter Mary became Burgundy's defender.

And indeed after the duke's death, there was not a man who wished them well, no matter who defended them. And judging from the way they acted, their sense seemed to have been as troubled as their prince's. For shortly after his death they rejected all good and sound advice and sought out all the ways that would be to their disadvantage. And they are in such a situation that their troubles are far from over, or at least they have reason to fear their return.

I tend to agree with the opinion of someone which I saw somewhere, which was that God assigns a prince to a region according to the degree of punishment or chastisement He wishes to inflict on his subjects, and He disposes the hearts of the subjects toward their prince according to how much He wishes to exalt or humiliate him. And thus, in regard to the house of Burgundy, He has made everything equal; for after one hundred and twenty years of long felicity and great wealth under three great, good, and wise princes, who preceded Duke Charles, God gave them this duke, who constantly maintained them in fierce wars, which involved much trouble and expense; and this took place in winter almost as often as in summer. Many rich and prosperous people were either killed or deprived of their possessions as a result of being captured. They began to incur great losses at the siege of Neuss, and this continued for three or four battles until his death—so much so that at the last battle, all the strength of his country was used up, and all his men, that is to say those who would have been willing and able to defend the position and honor of his house, were killed, destroyed, or taken prisoners.

And as I said before, it seems that this loss was equal to their former measure of felicity. For just as I have seen him great, rich, and honored, this was also true of his subjects; for I believe that I have seen and known the greater part of Europe. However, I have never known any territory or country, all things being equal, nor even one of still larger expanse, which was so abundant in riches, furniture, and buildings, nor so lavish in prodigality, expenses, feasts and entertainments as I have seen in Burgundy during the time when I was there. And if it seems to someone who has never been there in my time that I exaggerate, others who were there with me will perhaps say that I say too little.

But Our Lord, all of a sudden, caused the fall of this great and sumptuous edifice, this powerful house which had supported and educated so many worthy men, and which was honored far and wide in its time for its victories and glory, more than any other house in the vicinity. The Burgundians enjoyed this good fortune and the grace of God for one hundred and twenty years, while all their neighbors, such as France, England, and Spain, were suffering. And all of them, at one time or another, came to request their help, as you have seen from the experience of the king our master, who in his youth and during the lifetime of his father, King Charles VII, came to take refuge at their court for six years in the days of good Duke Philip, who received him cordially. From England I saw there the two brothers of King Edward, the duke of Clarence and the duke of Gloucester, who was later called King Richard [III]. From the other party, that of King Henry, who was from the house of Lancaster, I have seen all the members, or most of them, there. I have seen this house honored on all sides, and then suddenly fallen and turned upside down; it became more desolate and ruined than all its neighbors, both in prince and subjects. God has accomplished such works as these and similar ones before we were born, and He will continue to do so after our death; for one can be sure that the great prosperity of princes or their great adversity has its source in His divine ordinance.

10

To continue with my subject, the king, who had already established a postal service in the kingdom (which had never had any before), was soon informed of the duke of Burgundy's defeat; and he awaited further news at every hour, for he had been advised earlier of the arrival of the Germans and everything that depended on this. Many people kept their ears open in order to be the first to hear the news and report it to the king, for he usually rewarded the first to bring him important news, without forgetting the messenger besides. And he liked to speak about prospective news before it arrived, and said: "I shall give so much to the first man who brings me news of this." My lord of Bouchage and I received the first message about the battle of Morat, and we went together to inform the king about it. He gave each one of us two hundred silver marks.

My lord of Lude, who lodged outside the castle of Plessis, was the first to hear of the arrival of the horseman who brought the letters concerning the battle of Nancy of which I spoke. He asked the horseman to give him the letters, and he did not dare refuse because this lord had great authority with the king. The lord of Lude came very early in the morning, and it was just about daybreak, and he knocked at the door which was closest to the king. Someone let him in. He handed over the letters from my lord of Craon and others. The first letters did not confirm the duke's death, but some claimed that he had been seen fleeing and that he had made his escape.

The king at first was so overjoyed at the news that he hardly knew what face to put on. On the one hand, he was afraid that if the duke were taken prisoner by the Germans, he could persuade them to come to terms with him for a large sum of money, which he would easily have been able to give them; on the other hand, he was doubtful, if the duke had fled, defeated for the third time, whether he should take over his domains in Burgundy or not. And he thought that he might easily take them, since most of the worthy people in the territory had been killed in the above-mentioned battles. As to this point, he came to the resolution (which I believe few people knew except myself) that if the duke were alive and well, he would have his army, which was then in Champagne and Barrois, march immediately into Burgundy and seize the whole territory in this hour of great terror. As soon as he had taken possession of it he would send word to the duke that he was doing this merely in order to preserve Burgundy for him and to prevent the Germans from destroying it (for the duchy was held under his sovereignty, and he did not want to let it fall into the hands of the Germans under any circumstances) and that he would restore to him whatever he had taken. And he would have done it without any difficulty, although many people may find this hard to believe, because they do not know the reason behind this plan. But he changed his mind when he became certain of the duke's death.

As soon as the king had received the letters of which I spoke, which, as I said, did not mention the duke's death, he sent for all the commanders and several other high-ranking persons in Tours, and showed them these letters. They all appeared to be very joyful, but it seemed to those who observed them closely that many of them forced themselves to act in this manner, and that in spite of their conduct, they would have been happier if the duke's affairs had turned out differently. The cause of this might be that the king was greatly feared; and they suspected that if he were rid of so many enemies, he might want to make changes at home, particularly in their estates and offices: for many of his men had been engaged against him in the question of the Public Good and other causes concerning his brother, the duke of Guyenne.

After the king had spoken with them for some time, he went to hear Mass, and then had a table set in his room; and he invited all of them to have dinner with him. His chancellor [Pierre d'Oriole] was there, as well as other members of his council. As they dined, he continued to speak on the same subject. And I remember that several of us took notice of how the guests would eat and with what kind of appetite. But to tell you the truth, I do not know whether it was for joy or sorrow, but it seems that no one ate even half his fill. And this cannot be attributed to timidity at being seated at the king's table, because there was not one of the company who had not eaten with the king many times before.

When they had left the table, the king retired and gave certain persons some of the domains which had belonged to the duke, as if he had definitely been dead. He sent off the bastard of Bourbon, who was admiral of France, and myself [toward the north on January 11, 1477], and gave us full power to receive the homage of all who would accept to render it. He commanded us to leave immediately and to open all the letters sent by mail or messengers which we might encounter on the way, so that we might know whether the duke was dead or alive.

We left and went very fast, although we had the coldest weather which I had ever experienced in my life. We had not traveled half a day when we encountered a messenger; we ordered him to give us his letters, and thus we learned that the duke had been found among the dead by an Italian page and by his physician, named Master Lope, a Portuguese, who certified to my lord of Craon that the man was indeed the duke, his master, and the lord of Craon immediately notified the king of this.

11

After we had learned all these things, we proceeded as far as the suburbs of Abbeville, and we were the first to break the news to the partisans of the duke in this region. We found that the townspeople were already negotiating with my lord of Torcy, whom they had long held in great affection. The soldiers and officers of the duke negotiated with us by means of a messenger whom we had sent to them in advance. And since they were confident of coming to terms with us, they dismissed four hundred Flemings who were in the town. But when the people saw they had gone, they opened the gates to my lord of Torcy, and this was to the great disadvantage of the commanders and other officers of the town; for there were seven or eight of them to whom we had promised money and pensions, for the king had given us authority to do this. But they received nothing because the places were not surrendered by them.

The town of Abbeville was one of the places given up by Charles VII at the peace of Arras, all of which were to be returned [to the crown of France] in case of the absence of a male heir [in Burgundy]. Therefore it is not surprising that they let us in with no difficulty.[121] From there we proceeded to Doullens and we sent a summons to Arras, capital of

121. Charles the Bold's only surviving child was Mary. See p. 98, n. 6, on the importance of the Somme towns.

Artois, long the patrimony of the counts of Flanders, which had always been handed down to daughters as well as to sons.

My lord of Ravenstein and my lord of Cordes, who were in the town of Arras, and several other townsmen offered to come and speak with us at Mont-Saint-Eloy, an abbey near Arras. It was decided that I should go, and should take a few others with me; for we were almost sure that they would not do everything we wished; and for this reason the admiral refused to go.

Shortly after I had come to the appointed place, the lords of Ravenstein and Cordes arrived with several persons of quality and some officials from the town of Arras. Among them was their chief functionary, Jean de la Vacquerie, who was their spokesman; he has since become first president of the Parlement of Paris. At the time we requested them to open the gate in the name of the king, and to receive us in the town; for we pointed out that the king considered the place to be his by confiscation, along with the whole region, and if they refused to open the gate, they would be in danger of being taken by force, since their lord had been defeated and the whole territory was without means of defense, owing to the three lost battles.

The above-named lords sent word by Jean de la Vacquerie that the county of Artois belonged to my lady of Burgundy, the daughter of Duke Charles, and descended to her in direct succession from Countess Margaret of Flanders, who was countess of Flanders, Artois, Burgundy, Nevers, and Rethel, and who was married to the first Duke Philip [the Bold] of Burgundy, son of King John [II, the Good] and brother of King Charles V [of France]; and they begged the king to observe and continue the truce which had existed between him and the late Duke Charles.

Our words were moderate, for we had expected such an answer, but the principal reason for my going there was to speak privately with some of the individuals who had come and to try to persuade them to pass over to the king's side. I spoke to some of them, who soon after became good servants of the king.

We found the whole region greatly frightened, and not without reason; for I believe that in eight days' time they would not have been able to recruit eight men-at-arms; and as for other soldiers, there were not more than about fifteen hundred men, including both infantrymen and horsemen, who had escaped from the battle in which the duke had died; and they were now quartered near Namur and Hainaut.

Their former expressions and manner of speaking were much altered, for now they spoke softly and with much humility. I do not mean to imply that in the past they spoke more arrogantly than they should have, but it is true that when I was there they considered themselves so powerful that they did not speak to the king or of him with so much reverence as they have done since. And if people were always wise, they would be so moderate in their words in time of prosperity that they would not have cause to change their language in time of adversity.

I returned to my lord the admiral to give him a report of the proceedings, and there I was informed that the king was coming; he had set out soon afterwards and had had several letters written in his own name and those of his officers, in order to have troops assembled and come to him. By these means he hoped to reduce these territories, of which I spoke, to his obedience.

12

The king was extremely happy to realize that he had overcome all those whom he hated and who were his enemies. He had taken revenge on several of them, such as the constable of France, the duke of Nemours,[122] and many others. The duke of Guyenne, his brother, was dead, and he took over his succession. All those of the house of Anjou had died, such as King René of Sicily, Dukes John and Nicholas of Calabria, and then their cousin, the count of Maine, later count of Provence, and the count of Armagnac, who had been killed at Lectoure; and the king had obtained the domains of all of them, as well as their movable possessions.[123] But the house of Burgundy was greater and more powerful than all the rest, and had waged war against his father Charles VII for thirty-two years without a single truce with the help of the English; they had their territories bordering upon the king's, and their subjects were always ready to wage war against him and his kingdom. Therefore he was all the more pleased by the duke's ruin and his death, because he considered this to be more profitable to him than the destruction of all his other enemies combined. And he thought that for the rest of his life he would meet with no opposition in his kingdom or in neighboring lands. He was at peace with the English, as you have heard; he very much desired to remain so, and did everything in his power to maintain good relations between them.

122. Jacques d'Armagnac, duke of Nemours, was executed for lese-majesty on August 4, 1476. See p. 11 of the Introduction on how Commynes profited from this execution.

123. Again Commynes is inaccurate chronologically: the memorialist is speaking of events in January, 1477; King René died on July 10, 1480, and the count of Maine on December 11, 1481.

Yet although he was free from all fears, God did not allow him to manage this affair, which was of utmost importance, in the manner which would have obtained the most favorable results for him. For through marriage and friendship he could have easily annexed to his crown all these large territories, to which he otherwise could pretend no right; and he could have won the people over to his interest and have had them consent to all his requests through a marriage contract, owing to the great discomfort, poverty, and destruction which these territories had suffered. And thus he would have strengthened and enriched his kingdom by means of the long peace in which he could have maintained it; and he could have relieved it in many ways, particularly by not having his men-at-arms ride from one end of the kingdom to the other, which they did in former times and are continually doing to this day, quite often without very great need for it.

When the duke of Burgundy was still alive, the king had often told me what he intended to do if the duke should die, and he spoke very wisely. At the time he said that he would attempt to arrange a marriage between his son, who is our present king, and the duke's daughter, who has since become duchess of Austria. And if she would not consent to that (because my lord the dauphin was much younger than she was), he would then try to have her marry a young lord of his kingdom, so that he might maintain good relations with her and her subjects and recover peacefully the territories which he claimed were his. And he was still in the same frame of mind eight days before he heard of the duke's death. This wise resolution, of which I am speaking, was slightly changed when he received word of his death, and when he sent off my lord the admiral and myself. However, he did not say much about this; but he promised to several people lands and territories [which had belonged to the duke].

13

As the king was on the road, coming toward us, he received pleasant news from all sides. The castles of Ham and Bohain were delivered to him. The people of Saint-Quentin secured the town for him themselves and placed in it my lord of Moy, who was their neighbor. He was well assured of the town of Péronne, which was held by Guillaume Bische, and by means of us and others he had hopes that my lord of Cordes would be won over to his side. He had sent his barber to Ghent; the man was called Master Olivier [le Dain] and was born in a village near the town of Ghent. And the king had sent many other persons to several towns, with great hopes in all of them, for many served him better in words than in deeds.

As the king arrived near Péronne I went to meet him; and there Guillaume Bische and others brought him the homage of the town of Péronne, which made him very happy. The king stayed there that day. I had dinner with him that day as usual, for it was always his pleasure to have at least seven or eight people sit at his table, and sometimes many more. After dinner he withdrew, and he was not pleased with the little exploit which the admiral and I had performed; he said that he had sent Master Olivier, his barber, to Ghent, and that he would put this town into his hands; and that he had dispatched Robin d'Oudenfort to Saint-Omer, where he had friends who were capable of taking the keys of the town and placing his men inside. He sent others, whom he named, to other important towns, and he had me rebuked in relation to this matter by my lord of Lude and by others. It was not my place to argue with him or to speak against his wishes; but I told him of my suspicion that Master Olivier and the others whom he had named might not manage as easily as they thought to reduce these great towns to his obedience.

What made the king say these words to me was that he had changed his mind and that this good fortune which he had enjoyed at the beginning gave him confidence that from all sides everything would be surrendered to him. And he happened to be advised by some, and besides he himself was entirely disposed to ruin and destroy the house [of Burgundy] and to apportion its territories among several people; and he named those to whom he intended to give the counties, such as Namur and Hainaut, situated close to him; as for the other large territories, such as Brabant and Holland, he intended to help certain lords of Germany to obtain them; they would then become his friends and help him to put his wishes into execution. It was his pleasure to tell me all these things because I had formerly spoken to him and had suggested another course of action, which was described above, and he wanted me to understand his reasons, and why he had changed his mind, and why this procedure would be more useful for his kingdom, which had suffered greatly because of the power of the house of Burgundy and the large territories which they possessed.[124]

124. Commynes' lack of interest in institutional forms, illustrated in section 2 of the Introduction, makes this passage difficult to understand. Three questions of feudal law were raised for Louis XI by Charles the Bold's death. They can be easily understood by reference to the boundary line shown on the map in this volume. This line divides territories held by the king of France as ultimate suzerain from those held from the Holy Roman Emperor as ultimate suzerain. The first question was the rights of Louis XI to Burgundian territories on the French side

From the worldly point of view there was much to condone what this lord was saying; but as for the matter of conscience, it seemed to me otherwise. The king's sense was so great, however, that neither I nor others who were in his company could have had as clear an understanding of his affairs as he did: for without a doubt he was one of the wisest and most subtle princes who lived in his time. But in these important affairs, God disposes the hearts of kings and of great princes, which he holds in His hand, in such a way that they will proceed according to the events which He determines to bring about. For if it had been His pleasure that our king should have continued in the resolution which he had himself formed before the death of the duke, then without any difficulty the wars which have since taken place and are still continuing would not have occurred. But we were not worthy in the sight of God, either on one side or the other, of receiving such a long peace; and that was the cause of the error which our king committed, and not any failing of his judgment, for it was very great, as I have said.

I am elaborating on these things to show that at the beginning of such

---

of the line; among these territories were Flanders and Artois, mentioned in chapter 11. The second question was the disposition of Burgundian territories on the German side of the line, such as Brabant and Holland; as Commynes indicates here, Louis hoped that these territories could be divided up among various German lords. Whatever Louis accomplished in relation to territories on the German side had to be accomplished indirectly, since the French king had no legal basis on which to interfere in their disposition. But Louis could interfere directly in territories on the French side, since whenever succession took place in feudal territories, the new vassal was supposed to take an oath of fealty to his new lord. In most cases approval of the succession and acceptance of the new vassal was automatic. But if there was some dispute about the rightful heir, the dispute had to be adjudicated, and this raised the third question of feudal law for Louis. For Louis' hopes to break Burgundian power depended on whether Mary of Burgundy, Charles the Bold's only child, could inherit all her father's lands or not. If a vassal died without leaving any surviving children or grandchildren, his fiefs reverted to the lord to whom he owed fealty. The lord could then distribute them anew, to any vassal or vassals to whom he wished to give them. In the case of some fiefs, if a vassal died without leaving any male children or descendants of males, tradition allowed the fiefs to revert to the lord, even if a daughter of the vassal were living. Louis would have liked to see this tradition followed in all the lands of Charles the Bold. Indeed, Commynes believes that he had decided that Burgundian weakness was so great that "everything would be surrendered to him," so that he could parcel it out anew. But the tradition of a purely male succession was by no means established in all Burgundian territories, as Commynes points out in relation to Flanders in chapter 11. In territories where female inheritance was traditional, Louis would be violating feudal custom if he attempted to seize and dispose of them, whichever side of the boundary line they were on. Moreover, a tradition of Burgundian unity, of central institutions and concerns above and beyond the interest of component territories, had been replacing the notion that Flanders, Brabant, Burgundy, Franche-Comté and the rest were bound together merely by an important undertaking it is necessary to consult and discuss the matter seriously in order to be able to choose the better way; and it is especially important to recommend oneself to God and pray to Him, so that He may point out the best method. For everything proceeds from Him: and it is evident from writings and from experience. I do not mean to blame our king when I say that he erred in this affair, for by chance others, who were wiser and better informed than I, would be and were then of the same opinion as he was, although nothing was discussed about the matter, either there or elsewhere.

Chroniclers commonly write only things which reflect credit on those whose actions they record, and they omit many things, or they do not know about them sometimes as they truly happened. But I have decided not to speak of anything which is not true and which I have not seen or heard from such great people that they are worthy of being believed, and without having any regard to praises. For it is good to think that there is no prince so wise that he does not err once in a while, and even very often, if he lives long. And so their actions would appear, if one

---

feudal laws of inheritance (see notes 11 and 84 to the Introduction, pp. 9 and 39). One of the most dramatic expressions of this growing unity was Article 42 of the treaty of Péronne in which Charles and Louis agreed that under certain conditions Charles would no longer owe fealty to Louis (see p. 31 of the Introduction). If this article had become part of public law, Charles and his successors, not the French kings, would have become ultimate suzerains of the territories on the French side of the boundary line on the map. But of course Louis XI soon declared this article void, along with the rest of the treaty, and Charles was not in a position to force him to recognize it.

Commynes was only vaguely aware of juridical traditions and the politico-administrative unity of Burgundy. For example, he does not use the distinction of fiefs belonging to the Empire as opposed to fiefs belonging to France in the paragraph to which this note refers. Namur and Hainaut, like Brabant and Holland, owed allegiance to the Emperor, and yet, according to Commynes, Louis intended to seize the two former territories, while working indirectly with "certain lords of Germany" to dispose of the latter. The distinction in Commynes' eyes, and perhaps in Louis' too, lay in their relative proximity to French frontiers, not in feudal law—a graphic example of the moribund character of feudal rights in the fifteenth century. But if feudalism was dead or dying along the Franco-German frontier, the Burgundian upper class, for whom feudal institutions were still upon occasion profitable, was still very much alive. Their vested interests made a complete and sudden replacement of Burgundian power with French power impossible, especially in Charles the Bold's northern territories where centralization, as well as a common economy, had developed furthest. Commynes sensed this impossibility more surely than Louis XI, and so he favored the king's earlier plan, outlined in chapter 12, which would have brought Burgundian territories slowly under French control "through marriage and friendship." But Commynes was told to go home to his estates. As will be seen in Book 6 of the *Memoirs*, Louis was in this affair once more guilty of selling the bear's skin before it was caught. Emperor Frederick, teller of that fable, made the killing as far as the Burgundian succession is concerned.

always told the truth. The greatest senates and the greatest consuls in the world have indeed erred and still do, as it has been seen and is seen every day.

After the king had stayed in this village near Péronne, he decided on the next day to proceed to make his entry there, since the town had been delivered to him as I said before. This lord took me aside, as he was ready to leave, and he sent me to Poitou and to the borders of Brittany; and he whispered in my ear that if Master Olivier's enterprise did not succeed and if my lord of Cordes did not abandon his companions, he would have the territory of Artois burned in a place called Alloeue, along the river Lys, and he would immediately return to the Touraine region. I recommended to him several persons who had come over to his side by my means, in return for which I had promised them pensions and favors from him. He wrote down their names, which I enumerated, and he gave them what I had promised them. And so I took my leave of him this time.

My lord of Lude was very pleasing to the king in certain matters; he was very much interested in his own profit and was never afraid to trick anyone. At the same time he believed people rather readily and was often tricked himself. He had been educated with the king in his youth, he knew very well how to gratify him, and he was a very pleasant man. As I was about to mount on horseback he came to tell me the following words which he spoke seriously, in order to mock: "Now, are you leaving at the very moment when you should be making your fortune, or never, considering the great things which are falling into the hands of the king, and with which he can bring advantage and riches to all those whom he likes? And as for myself, I expect to become governor of Flanders and to turn myself into gold!" And he laughed heartily. I did not feel like laughing because I suspected that this came from the king, and I replied that I should be very happy if this were to come about, and that I hoped the king would not forget me; and so I left.

A knight from Hainaut had arrived there to speak to me not quite a half hour before [my departure], and he brought me news of several others to whom I had written, asking them to serve the king. The knight and I are related, and he is still living; therefore I do not wish to name him, nor those of whom he brought me news. Briefly, he proposed to me to deliver the principal localities and towns of the territory of Hainaut; and when I took leave of the king I said a word to him about it. He immediately sent for him, but he told me that neither this man nor the others whom I had named were the sort of people whom he needed. One did not please him for one reason, and another for another reason;

and it seemed to him that their offers were of no consequence and that he would surely obtain everything without their help. After I had taken leave of him he had the knight speak to my lord of Lude. He was amazed at this and soon left, without having entered into significant agreements, for the lord of Lude and he would never have come to terms nor to an understanding, since he had come in the hope of deriving advantage from this situation and coming into a fortune; and the lord of Lude asked him right away what the towns would give him in return for taking care of their affair.

Therefore I consider the king's refusal of these knights' offers and the contempt in which he held them to have been inspired by God: for I have seen him later in a situation where he would have esteemed them greatly if he had been able to come to terms with them; but by chance Our Lord may not have wanted to fulfill his desires in all circumstances, for certain reasons which I mentioned, or He did not wish him to usurp the territory of Hainaut, which was held from the empire [as a fief], both because he had no title to it and because of the ancient alliances and oaths which exist between the emperors and the kings of France. And this lord has since proved that he was aware of this, for he held Cambrai, Le Quesnoy, and Bouchain in Hainaut, but he gave back this part of Hainaut and restored Cambrai, which is an imperial town, to a state of neutrality.

Although I did not remain on the spot, I was kept informed of the happenings, and I could understand these things easily because of the experience and bringing-up which I had acquired on one side and the other; and I have since had confirmation of this by the mouth of those who were in charge of these affairs on both sides.

14

Master Olivier, as you have heard, had gone to Ghent, with letters of credence addressed to my lady of Burgundy, daughter of Duke Charles. And it was his duty to make secret remonstrances to her, so that she would accept placing herself in the hands of the king. This was not his principal mission [however], for he feared that it would hardly be possible for him to speak with the duchess alone; and even if he managed to obtain a private audience, he might not be able to persuade her to do as he suggested. But he intended to bring about some important change in the city of Ghent, realizing that it had always been so inclined, and that under Dukes Philip and Charles it had been kept in great fear, and that it had lost many privileges owing to the war which it had made against

337

Duke Philip, and the subsequent peace. And also another privilege concerning the making of their own law was taken away from them by Duke Charles, because of an offense which they had committed against him on the occasion of his entrance into their city on the first day that he came there as a duke. I spoke of this earlier in this account; therefore I shall say no more about it. All these reasons gave Master Olivier, who was the king's barber, as I said, much courage to pursue his objective. He spoke to certain persons whom he suspected would be interested in what he wanted; and he offered to have the privileges which they had lost restored to them by the king and to have other benefits given to them. But he did not go to their town hall to speak of this in public, because first of all he wanted to see what he could do with the young princess; however, he was able to find out something about it.

The above-mentioned Master Olivier, after he had been in Ghent for several days, was asked to come and deliver his message; he was admitted to the princess' presence, and he was dressed much more elegantly than his station would have warranted. He handed over his letters of credence. The lady was in her official chair, and the duke of Cleves was near her, with the bishop of Liége and other high-ranking persons, and a large number of attendants. She read his letter, and Master Olivier was invited to deliver his message. He replied that he had no other business except to speak to her privately. He was told that such was not the custom and that this was especially applicable in the case of this young lady, who was fit to be married. He insisted that he would say nothing further, except to her. They told him that they would force him to talk, and he became frightened. And I believe that when he came to present his letter he had not given a thought to what he should say, for it was not his principal business, as you have heard.

Several persons among this council found him ridiculous because of his low estate as well as the kind of language which he used. Those from Ghent were especially scornful, for he was born in a small village near the town, and he was subjected to all sorts of mockeries. And so he suddenly fled from the town because he had been warned that if he did not, he would be in danger of being thrown into the river; and I well believe that it would have happened.

Upon his departure from Ghent the said Master Olivier, who had styled himself count of Meulan, a little town of which he was captain and which is located near Paris, fled to Tournai. This town is neutral in that region, and it has great affection for the king, for it belongs to him and pays him ten thousand Parisian livres a year, but otherwise it enjoys complete freedom, and all sorts of people are welcome there; it is a beautiful town and a very strong one, as everyone in this region well knows. The churchmen and burghers of the town have all their assets and revenues in Hainaut and Flanders, for it borders upon both of these territories; and for this reason, during the ancient wars between King Charles VII and Duke Philip of Burgundy, they always used to give ten thousand livres a year to the duke, and I have seen them give as much to Duke Charles of Burgundy. At the time when Master Olivier entered the town, it was not paying anything, and it was enjoying great prosperity and peace.

Although Master Olivier's responsibility was too heavy for him, he was not so much to blame as those who had assigned it to him. His exploit turned out as was to be expected; yet he gave proof of sense and courage in what he did. For he realized that the town of Tournai was so close to the two territories which I mentioned that it could not possibly be nearer; and he understood that it was well situated to easily cause great damage to one or the other of these territories, provided that he could put into it men-at-arms whom the king had nearby (to which the townspeople would never have consented for anything in the world, for they never took sides for one party or the other, but remained neutral between the two princes). Master Olivier therefore sent word secretly to my lord of Moy, whose son was bailiff of the town (though he did not reside there),[125] that he should bring his company, which was stationed at Saint-Quentin, along with some other men-at-arms who were in that region. At the appointed hour he came to the gate, where he found thirty or forty men accompanying Master Olivier, who certainly had courage to have the barrier opened, partly by love and partly by force; and he put the men-at-arms inside: the people were rather pleased about this but the governors of the town were not. He sent seven or eight of them to Paris, and they never dared leave there as long as the king was alive. After these men-at-arms had entered, more came to reinforce them, and they have since done incredible damage in the two above-mentioned territories, such as plundering many beautiful villages and many fine farms which damaged [the possessions of] the townspeople of Tournai more than anyone else, for the reasons which I explained. And they made so many ravages that the Flemings came there and released the duke of Gelderland from prison (where he had been confined by Duke Charles) to make him their leader. And they came before the town, where they did not stay for very long, for they left in great disorder and fled, and lost many of their men there. And among

125. Jacques de Moy, son of the lord of Moy, did not become bailiff of Tournai until 1484.

the rest of the dead was the duke of Gelderland, who had placed himself at the rear guard in order to help his partisans resist the pressure of the enemy. But he was not well assisted and he died there.[126] Therefore the king gained honor from this by means of Master Olivier, and the enemies of the king reaped great misery. A much wiser and greater man than he might have failed to manage this affair properly.

I have spoken enough of the mission which was given by this wise king to this minor personage, who was unsuited for the management of so important an affair. And it does seem that God had troubled the king's sense in this respect, for as I said before, if he had not considered his objective as too easy to put into execution, and if he had toned down his passion and his desire for vengeance against that house [of Burgundy], there is no doubt that today he would hold all this territory under his jurisdiction.

15

Péronne was delivered to this lord by Guillaume Bische, a man of very low estate, native of Moulins-Engilbert in the Nivernais; he had been made rich and raised to a position of authority by Duke Charles of Burgundy—who had given him the command of this town because his property, called Cléry, was close by. It had been acquired by Guillaume Bische, who had built a very beautiful and strong castle there. After this lord [the king] had accepted the town, he received there several ambassadors from my lady of Burgundy; they included the greatest and principal persons who could assist her. And it was not a wise measure to have so many of them come together; but their grief and fear were so intense that they were at a loss as to what to say and what to do.

The above-mentioned delegation included their chancellor, named Guillaume Hugonet, a very notable and wise person, who had enjoyed considerable favor with Duke Charles and had derived many benefits from him. The lord of Humbercourt was also among them. I have often spoken of him in these memoirs and I cannot remember having seen a wiser gentleman nor one better suited for the management of important affairs. Also present were the lord of Veere, a great lord in Zeeland, the lord of Gruthuse, and many others, noblemen as well as churchmen and town officials.

Before hearing them, either in public or in private, our king took

126. See p. 250 above.

great pains to win each one of them over to his side. And he obtained from them humble words and respectful ones, as was to be expected from people who lived in fear. Those who had their lands in a locality where they did not have to fear seizure by the king, however, did not want to commit themselves in any way in regard to the king, unless the marriage of his son my lord the dauphin and the above-named lady were to take place.

The chancellor and the lord of Humbercourt, who had been accustomed to enjoy great authority for a long time and wished to continue to do so, and who had their property bordering on the king's, one in the duchy of Burgundy and the other at the entrance of Picardy, toward Amiens, lent an ear to the king and his offers and gave some promise of helping him by arranging that marriage; and then, after it was accomplished, they would agree to put themselves entirely in his service. And although this means of action would have been the best, it was not to his liking; and he was dissatisfied with them when he saw that, upon his refusal of the marriage, they did not wish to remain on his side. But he did not show his feelings because he wanted to make use of them in whatever way he could.

This lord was already kept well informed by my lord of Cordes; and, following his advice and counsel (he was commander and master in Arras), he requested the above-named ambassadors that they should have the citadel of Arras opened to him by the lord of Cordes. For at the time there were walls and ditches between the town of Arras and the citadel, and the gates were shut against the citadel; and now it is the other way around, because it is the citadel that is shut against the town.[127] After many remonstrances made to the ambassadors to the effect that it would be for the best and that the cause of peace would be furthered by this act of obedience, they consented to do it, particularly the chancellor and the lord of Humbercourt. And they delivered letters of discharge to the lord of Cordes and their consent that he should give up the citadel of Arras, which he did willingly. As soon as the king was inside, he had bulwarks of earth built against the gate and other places near the town; and by this arrangement my lord of Cordes withdrew from the town and had his soldiers march out with him. And everyone went wherever he pleased and took whichever side he wished.

127. Most medieval cities had a fortified castle, or citadel, at the center of the town where representatives of the feudal territory surrounding the city lodged. Very often, as at Arras here, town government and citadel government were at swords' points.

The lord of Cordes, who believed himself discharged from the service of his mistress by the consent which the ambassadors had given him that he should put the king inside the citadel of Arras, decided to swear allegiance to the king and to become his servant, considering that his name and his arms came from this side of the Somme, near Beauvais; for his name is Philippe de Crèvecoeur, and he is the second brother of the lord of Crèvecoeur. Moreover, these territories on the river Somme, of which I have spoken at length, which the house of Burgundy had occupied during the lifetime of Dukes Philip and Charles, reverted to the king without any trouble by the conditions of the treaty of Arras, according to which they were given to Duke Philip, to be enjoyed by him and his male heirs only; and Duke Charles had left only this daughter of whom I spoke. And thus Philippe de Crèvecoeur became the king's man without difficulty. Therefore he would not have been taken wrong for putting himself in the king's service if he had not already taken a new oath of allegiance to the lady of Burgundy and had not done homage to her for what he held [from the dukes of Burgundy]. This has been talked about, and will continue to be talked about in various ways, and so I am leaving it at the facts. All I know is that he had been educated, promoted, and put in high positions by Duke Charles, and that his mother had a hand in the education of the above-mentioned lady of Burgundy, and that he was governor of Picardy, seneschal of Ponthieu, commander of Le Crotoy, governor of Péronne, Roye, and Montdidier, and commander of Boulogne-sur-Mer and Hesdin for Duke Charles, when he died; and at present he still holds these same positions for the king in the same form and manner as the king our master gave them to him.

After the king had proceeded as I told you in the citadel of Arras, he left and went to besiege Hesdin, where he brought the lord of Cordes, who had held the place, as was said, only three days before; and his men were still there. They appeared as if they intended to hold it for the lady, saying that they had sworn allegiance to her, and they fired their artillery for a few days. They heard their master speak (and to be truthful those inside and out understood each other very well), and thus the town was delivered to the king, who then proceeded to Boulogne-sur-Mer, where the same thing happened. They held out for one more day, perhaps. Still, this would have been a dangerous trick if there had been men-at-arms in the region. And the king, who told me about it later on, realized this, for there were people inside Boulogne who were well aware of the situation and who were trying to put troops there, if they had been able to raise them in time, and to really defend it.

Book Five

While the king besieged Boulogne, which was for about five or six days, the people of Arras considered themselves betrayed to see themselves enclosed on one side and the other, where there were a great number of men-at-arms and considerable artillery; and they tried to find troops to garrison their town. And they wrote to this effect to neighboring towns, such as Lille and Douai. In the town of Douai were a few horsemen; among them were the lord of Vergy and others whom I do not remember. They were among those who had returned from the battle of Nancy. They decided to come and place themselves in the town of Arras; and they would form a body of soldiers from whatever they might find, such as two or three hundred horsemen, both good and bad, and five or six hundred foot-soldiers. The people of Douai, who were still a little bit proud at the time, urged them to leave in broad daylight, whether they liked it or not: this was a most unwise procedure to follow, and it turned out to their great disadvantage. For the country on the other side of Arras is as flat as one's hand, and is about five leagues away. Therefore if they had waited until night to march, they would have carried out their enterprise as they had intended.

As they were on their way, those who had remained in the citadel, such as the lord of Lude, Jean du Fou, and the marshal of Lohéac's men, were notified of their coming and they decided that it would be better to go forth and confront them, and risk everything, than to let them enter the town, for it seemed to them that they would not be able to defend the town once the others got in.

The enterprise of those whom I mentioned was very dangerous, but they carried it out bravely and they put the band that had come from Douai to rout. And almost all of them were either killed or taken prisoners; among them the lord of Vergy was captured. The king arrived there the next day, and he was greatly pleased with this exploit; and he had all the prisoners put into his own custody. He had several of the foot-soldiers put to death, in the hope of terrifying the few soldiers who were in the region. He had my lord of Vergy confined for a long time, because he did not want to swear allegiance to the king for anything in the world; and so he was closely guarded and shackled in irons. Finally, following the advice which his mother had given him, and after having been in prison for a year or more, he acted according to the king's good pleasure, which was the wise thing to do. The king restored all his own lands to him, as well as all those which he claimed, and he made him the possessor of a revenue of more than ten thousand livres and other nice offices.

Those who escaped from this rout, and they were few, entered the town. The king had his artillery, which was mighty and numerous,

advance and fire. Neither the moat nor the wall afforded much protection. The bombardment was great and everyone was terrified; and
they had practically no soldiers inside. My lord of Cordes had many
informers there; and, besides, since the king already held the citadel,
it was inevitable that he should also conquer the town. Considering this,
they surrendered the town under certain conditions, which were rather
poorly observed; and it was partly the fault of the lord of Lude. The
king had several burghers and many other persons of quality executed.
The lord of Lude and Master Guillaume de Cerisay derived much benefit from this, for the lord of Lude told me that at the time he gained
twenty thousand *écus* and two marten furs there. And the townspeople
loaned [the king] sixty thousand *écus*, which was excessive for them.
However, I think that the money was returned, because the people of
Cambrai lent forty thousand *écus*, which were definitely repaid to them
later. Therefore I believe that the other sum was also restituted.

16

At the time of the siege of Arras, my lady of Burgundy was in
Ghent, in the hands of these most unreasonable people; and this resulted in losses for her and profits for the king: for one person's loss
is another's gain.

As soon as they heard of the death of Duke Charles it seemed to them
that they had become liberated, and they seized all their magistrates,
who are twenty-six in all, and they put all or most of them to death;
and they gave as their reason the fact that on the previous day they
[the magistrates] had had a man decapitated, and although he had well
deserved it, they had no power to have done it, as they [the insurrec-
tionary townsmen] said, because their authority had expired upon the
death of the duke, who had placed them in the government. They also
executed many important and worthy people from the town, who
had been friends and partisans of the duke, among whom were several
who, in my time and in my presence, had helped to dissuade Duke
Charles from his intention of destroying a large part of the town. They
forced the lady to confirm their former privileges, which had been
canceled by the peace of Gavere, which they had made with Duke
Philip, as well as others which had been taken away by Duke Charles.
These privileges served no purpose except to make trouble between
them and their prince. And, besides, their principal inclination is to
have their prince weak; and they do not like any of them, from the
moment they become rulers, although quite naturally they are fond of

them during their childhood and before their accession to the government, as had been the case in regard to this lady, whom they had carefully guarded and loved until she became their sovereign.

It should also be understood that if at the time of the duke's death the people of Ghent had not made trouble and had been willing to try and defend the country, they might immediately have provided soldiers to place in Arras, and by chance in Péronne; but they thought of nothing except making this trouble.

However, as the king was besieging Arras, several ambassadors from the three estates of the lady's territories came before him, for there were certain deputies of these three estates in Ghent; but the people of Ghent managed everything as they pleased, because they held the lady in their power. The king heard them, and among other things, they said that the propositions which they had made and which were for the promotion of peace, proceeded from the wishes of the lady, who had decided to act under all circumstances according to the will and advice of the three estates of her country. In addition they requested that the king should desist from the war which he was waging in Burgundy as well as in Artois and that an appointment should be made for them to have a friendly peace conference; and while these talks were going on, the war should be suspended.

The king was already in a position of superiority, and he thought that his affairs might take an even better turn, for he was well informed that their soldiers were dead or dispersed everywhere; many of them had passed over to his side, and particularly my lord of Cordes, for whom he had great esteem, and not without cause, for he would not have been able to accomplish in a long time by force what he obtained only a few days before by his means, as you have heard. And therefore he did not pay much attention to their requests and demands. Besides, he was well informed, and he well realized that these people of Ghent were in such a state that they caused great trouble to their governing officials with the result that they were unable to give advice or orders for carrying out the war against him. For no sensible man, nor anyone who had been in a position of authority under their former princes, was consulted on any matter; instead they were persecuted and were in danger of being put to death. They especially hated the Burgundians because of the great authority which they had enjoyed in the past. And, furthermore, the king was well aware of that: for in such matters he saw as clearly as any man in his kingdom that the above-mentioned people of Ghent had always wanted to see their lord minimized, as long as they might in no way feel the effects of this in their country. And therefore he decided that as long as they had started to have divisions among themselves he would sink them even deeper in their dissensions, for he had to deal only with stupid people (burghers for the most part), who were particularly ignorant of the subtle procedures of which this lord was such a master; and he took the necessary steps to win and to carry out his design.

The king took up the matter of the phrase which the ambassadors had used, according to which their princess would not do anything without the deliberation and advice of the three estates of her country; and he told them that they were misinformed as to her intentions and those of certain other persons, for he was sure that she intended to manage her affairs by means of particular individuals who had no desire for peace, and that they would find themselves disavowed: the ambassadors were thrown into confusion by this, as persons not accustomed to conduct such important business and affairs. They promptly replied that they were absolutely sure of what they said and that they would produce their instructions if necessary. They were told that when it pleased the king they would be shown letters, written under such hands that they were above suspicion, in which it was stated that the lady wished to have her affairs managed by four persons only. They still insisted that they were quite certain of the contrary.

Thereupon the king had them shown a letter which the chancellor of Burgundy [Hugonet] and the lord of Humbercourt had brought with them when they had last come to Péronne; they were partly in the hand of the above-named lady, partly in the hand of the dowager duchess of Burgundy [Margaret of York], widow of Duke Charles and sister of King Edward of England, and partly in the hand of the lord of Ravenstein, brother of the duke of Cleves and a close relative of the young lady: thus this letter was written under three different hands. It ran only in the name of that lady, but it had been done only to give it greater weight. The document consisted of a letter of credence for the chancellor and Humbercourt; and in addition the lady declared that it was her intention that all her affairs should be managed by four persons—i.e., her step-mother the dowager, the lord of Ravenstein, and the above-named chancellor and Humbercourt; and she begged the king that any business which he might wish to transact with her might be handled by them, and that he should address himself to them and communicate the matter to no one else.

When these people from Ghent and the other deputies had seen this letter, they were very incensed about it, and those who communicated with them fomented their anger all the more. Finally the letter was handed to them, and they had no other message of any great substance: for they thought only of their divisions and of reorganizing their government, and they did not consider anything further, although they should have taken the loss of Arras much more to heart. But they were people with no experience in the management of important affairs, and most of them were burghers, as I said before.

They proceeded directly to Ghent, where they found the lady; and with her was the duke of Cleves, her close relative and a member of her house through his mother; and he was very old. He had been raised in Burgundy, that is to say in the house of Burgundy, from which he had always received a pension of six thousand Rhenish florins; therefore in addition to his capacity as a relative he sometimes came to court as an attendant. The bishop of Liége and several other persons were there to accompany the lady and to advance their particular affairs. For the bishop had come to obtain for his subjects the cancellation of dues of thirty thousand florins or so which they used to pay to Duke Charles, according to an agreement which was made between him and them after the war which they had had with each other, which I mentioned earlier. All these revolts had taken place because of the affairs and disputes of the bishop. For that reason there was no great need for him to pursue this matter, and he should have wished them [the Liégeois] to be poor (for he received nothing from his principality except the proceeds from a small estate), considering the greatness and richness of the territory and its piety.

The bishop was a brother of the two dukes of Bourbon, Jean and Pierre [de Beaujeu], who are at present ruling:[128] he was interested in a good table and pleasure, and he had poor judgment as to what was good or bad for him. He gave asylum at his side to Guillaume de la Marck, a fine and valiant knight, but a very cruel and ill-tempered one, who had always been an enemy of the house of Burgundy as well as of the bishop himself, and who had sided with the Liégeois. The lady gave him fifteen thousand Rhenish florins in the name of the bishop of Liége and of herself, in order to attract him to her side. But soon after-

---

128. Jean de Bourbon died in 1488; his brother Pierre de Beaujeu succeeded him as duke of Bourbon on April 1, 1488. Therefore, it is hard to see how they both ruled Bourbon "at present," since one was dead or the other not yet duke at any given time. But perhaps Commynes refers to the fact that Pierre, as husband of Louis XI's daughter Anne, the regent, was in effect ruling France along with his wife, while his brother ruled the duchy of Bourbon. In that case, Commynes would be writing this passage in 1488, which contradicts all other evidence about the circumstances of composition of the *Memoirs* (see p. 16 of the Introduction). The simplest way to solve the problem is to change the plural verb, "are ruling," to the singular, "is ruling," and blame Commynes' secretary for the mistake.

347

wards he turned against her and his master the bishop, and he attempted to make his own son bishop by force and by the help of the king. And since then he defeated the bishop in battle and killed him with his own hands, after which he had his body thrown into the river, where it remained for three days.

The duke of Cleves was there [at Ghent] in the hope of arranging the marriage of his eldest son and the lady, which he thought would be suitable for several reasons. And I believe that it would have been done if the young man had been personally pleasing to her and her servants: for he was of the same house and his duchy was adjacent and he had been raised there; so perhaps being seen too much and known too well caused his ill-success.

17

To return to my account, these deputies arrived in Ghent. The council meeting was called, and the lady was placed in her chair with several lords about her, in order to hear their report. They began to speak about the mission which she had assigned them, and they touched mainly upon the point which was going to serve their purpose. And they said that when they asserted to the king that she was resolved to act in all matters according to the advice of the three estates, he had replied that he was definitely sure of the contrary; when they persisted in their affirmations, the king offered to show them certain letters. The lady, who became suddenly agitated and incensed, immediately said that it could never have been true that this letter had been written or seen. Thereupon the speaker, who was chief functionary of either Ghent or Brussels, produced the letter from his breast and handed it to her in front of everybody. He showed himself to be a very bad man and a person of little honor to subject this young princess to such an affront, for it was most improper that she should have been treated so vilely; and if she had committed some error, she should not have been chastised for it in public.

It is not necessary to ask whether she was greatly mortified: for she had assured everyone of the contrary [to what the letter said]. The dowager [duchess of Burgundy], the lord of Ravenstein, the chancellor, and the lord of Humbercourt were present. The duke of Cleves and others had been given fine words about this marriage [between the lady and his son], and all of them were furious. Then great divisions took place among them and were declared. The duke of Cleves had always hoped, up to that time, that the lord of Humbercourt was on

348

his side, as far as this marriage was concerned, and he was very disappointed when he saw this letter; and so he became his enemy. The bishop of Liége did not like him, owing to the happenings in Liége, of which the lord of Humbercourt had been governor; neither did his companion, Guillaume de la Marck, who was with him.

The count of Saint-Pol, son of the constable of whom I spoke, hated the lord of Humbercourt and the chancellor because they had delivered his father into the hands of the king's servants at Péronne, as you have heard in the course of these memoirs. The people of Ghent detested them greatly, although they had never done them any harm, merely because they had seen them in positions of great authority. And surely they deserved them as well as any of those who lived in their time, either in these regions or elsewhere, and they had been good and loyal servants to their masters.

Finally, on the night following the morning during which this letter had been shown, the chancellor and the lord of Humbercourt were taken by the people of Ghent, although they had plenty of warning; but they did not know how to flee their evil fortune, as several others had. I well believe that their enemies, whom I mentioned, helped in their seizure.

With them they also took Guillaume de Cluny, bishop of Thérouanne (who died afterwards as bishop of Poitiers), and put all three of them together into custody. The people of Ghent followed somewhat the form of a trial, contrary to their usual procedure in matters of vengeance, and they ordered some of their jurists to question them; and with them was a member of the house of La Marck [Éverard, brother of Guillaume].

At first they asked them why they had the city of Arras given up by my lord of Cordes, but they did not dwell on this point very long, although they could find nothing else for which they might be blamed; but their passion did not allow them to stop there, for it was of no importance to them at the outset to see their sovereign divested of such a town, nor was their sense or judgment sufficiently well developed to realize the prejudice which might result for them in time. And they insisted on two points: first, on certain gifts which they alleged had been accepted by them [Hugonet and Humbercourt], and particularly in relation to a case which had been won by the city of Ghent because of the judgment pronounced against a private individual, and which had led to their receiving a donation from the city of Ghent.

To everything which touched upon this question of corruption they gave very good answers, and to the particular point raised by the people of Ghent that they had sold justice and had taken money from them, the men replied that they had won the case because their cause was just, and as for the money which they had taken, they had neither asked for it themselves nor had it requested by anyone else, but when it was presented to them they had accepted it.

The second point of their charge on which they insisted was that according to the above-mentioned people of Ghent, during the time of their tenure under the late Duke Charles, as his lieutenants and in his absence, in relation to several matters they had done many things contrary to the privileges and rights of the city, and that any man who acted against the privileges of Ghent should die. But these charges against these men were without foundation; for they were neither their subjects nor natives of their city, and so they would have been unable to break their privileges [since they were not bound by them]; and if the duke or his father had deprived them of some of their privileges, it had been after an agreement which had been drawn up between them, after the wars and dissensions. As for the remaining privileges which they had been allowed to keep, and which were greater than was necessary for their advantage, they had been well observed by them.

In spite of the manner in which these two fine and worthy men justified themselves of these two charges (for the principal one, of which I spoke at the beginning of this account, was glossed over), the aldermen of the city of Ghent, at a session in their town hall, condemned them to die, under the pretense of their infraction of the townspeople's privileges and their acceptance of money after having settled the above-mentioned case.

Upon hearing this cruel verdict the two lords were stunned, as it stands to reason, and they could see no way out of this situation because they were in their power. However, they appealed to the king in his court of Parlement, in the hope that it could at least postpone their death for some time, and that in the meantime their friends might help them to save their lives.

Before the sentence was pronounced they had been severely tortured, without any order of justice, and their trial lasted no more than six days. And in spite of their appeal, as soon as they received their condemnation, they were given only three hours time to confess and to put their affairs in order, at the end of which they were taken to the marketplace, where they were put on a scaffold.

When she was informed of this condemnation, the lady of Burgundy, who later became duchess of Austria, proceeded to the town hall and she begged and beseeched them in behalf of the two men; but it was to no avail. From there she went to the market-place, where all the people were assembled and in arms, and she saw the two men on the scaffold. The lady wore her mourning clothes and had only a bonnet on her head; she was dressed humbly and simply in order to move them to pity. And there she beseeched the people, with tears in her eyes and her hair disheveled, that they might take pity on her two servants and give them back to her.

A great part of these people were willing to have her wish granted and to let the men live; others were opposed; and pikes were lowered one against another, as for a combat. But those who wanted their death found themselves in the stronger position and finally they cried out to those on the scaffold that they should execute them. To conclude, both of them had their heads cut off, and the poor lady returned to her house in this state, very sad and dejected, for they had been the principal persons in whom she had placed her trust.[129]

After these people of Ghent had performed that exploit, they separated her from my lord of Ravenstein and the dowager [duchess], widow of Duke Charles, because they had signed the letter which the lord of Humbercourt and the chancellor had delivered [to the king], as you have heard. And they assumed complete authority and power over the poor young princess. For she could indeed be called poor, not so much because of the loss which she had already sustained in relation to so many important towns which had been given up and which were irretrievable, owing to the strong power under which they were placed: for by means of favor, friendship, or some arrangement she might still have entertained hopes; but she was particularly unfortunate in finding herself in the hands of the real enemies and persecutors of her house. And their actions, generally speaking, have always stemmed from stupidity rather than from malice. And it is always coarse tradesmen who most often have power and authority there, although they have no understanding of important affairs or of methods of governing a state. Their malice is directed only toward two things: first, they are eager to weaken and diminish the stature of their prince, and they will resort to all sorts of means to do so; and secondly, whenever they have done something wrong or have committed a great error and find themselves in the weaker position, they are second to none in humility, as they try to make a peace agreement, and in offering considerable gifts. And they know bet-

129. Commynes, as in the case of the battle of Nancy in 1477 and the interview of Péronne in 1468, dramatically telescopes events. On March 31, 1477, Mary of Burgundy made the attempt to save her counselors which the memorialist describes. On April 3, 1477, the counselors were executed.

ter than the people of any other town I have known how to find the right people to whom they may address themselves to manage their transactions.

While the king was conquering the above-mentioned towns, cities, and other places on the borders of Picardy, his army was in Burgundy, under the nominal command of the prince of Orange who still rules today, a native and subject of the county of Burgundy; but lately he had become an enemy of Duke Charles for the second time. Therefore the king made use of his services, because he was a powerful lord in both the county and the duchy of Burgundy, and, besides, he had important relatives and was well loved. But my lord of Craon was the king's lieutenant and had actual charge of the army; and it was in him that the king put all his trust. Indeed, he was a wise man and loyal to his master, but he was a little bit too interested in his own profit. When this lord approached Burgundy, he sent the prince of Orange and others before Dijon, to make the necessary remonstrances and request the people to render obedience to the king. They accomplished their mission so well, principally by means of the efforts of the prince of Orange, that the town of Dijon and all the others in the duchy of Burgundy rendered homage to the king; and several places in the county of Burgundy, such as Auxonne and some other castles, followed their example.

The prince of Orange was promised fine estates, and in addition all the places in the county of Burgundy which had come down to him from the succession of the prince of Orange his grandfather were to be put in his hands, although he was in litigation about them with the lords of Châteauguion, his uncles, who he claimed had been favored by Duke Charles. For their dispute had been argued in great solemnity before him for several days, and the duke, following the advice of many lawyers, gave a verdict against the prince, or so he said. Therefore he left the duke's service and came to join the king.

In spite of this promise, when the lord of Craon found himself the possessor of everything mentioned above, and had in his hands all the best places which were to have been allotted to the prince and were part of his grandfather's succession, he refused to give them up to the prince in spite of all the requests he could make. The king wrote to him several times about it, quite frankly, for he well knew that the lord of Craon was on bad terms with the prince. But he was afraid to offend the lord of Craon, for he had the whole region under his control; and he did not believe that the prince would have had the courage or the means to incite the territory of Burgundy to revolt, as he was to do later, at least to a great extent. But for the moment I shall leave this subject for another place.

352

After the people of Ghent had seized the government by force from the lady of Burgundy, put to death the two men of whom I spoke earlier, and dismissed whomever they pleased, they began to hire and fire people at will; they especially pursued and plundered all those who had best served the house of Burgundy, indiscriminately, without attention to those who in some things among others might have served that house badly. Among all people, they particularly picked quarrels with the Burgundians,[130] and they banished them all. They took as many pains to force them to become servants and subjects of the king as he himself did; and he persuaded them by means of attractive and shrewd arguments, very large gifts and promises, and also great force.

To begin with some novelty, they released from prison the duke of Gelderland, whom Duke Charles had confined there for a long time, for the causes which I mentioned earlier, and they made him commander of an army which they had improvised themselves, with forces from Bruges, Ghent, and Ypres, and they sent him before Tournai to burn the suburbs, although this was of very little utility to further the interest of their lord. It would have served the purpose better to send two hundred men and ten thousand francs in cash to help those who were already at the siege at Arras, provided that they had arrived in time, than to set up ten such armies, although they might have consisted of twelve or fifteen hundred well-paid men; for they could not do any more than burn a small number of houses in a region that was hardly important to the king, since he did not levy taxes there. But their understanding of such matters did not go so far. And I cannot think how God has so preserved the city of Ghent, from which have come so many evils and which is of so little use to the country and the public affairs of the territory in which it is situated, and much less to the prince. It is not like Bruges, which is a great receiving center for merchandise and a great place for foreigners, and in which, perhaps, more merchandise is traded than in any other European town; it would be an irreparable loss to have this town destroyed.

18

All things considered, it seems to me that God has created neither man nor beast in this world without establishing some counterpart to oppose him, in order to keep him in humility and fear. And therefore Ghent is well situated where it is, for those are the territories of Christendom the

130. "The Burgundians" refers to those from the duchy of Burgundy and the county of Burgundy (Franche-Comté), as distinguished from those living in the other possessions of the house of Burgundy. See p. 39, n. 84.

most given to all the pleasures to which man is inclined and also to the greatest display and expense. The people there [in Ghent] are good Christians, and they serve and honor God well.

And this is not the only nation to whom God has given some sort of thorn. For to the kingdom of France He has opposed England; to the English He has opposed the Scotch, and to the kingdom of Spain, Portugal. I do not want to speak of Granada, for the people are enemies of the true faith; however, so far Granada has caused much trouble to the kingdom of Castile. To the princes of Italy (most of whom hold their territories without title, unless it be given to them in heaven, and about that we can only guess) who rule their subjects rather cruelly and violently in regard to taxes, God has opposed the communes of Italy, such as Venice, Florence, Genoa, and sometimes Bologna, Siena, Pisa, Lucca, and others, which often are against the lords, and the lords against them; and each keeps an eye on the other so that neither may grow.

And to give particular examples, God gave the house of Aragon the house of Anjou as its counterpart; the Visconti, dukes of Milan, have the house of Orleans; the Venetians have these Italian princes, as I have said, and in addition the Florentines; the Florentines have their neighbors from Siena and Pisa, as well as the Genoese; The Genoese have their bad government and their lack of faith toward each other, and their party divisions occur in their very [family] alliances, such as the Fregosi, Adorni, Doria, and others. This is so evident that enough is known about it.

As for Germany, the houses of Austria and Bavaria have always been opposed, and the latter particularly is divided within itself. The house of Austria is also opposed to the Swiss. This division first started on account of a village called Schwyz, which could hardly number six hundred men, but now all the rest take their name from it, and the territory has prospered to such an extent that two of the richest towns belonging to the house of Austria, Zurich and Fribourg, are in their territory. They have won important battles in which they have killed several Austrian dukes. Many other party divisions can be found in Germany, such as the house of Cleves against the house of Gelderland, the dukes of Gelderland against the dukes of Jülich, and the Hanseatic cities, which are situated so far north, against the kings of Denmark.

And to speak of Germany in general, there are so many fortified places and so many people inclined to do evil and to plunder and rob, and who use force and violence against each other on the slightest pretense, that it is almost incredible. For a single man with only a valet to attend him will defy a whole city and even attack a duke, so that he will have a better excuse to rob him, by using a small castle on a rock, where he can retire and where he has twenty or thirty horsemen.

These people are hardly ever punished by the German princes, for the latter want to employ their services in time of need. But the princes inflict cruel punishment on the towns, when they can manage to do so, and they have often besieged and destroyed such castles. And these towns often keep a force of paid men-at-arms to protect them. Thus it seems that these towns and princes act in the manner which I have just described so that people will behave properly toward each other, and I should think that this mutual conflict is necessary not only in Germany but everywhere else.

I have spoken only of Europe, for I am not well informed of the situation in the two other parts of the world, Asia and Africa; but I have heard that they have as many wars and divisions as we do, and that they are carried on even more mechanically. For I have learned that in some localities in Africa they sell their own people to Christians, and this is borne out by the Portuguese, who have had many slaves and still do.

It may seem, therefore, that these divisions are necessary in all the world and that these dissensions and oppositions, which God has given and ordered for every estate and almost for every person, as I explained above, are also necessary. And offhand, speaking as an unlearned man who wants to hold only opinions which we should, it seems to me that this is so, and principally because of the stupidity of many princes, and also because of the wickedness of others, who have enough sense and experience but wish to use it evilly.

A prince or other man of whatever estate he may be, who has power and authority over others and is well educated, learned, and experienced will either be improved as a result, or else made worse: for great knowledge makes wicked men worse and good men better. However, it is probable that knowledge does men more good than harm, if only because it makes them conscious of their bad actions and ashamed of them; and that may be enough to prevent them from doing wrong, or at least from doing it too often. And if they are not naturally good, they will not wish to appear bad or willing to harm anyone. I have seen many such instances among great people, where they have abstained from many bad actions because of their learning, and often also because of fear of God's punishments, of which they are more aware than ignorant persons who have neither seen nor read anything.

Therefore I will say that those who are unwise for lack of having been brought up well—and perhaps also their temperament is involved here—do not understand at all the extent of power and lordship which

God has given them over their subjects; for they have not seen it, nor have they heard about it from those who know it. Those who do understand these things do not generally become close to such princes; and if some of those who are close do know, they do not want to talk about it for fear of displeasing them. And if anyone wishes to make some remonstrance to them, nobody will support him; at best he will be considered mad, and perhaps his words will be taken in the worst possible sense, as far as he is concerned.

Therefore one must conclude that neither our natural reason, nor our sense, nor fear of God, nor love of our neighbor will restrain us at all from doing violence to one another, or from keeping for ourselves what belongs to another, or from taking the possessions of others by all possible means. And if powerful lords hold towns or castles belonging to their relatives or neighbors, they will not return them under any circumstances. Once they have given a good pretense for keeping them, everyone in their entourage agrees with them, especially their closest companions and those who want to be in their good graces. I shall not speak of quarrels among the weak, for they have superiors who sometimes give justice to those involved (at least to the one who has a good cause) and who will pursue and defend an affair and spend a great deal on it. In the long run he will receive justice if the court (that is to say, the prince under whose authority he lives) is not against him.

Thus it is true that God is almost forced or summoned to show many signs and to beat us with many rods for our stupidity, and for our wickedness, which I believe is more likely. But the stupidity of princes and their ignorance are very dangerous and dreadful, for they are the source of the prosperity or adversity of their territories.

Therefore, if a prince is strong and has a great number of men-at-arms by the authority of whom he can obtain money at will to pay them and to spend on whatever he desires, without being concerned about the people, and if he refuses to restrain his mad and outrageous enterprises and expenses, and if everyone about him remonstrates with him, but to no avail, or worse still, incurs his wrath, who can remedy the situation if not God?[131]

God no longer speaks directly to people, and there are no longer prophets who speak with His tongue, for His faith is sufficiently ac-

131. In the remaining paragraphs of chapter 18 and in all of chapter 19 Commynes may frequently be observed defending his opposition to the policies of the French regency in the years after Louis XI's death. His emphasis on illegal trials and imprisonment, and the dismissal from office of "subjects who have served their predecessors loyally" suggests that he is referring obliquely to his own case, as I have indicated in n. 184 on p. 71.

cepted and understood and well-known to those who wish to hear it and understand it; and therefore no one will be excused by reason of ignorance, at least those who have had a sufficiently long life and have been endowed with natural sense. How would one punish these strong men, who use force to accomplish whatever they please, if God did not put his hand into it? Their least command is always made under penalty of death. Some of them punish people under the pretense of justice, and they have about them people of that profession who are always ready to comply with their wishes and who will represent a venial sin as a mortal sin. And if they do not have enough evidence against a man, they find ways of dissimulating part of the testimony of witnesses, so as to make the defendant powerless against their accusations and to ruin him with expenses; and they have an open ear for anyone who wants to make any charges against the person whom they have in custody and whom they wish to hurt.

If this method is not good enough to assure the success of their plan, they have others which take less time; and they say that it was necessary to punish the suspect as an example to others, and they conduct the trial as they see fit. In the case of others who have some power and who are their vassals, they resort to illegal seizure. For example, they say to one of them: "You have disobeyed me and have acted contrary to the homage which you owe me," and they proceed to take his possessions by force, if they are able to do so (or at least they try) and they make him live in great tribulation. As for one who is merely their neighbor, if he is strong and rough, they leave him alone, but if he is weak, he will not know where to hide himself, for they will accuse him of having supported his enemies, or they will insist on having their men-at-arms occupy his territory, or they will advance claims against him, or they will find occasion to destroy him, or they will support his neighbors against him and supply them with soldiers.

They will dismiss from office those of their subjects who have served their predecessors loyally, and replace them with new people, because they take too long to die. They will make trouble for clergymen with regard to their benefices, so that they may at least derive some profit from them which they will use to enrich someone usually in accordance with the whims of persons who have not been of any service to them, or of men and women who, under certain circumstances, can be very influential and enjoy credit with them. They cause their noblemen endless travail and expenses on account of the wars which they undertake on an impulse, without taking advice from or considering those whom they should consult before starting them: for they are the ones who will have to contribute their lives, their persons, and their possessions. Therefore they should know about it before these things begin.

To most of their people they leave nothing; and after having them pay more taxes than they should, they still give no order to the manner of life of their men-at-arms; the soldiers are constantly quartered throughout the country, without paying anything, and doing other evils and excesses which everyone of us knows about: for they are not content with their rations, and so they beat and abuse the poor people and force them to go and find bread, wine and other food for them; and if the good man has a wife or daughter who is beautiful, he would be wise to keep her out of sight.

However, since these men-at-arms are mercenaries, it would be very easy to put some order into the situation, and have the men paid every two months at the latest. Thus they would have neither occasion nor excuse to behave so violently under the pretense that they are not being paid; for the money is levied and is received at the end of every year. I refer to our kingdom, which is more oppressed and harassed in relation to this point than any other territory I know of; and only a wise king could remedy the situation. As for the neighboring countries, they have other modes of punishment.

19

To continue with my subject, is there any king or lord in this world who has the power, outside of his own domain, to levy a single *denier* on his subjects without the approval and consent of those who are to pay it, unless he does it by tyranny and violence? One might object that there are certain times in which it is not possible to wait for the convocation of an assembly because it would take too long to start the war and prepare it. To this I would reply that one should not be in such a hurry and that there is always enough time for such an enterprise. And I insist that kings and princes are much stronger when they undertake some affair with the advice of their subjects; and they are more feared by their enemies.

When it is a question of defending oneself, that cloud can be seen from afar, especially if they are foreigners; and then the good subjects cannot complain or refuse anything that is requested for the war. And in no case can it happen so suddenly that some persons cannot be called together, so that one can say: "This is not done without cause," without using any tricks or maintaining a small war arbitrarily and without any purpose, in order to have a cause for raising money.

I realize that money is necessary to defend the frontiers and to protect them, even when there is no war, so that they may not be surprised; but all this should be done in moderation. The sense of a wise prince will serve him well in such matters; for if he is good, he knows that there is a God, and a world, and what he can and should do and what he can do or leave alone. In my opinion, among all the countries in the world which I know of, the place where the public business is best managed, where the least violence is used against the people, and where no buildings are destroyed or demolished because of war is England; and misfortune and adversity befall those who make war.

Of all the kings in this world ours has least reason to say: "I have the privilege of levying on my subjects what I please." And those who ascribe these words to him to make him appear greater do him no honor; on the contrary, they cause him to be hated and feared by his neighbors, who would not want to live under his domination for anything in the world. But if our king, or those who want to exalt him or promote his reputation, were to say: "I have subjects who are so good and loyal that they never refuse me anything I request of them, and I am more feared and better obeyed by my subjects than any other prince in the world; my subjects endure all misfortunes and afflictions with more patience than any others, and bear less resentment for past sufferings," it seems to me that this would be very much to his credit, and I am sure that this is so. He should not say: "I take whatever I want and it is my prerogative, which I intend to keep." King Charles V [of France] never used such terms. As a matter of fact I have never heard any king say this, but I have heard it from their servants, who thought that they were doing their master a good turn. But, in my opinion, they misunderstood the interests of their lord, and they spoke this way in order to show humility before him and because they did not know what they were saying.

As an example of the goodness of the French, the first instance which comes to mind from our time is the convocation of the three estates in Tours [in 1484], after the decease of our good master, King Louis, may he rest in peace, which took place in 1483. It might have been thought at the time that such an assembly would be dangerous, and some persons of low estate and little virtue said then, and many times since, that it was a crime of lese majesty to consider having a meeting of the estates, and that it would only serve to diminish the authority of the king. But these are the very persons who commit a crime against God, the king, and the people. These words serve only those who are in positions of authority and esteem without having deserved it in any way, who are not qualified for their office, and who have never done anything except whisper in ears and talk about things of little value; these people are opposed to these great assemblies for fear that they may be recognized for what they are and that their practices may be condemned.

At the time everyone, whether of high, middle, or low rank, considered the kingdom to be very costly to maintain, for the people had endured and suffered for twenty years and more great and horrible taxes, and which amounted to some three million francs a year more than ever before. For Charles VII never levied more than 1,800,000 francs a year, and King Louis, his son, in the year of his death, raised 4,700,000 francs, not including funds for artillery and other supplies. And it was indeed pitiful to see and hear of the poverty of the people. But one good thing about our good master was that he did not hoard anything in the treasury; he collected everything and spent everything. He built large edifices to fortify and defend the towns and other places of the kingdom, and he did this to a much larger extent than all the kings who preceded him. He was very generous to the churches. In certain respects it would have been better if he had been less liberal, because he robbed the poor to give to those who had no need of it. In short, no one is perfect in this world.

And in this kingdom, which was so oppressed in many ways after the death of our king, was there any division against the king who now reigns? Did princes and their subjects rise up in arms against their young king? Did they wish to replace him with another? Did they wish to deprive him of his authority? Did they want to restrain him so that he would be unable to perform his role as a king and issue commands? Certainly not. Still, there were some people vainglorious enough to say that such things would have happened, had they not prevented it. People did the opposite of everything I said in my questions: for all of them came to him, whether they were princes, lords, or ordinary townsmen; all of them acknowledged him as their king and swore allegiance to him. The princes and the lords made their requests humbly, on their knees, handing in their demands in the form of petitions, and they established a council to which twelve of them were named. And then the king, who was only thirteen years old, gave orders, according to the advice of this council.

At the above-mentioned assembly of the three estates, certain requests and remonstrances were made with great humility for the good of the kingdom, always remitting everything to the king's good pleasure and that of his council, and granting him whatever was asked of them, and whatever was shown by written documents to be necessary for the king's expenses, without saying anything. And the sum requested was 2,500,000 francs, which was enough, and all that heart could desire, and, if anything, it was too much rather than too little, unless something else should come up. And the estates begged that at the end of two years they should meet again, and in case the king did not have enough money, they would grant him as much as he pleased; and if he were engaged in war or if anyone were to offend him, they would put at his disposal their persons and their possessions without refusing him anything that he might need.

Is it with such subjects, who give so liberally to him, that the king should allege a privilege of being able to take at his pleasure? Would it not be fairer to God and to the world to raise money in this manner than with unordered will? For no prince can levy taxes otherwise than by authorization, as I said, unless he does it by tyranny and is excommunicated. But many are so stupid that they do not know what they can do or not in this respect.

On the other hand, there are people who offend their lord and refuse to obey him or provide for his needs; instead of helping him, when they see him entangled in some affair, they despise him or they rebel against him or disobey him and commit other offenses which are contrary to their oath of fealty.

When I refer to kings or princes, I mean them and their governors; and when I say people, I mean those who have high positions and dignities under their authority. The greatest misfortunes generally proceed from the strongest, for the weak seek only to have patience.

I include women as well as men, because women are sometimes and in certain places put in a position of authority, either by their husbands' love, or for the administration of their children's affairs, or because their territories were part of their dowry. If I were to speak of the middle estates of this world and the low ones, it would take too long. It will be sufficient to speak of the high-ranking people, for it is through them that God's power and justice are made known. For if misfortunes befall a poor man or one hundred of them, no one worries about this, for it is attributed to his poverty or lack of proper care, or if he drowns or breaks his neck because no one was there to save him, people hardly talk about it. When calamity befalls a great city, however, the reaction is not the same; yet it does not arouse so much commotion as in the case of a prince.

One might ask why the power of God is more manifest against great people than against persons of low rank. It is because the humble and the poor find enough to punish them when they deserve it. Furthermore, they are frequently chastised when they have done nothing wrong, either to serve as examples for others because someone wants to get their possessions, or perhaps because of an error on the part of the judge. At other times they have deserved their punishment and justice must take its course. But as for great princes and princesses, their rich governors and provincial counselors, disorderly towns who disobey their lords and governors, who will investigate their conduct? Assuming that evidence can be gathered against them, who will take it to a judge? Who will presume to judge their case, consider the information, and give a verdict against them (I am speaking of the bad ones, not the good, for there are very few of the latter)? And what are the reasons for which these people and all the rest commit all these enormities which I have mentioned, and many others about which I shall be silent, for brevity's sake, without any consideration for divine power and justice? In these cases I say it is lack of faith, and in the case of ignorant persons, it is lack of both sense and faith, but principally of faith, from which it seems to me that all the misfortunes of the world derive, and especially the afflictions which cause people to complain of being hurt and oppressed by others more powerful than they are.

For if a poor man, who has true and good faith in God, and who firmly believes the tortures of hell to be as they really are, and who also has wrongly possessed himself of someone else's property, or whose father took it, or his grandfather, and he possesses it now, whether it is a duchy, county, city, castle, furniture, a field, a pool, [or] a mill, depending on each person's rank believes firmly, as we all should, that: "I shall never enter paradise if I do not give full satisfaction and if I do not give back what I truly know belongs to others," is it possible that any king, queen, prince, princess, or any other person of whatever quality or condition they may be in this world great or small, man or woman, living on this earth would in true and good conscience (as I said before) retain anything from his subject, or subjects, or anyone else, whether a close or distant neighbor, or would want to put him to death wrongly and unjustly, or keep him in prison without reason, or rob some to make others rich (which is their most common occupation) or act dishonorably toward their parents or servants to further their own pleasures, as with women, or do anything similar? By my faith, no! It would be incredible. Therefore, if they had true faith and believed what God and the church command us under penalty of damnation, knowing that life is so short and the pains of hell so horrible and without end or remission, would they be as they are? One must conclude that they would not, and that all evils come from lack of faith.

Book Five

For example, when a king or prince is held as a prisoner and fears that he may die in prison, does he have anything in the world so dear to him that he would not give it up in return for freedom? He gives not only his possessions but also those of his subjects, as you have seen in the case of King John [the Good] of France, who was captured by the prince of Wales at the battle of Poitiers [in 1356]. The king paid three million francs and surrendered all of Aquitaine, at least the part of it which he held, and several other cities, towns, and other places, which amounted to a third of his kingdom; and he impoverished the kingdom to such an extent that for a long time they circulated as currency something like leather which had a small silver nail in the middle. All this was given by King John and by his son Charles the Wise, for the ransom of the captured king. If they had refused to give up anything, the English would not have put him to death, but at worst they would have imprisoned him. And even if they had killed him, the agony of the execution would not have been equal to the one hundred thousandth part of the least torment of hell.

Therefore he gave up everything which I mentioned, and he ruined his children and his kingdom because he believed what he saw and knew that he would not be freed otherwise.[132] But perhaps when people commit such acts as will bring upon themselves the sort of punishment which befell the king, his children, and his subjects, they do not have firm faith and understanding of the offense which they commit against God and His commandments.

For there is no prince (or few) who, if he holds a town belonging to his neighbor, would restore either in view of any possible remonstrance or of any fear of God, or even to avoid the torments of hell. Yet King John gave up so much merely to get out of prison. Therefore I maintain that it is lack of faith.

I asked earlier about who would give information about the great, who would accuse them before a judge, and who would be the judge who would punish the wicked. My answer to this is that the information which will be brought against them will be the complaints and clamors of the people whom they afflict and oppress in so many ways without having any compassion or pity for them, the dolorous lamentations of the widows and orphans whose husbands and fathers they have put to death, to the detriment of their survivors, and in general the protesta-

132. Commynes' notion of the circumstances surrounding John the Good's imprisonment is based on popular legend rather than historical facts. Leather money never existed, and John the Good was so far from desiring his freedom in order to return to France that he chose a pretext to go back to London after his release, and died there.

tions of all those whom they have persecuted either in their persons or their possessions. This will be the accusation, and the great cries of the people, their complaints and their pitiful tears will bring it before Our Lord, who will be the true judge of the case, and perhaps He will not defer their punishment until the next world but will chastise them in this one.

Therefore we must assume that they will be punished because they have refused to believe and have been lacking in true faith and trust. Thus we must say that God has to show His will by means of examples and instances, so that they and everyone else may be convinced that their punishments are the result of their cruel offenses, and He must show upon them His force, His virtue and His justice. For no one else in this world has this power except Him.

At first God's punishments do not seem so great because they are distributed gradually; but they are never sent to any prince nor to those who are in charge of his affairs, nor to governors of his large territories without serious and dangerous consequences for their subjects. I do not call these things misfortunes unless their subjects are unfavorably affected by them. For such mishaps as falling from a horse, breaking one's leg, or running a high fever are curable; and such accidents are good for princes because they make them wiser. I call them misfortunes when God is so offended that He will not endure these wicked acts any longer, and will manifest His power and divine virtue. First of all He attacks their understanding, which is a great affliction for those who are so affected. Then He troubles their house and allows division and dissension to arise in it. The prince falls into such disgrace with Our Lord, that he shuns the advice of the wise and raises to high positions persons of little experience, who are unwise and unreasonable, but who flatter him and agree with everything he says. If he wants to impose a new tax of one *denier*, they propose two. If he threatens a man, they say that he should be hanged; and thus they act in all other matters. They advise him to make others fear him above all, and to show himself proud and courageous; and by this means they hope to be feared, as if authority had been their inheritance.

Those whom princes by such counsel have banished and dismissed, although they have served them for many years and have many friends and acquaintances in their territories, are very discontented, and on their account many of their friends and well-wishers are equally dissatisfied. And perhaps they may be so hard pressed that they will be forced to defend themselves or to escape into the territory of a small neighbor, who by chance might be an enemy hostile to the prince who discharged them. When there is internal dissension, outsiders step in. Is there any plague and persecution so great as war between friends and those who know each other, and is there any hatred so mortal?

It is easy to defend one's country against foreign enemies when there is unity at home. The invaders have no informers nor correspondence there. Do you believe that an unwise prince, surrounded by foolish advisers, can foresee remote misfortunes which may result from dissension among his subjects? Or that he realizes that this will be to his disadvantage? Or that this proceeds from God? No one has a better table, nor a better bed, nor more horses and clothes; and his retinue is much increased, for he attracts people to his court by promising them and giving them the spoils and positions of those whom he has banished, and adds his own personal gifts, so as to increase his reputation. But when he least suspects it, God will raise an enemy against him, and by chance it may be someone of whom he has never heard. Then thoughts and great suspicions about those whom he has offended will come to his mind, and he will begin to be afraid of various other people who wish him no harm. He will not make God his refuge but will rely on his army.

20

Have we not seen in our day such examples around us? We have seen King Edward IV of England, who died only recently, the head of the house of York. Had he not destroyed the house of Lancaster, under which he and his father had lived for a long time, and had he not rendered homage to King Henry VI of England, who was of Lancastrian lineage? Since then Edward kept him a prisoner for many years in the castle of London, capital of the kingdom of England, and finally put him to death.

Have we not seen also the count of Warwick, administrator and principal governor of all the affairs of King Edward (who had all his friends put to death, and particularly the dukes of Somerset), at length become the enemy of King Edward his master, give his daughter in marriage to the prince of Wales, son of King Henry VI, try to reestablish the house of Lancaster, and suffer defeat in the battle where he died together with his brothers and relatives? The same thing happened to many lords of England, who for a time had caused their enemies to die. Later the children of these people took revenge, when time turned in their favor, and they killed the others.

One can well imagine that such plagues are brought about by nothing except divine justice. But as I said elsewhere, the kingdom of England enjoys one particular grace above all other kingdoms, that neither the country nor the people are destroyed; neither are their buildings burned nor demolished. For the fortunes of war befall only the soldiers, and especially the noblemen. Thus nothing is perfect in this world.

After King Edward had had the upper hand in all his affairs in his kingdom, and after he had obtained fifty thousand *écus* per year, which were paid to him in his castle of London, and had become so rich that no one could have exceeded him in wealth, he suddenly died, apparently out of melancholy at the [proposed] marriage of our present king with my lady Margaret, daughter of the duke of Austria. As soon as he received the news of this, he became ill. For then he found himself disappointed as to the marriage of his own daughter, to whom they had given the title of my lady the dauphiness; and the pension which he received from us, and which he called tribute, was canceled; but it was neither pension nor tribute, as I explained before.

[Upon his death] King Edward left his wife and two handsome sons; one was called the prince of Wales, and the other the duke of York. The duke of Gloucester, the late King Edward's brother, administered the government for his nephew, the prince of Wales, who was then about ten years old, and rendered homage to him as his king; he took him to London, pretending to have him crowned. But it was also to remove the other son from the sanctuary of London, where he was with his mother, who was suspicious of the duke.

Finally by the assistance of a bishop called the bishop of Bath—formerly King Edward's chancellor, but later dismissed by the king, who held him in prison and then still took his money—he executed the exploit which I shall describe later, at the time of his deliverance. The bishop told the duke of Gloucester that King Edward had once been so much in love with an English lady that he promised to marry her, on condition that she would first give herself to him; and she consented. The bishop claimed that he had performed the marriage with only the two of them and himself present. He was a man of honor, and so he kept the matter secret and helped persuade the lady to do likewise. Thus no one knew about it. And since then King Edward, again falling in love, married the daughter of an English knight named my lord Rivers; she was a widow and had two sons.

At the time I am speaking of, the bishop of Bath revealed this matter to the duke of Gloucester and helped him in the execution of his evil plan. The duke had his two nephews murdered and made himself king, under the name of King Richard [III]. He had the two daughters declared illegitimate at a session of parliament and had them denied the right to wear the royal coat of arms; and he had all of his late brother's loyal servants put to death, at least those whom he could lay hands on.

His cruel reign did not last long; for while he was at the height of his pride, and had more authority than any of his predecessors of the last one hundred years, he had the duke of Buckingham put to death and assembled a large army in readiness to fight, but in the meantime God sent him an enemy who had no power. It was the count of Richmond, who had been a prisoner in Brittany, and who is now king of England [Henry VII]; he is of the house of Lancaster, but was not the next in line to the crown, regardless of what was claimed (or so I have heard). The count of Richmond told me, not long before he left our kingdom, that since the age of five he had been guarded as if he were a fugitive or in prison. He was a prisoner of the late Duke Francis for fifteen years or so in Brittany, having fallen into the hands of the duke as a result of a rough tempest, as he was fleeing to France with his uncle, the count of Pembroke. I was at the duke's court when they were taken. The duke treated them gently, as far as prisoners go, and upon King Edward's death, he supplied the count of Richmond liberally with men and ships; and with the help of the duke of Buckingham (who died later on account of this), he sent him to land in England. There was a great storm and the winds were contrary; and so he returned to Dieppe, and from there he went back by land to Brittany.

Upon his return to Brittany, he was afraid of becoming a financial burden to the duke, for he had some five hundred Englishmen in his retinue, and he also feared that the duke might be reconciled with King Richard, which would have been to his disadvantage; and indeed bargains were being made. Therefore he left with his men without taking leave of the duke.

A short time later he was given three or four thousand men, but only their passage was paid. And our present king gave those who were with him a large sum of money and several pieces of artillery. He was conducted by ship from Normandy to land in Wales, of which he was a native. King Richard marched forth to encounter him, but an English knight, named Lord Stanley, joined the count of Richmond. He was the husband of the count's mother and brought him a reinforcement of some twenty-six thousand men. A battle was fought: King Richard was immediately killed, and the count of Richmond was crowned king of England on the battlefield, with the crown that King Richard had worn.

Can one speak of fortune in this case? It is the true judgment of God. But to make it more evident, as soon as King Richard had his two nephews cruelly murdered, as I mentioned earlier, he lost his wife. Some say that he had her slain. He had only one son, who died soon after.

This matter would perhaps have better served later, when I shall speak of King Edward's death, for he was still alive at the time with which this chapter deals, but I have done it in order to continue with what I was saying in this digression.

Similarly, we have seen many changes in the kingdom of Spain, after the death of the late king, Don Henry, who was married to the sister of the late king of Portugal, and whose union was blessed with a beautiful daughter. She did not succeed him, however, and was deprived of the crown under the pretense that her mother had committed adultery. And this was not allowed to pass without dissension and cruel wars. For the king of Portugal wanted to support his niece, and he was assisted by several lords of the kingdom of Castile. However, King Henry's sister, who was married to the son of Don John, [that is, Ferdinand,] the king of Aragon, obtained the kingdom and possesses it to this very day. And thus this judgment and distribution were made in heaven, where enough others are also made.

You have seen, not long ago, the king of Scotland and his thirteen- or fourteen-year-old son at war against each other. The son and his partisans won the battle, and the king was killed on the spot. He had had his brother put to death, and he was suspected of having caused the death of several other persons besides his brother.

You can see also the duchy of Gelderland out of the hands of its traditional rulers, and you have heard of the ingratitude of the late duke toward his father. I could mention many other similar cases, which can easily be recognized as divine punishments. These are the sources of wars, which in turn give rise to mortality and famine. And all these misfortunes proceed from lack of faith. It must therefore be realized, considering the wickedness of men, and especially of the great, who neither know that there is a God nor believe in Him, that it is necessary for every lord or prince to have his contrary, to keep him in fear and humility; otherwise nobody could live under their rule or even near them.